Treatment or Torture

G. SEABORN JONES

Treatment or Torture

The Philosophy, Techniques, and
Future of Psychodynamics

TAVISTOCK PUBLICATIONS
London · New York · Sydney · Toronto · Wellington

First published in 1968
by Tavistock Publications Limited
11 New Fetter Lane, London E C 4
Printed in Great Britain
in 11 pt Bembo
by The Camelot Press Limited,
London & Southampton
© *G. Seaborn Jones 1968*

1 · 1

SBN 422 71980 3

Distributed in the United States of America
by Barnes & Noble Inc.

Contents

16 The General Testing Principle   223

17 The Science and Philosophy of Psychodynamics   239

18 Training through Analytic Groups   254

19 LSD Treatment   269

20 The Practical Problem of Furthering the Science of
     Psychodynamics   281

21 Aggression and Rationality   287

    BIBLIOGRAPHY   303

    NAME INDEX   313

    SUBJECT INDEX   315

Acknowledgements

I wish to express my profound gratitude to Dr H. Ezriel for convincing me that psychoanalysis and group analysis can be made scientific.

I have also benefited from innumerable lively and inconclusive arguments with Professor A. J. Ayer about the philosophical problems dealt with in this book.

Miss Pearl Katz has greatly assisted me in the preparation of the manuscript with her tireless and devoted encouragement and hard work.

Mr John Harvard-Watts and Miss Diana Burfield are to be thanked for showing sympathetic flexibility in handling an interdisciplinary manuscript, which, in less capable hands, might easily have been torn in two to fit into academic pigeon-holes.

The author is obliged to the publishers and others concerned for permission to quote from the works listed below:

George Allen & Unwin Ltd and Oxford University Press, in respect of *The A.B.C. of Relativity* by Bertrand Russell; George Allen & Unwin Ltd and International Universities Press in respect of an article by Melanie Klein in *Psycho-Analysis Today*, edited by Sandor Lorand (copyright 1944); Ballière, Tindall & Cassell Ltd in respect of 'Hypothesis to explain Trauma Re-enactment Dreams' by J. O. Wisdom; Cambridge University Press in respect of *The Nature of the Physical World* by Sir Arthur Eddington, 'Experimentation within the Psychoanalytic Session' by Henry Ezriel, and *Physics and Philosophy* by Sir James Jeans; Sigmund Freud Copyrights Ltd, the Institute of Psycho-Analysis, George Allen & Unwin Ltd, the Hogarth Press Ltd, and Basic Books, Inc., in respect of *The Interpretation of Dreams*, Vol. 4 of the Standard Edition of *The Complete Psychological Works of Sigmund Freud*; William Heinemann Ltd and Collins-Knowlton-Wing, Inc. in respect of *Battle for the Mind* by William Sargant; Hogarth Press Ltd and International Universities Press, Inc. in respect of *The Ego and the Mechanisms of Defence* by Anna Freud; Hutchinson Publishing Group Ltd and Dryden Press, Inc. in respect of *Schools of Psychoanalytic Thought* by R. L. Munroe; Hutchinson Publishing Group Ltd and Barnes & Noble, Inc. in respect of *The Concept of Mind* by Gilbert Ryle; the author, Hutchinson Publishing Group Ltd, and Basic Books, Inc. in respect of *The Logic of Scientific Discovery* by Sir Karl Popper; Hutchinson Publishing Group Ltd, in respect of *The Philosophy of Science* by Stephen Toulmin; the author and Methuen & Company Ltd in respect of *Foundations of Inference in Natural Science* by J. O. Wisdom; the author, Routledge & Kegan Paul Ltd, and Basic Books, Inc. in respect of *Conjectures and Refutations* by Sir Karl Popper; Routledge & Kegan Paul Ltd and Humanities Press, Inc. in respect of *Methods and Criteria of Reasoning* by R. Crawshay-Williams; Routledge & Kegan Paul Ltd in respect of *Biological Principles* by J. H. Woodger.

Preface

This book is intended for students and teachers of philosophy, of scientific method, of medicine, of psychiatry, of psychoanalysis, of education theory or of academic psychology, and for the general reader.

The student of philosophy will find clear explanations and examples of all the recognized logical fallacies, as well as several which have been identified and named by the author. He will also find a full discussion of the main philosophical problems. He may find some of the explanations of psychoanalytic theory far-fetched, if he has no experience of the subject, while the psychoanalyst, on the other hand, may find a few of them over-obvious. Their indulgence, however, will be repaid by the less obvious conclusions.

If the general reader with a distaste for technical argument, whether philosophical or scientific, skims (but not skips) a few pages here and there, he will still be able to follow the reasoning of the book without serious loss, and to agree or disagree with its conclusions.

Introduction

The purpose of this book is to lay the foundations of the science of psychodynamics. In order to do this, several related questions have to be answered. What are the methods of science? Can we distinguish between those which are fruitful and those which are barren? Can the scientist be completely objective? Is there any safeguard against shared delusions? How can rationality be achieved if human beings have little insight into their own motives? Can the scientist be sure of his 'facts'? If so, why do the most advanced scientists speak only of 'models' and 'tentative hypotheses' and not of 'facts'? Is psychoanalysis a science? If so, why are there conflicting 'schools'? Do we have to choose between psychoanalysis, modern Pavlovian psychology, Western academic psychology and the drug treatment used by some psychiatrists, as the basis of psychodynamics? Are the techniques of modern philosophy relevant to these problems?

Psychoanalysis has shown that human beings have much less insight into their own motives than they would like to believe, and that much of their supposed rationality is rationalization. The philosophical and the psychoanalytic approaches to confusions and fallacies are complementary. Philosophy attempts a formal explanation (What kind of fallacy is this?); psychoanalysis a causal explanation (Why does this person need to believe this now?). A student can be trained by a philosopher to think more clearly, and may even be induced to discard deep-rooted convictions when they are shown to lead to contradictions. But the winner of a philosophical argument may be the one with the most sophisticated, coherent, and persuasive rationalizations of unconscious wishes and fears.

Where fundamental convictions conflict and the disputants are more or less equally intelligent and articulate, there is little likelihood of conversion by 'proof'. The convinced optimist, pessimist, Christian, Communist, patriot, pacifist . . . may be what he is out of deeply buried emotional needs, and if he is free from painful doubts or symptoms he will be immune to the influence of alien opinions, whether religious, philosophical, ideological, or psychoanalytic. The implication for philosophy is that there is limited scope for philosophical persuasion; the implication for psychoanalysis is that a student needs some strong incentive to induce him to investigate the origins of his attitudes and beliefs.

The problem of rationality has four aspects: first, the book demonstrates that there is no safeguard against shared delusions or illusions; second, 'certainty', whether of facts or of definitions, is either delusory or banal; third, new philosophical problems are created whenever a new discipline or a new approach to a discipline introduces novel ways of using language; and, fourth, the principles and criteria that have been proposed for distinguishing between sense and nonsense, or between the scientific and the unscientific, though powerful tools in the analysis of theories, do not stand up to logical analysis. The criterion which has had most influence on the philosophy of science is the falsifiability criterion for the demarcation of the scientific and the non-scientific. Professor Popper's formulation of this criterion is examined in detail. Although it plays an important part in the testing of theories, it is found to fail as a criterion. Falsifiability is neither a sufficient nor a necessary condition of scientific status.

The ground is prepared for defining the science of psychodynamics by exposing the fallacy of Behaviourism; by analysing the problems of communication; by distinguishing twelve kinds of psychoanalytic hypotheses and showing whether or how they can be tested; by identifying the unconscious mechanisms which influence our thought, and relating them to philosophical fallacies; by answering the question whether 'the will is free'; and by summing up all the arguments that deal with the scientific status or reliability of theories and hypotheses in the general Testing Principle, which applies equally to science and philosophy. This principle is not logical, but psychological, and the argument makes clear that any formal principle based on logic is bound to fail.

An outline is then given of the subject-matter and scope of the science of psychodynamics.

Finally, since the theoretical problem of deciding the programme of the science is not independent of the hitherto unsolved problem of applying university techniques of teaching and research to psychodynamics, a practical solution, based on the author's experience of analytic group training, is put forward.

I

The Relation between Philosophy and Science

Many modern philosophers believe that the discipline of philosophy is independent of the scientific disciplines. The distinction between 'factual disputes', 'disputes about values', and 'purely verbal disputes', which plays an important part in modern philosophy, suggests that 'facts' are independent of value judgements and of the various ways of referring to them. I am stating a 'fact' when I say that light travels at 186,000 miles per second; I am making a 'value judgement' when I say, 'This sunset is beautiful'. The purist would not say that the statement 'Light travels at 186,000 miles per second' is a fact; he would say that it is a true statement referring to a fact, or that it is a true factual statement. The fact is 'out there', waiting to be described. The speed of light is thought of as a physical fact; my finding the sunset beautiful as a psychological fact.

The significance of a distinction is best brought out by examining marginal examples. Let us consider the statement, 'Light consists of photons'. Is this a statement of fact? The rival theory that light consists of waves makes us hesitate. We may say that the statements, 'Light consists of photons' and 'Light consists of waves' cannot both be true factual statements; therefore they are hypotheses, one of which will be confirmed and the other refuted by further scientific investigation. Then we shall discover the 'fact'. Or we may say that 'photons' and 'waves' are 'convenient fictions' of equal explanatory value, so that neither statement is a statement of fact. Or we may say that both statements are true factual statements which only seem to be contradictory. We then have a choice between saying that the 'fact' is not known and may never be known, saying that there is no fact to be discovered but only two ways of describing and explaining phenomena, or saying that 'the fact' cannot be uniquely described.

The above example may suggest that what we all agree to call a fact is that to which a well-confirmed and universally accepted hypothesis refers. We may note in passing that the speculations about the universe of earlier philosophers, such as Democritus and Leibniz, are not independent of science, but are considered as confirmed or disconfirmed by scientific discoveries. There is, however, no universally accepted hypothesis referring to my finding the sunset beautiful. I may make no statement at all and still believe that my reaction is a fact.

OSTENSIVE DEFINITION

Bertrand Russell (1954, p. 159) says, '"Fact", as I intend the term, can only be defined ostensively. Everything that there is in the world I call a "fact". The sun is a fact; . . .'. And later he says, 'I mean by a "fact" something which is there, whether anybody thinks so or not'. But I find that 'something which is there, whether anybody thinks so or not' is something *I* cannot think about. To say that the sun is a fact whether anybody thinks so or not is to use a conceptual system to try to escape from the conceptual system. It is like throwing a ball, and while throwing it saying, 'The ball is leaving my hand whether I am throwing it or not.' This statement is not precisely self-stultifying; perhaps it could be called somewhat disingenuous.

Most of us believe that events occurred before there were conscious beings to observe and describe them, that events occur which no one can observe and which will go on occurring when the human race ceases to exist. It may seem innocuous to state as a 'fact' that the sun was shining before there was anyone to see it shine. But 'shine' is a word invented by people with eyes, and physicists try to eliminate the anthropomorphic implications from statements of fact. It seems even more innocuous to state as a fact that there was a sun before there was anyone to see it. But our belief that there is an object called 'the sun' is derived from our belief in the continuity of a series of space–time events which have certain effects on our bodies and our instruments. Although the word 'sun' has not changed in the last 500 years, and is considered a correct translation of *sol* or ἥλιος, our conception of what the word refers to has changed radically as a result of scientific discoveries. This example illustrates two semantic points which need to be distinguished: first, that the sentence, 'The sun is setting', as used by a superstitious Greek or Roman, is semantically distinct from the same sentence as

used by a modern physicist; and, second, that even the most sophisticated scientific conception of 'the sun' is not free from an anthropo-
centric element. The events in a certain space–time 'region' of the
universe are conceptually isolated from near-by events because they
have certain effects on our bodies and instruments, and the series of
such events through millions of years is conceived as an 'object' and
described by a noun, 'sun'. If our retinas were sensitive to radiant
energy of some other range of wavelengths than 400 to 760 perhaps
our conceptual system would be different.

Bertrand Russell goes on to say (ibid., p. 160), 'Physical facts, for
the most part, are independent, not only of our volitions, but even of
our existence'. Now all of us except the extreme sceptic admit that
there is *something* which is independent of our existence, but when we
try to think about or describe *what* that something is we inevitably do
so in terms of a constantly changing conceptual system. Whenever we
think, speak, or write of a 'fact' we do so in words or mathematical
symbols which play a part in language, and the part they play changes
as the language develops. The development is both ontogenetic and
phylogenetic. The sentence, 'The sun is setting', as used by a four-year-
old child, is pragmatically (see p. 11) distinct from the same sentence
as used by the same person when he becomes a science graduate. The
part played by the word 'mind' in the English language changes both
in the usage of the child as he becomes more sophisticated, and in the
usage of scientists and philosophers as they become more and more
critical of Descartes.

'MIND'

The word 'mind' is interesting both to philosophers and to scientists
because it is frequently used, it seems to refer to something important,
and it does not fit comfortably into sophisticated language. Can we
say, 'The facts are there, they are what is and what happens, and we
have to adapt our language to describe them adequately'? Perhaps
this is somewhat like saying, 'The statue is there and I have to chip
away the stone to reveal it'. The analogy is not, of course, a very close
one. The sculptor, if successful, creates a figure which will be thought
'true to life' or a work of imagination which will be thought powerful; the writer creates either an imaginative work which will be
thought beautiful or a theory which will be thought true. There is no
connection, it may be said, between creating works of art and 'discovering' facts. There may be some marginal examples to make us hesitate:

is Gibbon's *Decline and Fall* a factual account or a work of art? but the difference is fairly clear-cut.

Let us consider the work of Dostoevsky, Freud, and the philosophers who have written about 'Mind'. Dostoevsky wrote novels which did not purport to describe facts. Some of his writing is like biography, with the difference that his characters did not exist as he describes them. Yet we take them seriously, say that they are 'true to life', and feel that he has taught us something about mental processes. He studied his own and other people's thoughts, feelings, and behaviour, re-organized (probably in part unconsciously) his experience, and created imaginary characters who contribute to our understanding of real people. Freud studied his own and other people's dreams, thoughts, feelings, and behaviour, reorganized his experience, and created a theory to explain what he had studied. His case-histories are about real people, but they sometimes read like extracts from novels because details are included which had formerly seemed significant only to artists. The understanding which was implicit in Dostoevsky is explicit in Freud.

How should we describe the introduction of such terms as 'id', 'ego', and 'superego'? Did Freud discover new facts and introduce new terms to refer to them? Did he discover the 'fact' that a large part of our mental processes are unconscious? Dostoevsky's novels show clearly that the author had a profound understanding of unconscious fear, rage, and guilt. *The Idiot*, for example, is a consistent portrayal of a character, Prince Myshkin, whose extreme sufferings on behalf of others make all contact with reality intolerable for him and force him to retreat into madness. The story of his life would be inexplicable without some insight into unconscious processes. Shakespeare reveals similar understanding in his portrayal of Hamlet. Freud did not 'discover' the unconscious, just as he did not 'discover' the phenomena of infantile sexuality. The sexual activities of infants have always been seen, if not recognized, by those who have had the handling of them. He studied his own dreams and what other people said, in the way that earlier scientists had studied physical phenomena, and invented a conceptual system which made his data intelligible. The 'id', the 'ego', and the 'superego' do not refer to entities, and whatever 'facts' are revealed in his writings are not independent of the terminological system he uses to describe them.

What are philosophers doing when they write about 'Mind'? They point out discrepancies between common-sense, philosophical, and scientific ways of talking, they criticize earlier philosophical theories,

they show differences and resemblances between various classes of statements, they reveal that certain ways of talking lead to paradoxes and
try to solve them, and they suggest that some uses of language are less
misleading than others. In short, they explain, or clarify, or revise the
relevant use of language. They may not adduce new 'facts', but they
do take into account whatever relevant scientific knowledge is known
to them, and hence the scientific uses of language. Any philosopher
who discussed the logic of 'I can see a far-distant star' without knowing
that light took, say, a thousand years to reach us from the star, would
be incompetent. In the same way a philosopher who knew nothing at
all of the effects on mental activity of physiological changes in the
brain, or of the physiological effects of love, grief, or despair, would
be seriously handicapped in a discussion of the mind–body problem.
This is not to say that he must be an expert in several related scientific
subjects. He could hardly be. But ignorance of certain relevant discoveries and theories may invalidate his argument.

If it is possible that scientific discoveries may invalidate philosophical
theories, is it possible that philosophical discoveries may invalidate
scientific theories? Let us consider the statement 'The mind and body
interact'. This looks like a factual statement, and many philosophers
and scientists would probably maintain that there is a 'fact' to which it
refers. Let us now suppose that a philosopher, drawing upon uses of
language in many fields, were to demonstrate that there is nothing to
which the term 'mind' refers, and were to persuade all philosophers
and scientists to follow him in excluding the term from their technical
vocabulary. There would then be a temptation to say that the 'facts'
are just as they always were; the change has been merely verbal; we
have adapted our technical language and it is now in conformity with
the 'facts'.

HOW 'FACT' IS USED

Perhaps we have now discovered how the term 'fact' is used. *What I
am prepared to call a 'fact' is that to which each of the hypotheses I have
recently found completely convincing refers.** I may cease to believe the
hypothesis, 'The mind and body interact', either because a scientist
makes some discovery that convinces me their apparent interaction is
delusory, or because a philosopher convinces me that in making the
statement I have been making a 'category mistake'. In *The Concept of
Mind*, Ryle says, 'Descartes left as one of his main philosophical

---

* 'Fact' is also used to describe the hypotheses themselves.

legacies a myth which continues to distort the continental geography
of the subject. A myth is, of course, not a fairy story. It is the pre-
sentation of facts belonging to one category in the idioms appropriate to another. To explode a myth is accordingly not to deny the
facts but to re-allocate them. This latter statement suggests that the
'facts' remain unchanged when we have learned to think and talk
about them in a quite different way. If we accept this (very general)
view, we must believe that if I am dissuaded from my conviction that
the mind and body interact, as a result of a scientist's discovery, I shall
'deny the fact'; if, however, I am dissuaded by a philosopher's argument, I shall 're-allocate' it. But what is the 'it' to be re-allocated?

It may be said that all the phenomena formerly referred to by the
statement 'the mind and body interact', such as the effects of mescaline
on perception, or the physiological effects of bad news, can now be
referred to in reformed terminology by some new statement or set of
statements. Therefore the 'facts' have not changed but have been re-
allocated. This will not do. If 'the mind and body interact' is an
invalid statement because it exemplifies a category mistake, it cannot
be equivalent to a set of statements such as 'mescaline affects perception', etc., which do not obviously exemplify category mistakes. We
cannot say that the facts to which the invalid statement referred have
been re-allocated because we cannot confidently say to what 'facts' it
referred. This is not to say that it was meaningless. A statement may be
invalid without being meaningless. If a foreigner, describing a visit to
London University, said, 'All the colleges *and* the University are being
redecorated', he would be guilty of a category mistake, but his statement might be just as meaningful and informative as the proper statement. He might simply be using the term 'University' to misdescribe
the Senate House. If, however, he said, 'All the colleges are being
redecorated but the University is not', his remark would be meaningless to anyone who did not know that he was misdescribing the Senate
House.

The above examples are given to illustrate two main points: first,
that *we cannot by inspection decide whether any given sentence embodies a
category mistake*. I am not making a category mistake when I say 'The
sun is rising'; I may not even be making a category mistake when I
say, 'Minds and bodies interact'. I may have emancipated myself from
the 'two worlds myth' but found that the statement, 'There is interaction between those phenomena described by psychologists and those
described by physiologists, chemists, and physicists' is a somewhat
unwieldy alternative. We have to consider who is speaking, to whom,

and in what situation, and what common knowledge can be assumed by speaker and listener.

The second point is that it is difficult, if not impossible, to give a reference to the term 'fact' which will be independent of the language used to think, speak, or write about 'facts'. The conception of the 'world of facts' changes individually with education, and sociologically with every advance of science and philosophy. What then remains of the distinction between a 'factual' and a 'verbal' dispute or mistake? If we know that the revolution of the earth causes the sun gradually to appear we are not making a 'verbal' mistake when we say 'The sun is rising'. If our misinformed foreigner says, 'The big building next to the British Museum is the University' we might be inclined to call his mistake a category or 'verbal' mistake. If he said, 'The big building next to the British Museum is *called* the University' we would call it a 'factual' mistake. Implicit language mistakes are 'verbal'; the same mistakes when explicit are 'factual'.

In *The Concept of Mind* (p. 22) Ryle says, '. . . the phrase "there occur mental processes" does not mean the same sort of thing as "there occur physical processes", and, therefore, . . . it makes no sense to conjoin or disjoin the two'. Suppose I now conjoin the two and say, 'There occur mental processes and there occur physical processes.' If this makes no sense, what kind of nonsense is it? If it is a category mistake or a logical mistake, how can I correct it? The analogue suggested by Ryle does not help us. It is, 'She came home in a flood of tears and a sedan-chair'. First, this joke is not meaningless: it means the same as the correct expression; and, second, it is easily amended to 'She came home sitting in a sedan-chair, in a flood of tears'. Why do we not call 'bursting into floods of tears' or 'being on the horns of a dilemma' category mistakes, but allow them as metaphorical expressions? Because everyone has consented to talk in this way and there is little danger of misunderstanding.

Suppose I go on to defend my 'nonsensical' statement, 'There occur . . .'. By 'mental processes' I mean both what I find going on by introspection and memory, and unconscious mental processes as studied and described by psychoanalysts; and by 'physical processes' I mean what is described by physicists; and I leave open the question how far the two sets of hypotheses do or will coincide. To call dreaming a physical process may not be a mistake but there is at present no point in doing so; it would be unenlightening, because physicists cannot put forward hypotheses to describe and explain what is going on when I dream. If they could, as some day they might, calling a dream both a mental and a physical process would be like calling the Spanish Civil War both a political and an economic process. Neither *need* suggest a two-worlds myth; both *can* quite legitimately suggest that a set of hypotheses from one discipline coincides (at least partially) with a set from another discipline.

One of the most prolific authors of 'category mistakes' in English was Shakespeare. ('Sleep, that knits up the ravell'd sleeve of care'; 'And where care lodges, sleep will never lie'; 'Patience is sottish, and impatience does/Become a dog that's mad'.) How do we distinguish between category mistakes and figurative or poetic language? Figurative language is the deliberate and successful allocation to a single category, of concepts usually assigned to different categories. Category mistakes are such allocations when they are unwitting and unsuccessful. It is impossible to judge from the grammar or 'logic' of an utterance, unless 'logic' here means 'pragmatics', whether it is a category mistake or not. Wit, jokes, illuminating paradoxes, poetic images, and established idioms are not category mistakes but *category fusions*. 'Du sublime au ridicule n'est qu'un pas.' 'D'accord, le Pas de Calais.' Here we have a metaphor taken literally and resulting in wit. 'Le propriété c'est le vol' is logically invalid, but it comes off: it is a successful paradox. 'Bubbling over with excitement' is a valid idiom.

I suggest, therefore, that whether to say, 'There are both physical and mental processes' is a category mistake or not depends on the context and on the philosophical standpoint of the speaker. If he believes that he is referring to two distinct and independent series of events, it *is* a category mistake; if he is using the sentence as logically analogous to 'There are both political and economic events', it is not. Further, the question whether any utterance is a category mistake can be settled, not by considering the sentence, but by considering the standpoint and intention of the speaker and the linguistic and situational context of the utterance.

At this point, a philosopher might object that the foregoing analysis of 'fact' and 'category mistake' is not philosophical but psychological. Instead of explaining what 'fact' meant, I found myself forced into autobiography (see p. 7). I have always used the term 'fact' when I have been convinced of the truth of some hypothesis, such as, 'Father Christmas brings presents every year'. I reluctantly abandoned this hypothesis in favour of a much less exciting one, and I have since abandoned many others: some because I decided they were false; some because I decided they were meaningless (to me). In each case what had seemed to be a 'fact' ceased to seem so. There is no reason to think that I shall not go on changing my opinions, or that science will make no further progress. It is likely that in a few hundred years the 'facts' described by Einstein, Russell, and Freud, will undergo revision as the 'facts' described by Newton have been revised.

SEMIOTIC

If logical terms such as 'category mistake', 'analytic', 'descriptive', 'performative', and so on, refer, as I maintain, not to sentences or statements but to utterances-in-context or to classes of such utterances, then the distinction between philosophy and psychology becomes much less clear than is supposed. Let us consider the statement: '"He has improved in mind and body" exemplifies a category mistake.' This is a shorthand statement which is misleading as it stands and needs to be expanded in order to be valid. Thus, 'If anyone says "He has improved in mind and body" in a situation where it is clear that "mind" and "body" are being used as if they referred to two separate entities of the same kind, then he is making a category mistake.' Is this a philosophical or a psychological or a sociological statement? Similarly, it would be wrong to say that 'Not Guilty' is a performative or ascriptive expression. We need to say, '"Not Guilty" is a performative expression when spoken by the foreman of a jury in a particular situation.' We could expand still further and say, 'Whenever the foreman of a jury says "Not Guilty" to the judge after the return of the jury, he is performing and not describing: he is changing the situation.' This longhand statement looks curiously like a sociological statement.

Before we try to discover the relationship between philosophy and psychology, let us link this question with the distinctions between the three branches of semiotic: pragmatics, semantics, and syntactics, as formulated by C. W. Morris in his *Foundations of the Theory of Signs*. Pragmatics, the theory of the relations between signs and those who produce or receive and understand them, comprehends psychology, sociology, and the history of the use of languages. The longhand statement quoted above is a pragmatic statement: it may therefore be called a sociological statement. Semantics, the theory of the relations between signs and their designata, is an abstraction from pragmatics. In *The Concept of Mind* (p. 130) Ryle points out, 'Verbs like "spell", "catch", "solve", "find", "win", "cure", "score", "deceive", "persuade", "arrive" and countless others signify not merely that some performance has been gone through, but also that something has been

brought off by the agent going through it. They are verbs of success.'
He is here doing semantics. His observation could be expanded into
the language of pragmatics: 'When people use verbs like "spell"', and
so on; but in this example we feel that such transcription would be
pointless. What, then, is the difference between this example and the
'Not Guilty' example?

The abstraction from the psychology or sociology of utterances to
the semantics of words and sentences is innocuous *as long as the differences between individual speakers and listeners, and individual contexts, are
insignificant*. The danger of such abstraction, as the example 'He has
improved in mind and body' has illustrated, is that *sentences* or *statements*, instead of *utterances*, tend to be classified as 'analytic', 'descriptive', 'performative', 'category mistakes', and so on. Semantics, then,
is shorthand pragmatics, which should always be susceptible of transcription into pragmatic form. The transcription, for example, of
'"He has improved in mind and body" is a category mistake' into
pragmatic form is uninteresting *only* if *any* person, *whenever* he uses the
sentence 'He has improved in mind and body', is making a category
mistake.

Syntactics, the theory of the formal relations among signs, is of two
kinds. If a logistic system is not intended to have any interpretation it
has no direct bearing on science or ordinary language. If it is so
intended, it is an abstraction from semantics and should, like semantics,
be susceptible of transcription into pragmatics. Let us take as an
example the relation of exclusive disjunction – $p+q$ (p or q but not
both). Whether or not two given sentences can be substituted in a
syntactic formula to form a valid semantic statement can be decided
only by a *pragmatic* study of the uses of those sentences.

Take the sentence: 'The statement that evolution is due in part to
the hereditary transmission of characters acquired or modified by use
or disuse is incompatible with the statement that evolution is due solely
to random variations and natural selection.' This is a statement in
semantic form of the exclusive disjunction of possible versions of the
neo-Lamarckian and the Darwinian hypotheses. Now suppose I try to
explain what I mean by 'random variations'. 'Random'* usually means
'unplanned', 'unguided', 'unpredictable', or 'not according to rule'. If
I say that variations are 'random', can I mean any more than that no
scientist has been known to predict them or to suggest a hypothesis to
account for their occurrence or to point out any regularities in their

* The term 'random' is systematically equivocal. No attempt is made here to deal
with it in its complexity.

occurrence? Do I also mean that no scientist ever will? If so, my statement is rash.

I call a toss of the coin 'random' if I believe that the thrower lacks either the skill or the will to control the toss in such a way that the result is predictable, and if there is no suspiciously long run of heads or tails. But I would call the throws random if a clever juggler got the trick of controlling them (a trick which he kept to himself) and deliberately got heads and tails in roughly equal proportions. Only he would know they were not random. They would seem random to me *because of my ignorance of his skill.*

If I am modest, then, I can say no more than that I know of no causal explanation of biological variations, no regularities in their occurrence, and no correlation with other events except some non-specific and unquantified correlation with radiation. One of the causal factors might be, and equally might not be, modification of characters by use or disuse.

It follows, therefore, that the relevant terms can be used in such a way that the hypotheses are not incompatible. If that is so, the semantic statement is either descriptive and inadequate, or recommendatory. If recommendatory, it is like 'We should not use this hypothesis as equivalent to that', or 'Anyone who uses language in this way is in a muddle', or 'I disapprove of this kind of talk'. The recommendatory use of semantics is often difficult to distinguish from the descriptive, and transcription into pragmatics has the merit of revealing the 'cash-value' of more abstract statements.

Let us now consider the 'cash-value' of statements about psychology and psychoanalysis. Both philosophy and the sciences are concerned with the formation, criticism, and testing of general theories. When a philosophical theory conflicts with a scientific one, by what criteria should we choose between them? In the chapter on 'Psychology' in *The Concept of Mind*, a chapter whose brevity he explains by his denial that '"psychology" is the name of a unitary inquiry or tree of inquiries', Ryle remarks, 'Indeed, so deservedly profound has been the influence of Freud's teaching and so damagingly popular have its allegories become, that there is now evident a strong tendency to use the word "psychologists" as if it stood only for those who investigate and treat mental disabilities.' He goes on to consider and reject the following view: 'Granted that there are hosts of different ways in which the workings of men's minds are studied, psychology differs from all the other studies in trying to find out the causes of these workings.' He rejects this view on the ground that 'not all, or even most, causal explanations of human actions and reactions are to be ranked as psychological. But, furthermore, not all psychological researches are searches for causal explanations. . . . So, as it must be styled "psychological research", "psychological research" cannot be defined as the search for causal explanations.'

Let us now contrast this opinion with that of Freud (1923b, p. 235):

'Psycho-analysis is the name (1) of a procedure for the investigation of mental processes which are almost inaccessible in any other way, (2) of a method (based upon that investigation) for the treatment of neurotic disorders and (3) of a collection of psychological information obtained along those lines, which is gradually being accumulated into a new scientific discipline.'

Before we try to choose between these views, there are several points in Ryle's argument which should be considered separately. First, there are many people who are not sure how to use the terms 'psychologist', 'psychiatrist', and 'psychoanalyst'. This is a true sociological observation. Second, it is also true that not all causal explanations of human actions are to be ranked as psychological. 'I shouted because he trod on my foot' is an example. Third, it is also true that not all psychological researches are searches for causal explanations. Research into the distribution of the kind of intelligence that can be measured by tests is an example. None of these true remarks seem to be relevant to the question whether psychology is becoming a scientific discipline.

What, then, does 'psychological research' mean? The research into the careers of a group of highly intelligent children carried out by L. M. Terman (1929-59) in California was 'psychological'. Was Freud's work psychological research? The peculiarity of the psychoanalytic method is that research and therapy are a single activity, although they are logically distinct. This has given rise to two alternative criticisms: that the method has had some therapeutic success but the explanations are fanciful 'allegories'; and that the method has contributed a great deal to the explanation of human behaviour but is of little therapeutic value. Clearly, therapeutic success is not a criterion of the validity of aetiological theories. A doctor administering a drug may obtain a real or apparent therapeutic success while maintaining a false theory. There are three possibilities: he may be right about the cause of the disease and find that the drug is efficacious while putting forward a false hypothesis to account for its efficacy; he may be wrong about both the cause of the disease and the effect of the drug but be right in maintaining a correlation between the administration of the drug and the patient's improvement; or the 'therapeutic success' may be no more than a lucky coincidence between the treatment and a spontaneous remission of the illness.

Before we consider how differences of opinion about psychology can be settled, a few words must be said about the terms 'research', 'diagnosis', 'explanation', and 'interpretation'. Everyone is concerned, for part of his waking life, with psychological problems. 'Why did he lose his temper?' 'Why does she invariably quarrel with anyone who attracts her?' 'Why is he unable to make productive use of his talents?' 'Why is he incapable of understanding this simple logical point?' Common sense tries to answer such questions and its answers are often re-statements of the problem in different form. 'His talents are wasted because he is lazy.' 'He cannot understand because he is stupid.' The difference between the common-sense and the scientific answer is like the difference between 'The apple falls because it is heavy' and the Newtonian explanation. If we think we have found a shrewd answer to a psychological question, such as 'He lost his temper because you nearly exposed a fallacy upon which his self-respect depends', we do not think we are doing scientific research or making a medical diagnosis. Yet psychological research, like physical research, consists in finding more and more comprehensive answers to more and more 'why' and 'how' questions.

INTERPRETATIONS

The term 'diagnosis' is associated with medicine and dissociated from 'research'. Yet a profound diagnosis of a single severe case of schizophrenia would constitute psychological research of great explanatory power. In psychoanalysis, diagnosis *is* research. There is also a very close connection between diagnosis and therapy, but although they are processes which are carried on *pari passu* they cannot be equated. The reason is that an analysis which is therapeutically unsuccessful may provide a valuable contribution to aetiological explanation. The cause of failure, such as premature termination, may be theoretically irrelevant. The connection between diagnosis–research and therapy is complex. An interpretation given by an analyst in a session is, from one point of view, an item of explanation (and therefore of tentative diagnosis or research); from another point of view it is an intervention which may change the situation. It may be a therapeutic factor. In philosophical terms, an item of explanation, when given outside the analytic situation, is descriptive; when inside, it is both descriptive and enactive* and needs to be both true and timely to have therapeutic value. An interpretation, then, is a hypothesis, an item of diagnosis, and an item of explanation. It may be objected that a hypothesis which changes the situation is not a valid hypothesis; that there is a parallel between the intervention of the analyst and the intervention of the physicist who tries to ascertain the position and the velocity of an electron. To study its position he has to use short gamma-rays which disturb its motion, and to study its velocity he has to use long waves which are too coarse to determine its position.

At this point we must distinguish between the controlled intervention of the analyst (giving interpretations) in an analytic session, and the use of hypotheses to account for the effect of enactive interpretations on subsequent behaviour. Perhaps a parallel with biophysics, though potentially misleading, may serve to illustrate this point. If current research into the effects of radiation on genetic mutations were to reach the stage where the effects of controlled experiments on mutations could be accurately predicted, then we should have a set of scientific hypotheses relating to the process of the physicist's intervention in 'random' mutation. This might lead to a fuller understanding and explanation of non-induced, random mutations, and eventually to the dropping or restricting of this use of the word 'random'. The intervention of the physicist would be parallel to the intervention of the analyst, and biophysical hypotheses to account for the effects of the intervention would be parallel to psychological hypotheses to account for the effects of the analyst's intervention.

Until recently psychoanalysis, in the sense of scientific psychology, was explanatory and not predictive. There is a close, but not complete, parallel between explanation of human behaviour and explanation of the evolution of species. Both Darwin and Freud accumulated data in support of hypotheses which encountered strong emotional resistance. Both were unable to conduct controlled experiments by which their hypotheses could be tested. Even embryology, which seemed to many

* The term 'performative' is used by J. L. Austin (1946, p. 171) to distinguish a use of language which may seem to be, but is not, 'descriptive' or 'informative'. 'I know' or 'I promise' do not describe the state of mind of the speaker. When a descriptive or an informative sentence is used to achieve a certain effect, or is likely to do so, and the effect is more important than the description or information, I suggest the term 'enactive' to describe the use of language.

The many uses of language shade into each other, and no pedantic system of 'categories' is being proposed.

A full list of the important philosophical distinctions between the *predominant functions* of utterances (and hence by abstraction to the semantic level, between the predominant functions of sentences) will be found in the Index under 'Uses of Language'.

THE RELATION BETWEEN PHILOSOPHY AND SCIENCE 17

scientists to verify the evolutionist's case, merely strengthened it, and offered no 'proof' in any rigorous sense of the term. Both succeeded in convincing some and failed to convince others. Both were concerned with genetic explanation rather than with precise explanation of concurrent events. The divergence lies in the 'publicity' of Darwin's data and the 'privacy' of Freud's (in one sense of that term). Darwin investigated nothing that could not have been investigated by other observers; Freud's data were his own dreams and thoughts, only part of which he could bring himself to reveal, and the confidential revelations of his patients, whose privacy and anonymity he had to respect. Psychoanalytic explanation based on 'public' evidence, such as Leonardo's biography or *Hamlet*, cannot claim a higher scientific status than shrewd speculation, since it is untestable analogical extrapolation from clinical experience.

The divergence lies not only in the accessibility of the data but also in the genesis of conviction. Belief in some form of evolutionary theory gradually spread because it accounted for innumerable phenomena which were otherwise scientifically inexplicable. Conviction came, if it came at all, from reading the relevant literature. Psychoanalysis, on the other hand, is seldom convincing to anyone who has not experienced, over and over again, a close connection between a specific interpretation and a related physical or mental change. A study of the literature may lead to a conviction that 'there's something in it', but it is unlikely to induce the reader to entertain as scientifically respectable the most important psychological hypotheses: those relating to the details of the phantasy life of both 'normal' and 'abnormal' individuals.

2

Psychoanalysis and Physics

Until recently, then, psychoanalytic theory has had a weaker claim to 'scientific respectability' than the theory of evolution, and both have had a weaker claim than the sciences which can conduct controlled experiments and make precise predictions. It is true that the 'exact' sciences have proved to be less exact than was believed, but at the macroscopic level their exactitude is still impressive. Before we go on to consider how the situation has changed, it will be useful to examine the distinction between the descriptive and classificatory sciences like natural history, and the exploratory sciences like physics. In *The Philosophy of Science* (1953, p. 53) Stephen Toulmin has given succinct expression to this distinction: 'Natural historians . . . look for regularities of given forms; but physicists seek the form of given regularities.' And on p. 34: 'The heart of all major discoveries in the physical sciences is the discovery of novel methods of representation, and so of fresh techniques by which inferences can be drawn – and drawn in ways which fit the phenomena under investigation.' He suggests that the acceptance of a model in physics is justified in the first place by the way in which it helps us to explain, represent, and predict the phenomena under investigation: that the model is more than a simple metaphor but that it may be necessary, as the science develops, to modify the model or to invent new models to deal with new problems.

Psychoanalysis, in this respect, is like physics and unlike natural history. The phenomena of dreams, for example, have, like the phenomena of light, been available for scientific study for thousands of years, but both sets of phenomena remained unintelligible until the appropriate methods of representation and techniques for drawing inferences were devised. Toulmin has pointed out (ibid., p. 79) that as soon as a formula's fruitfulness has been established it comes to be treated as a law, i.e. as something of which we ask not 'Is it true?' but 'When does it hold?' Now it may be thought that psychoanalysis is a discipline in which no law can be formulated – either because it is conceived as a genetic discipline like archaeology, or as a non-quantitative, non-mathematical discipline. Freud contributed to this belief by his use of the analogy with archaeology: he believed for many years that he was 'digging up the past'.

GENETIC AND AHISTORICAL METHOD

The distinction between the genetic method and the dynamic, ahistorical method is clearly explained by Dr Henry Ezriel (1956–7):

> 'The customary method of investigation in the natural sciences is to observe events in the "here and now", i.e. while they are taking place in front of the observer, either spontaneously or under experimental conditions set up by him. It is then possible to identify "dynamic, ahistorical" causes, i.e. the kind of conditions which have to operate in the "here and now" of *any* situation in order to bring about a certain event. In contrast with this, the historian or archaeologist, using a genetic method, reconstructs *particular* past events' (p. 34).

He points out that psychoanalysis is an ahistorical, dynamic method and not a genetic one. Here it may be objected that the analyst's purpose is to discover what events in the history of the individual were causal factors in the development of the disturbance, and so the method must be a genetic one. An analogy with physics may help to clarify the point. If a scientist computes the amount of radioactive carbon present in organic remains, he is studying here-and-now events; his findings may be a contribution to archaeological dating, and if the scientist's interest is primarily in the date of death of the organism, the radio-carbon method may be thought of as a genetic, historical method. If, however, the interest were in the process of radiation, its investigation would be thought of as a piece of dynamic research. The psychoanalyst, too, is investigating here-and-now processes, and, since the unconscious fears which are revealed originate in the past, he can, like the archaeologist, speculate about the approximate date of the origin of specific fears by correlating his findings with what is known of children and adolescents. Whether he thinks that his work is genetic or dynamic depends on the direction of his interest and on the theory he maintains. The following argument suggests that the more fruitful approach both therapeutically and heuristically is the explicit recognition that the analyst is both investigating and intervening in here-and-now processes.

Ezriel argues that what the analyst uncovers is

'. . . not a replica of actual events in the patient's past life, but *unconscious structures active in the present* though formed in the past out of both phantasies and correct or distorted memories of actual events' (op. cit. p. 32).

'In keeping with Lewin's (1936, p. 34) thesis that only such forces as exist at a certain time can have effects at that time, genetic explanations are valid only because they include ahistorical dynamic causes. It could, for instance, be said that the genetic "cause" of the submissive behaviour of one of my patients towards me in treatment is that a rebellious attitude which he adopted in his childhood towards his father happened to be followed closely by his father's death, and thus made him believe that it was his attitude that was responsible for the disaster. This genetic proposition, however, is valid only because it tries to explain the patient's behaviour at two points in his life, in his childhood and now, each time by reference to dynamic propositions which are based on the same ahistorical dynamic cause of his submissiveness, i.e. that to him *events show that rebellious behaviour leads to the death of the person on whom one's welfare depends.* In childhood this dynamic cause operated in external reality when – in addition to other causes – his father's death made him substitute a submissive for a rebellious attitude; the same dynamic cause operates here and now in the psychical reality of his unconscious phantasies and makes him adopt a submissive instead of a rebellious attitude towards me in treatment. This last statement can, however, be formulated as an ahistorical dynamic proposition in the here and now, which explains this particular aspect of the patient's personality by reference solely to his present unconscious structures – (unconscious object relationships) without any reference to the past' (pp. 35–6).

'It ought to be possible for the analyst . . . to control the antecedent variables by selecting them from the pre-interpretation material and incorporating them in his interpretations, and to make predictions about the patient's responses to these interpretations. The psychoanalytic session thus becomes an experimental situation in which hypotheses can be tested through direct observation of the patient's behaviour.

Experimentation in the psychoanalytic session therefore depends on the analyst's ability to select the antecedent variables, i.e. to identify the patient's unconscious object relationships which are determining his behaviour towards the analyst' (p. 38).

DIFFERENCES BETWEEN PHYSICS AND PSYCHOANALYSIS

The importance of this theoretical advance can easily be overlooked. Because therapy, diagnosis, and scientific research are temporally coincident, there is a tendency to feel that experimentation in psycho-analysis cannot be 'pure science', or that successful research can be achieved only at the expense of therapy. Before trying to disentangle the logically distinct elements in a single process, it may be interesting to ask how this process resembles and differs from experimentation in physics. The first obvious difference is that physics, being a highly developed science, has a large number of laws, or, in Ryle's phrase, 'inference-tickets', at its disposal, whereas psychoanalysis has very few, and tentative, ones. The second is that psychology is not primarily quantitative. The third is that there is usually a clear division between pure and applied physics, and for pure research experiments can often be designed to fit particular theoretical problems. The fourth is that where controlled experiments are impossible, as in astronomy, the configuration of (macroscopic) elements is relatively simple, whereas in psychology it is very complex. The fifth is the difference in accessibility of evidence, although this is now being eliminated by the use of electrical recordings. Any observer who understands the theoretical techniques of psychoanalysis can now make an independent judgement of (a) the validity and (b) the efficacy of interpretations, and (c) the validity of hypotheses about the effects of the interpretations, when-ever electrical recordings are used.

RESEMBLANCES

The first resemblance between psychoanalysis and physics is that the phenomena which attracted the scientist's interest to begin with were everyday phenomena, such as light and dreams, which were generally thought either to have been explained, or not to need explanation, or to be inexplicable. The second is that both sciences began by introduc-ing new inferring techniques. Regarding light as something that travelled in straight lines was the foundation of the physical theory of light; regarding dreams as attempted wish-fulfilments was the starting-point of the psychological theory of dreams. In grander terms, the Principle of the Rectilinear Propagation of Light and the Principle of the Attempted Wish-fulfilment Function of Dreams were discoveries which enabled a series of new inferring techniques to be introduced. Their heuristic value was independent of the problem of defining the terms occurring in the principles. It is doubtful whether the term 'light' has ever been satisfactorily defined, and a moment's reflection will reveal that what Freud studied was not 'dreams' but memories of dreams. (There is good reason for saying that no one ever knows precisely what he has dreamt, since we cannot tell what part is played by the elaboration of memories of dreams as we return to consciousness.) The heuristic value of the two principles was also independent of the truth of the statements, 'Light travels in straight lines' and 'All dreams are attempted wish-fulfilments'.

The third resemblance is that both the physicist and the psychoanalyst seek (in Toulmin's words) 'the *form* and the *scope* of regularities which are found to happen, not universally, but at most on the whole'. Snell's Law describes the regularities, under similar conditions, of the refraction of light within a wide range of transparent substances, but it makes sense to speak of the scope of Snell's Law because in the case of some substances refraction is 'anomalous'. Later on we shall examine two psychoanalytic laws and consider how they are like and unlike physical laws. Psychoanalysis studies the form and scope of regularities in the dream-memories, phantasies, and behaviour not only of 'abnormal' patients, but also of 'normal' doctors and other trainees.

The fourth resemblance is the introduction of models which help us to explain, represent, and predict the phenomena under investigation. An example is the id-ego-superego model. In both the physical sciences and psychoanalysis 'the regularities we find in any particular field of phenomena are represented in a way which is application-neutral' (Toulmin, 1953, p. 122). In comparing physical theories with maps, Toulmin points out that a satisfactory map is route-neutral, and that 'though the preparation of itineraries may in fact often be applied cartography, it need not be. Itineraries preceded maps'. To discuss the cause or cure of a particular neurotic illness is like discussing an itinerary: it is applied psychoanalysis.* To represent psychological regularities in a way that is application-neutral is pure psychoanalysis. If Toulmin is right in saying that 'the determinate . . . is that for which a place can be found on the map', then psychoanalysis has had the effect of showing that many more psychological phenomena are determinate than was formerly supposed.

The fifth resemblance is that in both sciences the discovery of new techniques and theoretical advances proceed *pari passu*. The introduction of the technique of child analysis by Melanie Klein was accompanied by changes in the theory of psychic development, and hence in

---

* Many psychoanalysts use the term 'applied psychoanalysis' where I have used 'extrapolation from clinical experience'. For example, Part Two of *New Directions in Psycho-Analysis* (Klein *et al.*, 1955) consists of papers applying psychoanalytic findings to ethics, aesthetics, literature, etc. This double use of the term 'applied' should not cause confusion, provided that it is not assumed that all analytic work except studies in related disciplines is 'pure'.

the id-ego-superego model. The technical change from the attemp
reconstruct the psychic history of the individual to the attempt to giv
here-and-now interpretations of the transference situation is accompanied by a theoretical shift of emphasis from genetic to ahistorical
explanation, which facilitates the formulation of application-neutral
principles or laws.

Sixth, the following remarks of Toulmin's about physics can be
applied verbatim to psychoanalysis: 'The difference between laws and
generalizations is connected with . . . the fact that natural historians
are committed for the most part to the everyday classification of their
subject-matter, whereas it is open to physical scientists to reclassify
theirs as they go along: "What is or is not a cow is for the public to
decide". . . . In formalized sciences such as physics, by contrast, the
terminology is not fixed beforehand, least of all by the public. Theories,
techniques of representation and terminologies are introduced together,
at one swoop' (1953, pp. 145-6).

What is or is not unconscious guilt is as hard for the layman to
decide as what is or is not anomalous refraction, and as different from
what is or is not a cow. It is highly probable that the techniques of
representation and terminology of psychoanalysis will undergo similar
changes to those of physics.

Finally, the psychoanalyst is like the physicist in that his *presumptions*
(not assumptions) are only *initial* presumptions. He presumes (a) that
the existing theories will, between them, suffice to explain the behaviour of each fresh system of phenomena which he chooses to study,
and (b) that any fresh system will resemble most closely in behaviour
those systems which it most resembles in structure (cf. Toulmin, 1953,
p. 147). He has to be on the look-out for deviations, and when he finds
them he has to try to discover how the existing theories can be modified
or supplemented to account for them.

THERAPY, DIAGNOSIS, AND RESEARCH

Having briefly considered how pure psychoanalysis is like and unlike
pure physics, we can now return to the logical distinctions between
therapy, diagnosis, and research.

Although successful therapy tends to make the layman think, 'There
must be something in it', it is not, as we have seen, an adequate
criterion of correct explanation. If a doctor, confronted with a
mysterious new disease, says, 'Try penicillin', and penicillin works, his
contribution to pure science is simply the isolated datum, 'Somehow

this disease'. And so, *mutatis mutandis*, for a doctor who

23

to

—nding a drug which cured schizophrenia. The social
—covery would be enormous; its value for pure science
—n how comprehensively the effect of the drug could

—zriel's article: he distinguishes between three kinds of
relations in the psychoanalytic session—the *required*, the *avoided*,
and the *calamity*. For example, the patient mentioned before 'adopted a
submissive behaviour pattern (required relationship) and avoided
being rebellious because he feared that rebellious behaviour would lead
to the death of the person on whom his welfare depended'. Ezriel
believes that the essence of psychoanalytic therapy is 'a process of
reality testing. . . . The interpretation enables the patient to test his
unconsciously determined fears in external reality when the avoided
relationship materializes by being made explicit by the analyst. . . .
He is thus helped to assess the true effects of the avoided relationship
and, comparing them with the unconsciously expected calamity and
realizing that the latter has not materialized, he becomes capable of
giving less disguised expression in external reality to his hitherto
avoided behaviour pattern' (1956–7, p. 39).

ROGERS ?

From this we can see that the interpretation is (a) a hypothesis, and,
if true, is (b) an item of diagnosis and (c) a therapeutic factor, that is, an
intervention, something which changes the situation. Pure psychology,
therefore, as opposed to applied, will consist of laws and theories
relating to the interaction of words and actions of analyst and patient,
and, by extrapolation, to the thoughts, words, and actions of people in
general. Similarly, the physicist extrapolates from the results of controlled experiments with light to the behaviour of light in general,
with the proviso that deviations are always possible.

Before we return to the problem of the changing terminologies of
philosophy and science, let us consider two psychoanalytic laws proposed by Ezriel in relation to Toulmin's distinction between four
classes of statement which he suggests have been confused by philosophers. He distinguishes between:

'(i) abstract, formal statements of a law or principle – e.g. Snell's Law;
(ii) historical reports about the discovered scope of a law or principle – e.g.
the statement that Snell's Law has been found to apply to most non-crystalline
substances at normal temperatures;
(iii) applications of a law or principle to particular cases – e.g. the statement
that . . . the sunlight getting over a certain wall is travelling to the ground
behind the wall in a straight line;

(iv) conclusions of inferences drawn in accordance with a law or principle – e.g. the conclusion that, the angle of incidence and refractive index being what they are, the angle of refraction must be 36°; or the conclusion that, with the sun at 30°, the shadow of a 6 ft. high wall must be 10 ft. 6 in. deep' (Toulmin, 1953, p. 90).

Now to examine Ezriel's two laws:

'The first law is: if we set up a field by putting together a patient in need of treatment and a therapist presumed to be capable of satisfying this need, and if the therapist assumes a passive, non-directive role, then the patient will display in his words and actions a manifest form of behaviour from which, by applying certain operational rules, three kinds of object relations can be inferred: (i) the required relationship, which he has to adopt to escape from (ii) the avoided relationship, which he believes will lead to (iii) a calamity.

The second law is: if the analyst then gives a here-and-now interpretation – that is, points out the hidden dynamics of the patient-analyst relationship in terms of these three object relations and their connection, by means of a "because" clause – the subsequent material produced by the patient will contain the avoided object relationship in a clearer, i.e. less repressed form' (Ezriel, 1956–7, p. 40).

These are abstract statements of laws, class (i). The question of their being true or false is less interesting than the question: what is their scope and their heuristic value? An example of Toulmin's class (ii) statements would be: 'Ezriel's Laws have been found to apply to groups of patients as well as to individuals.' An example of class (iii) would be: 'X is being more rebellious to the analyst as a result of the interpretation, which pointed out that he was being submissive because he unconsciously feared that rebelliousness would lead to a calamity.' An example of class (iv) would be: 'If X is carefully avoiding a quarrel with the analyst in spite of considerable evidence of suppressed hostility, then he must fear the consequences of the open expression of his feelings.'

The second and third classes are empirical statements. The first, the abstract statements of laws, are certainly *based* on experience, in the sense that time and time again analysts have found evidence of powerful unconscious fears of some indescribable calamity, sometimes rationalized as fears of death, of war, of madness, of revenge inflicted by enemies, and so on: unconscious fears which are not modified by the temporary mitigation of the 'rational' fears; and have found that interpretations are often followed by clearer manifestations of the 'avoided object relationship'. But the laws will stand or fall by their usefulness as techniques for making precise inferences, and not by their truth or falsity. Philosophers disagree about whether law-like statements should be called empirical statements; the dispute is not important if all the relevant distinctions are recognized.

The 'must' in the example of class (iv) is the scientific 'must' which puzzled Hume. When we say, 'If the water has been raised to 212°F it must be boiling', we say it with the tacit qualification, 'If all the conditions are satisfied for the application of the principle: water boils at 212°F.' The same applies to the statement: 'The sun must have risen now in Australia.' To quote Toulmin (p. 94):

> 'The important thing is not to confuse the questions, what theory *has been found* reliable in a given field, and what phenomena, according to this theory, *must* occur in any given circumstances. When one is talking *about* a theory – whether establishing it, or identifying a system as one to which it applies – one is concerned with what has been found to be the case, not with what must be; but when one is talking *in terms of* a theory – applying it to explain or foretell the phenomena occurring in such-and-such a situation – one is then concerned with what, according to that theory, must happen in that situation.'

This point is relevant to my example of class (iv): 'If X is carefully avoiding a quarrel . . .'. A sharp critic may have objected, 'But why "must"? Why couldn't he be avoiding a quarrel out of politeness, or laziness, or kindness? Surely fear is not the only motive for an eireni-con?' The answer to such a critic reveals a philosophical difficulty which is due to the special status of psychological terminology. Although the terms 'politeness', 'laziness', 'kindness' and their like occur in analytic sessions, they are not used to explain behaviour in the *theory* as they are in everyday speech. They are used to refer to the explicandum rather than the explicans. 'He fails his examinations through laziness' would be regarded by an analyst as a pseudo-explanation just as trivial as 'His throat is inflamed because he has laryngitis'. The reason for this is that the emotions evoked by a successful analysis are the primitive, pre-social emotions of great intensity, so that politeness, kindness, or apathy, are regarded in explanatory theory as defences against primitive emotions such as love, hate, fear, and guilt.

The philosophical problem is that psychoanalytic theory is misleadingly intelligible to the layman. To understand the terminology of physics or biology it is necessary to study the techniques from which the technical language has evolved. In psychoanalysis a short cut is possible, so that it may appear that there are no technical terms apart from a score or two of words for which definitions are provided.

There are two further complicating factors: first, many of the terms used for conscious mental processes are given a theoretical application to unconscious processes; and second, many of the problems the analyst tries to solve are problems to which the layman offers a rival solution which *feels right* to him. It is more difficult for an intelligent man to admit to a doctor, 'If you were given a chance to study my words and behaviour you would understand my mental processes and my problems better than I do' than to admit, 'If you were given a chance to study my body you would understand better than I what is going on in it.'

The analyst has one foot in common-sense language and the other in technical terminology. This is not a problem with interpretation, since he interprets mainly in the idiom of the patient, but it is a problem for the psychological theorist and the philosopher. Here we may revert to an earlier example and draw what may seem a wild analogy between the conceptual change underlying the child's and the adult's use of the sentence, 'The sun is rising', and the conceptual change underlying the lay and the psychoanalytic use of the sentence, 'He is afraid'. The lay criteria would be something like: 'He says he is afraid'; 'He is sweating'; 'He has good reason to go into the burning building but he is not going in'; and so on. The psychoanalytic criteria would include these but add many others, such as: 'He has high blood-pressure'; 'He has a duodenal ulcer'; 'He fails his examinations'; 'He is frequently impotent'; and so on. This is not to suggest that symptoms are related to fear in any direct or simple way, or that unconscious and conscious fear cannot be distinguished, but that the term 'unconscious' is often omitted in explanatory theory as superfluous.

3

Behaviourism

It is time to recapitulate and to reconsider several unanswered questions. We noted that Ryle claimed that he was re-allocating rather than denying facts. I suggest that this way of talking is a residue from the metaphysical theory of logical atomism once proposed by Russell and Wittgenstein, according to which language had meaning through a structural similarity of sentence and fact, and 'facts' were 'out there' waiting to be pictured or referred to. The thesis of this chapter is that uses of language are successful or unsuccessful for certain purposes, and that it is misleading to speak of 'facts' as if they were independent of ways of thinking, talking, and writing. Our languages, both at common-sense and technical levels, are constantly changing, and even when words or sentences remain unchanged ('the sun is rising') their uses undergo a semantic (and hence a pragmatic) change. When a philosopher successfully demonstrates that a certain way of talking is pointless, and persuades his contemporaries to abandon it, he changes language in such a way that the sentences which it was formerly thought could be used to describe, ask questions, and so on, are now regarded as curious relics, like abandoned castles. Many of our present-day utterances are believed to be factual, but this is not to say that there are 'facts' to which they refer or which they describe. I do not think that anyone believes that there are 'questions' out there in the world to which sentences used for interrogation 'refer' or 'correspond'.

THE STATUS OF PSYCHOLOGICAL THEORY

When Freud and Ryle disagree about the status and future of psychological theory whom should we follow? Those theories have the strongest claim to be studied, and clarified by philosophical analysis, which have the greatest explanatory value, and not those which have the most consistent terminologies. Those philosophical methods have the strongest claim to be adopted which are most fruitful, that is, most successful in resolving philosophical puzzlement. Philosophers have a natural tendency to study the language of other philosophers, living and dead. If it is true, however, as I maintain, that languages, philosophical and scientific techniques, and literary and scientific conceptual systems are all changing by progressive interaction, then those disciplines whose techniques initiate the most important changes in our ways of thinking, talking, and writing, should be counted among the proper objects of philosophical clarification. Freud and his followers have thrown more light on human thinking, feeling, and behaving, than any other writers in history. For this reason, and also because the terminology of psychodynamics has not yet been made precise and consistent, psychoanalysis is a field in which the most modern philosophical method may be expected to be especially fruitful. We cannot follow Ryle in his opinion of psychological theory (1949), but we can follow him in his method of studying the way language works, with a minimum of preconceptions, and pointing out resemblances and differences between various uses of language. In the psychological field this could best be done by psychoanalysts with the time, interest, and flair for critical examination of the theory, but of those analysts who have a philosophical bent most, to judge by recent literature, are too hardpressed by clinical work to devote much time to the philosophy of psychoanalysis. Hence the need for the small stream of philosophical psychoanalysts to be augmented by a tributary of psychoanalytic philosophers.

The view I am advocating, that the uses of language are constantly changing as new discoveries are made, new techniques introduced, new insight gained, and new principles and laws formulated, implies that philosophy and science are constantly influencing each other. Let us consider as an example the theory and programme of Behaviourism.

Ryle says (p. 328): 'The behaviourists' methodological programme has been of revolutionary importance to the programme of psychology.' This statement is unquestionably true. The decision never to assume that ancient remains are a clue to unseen past events would be of revolutionary importance to archaeology; never to infer from seen to unseen clouds – to meteorology; never to trust a microscope – to cytology; never to trust instrument readings – to physics; never to trust a telescope – to astronomy. The decision never to use the most important (though not easily decipherable) clue to what people think and

feel, namely, what they say spontaneously in a controlled situation, is
for a psychologist a self-denying ordinance which stops the science
before it starts. Unfortunately behaviourism is not merely an eccen-
tricity of certain academic psychologists: it has had a considerable
influence on modern philosophy. At the end of *The Concept of Mind*
Ryle says, 'Thinking, on the one view, is identical with saying. The
holders of the rival view rightly reject this identification, but they
make this rejection, naturally but wrongly, in the form that saying is
doing one thing and thinking is doing another.' He is concerned to
expose the terminological malversation (his phrase) of epistemologists,
and he does so with brilliance and cogency. Four of the major fallacies
which have beset philosophy are: the Epistemologist's Fallacy, the
Fallacy of Unrestricted Scepticism,* the Fact-finding Fallacy,† and
the Behaviourist Fallacy.‡ From the first two Ryle is immune:
from the second two his immunity is (or was) incomplete. The Epistemologist's Fallacy is of little interest outside technical philosophical discussion; the other fallacies will be fully elucidated in
Chapter 15.

THE EPISTEMOLOGIST'S FALLACY

Ryle points out (1949, p. 317) that the phrase 'theory of knowledge'
could be used to stand either for the theory of the sciences, i.e. the
systematic study of the structures of built theories, or for the theory of
learning, discovery, and invention. He demonstrates by a series of
convincing examples that

'. . . these separate intellectual processes postulated by epistemologists are
para-mechanical dramatizations of the classified elements of achieved and
expounded theories' (p. 291).

'Now the great epistemologists, Locke, Hume and Kant, were in the main
advancing the Grammar of Science, when they thought they were discussing
parts of the occult life-story of persons acquiring knowledge. They were
discussing the credentials of sorts of theories, but they were doing this in
paraphysiological allegories. The recommended restoration of the trade-
names of traditional epistemology to their proper place in the anatomy of
built theories would have a salutary influence on our theories about minds'
(p. 318).

In short, his whole chapter on 'The Intellect' is a stimulating and convincing refutation of the Epistemologist's Fallacy.

* Defined p. 202.   † Defined pp. 203–4.   ‡ Defined pp. 204–6.

THE MIND AS A PRIVATE STAGE

He then goes on:

'One of the strongest forces making for the belief in the doctrine that the mind is a private stage is the ingrained habit of assuming that there must exist the "cognitive acts" and "cognitive processes" which these trade-names have been perverted to signify. . . . The imputed episodes seemed to be impenetrably "internal" because they were genuinely unwitnessable. But they were genuinely unwitnessable because they were mythical. They were causal hypotheses substituted for functional descriptions of the elements of published theories' (p. 318).

This last sentence is the clean blow which lops off the Epistemologist's Fallacy's head. But are there not other reasons for thinking of the mind as a private stage? Are there not reasons which would occur to the 'plain man' who has never heard of epistemology? Suppose I have committed a murder. I am cautious and never speak about it, never hint at it, to anybody. No one suspects me: I am a good actor and I behave quite unconcernedly when the newspaper reports are discussed. I often think about the murder; I re-enact it in my mind, I rehearse possible conversations with detectives in case I may fall under suspicion, and I make plans for a rapid getaway in the event of anything going wrong. If all goes well the secret will die with me. It may be said that what is taking place is not secret thinking but an interior dialogue or monologue, but surely this would be to elevate a metaphor into an unenlightening philosophical theory. Thinking without speaking *is* sometimes like talking to oneself, but it is still thinking. Private thinking may be completely and for ever inaccessible to all but the thinker. If Galileo had been content merely to *think* the blasphemy, 'Eppur si muove', no one would have known that he had formulated the heliocentric hypothesis.

BEHAVIOURISM

Instead of trying to persuade the behaviourist that people sometimes think in private, we should ask why the programme of Behaviourism has had so great an influence on academic psychology and even on philosophy. Both disciplines were profoundly impressed by the success of physics and the failure of psychology in the nineteenth century. It may be, therefore, that the academic psychologist, trying to account for this disparity of achievement, decided, or felt, that the physicist's success was due to his use of techniques of quantitative measurement, of controlled experiments, and of methods of decisive validation of hypotheses. He may have felt that the psychologist's failure was due to his lack of similar tools and to the inadequacy and deceptiveness of introspection. Some psychologists also felt a profound respect for the quantitative technique devised by Pavlov, and may have believed that a path would soon be found leading from canine physiology to human psychology. The result was that the academic psychologist forswore introspection, focused his interest on stimulus–response situations, looked about for anything that could be called 'behaviour' and could be measured, devised controlled experiments which might one day throw some light on the interesting problems of human psychology, and formulated hypotheses and laws relating to his experiments. Examples of such laws are Kirschmann's Law, that the saturation of a colour induced by chromatic contrast is proportional to the logarithm of the saturation of the contrast-inducing colour, and Fechner's Law, that the sensation is proportional to the logarithm of the stimulus. The paradoxical result of the behaviourist's programme has been that the work in academic and educational psychology which has thrown most light on human psychology is the kind of investigation in which precise validation is, for the most part, impossible – such as Rorschach testing, which is a valuable diagnostic tool; Gestalt theory, as developed by Köhler, Koffka, and Lewin; intelligence and aptitude testing; Piaget's empirical studies of the learning process in children, and so on. The rest is largely a minor extension of neurology and optics. It may be objected that intelligence testing is precise and can be validated. It is true that arithmetic is used, and arithmetic suggests precision, but recent discoveries regarding intellectual inhibition suggest that intelligence tests are best described as extremely useful rough-and-ready clues to a wide, but limited, range of capacities.

The behaviourist's response to the stimulus of Freud's work was a complex of contempt, anger, and fear: contempt, because Freud claimed to be laying the foundations of the dynamic science of psychology by studying his own dreams and the supine murmurings of neurotic patients, and because public validation of his hypotheses was impossible; anger, because psychoanalysis began to be taken seriously as a rival method of psychology; and fear, lest Freud might be on the right track. This is not of course true of academic psychologists in general, but only of extreme behaviourists for whom the renunciation of introspection and retrospection, and of inference from behaviour to mental processes, was an article of dogma. The psychoanalyst does study behaviour: the verbal and other behaviour of patients and students; but it is only when he uses expressed thoughts and feelings as clues to the unexpressed that he can offer explanations of human behaviour.

We can now detect the provenance of the Behaviourist's Fallacy. It was due to a misunderstanding of the kinds of scientific procedure that lead to success. There are many different motives for scientific investigation as well as many different purposes, methods, and kinds of success. The successful attempt to control the energy released by atomic fission was stimulated by the desire to possess a devastating weapon, which shows itself in the allocation of vast sums of money for a crash programme of research, by the ambition to anticipate rivals in achievements of pure research, by scientific curiosity, by the need for a supplementary source of electric power, and so on. It is impossible to apportion the various motives in their order of importance between the physicists, engineers, politicians, and others concerned in the enterprise. Some of the methods used were those of pure science, some of applied, and no doubt there were many for which the dichotomy would be too crude. The theoretical solution of the problem of discovering under what conditions a nuclear chain reaction would be initiated is one kind of scientific success; the theoretical solution of the practical problem of controlling nuclear fission for the purpose of a limited explosion is another kind of success; the making of an atomic bomb is another kind; the solution of the theoretico–practical problem of controlling fission for generating electricity is another kind; and so on.

The motives, purposes, methods, and successes, of Harvey, Watt, Darwin, Mendel, and Fleming, to pick names at random, cannot be assimilated and described in terms of a simple formula for scientific method. Sometimes a comprehensive hypothesis, sometimes a technique, sometimes a discovery, is the major innovation. Sometimes there is a large, sometimes a small, element of luck. There is, however, something which they all have in common: they all make assumptions which go far beyond the scope of their observations and experiments, and statements which are not entailed by the statements recording their observations. This is not to say that scientists always recognize the disparity in scope between assumptions and tests. It has been said of the theory of evolution, for example, that no hypotheses are admissible if they are so formulated as to preclude the possibility of empirical test *in principle*.

Now it seems to me that the *biogenetic hypothesis*, however formulated, is such as to preclude the possibility of empirical test for three reasons: first, palaeontological evidence, however convincing, is no more than a collection of clues to past events; second, many organisms have perished without leaving any trace; and third, the evidence of embryology is indirect and inconclusive. The insistence on testability in principle would exclude a hypothesis which is held by the majority of scientists, which cannot be scientifically tested, and for which I personally cannot imagine any scientific test in the future. 'In principle' may mean something more than 'imaginable', but I have yet to find a satisfactory explanation of the phrase.

There is good reason for believing in the theory of evolution on the basis of the inconclusive evidence, for believing that a particular metal always melts at x degrees under pressure condition y on the basis of one or two experimental tests, for believing that there are currents at the bottom of the Pacific Ocean as well as at its surface, for believing that unobservable nuclear fission took place when the first atomic bomb was exploded, for believing that other people dream as well as oneself. When visible events occur in a seismometer it is assumed that correlative events are occurring somewhere on the earth's crust; that when they do so in a Geiger counter invisible, microscopic events are occurring which we call radiation. There is good reason of the same kind for believing that when events occur in the electroencephalograph there are correlative events occurring in the subject's brain

The reason why the last statement has a less impressive ring than its precursors is that electroencephalograms cannot, at their present stage, be used to make precise predictions, and no adequate *account* can be given of the events to which EEG readings correspond, whereas seismograms and Geiger–Muller counter readings can be explained and can be used to make predictions. The difference may prove to be simply one of degree. From a GM counter reading it can be predicted that if a human being enters a certain area he will probably suffer from radiation sickness. From an EEG reading it can be predicted that X will probably have epileptic fits. If the precision and range of predictions based on EEG readings were greatly augmented, and a convincing explanation of the readings provided, the relation of the observable readings to the unobservable phenomena would be closely analogous for GM counter and EEG.

Reichenbach, in his *Philosophic Foundations of Quantum Mechanics* (1944), described unobserved interpolations and extrapolations as 'interphenomena'. Both Behaviourism and Operationalism fail to recognize that interphenomena play a more important part in scientific explanation than do particular observations. This is not to say that the scientist can give an adequate *description* of interphenomena, but that without a belief in the validity of interpolation and extrapolation scientific explanation and prediction would be impossible.

The criticism of operationalism has been well expressed by J. O. Wisdom in *Foundations of Inference in Natural Science*:

'What is faulty is what is new: the twist given to such a process of defining, that the meaning is given, not merely revived, by the operation. Perhaps the most serious aspect of the doctrine is the implication that one important kind of definition provides the only way of using words correctly; and this leads some – e.g. classical behaviourists who are incompletely emancipated from metaphysics and therefore afraid of being found guilty of having a metaphysical attitude – to lose sight of the role of non-instantial concepts, which cannot be defined operationally' (1952, p. 83).

The events to which EEG readings correspond cannot, at the present stage of science, be described; the events to which seismograms correspond may be interphenomena (if they are not directly observed) or directly seen occurrences, and both classes can be described in macroscopic terms; the events recorded by Geiger counters can be described, but not without using 'non-instantial' terms. Modern physicists do not claim to know 'what an electron is'; they are content to experiment, to take readings from instruments, to arrange symbols in patterns, and to use the patterns to explain and predict.

CRITERIA OF SCIENTIFIC STATUS

One of the criteria frequently suggested for deciding the claim of a discipline to scientific status is the use of quantitative experiments. J. O. Wisdom (1952, pp. 10–16) has described several experiments which are unquestionably scientific but which are solely concerned with qualitative change, such as Pasteur's experimental test of the hypothesis of spontaneous generation, Rabaud's investigations into the methods of orientation of birds, bees, and ants, the discovery of argon by Rayleigh and Ramsay, and Davy's refutation of the 'electric acid' hypothesis. These examples are sufficient to show that science is not necessarily quantitative.

Another criterion sometimes proposed is the use of controlled experiments. The example of astronomy, where controlled experiment is impossible, is sufficient to show that science cannot always control its data. There are many highly probable hypotheses relating to the sun and the planets, although man has not yet succeeded in experimentally controlling their movements.

A further criterion suggested is the susceptibility of the discipline's hypotheses to objective 'public' tests, by which they can be refuted or shown to need modification. This is the demand which gives plausibility to *methodological* Behaviourism. Let us therefore consider whether the demand for 'public' tests is legitimate; if it is based on a confusion, this demand is not a sound reason for embracing Behaviourism.

A convenient starting-point is J. H. Woodger's antithesis between 'public' and 'private' facts (1929, pp. 459 ff.). As examples of the first he gives 'There is a jug on this table', 'This frog has four legs', and 'All brains consist chiefly of nerve-cells and processes'; as examples of the second, 'I am now seeing a red patch', 'I am now remembering a telephone number', and 'I am now thinking of the next general election'. He maintains that it is to the first type that the propositions of natural science belong, and that facts of the second type are 'evidently of a different nature and do not form part of the subject-matter of natural science (as here understood)'. He goes on:

> 'If it *is* the case that "a jug is on this table" there is no theoretical obstacle to the possibility of any number of people knowing it. But if it is the case that "I am now remembering a telephone number" it is not possible for anyone else to know it unless I choose to tell them, and even so they cannot be certain that I am telling the truth. Thus in the second case the facts are "strictly private" to one knower, and other knowers can only know them at second hand and with some element of uncertainty. Correlated with the difference of accessibility of the two types of facts is the difference in the way in which they are known. Facts of the first type are known through sense, those of the second are not, – they are only known "immediately" or "introspectively". Now the antithesis between "mind" and "body" rests upon the existence of these two types of facts, and on the difficulty of bringing them together on to the same epistemological footing.'

Before we examine Woodger's conclusions, let us look more closely at 'public' and 'private' 'facts'. If someone says to me, 'I'd forgotten your telephone number, but now I've just remembered it', and then goes on to give the correct number, I can suspect that he had remembered it all the time (though this would be a little unreasonable), but I cannot suspect that he did not remember it at the time of giving it.

This is not to say that remembering it *is* just saying it correctly: to suppose so is to make a different kind of behaviouristic mistake. He could have remembered it and said nothing, and no one would have known that he had done so but he himself. The reason I know that he remembered it is that the chance of hitting on the right number at random is very small, just as the chance of predicting at random the appearance of Neptune at a given time and position is very small. Now, is the 'fact' asserted by the statement, 'I remember your telephone number', followed by the giving of the number, a 'public' or a 'private' fact? If we mean: is the item of knowledge obtained 'immediately' or 'through sense', the answer is 'immediately'. If we mean: can anyone check the truth of the statement, the answer is 'yes'. So we find that the class of 'facts' which are 'public' in the sense of being 'available to anybody' does not coincide, as Woodger thought, with the class of 'facts' which are 'public' in the sense of being 'known through sense and not immediately.'

There are three possibilities here: First, a person may remember a telephone number and say nothing about it. Then the remembering cannot be a piece of scientific evidence except for a theory of his own. Second, he may remember it and say, 'I've just remembered that telephone number but I'm not going to tell you what it is.' Here too the remembering cannot be used as evidence except by himself *because it cannot be correlated with any other evidence or theories* (except possible evidence of his known habitual truthfulness). Third, he may remember it and say it. Here the remembering is still 'private', but what he says can be *correlated* with other evidence as to the correct number. *Correlation, and not 'publicity' is the prerequisite of scientific usefulness.*

Now I may have a private psychological theory by which I predict that I shall remember an incident from my childhood which I have forgotten but which my parents have described to me. If I remember it, the remembering will be relevant evidence – private evidence. If I publish the theory, the account of the remembering will be scientific 'public' evidence if my word is accepted as to its veracity. If I describe the memory in detail, and the details are *correlated* with independent evidence of which I knew nothing, then the description becomes fully established scientific evidence, 'private' or 'public'. *Correlation*, therefore, may be 'private' or 'public'.

This is an important point, marking one of those inconspicuous crossroads in philosophy where it is easy to take the road to absurdity. Suppose that identical twins claimed to be able to read each other's thoughts at will, whether together or separated, and they are tested by two scientists communicating with one another by radio telephone. At various times and places scientist A asks the first twin to say something and immediately afterwards scientist B asks the second twin to repeat the remark. The statements are collected and correlated and found to correspond exactly. Would this be a valid scientific test of the claim? If the appropriate precautions were taken to exclude alternative explanations, I maintain that the probable hypothesis would be established that the twins were capable of *some* extrasensory communication. This does not mean that the scientists would know 'they can communicate directly' *in the same way* that the twins would know 'we can communicate directly'. Scientists do not know of Q that he is blind in the same way that Q knows he is blind, but this fact is quite irrelevant to the scientific validity of the statement, 'Q is blind'. No one but R knows that 'R had a glimpse of Neptune' in the same way that R knows it, but for some reason the difference in ways of knowing in this and all other examples of observers' reports is disregarded as unimportant, while the difference between X saying that he is in pain and Y saying that X is in pain arouses perennial philosophical anxiety.

So far as scientific usefulness is concerned the important distinction is not between 'public' and 'private', but between 'correlatable' and 'uncorrelatable'. Those reports of 'private' experiences are unreliable which are suspected of *failure of correlation with independent evidence*, of being falsehoods, inaccurate memories, misdescriptions, hallucinations, and so on; and all so-called 'public' facts are based on the private memory of observers and depend on their truthfulness.

To return to Woodger: 'It is just as illegitimate to introduce private facts into an exposition of human cerebral physiology as it is in the case of lower animals' (1929, p. 461). Suppose that two physiologists are trying to find out which areas of the brain are associated with visual, auditory, and tactile sensations. They both have their skulls trephined, and they direct an electric current on various areas of each other's brain. M asks N what he sees, hears, or feels when areas A1, A2, and A3 are stimulated, and N's reports are recorded verbatim. Then N asks M the same questions, and M's reports are recorded and compared with N's. A series of similar experiments are carried out with other pairs of physiologists, and the data show a high degree of correlation. Can the scientific findings of these experiments be adequately described without introducing 'private facts' into the exposition? And why should M's reports of what he sees, hears, and feels be less reliable scientific data than his reports of his stimulation of such-and-such areas of N's cortex?

Woodger is not an extreme behaviourist. Indeed, this is one reason why his ideas are worthy of careful consideration. He says:

'But it does not follow from this that a study of private facts, even in other human beings than ourselves, is impossible or valueless. Here I should dis-agree with the extreme behaviourists who are not content with their own methodology but, as is the way with human beings, must carry the war into what they erroneously suppose to be the enemy's camp, and set up an "antithesis". The success of the psychoanalytical procedure shows that it is possible to study private facts scientifically. But the success of this procedure has depended on the fact that they have done what the behaviourists have done – they have refused to mix their facts with the other type of facts. So long as you adhere to public or to private facts and keep them pure, all goes well – you remain all the time on one epistemological plane. If this is done the behaviourist need have no quarrel with the psychologist. His is the easier task because public facts are directly accessible and afford a safer basis for generalization. But he is in no position to throw stones at those who choose the more difficult task. A theory relating to private facts of a given individual *can* be verified *for that* particular individual in spite of the difficul-ties' (ibid., p. 461).

It would be easy to misrepresent Woodger's thought in this pas-sage. I do not know what it is to 'remain on one epistemological plane'. I suspect, however, that he is doing what the extreme behaviourists do much more blatantly: 'setting up an antithesis' (this time between 'public' and 'private' facts), and exonerating the psychoanalyst from trespassing on 'public' property. But the analyst studies behaviour, and a recording can make the patient's verbal behaviour 'public' in the sense that it can be studied by other analysts. He can, if he so wishes, study the patient's blood-pressure graph, which is as 'public' as any other scientific data, and he may use the correlation between rises and falls in the blood-pressure level at successive stages of the analysis to throw light on the effects of the interpretations. He may or he may not, but why should he be locked in his 'private' garden? He may use Rorschach tests for diagnosis or as a guide to progress. Are they 'public' or 'private' data?

The 'public'–'private' antithesis is a product of confusion. All scientific knowledge falls short of certainty for two reasons: because any hypothesis may be refuted or modified, and because all but a tiny fraction of any man's knowledge depends on fallible memory, fallible reports, fallible observations. I have read of the discovery of Neptune, but why should I believe it? The observers may have been deceived by a wish-fulfilling hallucination. They may have seen nothing and

D

lied out of loyalty to their colleagues. A rumour put about by a
scientific faction may have beguiled the authors I have read, and so on.
'But,' the reader may object, 'the observation can be repeated at any
time.' Well, I could not repeat it. I would not know where to turn
the telescope. And if an astronomer arranged it for me he could easily
deceive me. How do I know he is not in the conspiracy?

Why does 'I have just had a pain' seem more 'private' that 'I have
just seen Neptune'? If Neptune had been visible from the earth for
only one day, and was never again to be visible, and if only one
astronomer had seen it, the two statements would be epistemologically, though not logically, comparable. Yet if the astronomer's integrity
were not in dispute, and the observation confirmed an otherwise
convincing theory, the second statement would not be rejected on the
grounds of its privacy.

Some of my thoughts are 'private' in the sense that I could, if I
wished, keep them to myself for the rest of my life. I have 'private
access' to them, and they are inaccessible to science (except perhaps to
a scientific torturer). Some of the 'facts' I speak about are 'private' in
the sense that to me they are more than bare facts. If I say, 'I remember
the island of Ibiza' and you believe me, the bare fact (which is not
independent of the way it is expressed) is public, but my utterance is
accompanied by a particular memory which is private. For science,
however, my utterance is a satisfactory datum whose reliability can
be tested. My unconscious wishes and fears are 'private' in the sense
that they play an important part in my experience although I cannot
describe them or become fully aware of them. They are 'public', however, in the sense that electrons are 'public', in that they are inferred by
interpolations from my behaviour, just as electrons are inferred from
the behaviour of instruments, and in that the interpolation is more
successfully effected by a scientist (or scientists) than by me.

Once the analyst's guesses have been confirmed by specific changes in
my feelings (private unless reported) and behaviour (public) I become
aware of my unconscious thoughts and wishes, but whether I do so
'immediately' or inferentially it is difficult to say. Such awareness is
usually inferential at an early stage and more direct at later stages.

VALIDATION

It would be wrong to give the impression that a little clear thinking
can quickly clear up all the puzzles connected with the method
of validation of psychoanalytic theory. The difficulty of validating

'paradoxical unconventional descriptions of what is known' has been described by John Wisdom in *Philosophy and Psychoanalysis*:

> 'Because they are unconventional convention does not link the words of the description close to the facts. In this sense the proof of them must be incomplete. But this doesn't mean that the proof of them must be incomplete like the proof of a prediction. In other words the way in which the proof of *these* statements is different from conventional demonstration does not make these statements precarious, dubious, uncertain' (1953, p. 268).

Unfortunately even Wisdom speaks of 'linking words to facts', as if the 'facts' were 'out there' like the guide picture of a jigsaw puzzle. One of the main theses of this chapter is that *new ways of talking, writing and thinking, when tested and established, initiate new facts.** The facts are not independent of our methods of abstraction; nor are factual statements arbitrary or 'merely conventional'. It would be misleading to say that the fact that hereditary factors are transmitted through chromosomes is independent of man's methods of studying genetics. But for the contingent fact, for example, that there is a portion of the nucleus which is readily stained, and which has been given the name 'chromatin', the term 'chromosome' and its correlative concept might not have been introduced. If only certain parts of what we now call the chromosomes had been stainable, those parts would have been called 'chromosomes' (or some such term) and their dance in the nucleus would have had a different choreography. The description of the process of mitosis would have been 'factual' in the same way that the current description is 'factual'. The statement 'hereditary factors are transmitted through the chromosomes' would have had just as strong a claim to the title 'factual' if 'chromosome' had had that different denotation as it has with the current denotation.

It would be equally misleading to say that there would have been no chromosomes if man had not invented them. There would be *some* space–time events, but the form of the factual descriptions of those events (and therefore the form of the 'fact') depends on our methods of abstraction. To put this difficult point paradoxically, chromosomes, like the blue of the sky or the sourness of lemons, are neither mind-dependent nor mind-independent. (This is one of the key problems of philosophy, and in Chapter 15 I shall attempt to elucidate the paradox.)

It can be seen, therefore, that my objection to the antithesis 'public' and 'private' facts is that it is too crude, and that it is a source of

---

* This point will be elaborated later.

important philosophical fallacies. What is known or perceived 'immediately', like a pain, or a small patch of light described as a new planet,*
should not necessarily be given a special epistemological status and
called 'private'. The perception is 'private' in the sense that no one but
the percipient can have exactly that experience, but the description of
the perception may have the same epistemological status as any other
scientific report. Scientific knowledge is *abstract* knowledge, and if
the report abstracts in a way that is adequate to the current scientific
purpose, if it can be *correlated* with other reports, and if the likelihood
of falsification, misdescription, or hallucination can be disregarded,
then this is a report of scientific value.

* When an observer reports that he has 'seen a patch of light', he may be unwittingly
referring to a 'private' experience. He may have had a hallucination. If we accept his
claim that he has seen Neptune, *we decide* that he has reported a scientifically valuable
observation. We may decide this because he is a reliable observer *and* because what he
reports is what a scientific theory would lead us to expect. The phrases 'facts known
through sense' and 'facts known immediately' are misleading. *Only when we accept the
claim that the observer's reported experience was correlatable with other reports or with theoretical
assumptions do we call the seeing of Neptune a 'fact'.*

4

Conveying and Describing

I suggest that we should totally reject the dichotomy 'public' and 'private' 'facts', and try to distinguish the main kinds of situations in which events, experiences, sensations, states, moods, dispositions, tendencies, are:

1 known or felt but not conveyed or described;
2 conveyed only in a non-discursive form;
3 described, conveyed, or indicated in everyday language or in conventional technical language;
4 described in unconventional, puzzling language.

Various kinds of problems arise when we try to judge the importance of different sorts of experiences or to link them with theories or with other experiences.

EXPERIENCES NOT CONVEYED

1(a) I have experiences, and I have reason to believe that others have experiences, which cannot be adequately conveyed: the indescribable atmosphere of a dream; rare states such as that of ecstatic love for which the right words cannot be found; moods when listening to music; the sensation, after taking mescaline, of the immeasurably heightened significance and the immeasurably widened range of colours and intensities of light – the impression of being able to see all about one what the greatest artists have tried and failed to convey;* mystical experiences; psychotic experiences such as the elation which John Custance tried to communicate in *Wisdom, Madness and Folly* – a

---

* Aldous Huxley's *The Doors of Perception* now seems to me a brilliant but only partially successful attempt to describe such an experience.

manic exhilaration from which the author 'escaped' back into humdrum normality. Such experiences seem to be of major philosophical importance, but they slip through, tangle, or break the net of language.

1(b) Wittgenstein has pointed out (*Philosophical Investigations*, 1953, p. 78) that saying how the word 'game' is used or how a clarinet sounds is quite different from saying how many feet high Mont Blanc is. 'Describe the aroma of coffee', he says (ibid., **610). 'Why can't it be done? Do we lack the words? And for *what* are words lacking?'

1(c) We have reason to believe that some events occur for which we can offer no adequate description, not because they are not subject-matter for science, but because of the limitations of scientific technique: processes in the brain when we think or dream; changes in neurological processes coincident with the onset or cure of psychogenic blindness or paralysis. We can *postulate* a neurological change, because before paralysis stimulus *s* was invariably followed by response *r*, while since paralysis *r* never follows *s;* but the change cannot be adequately *described*, much less explained, in neurological terms. The psychological description and explanation, whose accuracy is supported but not *proved* by the cure of the paralysis, is not a *substitute* for the awaited neurological account but a *complement*, just as economic and political histories are complementary. The psychological account *is not an account of the postulated neurological processes.*

1(d) There are innumerable events, feelings, moods, which could be described but are not: I had a twinge of toothache a few moments ago; I have committed a murder which no one suspects; X secretly loves A, hates B, feels jealous of C, and so on.

EXPERIENCES CONVEYED NON-DISCURSIVELY

2(a) There are forms of communication which seem as important as linguistic communication but which cannot be adequately related to language: Schubert's great quintet, Beethoven's last quartets, the paintings of Rembrandt. . . . We may feel a certain tension or frustration: language should be able to embrace more than it does.

2(b) Some experiences and thoughts are conveyed or described – sometimes very beautifully described – but in idiosyncratic rather than in common-sense or scientific language: lyric poems; Shakespeare's plays; novels, in which experiences are attributed to fictitious characters; forms of literature or conversation which are revealing but devoid of testable reports.

EXPERIENCES CONVEYED IN EVERYDAY LANGUAGE

Now we come to description.

'Think how many different kinds of thing are called "description": description of a body's position by means of its co-ordinates; description of a facial expression; description of a sensation of touch, of a mood' (Wittgenstein, 1953, **24). 'What we call "descriptions" are instruments for particular uses. Think of a machine drawing, a cross-section, an elevation with measurements which an engineer has before him. Thinking of a description as a word-picture of the facts . . . one tends to think only of such pictures as hang on our walls . . . (. . . as it were, idle)' (ibid., **291).

Consider the following contexts in which people purport to describe, inform, explain, direct:

3(a) People give information, directions, instructions, in conventional, unpuzzling language, without being suspected of making mistakes or telling lies: the form and specificity of the description is appropriate to the purpose of the communication: the subject-matter *could* be described in other ways for other purposes.

3(b) People give accurate, checkable information about observed events in conventional scientific language. The mathematical and technical terminologies are incomprehensible to all but a small minority, but the majority accept the account given by scientists because of the demonstrable success of their operations. The part played by 'success-prestige' in our assessment of scientific description may be difficult to estimate, or to admit.

In *all* 3(a) and 3(b) situations, the language, whether common-sense or technical, may be unpuzzling because *although there are certain unwarranted assumptions, no one notices or questions them* ('The earth is flat', phlogiston, the ether, Newtonian energy and momentum, etc.). Dramatically successful talk is likely to escape criticism.

3(c) Logically distinct but inseparable from 3(b) situations: scientists describe or indicate events in conventional language (including mathematics) by interpolation and extrapolation: dangerous radiation occurring in certain areas as a result of atomic fission, inferred from Geiger counter evidence combined with lawlike descriptions of the process of fission; the process of evolution of organisms, whose description is yielded by the precarious interweaving of interpolations from palaeontological data with extrapolations from embryological reports.

What is important to notice is that it is *a matter of judgement* on the part of the scientist to decide how far he can go in filling in the gaps in the story suggested (for example) by his palaeontological clues or in extrapolating from his embryological data.

3(d) People unwittingly misdescribe in unpuzzling language. Memory is fallible; knowledge of self and others is limited. Childhood memories may be memories of phantasies rather than of real events; false theories are imposed on history and current affairs; people delude themselves: 'I have done my best to make my son a success', where it is clear that he has done his best to make him a failure; 'I want my daughter's marriage to be happy', where it is obvious that she is doing all she can to break it up; the various forms of illusion, delusion, self-deception, rationalization, and sentimentalizing.

3(e) People tell lies in unpuzzling language: we doubt a man's veracity because of his manner of reporting, or because his story is internally inconsistent, or because there is conflicting evidence, or because he has a motive for lying (or for several of these reasons). We always look for a motive and when we find none there is a problem: a psychoanalytic problem.

EXPERIENCES CONVEYED IN UNCONVENTIONAL LANGUAGE

So far we have considered situations where the language is not *prima facie* problematic. We now come to situations where, in addition to the problems of 3 – (the uneliminable possibility of unsuspected false assumptions, fallible judgement, unwitting or deliberate mis-description) – there is unmistakable semantic bewilderment.

4(a) A scientist or philosopher devises a new technique, questions well-established assumptions and definitions, or introduces new concepts and new ways of organizing phenomena. The shift in point of view is comparable to the shift from one map projection to another: say from the cylindrical orthomorphic (Mercator's) to the cylindrical equal-area projection. In some cases the shift is relatively slight (near the equator); in others (near the poles) it is enormous, because one (Mercator's) preserves local shape at the expense of area, while the other preserves local area at the expense of shape.

Map projections, however, are *chosen*, and the choice depends on the *use* to which the map is put. Mercator's, for example, is the most useful projection for navigators at sea; an equal-area projection for statistical purposes – to show density of population, incidence of rainfall, etc.; Clarke's perspective projection for conveying a general idea of the shape of continents; and a polar perspective projection for the strategic planning of Air Forces. Because a choice can be made, and because it is clear to geographers that a choice *has* to be made, the attempt to find *the veridical map* which would be suitable for all purposes can be shown to be naïve.

A special technical terminology, however, or a special non-technical way of using language for certain purposes, is not thought of as a projection at all. Hence the temptation into which some scientists have fallen, to regard the language of psychoanalysis as a provisional make-shift, to be superseded by a 'monistic frame of reference' (Barnett, 1955). As Woodger has pointed out in his valuable advice to medical students:

> 'What is important is that our talk should be *successful*, and, as the history of science shows, scientific talk has often been successful when the people who did the talking did not know what they were talking about . . . from the point of view of the doctrine of limits, the early users of the differential calculus did not know what they were talking about. But this did not prevent their talk from being successful in mechanics' (1956, pp. 138–9).

Rejecting Barnett's proposal that the exponents of related disciplines should abandon their own language in favour of the language of ethology, Woodger remarks: '. . . you cannot express *all* you want to say in the language of ethology because its vocabulary is not big enough, and so psychology cannot be a part of ethology' (p. 140).

4(b) This brings us to the second source of semantic bewilderment: the reconciliation of overlapping or alternative forms of description. Different kinds of valid description, with different terminologies and different frames of reference, are available for one section of space–time – the Russian Revolution, of which a political or an economic or an economico–political history can be written; the changes which occur in a particular woman at the menopause, which are theoretically describable in endocrinological, physiological, chemical, physical, or psychological terminology, or which might be described by a student of psychosomatic medicine in terminology derived from three or more disciplines; the development of a single human embryo, which may be described in embryological, anatomical, physiological, chemi-cal, or physical terminology, but which cannot be adequately des-cribed in terms of pure physics.

I shall call these descriptions *language projections.** The task of recon-ciling the overlapping language projections applicable to the Russian

---

* For explanation of the concept 'language projection' see pp. 199–200.
For full list of types see Index under 'Language Projections'.

Revolution seems less problematical, both scientifically and philosophically, than the problem of reconciling the language projections applicable to the menopause. Why is this so? Partly, perhaps, because no attempt is made to describe more than a limited selection of the series of events called 'the Russian Revolution', whereas a scientific account is often felt to be inadequate if incomplete. Partly because economic and political inquiries go hand in hand, and each language projection is familiar to students of the other. Partly, too, because the problem of reconciliation of language projections may seem more acute when we are seeking lawlike hypotheses and predictions. Above all, because the thought-feeling-motive language projection is more difficult to reconcile with language projections of the physical sciences than any other.

It is for this reason that I shall now try to explore the relationship between the thought-feeling-motive language of ordinary speech and of literature, the language of psychoanalysis, and the language of the physical sciences.

In the examples to be given below ('Psychoanalysis as Fear-reduction', p. 49), let P be the language of the physical sciences *plus* that part of language ('The sun is rising', 'Snow is falling') whose *full meaning* could be expressed in the language of the physical sciences;
let TFM be the class of statements, in ordinary language, about people's thoughts, feelings, motives etc. (corresponding roughly to Woodger's 'person language' statements) which cannot be transposed into P;
let TFME be the extension of TFM which results from the introduction of the psychoanalytic concept 'unconscious', and from the consequent broadening of such concepts as 'fear', 'rage', 'guilt', 'jealousy', 'need', etc.

Woodger has pointed out that 'as soon as we deal with persons a new source of information is open to us: we know about persons, so to speak, at first hand, by *being* persons; part of what we get is *of* ourselves and yet is not got by seeing, feeling, hearing, tasting or smelling' (ibid., p. 140).

In the following examples I shall try to make a distinction between the kind of *language* we use and the way we get our information. This is not easy; and whatever device may be used to show the difference between 'direct awareness' and 'inferential knowledge' is open to devastating philosophical objections. At this point it is necessary to stress that the ways of talking represented by P, TFM, and TFME, do *not* correspond to three ways of getting to know something.

PSYCHOANALYSIS AS FEAR-REDUCTION

The examples chosen are all directly or indirectly concerned with fear and its symptoms. The hypothesis I wish to defend, that the therapeutic efficacy of psychoanalysis is due to the gradual reduction of fear, is defensible only if 'fear' is understood in an extended sense: understood, that is, as 'the conscious feeling of fear together with symptoms of fear'. As symptoms of fear diminish, the conscious feeling of fear may increase; but 'fear' in the extended sense may be lessened.

1 He is trembling	P	e*
2 He feels frightened without knowing why	TFM	e
3 He feels frightened because he has an unconscious impulse to kill	TFME	e
4 His pulse rate is 90 per min.	P	e
5 He can feel his heart thumping but he does not feel frightened and thinks there must be something wrong with his heart	TFM	e
6 His rapid pulse is due to unconscious fear of the doctor but he is not allowing himself to feel conscious fear	TFME	e
7 He does not travel in underground trains	P	d†
8 Whenever he tries to get into an underground train he suffers from acute anxiety	TFM	d
9 His fear of underground trains and tunnels is due to an unconscious fear of what they symbolize	TFME	d
10 His blood pressure is often below normal	P	d
11 When he is frustrated he gets depressed instead of angry	TFM	d
12 He often gets depressed because he has an unconscious fear of giving way to uncontrollable rage	TFME	d
13 He sweats and groans in his sleep	P	d
14 He has nightmares	TFM	d
15 His terrifying dreams are a re-enactment of a situation which was traumatic because an unconscious wish coincided with an unconscious fear	TFME	d
16 He never leaves his room	P	d
17 Whenever he tries to leave his room he has an anxiety attack	TFM	d
18 He cannot leave his room because he has an unconscious fear of attacking someone or being attacked	TFME	d
19 After the explosion he had diarrhoea	P	e

* Episodic. † Dispositional.

20 After the explosion he had diarrhoea but did not feel afraid	TFM	e
21 His diarrhoea was due to unconscious fear	TFME	e
22 He has frequent peristaltic disturbances without apparent physical cause	P	d
23 Sometimes when he has peristaltic disturbances he feels anxious, sometimes not	TFM	d
24 His peristaltic disturbances are due to fear, sometimes conscious, sometimes not	TFME	d
25 He is sometimes impotent	P	d
26 He is impotent when he feels anxious	TFM	d
27 His impotence is due to an unconscious fear of attacking or being attacked by a woman	TFME	d
28 Little Hans avoids horses*	P	d
29 He is afraid of horses	TFM	d
30 His fear of horses is displaced from an unconscious fear of his father	TFME	d
31 Little Hans no longer avoids horses but he avoids his father	P	d
32 His fear of horses has been displaced by a fear of his father	TFM	d
33 His unconscious fear of his father has been made conscious and has replaced his fear of horses	TFME	d

* See Freud (1909) and Anna Freud (1949, pp. 75–6).

RELATIONSHIP BETWEEN P, TFM, AND TFME

All the statements in P and TFM are such as might appear in a doctor's notes. None of the statements in TFM or in TFME could be transposed into P without loss. All the information in TFM, some of that in P, but none of that in TFME could have been obtained by asking the patient. There is no sharp dividing line between TFM and TFME, as psychological insight is sometimes expressed in everyday idiom: 'Deep down you *are* afraid'; 'You *are* angry although you deny it'; etc. Such remarks, which presuppose unconscious feelings without explicitly referring to them are for the present purpose to be classed with their explicit counterparts and included in TFME.

We can now come to the point of these distinctions. TFME *is not* a rough-and-ready provisional tool, to be abandoned, like the hand-loom and the paddle-wheel, when science makes its next seven-league stride. It is a tool to be scientifically improved, but it is in itself a tool of science. However modified, it must remain an extension of TFM in order to perform its function: to change the situation by linking up elements that are dissociated. Little Hans (Freud, 1909, Anna Freud, 1949, pp. 75–6) loses his fear of horses when he is told (truly), and recognizes, that 'deep down' he is afraid of his father. Somatic symptoms are modified or eliminated when they are shown and recognized in TFME to be a part of a syndrome – 'fear', 'rage', or 'guilt' in their extended senses. It is a function which P will never be capable of performing.

The relationship between the three ways of talking is represented in the following diagram:

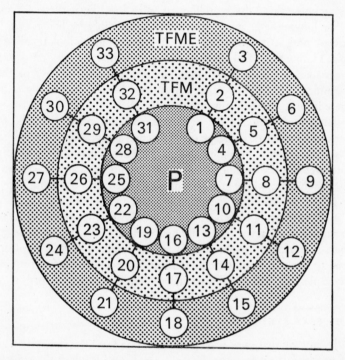

On the other hand, information and ideas expressed in P, TFM, *and* TFME are suitable material for suggesting hypotheses to be used in interpretations. It does not matter where a guess originates if it can be used and tested, directly or indirectly, in the clinical situation. Clues may be provided by the correlation of blood-pressure charts with reports of changes in the patient's sensations; and clues may be provided by Dostoevsky or Proust as well as by Freud and his followers.

In order to show that language projections P, TFM, and TFME do not correspond to three ways of getting to know or being aware, all that is needed is to rewrite examples 1–33 in the first person:

1 I am trembling   P   e
2 I feel frightened without knowing why   TFM   e
3 I feel frightened because I have an unconscious impulse
   to kill   TFME   e
                                                              (and so on)

The distinctions between P, TFM, and TFME remain unchanged,* but the answers to the question 'How do you know?' are different. I may know that I am trembling either by direct kinaesthetic sensation or by looking (e.g. at an injured leg); or possibly by being told, if I haven't noticed it. I may know that *he* is trembling by looking or being told. I know that I feel frightened 'directly', though I may misdescribe the sensation (there is no claim to incorrigibility for any of these examples). I know that *he* feels frightened because he has said so and there is no reason to doubt his word.

The examples in TFME may look somewhat bizarre in the first person. They mark the stage of intellectual acceptance of a hypothesis based on evidence brought together by what I shall call a 'focusing'† interpretation: acceptance before there is any conscious awareness of the assumed impulse. I get to know that I have an unconscious impulse to kill in the same way that I get to know that *he* has: by considering a mass of indirect evidence. This is true of ten of the eleven TFME examples when rewritten in the first person. In the last example (33), there is an element of direct awareness. In practice, TFME admissions tend to be made with some discomfort, in a tentative form: 'I suppose my rapid pulse must be due to unconscious fear of the doctor.'

THE FEAR SYNDROME

Why not say that there is palpitation but no fear? Because it is an aim of psychoanalysis to *reveal* fear as a *syndrome* including the evidence expressible in P and the evidence expressible in TFM; to connect up the carefully isolated situations where the patient (a) is aware of fear; (b) escapes conscious fear by rituals, denial, or avoidance (zoophobia, claustrophobia, agoraphobia, etc.); (c) has palpitation, indigestion, and

---

* In the physical account, 'I', like 'he', would have to be replaced by the description of an organism identified by co-ordinates.

† For definition see p. 95.

other physical symptoms; (d) is impotent; and so on. In short, TFME can be used to include more and more of the syndrome and so make it conscious *as a syndrome*, as a step towards discovering the causes.

The terms 'unconscious fear', 'unconscious rage', 'unconscious guilt', 'unconscious wish', 'unconscious need', raise distinct philosophical problems. 'Need', for example, is a term which may appear in both P and TFM: 'I need a drink', 'I need your advice', 'He needs Vitamin C', 'The plants need water'. I may feel a direct need for air in a blocked mine, or I may know I need a blood-transfusion because the doctor has told me so. There is nothing puzzling about plants, animals, or people needing things without knowing it. A primitive tribesman may not know that he needs aureomycin, but we do not call his need 'unconscious'. 'Unconscious need' is semantically distinct from 'unconscious fear'; becoming aware of a need is different from coming to feel fear, rage, or guilt. It is also recognition of a pattern, but the recognition may not be accompanied by a specific *feeling* of need.

Is there a specific feeling of need? Or is the feeling that of wanting? 'I want your advice and if I don't get it I'll be in a quandary.' Sometimes 'I need' means 'I want and I know it is necessary', but sometimes it means '*I must have*' (a drowning man gasping for air). However, a man may recognize a need without wanting what he needs. He may be forced by a mountain of evidence to recognize that he needs to suffer: to suffer illness, hardship, accidents, humiliation, failure, or imprisonment: any one of the misfortunes which are consciously abhorred. (Although illness may sometimes be consciously desired.) The need is hard to recognize because irrationality is hard to admit. But the recognition is more like a discovery in the physical sciences than direct awareness. It may be more like recognizing someone else's jealousy than becoming aware of one's own.

On the other hand, an unconscious need may be transformed into a conscious desire. A girl who has for many years been honestly assuring herself and others that she hates children and does not want any of her own may come to recognize a pattern of behaviour, such as extreme carelessness about contraception, which becomes intelligible only when an unconscious need for children is assumed. This recognition may (and may not) be followed by a conscious longing for children. We speak of unconscious need when we detect *anomalies* in a person's behaviour. There is no anomaly in the failure of a primitive man to be aware of his need for aureomycin.

PATTERN AND FEELING

In brief, *becoming aware of a pattern is logically distinct from becoming aware of the feeling which the pattern leads us to expect, and either form of awareness may occur without the other.*

Becoming intellectually aware of a pattern is like (and unlike) learning to identify tissue as seen through a microscope. It is *learning to see and to recognize.* Although we use an extension of TFM to describe the patterns, the intellectual process is that of connecting clues and weighing evidence. Intellectual evidence is important *as a precursor to changes in feelings and behaviour.* A pilot flying over mountains in thick cloud is trying to distinguish clouds from mountain peaks. Identifying a peak directly ahead is an intellectual preliminary to immediate changes in feelings and behaviour.

NEED AND WISH

There is an important philosophical distinction between 'need' and 'wish'. Let us examine one of the few major *philosophical* contributions to the theory of psychoanalysis since Freud: J. O. Wisdom's 'Hypothesis to Explain Trauma Re-enactment Dreams' (1949).

He suggests that all dreams are *need*-fulfilments, and he distinguishes between pleasure–need and punishment–need. Trauma re-enactment dreams are repeated because the essence of a traumatic experience is that it portrays an entire conflict too faithfully.

Wisdom explains trauma dreams as follows:

'The absence of manifest distortion means that the supposed pleasure-need and the evident punishment-need are expressed in the same content, so that there is a common aim of both needs (destruction) and a nearly common object (the enemy object identified with the self, or part of it)' (p. 20).

Is it a departure from normal usage to speak of the 'aim' and 'object' of a need? If so, is the departure justified? If I wanted to kill someone, would I call him 'the object of a pleasure-need'? No: but it is easy to see why Wisdom prefers 'need' to 'wish'; it is neutral as between the pleasant and the unpleasant.

The first detailed analysis in Freud's *The Interpretation of Dreams* (1900), that of the famous dream of Irma's injection, provides an interesting example:

'The dream acquitted me of the responsibility for Irma's condition by showing that it was due to other factors – it produced a whole series of reasons. The dream represented a particular state of affairs as I should have wished it to be. Thus its content was the fulfilment of a wish and its motive was a wish' (pp. 118–19).

The latent dream–thought might be expressed as a counter-factual wish–statement referring to present time: 'I wish there were no possible grounds for blaming me for her condition.' If we decide to use 'need' language we shall have to say: 'The content of the dream was the fulfilment of a pleasure-need and its motive was a pleasure-need.' The translation is artificial, but that is not a decisive objection. What I suggest *is* a decisive objection is *that we should lose an important distinction between 'need' and 'wish'*. We want to be able to say, for example, 'She *needs* to have a child, and sometimes she *wishes* she could have one; sometimes she *fears* having one.' Wishing and fearing are compatible, and are independent of needing. We may *wish* to be independent although we are *afraid* of being independent and *need* to be dependent. The conscious wish to be independent may be accompanied by a conscious fear of being independent and a *disguised* wish to be dependent. A child may *wish* that a rival were dead, be *afraid* of acting upon the wish, and *need* the rival to be alive.

The difference between 'wish' and 'need' is like the difference between 'believe' and 'know': 'need' and 'know' have a reference *beyond* the mental state of the one who wishes or believes. I may believe without knowing, and wish without needing. But the parallel is imperfect: I can need without wishing, but I cannot know without believing.

Let us consider Wisdom's hypothesis:

'A dream or Perceptualization during sleep is either an undistorted Perceptualization of the fulfilment of a pleasure-need alone, or a Perception of it distorted by Condensation, Displacement, and Symbolization, and modified by Secondary Elaboration, in both cases to preserve sleep against disturbance by a physical stimulus whether external or in the body, OR a Perceptualization of both pleasure- and punishment-needs, distorted by the same distortion mechanisms, to reduce pressure from the punishment-needs by distortion of all needs and by initial Perceptualization of the pleasure-needs alone, with the aim of preserving sleep against disturbance by punishment-needs aroused by the unperceptualized pleasure-needs' (1949, p. 20).

When I first read this hypothesis I found it particularly impressive because I had recently had the following dream: someone – unidentified – is being tortured, and although I am horrified, the horror is exciting and even pleasurable. As the dream continues the horror increases, and I gradually realize that the victim is myself. Pleasure gives way to extreme anxiety.

I would describe the dream as beginning with a wish-fulfilment (disguised) and changing into a (talion) fear-fulfilment. It seems to me that Wisdom's hypothesis could be rewritten, substituting 'wishes' for 'pleasure-needs' and 'talion fears' for 'punishment-needs' without loss of his valuable insight and with a double gain: the description and explanation not only of the dream of Irma's injection but of many dreams recorded by Freud and other analysts could be retained in their present form; and we could keep the important distinctions between 'need' and 'wish', and 'need' and 'fear'; and between 'unconscious need', 'unconscious wish', and 'unconscious fear'.

'Need-fulfilment' is an odd phrase. We usually speak of *satisfying* or *appeasing* a need, and we often want to contrast the satisfaction of a need with the wish-fulfilment of dreams and day-dreams. I now suggest that we should contrast the appeasement of a punishment-need with the fulfilment of a talion fear in dreams and day-dreams. Freud was the first to point to '... the cure or improvement of severe neuroses which we sometimes observe after real accidents: all that matters is that the patient should be wretched – in what way is of no consequence' (1940, Chapter Six). There are many examples in the literature of psychoanalysis of dramatic changes from depression or acute anxiety to peace of mind or even happiness, after some serious misfortune such as physical injury or imprisonment. In such cases we would speak of *the appeasement of a need for punishment* which was due to unconscious guilt. Anxiety dreams or nightmares, on the other hand, we would describe as fear-fulfilments: talion fear-fulfilments.

In *The Interpretation of Dreams* Freud spoke of 'counter-wish dreams', which he attributed to two motives:

> 'One of the two motive forces leading to such dreams is the wish that I may be wrong. These dreams appear regularly in the course of my treatments when a patient is in a state of resistance to me; and I can count almost certainly on provoking one of them after I have explained to a patient for the first time my theory that dreams are fulfilments of wishes' (pp. 157-8).

This is a part of Freud's theory which understandably provokes critics of psychoanalysis to protest: 'Of course, it's "Heads I win, tails you lose!" If you produce a counter-example to the hypothesis that all dreams are wish-fulfilments, they'll say you deliberately dreamed your anxiety dream to refute them!'

This kind of criticism should, I believe, be taken very seriously by psychoanalysts. I remember my own surprise when I first noticed that Freud simply stated his conclusion, as if the matter were settled. Yet the phenomenon he describes is a genuine discovery: in the phase of negative transference a patient may not only have 'counter-wish' dreams: he may suffer an exacerbation of symptoms in order to demonstrate the inadequacy of the therapist. The problem for the scientific analyst is clearly to state the criterion by which the various kinds of anxiety dreams can be distinguished.

Freud goes on to discuss 'the second motive for counter-wish dreams':

'There is a masochistic component in the sexual constitution of many people, which arises from the reversal of an aggressive, sadistic component into its opposite. Those who find their pleasure, not in having *physical* pain inflicted on them, but in humiliation and mental torture, may be described as "mental masochists". It will at once be seen that people of this kind can have counter-wish dreams and unpleasurable dreams which are none the less wish-fulfilments since they satisfy their masochistic inclinations. I will quote one such dream, produced by a young man who in his earlier years had greatly tormented his elder brother, to whom he had a homosexual attachment. His character having undergone a fundamental change, he had the following dream, which was in three pieces: I. *His elder brother was chaffng him.* II. *Two grown men were caressing each other with a homosexual purpose.* III. *His brother had sold the business of which he himself had looked forward to becoming the director.* He awoke from the last dream with the most distressing feelings. Nevertheless it was a masochistic wishful dream, and might be translated thus: it would serve me right if my brother were to confront me with this sale as a punishment for all the torments he had to put up with from me (1900, p. 159).

My own dream, mentioned above, is similar to this dream in that it might be translated: 'It would serve me right if *I* were tortured . . .'. But is 'it would serve me right' the natural expression for a *wish*? I suggest that it is rather the expression of a (talion) fear which is linked with a (guilty) wish.

When we have made the necessary distinctions between needs, wishes, and fears (conscious and unconscious), we may still feel dissatisfied with the existing framework for the explanation of dreams. There are dreams, phantasies, and perversions, the scientifically invaluable clue to unconscious phantasies, which it would be artificial to attribute to wishes or fears. In the first of *Three Essays on the Theory of Sexuality* Freud described neuroses as 'the negative of perversions'; he meant that neurotic symptoms are due in part to the repression of impulses which if acted upon would constitute a perversion. It must be emphasized, in view of the widespread tendency – itself a defence technique – to identify psychoanalysis with *abnormal* psychology, that repressed 'perverted' impulses are extremely common, and account for the feeling, often experienced by one or both partners, that something is *lacking* in the 'normal' sexual relationship between a man and a woman. This feeling may be due to repressed sadistic, masochistic, or homosexual impulses, or to the *lack* of some other element of an unconsciously *required* total situation. The required situation may be determined by a fixation in infancy or childhood, and may be clearly reconstructed by the victim of a perversion. If such a person demands to be chained to the bed, for example, the chaining is a *sine qua non* of complete sexual satisfaction, and the correlative impulse in someone who is not perverted might appear in a dream about being chained. Such an element in a dream, I suggest, is not a wish- or fear-fulfilment, but a *lack-fulfilment*, because the element is neither directly wished for nor feared but *required*, and such an element in a perversion, when physically enacted, is the *provision of a lack*. By using these terms we keep the important distinction between the very different worlds of phantasy and action, while stressing the pain–pleasure *neutrality* of such requirements.

THE NEED HYPOTHESIS

The discussion can be summed up in the form of a hypothesis of wider scope, the *Need Hypothesis*, which keeps as close as possible to the natural use of the terms:

A. If a *need* does not arouse fear or guilt it will manifest itself either in action tending to satisfy it or in *wish-fulfilment* dreams or phantasies;

B. If a need (such as the need for *complete* sexual satisfaction) takes such a form in conscious or unconscious phantasy that it arouses fear or guilt, whether in the form of conscious feelings, somatic symptoms, or behavioural manifestations (such as rituals or avoidance), then

(*i*) there will be partial or total inhibition of the active satisfaction of the need (e.g. intermittent or chronic, partial, or total impotence or frigidity);

(*ii*) when the need is only partially satisfied in action a *lack* will be felt, which may be manifested in attempts to *supply the lack* itself in perverted action, or to *appease* the lack with substitute *lack-fulfilment* dreams or phantasies;

(*iii*) there may also be a *need* for suffering, which may be *appeased* or *satisfied* by accidents, illnesses, failures, and other misfortunes;

(*iv*) there will be linked wishes and fears (usually talion fears) which can be inferred from anomalies in thought, feeling, and behaviour;

(*v*) the lacks, wishes, and fears will appear as percepts in dreams and phantasies, more or less distorted by condensation, displacement, substitution, and secondary elaboration;

(*vi*) the lack-, the wish-, or the fear-element may predominate in consciousness according to changing conditions, such as traumatic experiences, suffering which appeases guilt, and the effects of interpretations, including the desire to prove the analyst right or wrong;

(*vii*) all three elements will normally be distorted, the lack and the wish because they are unacceptable to the ego (ego-dystonic), and the fear partly because it is a clue to the lack or wish;

(*viii*) if an actual experience corresponds very closely to the fulfilment of a lack or wish that is linked with a powerful talion fear (the enemy object being identified with the self, or part of it), the experience will be traumatic, and may be re-enacted in dreams with relatively little distortion, *the re-enactment itself being a form of suffering*;

(*ix*) as lacks and linked wishes and fears are made conscious and related to each other, the direct and indirect manifestations of irrational fear are gradually reduced.

The above need hypothesis is not the kind of scientific hypothesis which can be submitted to a crucial experiment, although it can be demonstrated (see pp. 262–8). It is a *philosophico-scientific* attempt to sum up a wide variety of psychoanalytical findings in the most appropriate and least misleading language. It is like an attempt to sum up a wide variety of biological findings in an evolutionary hypothesis, an attempt which is as much philosophical as scientific. Neither kind of hypothesis is liable to outright refutation; both kinds are liable to criticism and revision. The question of 'proof' does not arise, except in the sense of 'convincing a large proportion of scientists'; whoever believes that evidence of evolution was put on earth to test our faith, or that the succession of interpretations and predicted symptom-changes is not an aetiological but a coincidental sequence, will retain his logically impregnable position.

Part of the need hypothesis will be *supported* if it can be accurately predicted that interpretations of a certain kind will have the effect of making the wish- or lack-element conscious, while those of another kind will make the fear-element conscious; and if the cumulative effect of interpretations is to make lacks, wishes, and fears conscious and to relate them to each other, with a consequent reduction in the total direct and indirect manifestation of irrational fear.

It remains to answer the objection that the analyst cannot be proved wrong. It can be met only by a detailed study of interpretations and their effects. The analyst *can* be proved wrong, but not in the way Freud's patients tried to prove him wrong. They tried to demonstrate, by allowing only fears to consciousness, that the fears were not linked with guilty wishes; this technique certainly could not disprove the wish-fulfilment or any other theory. *The analyst can be proved wrong when he makes predictions about the effects of interpretations and these predictions are falsified.*

EMPATHY

On pp. 46 and 47 above we noticed two sources of semantic bewilderment: the introduction of new concepts and the overlapping of language projections. A further source is the important part played by *empathy* in psychoanalysis.

Indescribable experiences, however important, are necessarily ignored by most sciences. The *prima facie* incoherent talk of psychotics is carefully studied by psychoanalysts and, by virtue of its resemblance to the reported dreams of normal people, can be in part deciphered. Now that the major discovery has been made – that such talk *is* decipherable – there is good reason to suppose that increasingly skilful hieroglyphists will make increasing ranges of speech intelligible. But the experience itself, as distinct from the descriptions given by the patient and from the scientist's abstract descriptions, will be for ever private and incommunicable. There is a sense of the word 'understand' in which X, who has just recovered from the manic phase of manic-depressive psychosis, understands Y's manic state better than Z, the psychoanalyst; and there is a sense, the abstract scientific sense, in which Z understands the manic phase better than either X or Y. Hence the pseudo-paradox that an analyst who has suffered from a severe neurosis is likely, provided that he has recovered from professionally incapacitating symptoms, to be more perceptive, *ceteris paribus*, than one who has not suffered from a neurosis. His understanding of his patients is both scientific (abstract) and *empathic*.

SUBJECT-MATTER AND HYPOTHESES

A further source of confusion is the failure to distinguish between the subject-matter of science and the scientific hypotheses relating to that subject-matter. Idiosyncratically described and unwittingly mis-described experiences constitute the major part of the material from which the analyst tries to abstract a coherent theory. Hence his scientific interest in all forms of literature, including plays, novels, biography, and autobiography. A psychoanalyst's speculations about historical personalities, based on extrapolation from clinical findings, are com-parable to the geneticist's speculations about evolution. They are valuable for their insight, they are precarious, and they are to be judged by less rigorous standards than laboratory or clinical work. The same could be said of the astronomer's tentative speculations about distant stars. *But we value the biologist's and the astronomer's speculations more highly than the layman's.*

HETEROGENEOUS DESCRIPTION

The problem of new concepts such as evolution, relativity, and the unconscious, and the problem of overlapping language projections, are related to, but distinct from, the problem of heterogeneous description. By 'overlapping language projections' I mean the description of one section of space–time in different terminologies with different frames of reference. An example would be a physiological and a psychological description of the effects of an injection of morphine. By 'hetero-geneous description' I mean the use in one discipline of technical terms adopted from other disciplines. 'Inhibition', for example, has a use in neurology and in psychoanalysis. In *Inhibitions, Symptoms and Anxiety* (1926), Freud describes 'inhibition' as '. . . the expression of a *restriction of an ego-function*' (p. 89), and says that inhibitions 'are restrictions of the functions of the ego which have been either imposed as a measure of precaution or brought about as a result of an impoverishment of energy' (p. 90). The ego, which he describes as the organized part of the id, has 'functions', such as 'the keeping down of the instinctual claims of the id', 'protecting itself from dangers by means of anxiety', 'interposing, between the demands made by instinct and the action that satisfies it, an intellectual activity . . .'; and it has to 'maintain great expenditures of energy upon anti-cathexes'. In *New Introductory Lectures* (1933, Lecture XXI), he describes the ego as 'that portion of the id which was modified by the proximity and influence of the external world, which is adapted for reception of stimuli and as a protective shield against stimuli' (p. 75).

Freud has been accused of trying to make his theory sound scientific by misappropriating biological and physical terms. This criticism misses the point. The criterion of success in devising an original terminology, as in devising an original technique, is its organizing and heuristic value. The origin of original terms is irrelevant. The only valid criticism of Freud's theory would be a demonstration that a revision of his terminology would achieve more successfully and more consistently *all* that Freud and his followers have set out to do.

Freud took terms from physiology ('inhibition' and 'function'), from physics ('energy') and from biology ('instinct'); he personified the id, the ego, and the superego, and even talked of an abstract psychological 'organization' developing out of the cortical layers of another abstract psychological entity. It would not be surprising if physiologists, physicists, biologists, economists, and academic psychologists, not to mention philosophers, were to throw up their hands in despair at such a terminological tangle. Yet this would be a most important mistake. When hacking his way through the jungle of human psychology which he was the first to chart, Freud picked up every tool that lay to hand, sharp, blunt, standardized, or home-made, and he adapted or re-fashioned each as he went along. It is doubtful whether he could have penetrated so far by any other means. The explanatory power of his writings is so incomparably great that a philosopher or scientist of discernment has to emancipate himself from his horror of 'category-mistakes' and study the difficult philosophical problem of hetero-geneous description.

Is it a 'fact' that 'the ego protects itself from dangers by means of anxiety'? Or that it 'keeps down the instinctual claims of the id'? The question reveals our hesitation to apply the term 'factual' to any original, unconventional, tentative generalization, however well it organizes a wide range of phenomena. The hesitation is partly due to scientific caution, as when we withhold the label 'factual' from 'all hereditary characters are transmitted through genes'. It is also due to semantic bewilderment, as when we withhold it from 'Property is theft', or 'Sleep, that knits up the ravell'd sleeve of care'.

It may now be objected that I am making too much of the impre-cision of young scientific theories, and that if and when we can translate 'the ego protects itself . . .' into precise, universally accepted scientific language, we shall have discovered a 'fact' which has always been there, whether we knew it or not. It is true that if and when we succeed we shall be able to put our new factual statement into the past tense or into the timeless present. It will then describe a 'timeless fact', just as Aristotle's statements did for so many centuries. If it remains unchallenged, it will be by reason of the changelessness of psychological theory. In other words, psychology will have ossified.

CONCLUSION

The conclusion I wish to draw from this discussion is that what we call true factual statements are simply hypotheses which we feel no scientific or philosophical need, at the present time, to question or modify. When we lose confidence in their validity we either drop them altogether except as jokes ('she is a witch', 'the devils have left his body'), keep them with a changed semantic value ('the sun is rising', 'spring tides are caused by the combined attraction of the sun and moon'), or modify their form or scope ('the human body is opaque *except* when X-rayed', 'the earth goes round the sun *if* we take the sun as a fixed point of reference', or, equally valid, 'the sun goes round the earth *if* we take the earth as a fixed point of reference').

5

Hypotheses and Interpretations in Psychoanalysis

PSYCHOANALYSIS: TECHNOLOGY OR SCIENCE

The problem of testing psychoanalytic theory is in some ways like, and in other ways unlike, the problem of testing other scientific theories. Let us first consider the approach of J. O. Wisdom, who maintains (1956) that psychoanalysis is primarily a technique and a technology and only secondarily a science. He makes an interesting set of distinctions between the three types of hypothesis which constitute the theory of the unconscious and the three types of hypothesis constituting the theory of the transference. I shall try to summarize these distinctions, but the article itself should be consulted.

The theory of the unconscious consists of:

1. the hypothesis of the unconscious;
2. (a) the guise hypothesis (that unconscious ideas – using 'ideas' to cover wishes, fears, etc. – influence *all* the patient's ideas);
(b) the genetic hypothesis (that childhood networks of ideas influence adult ideas);
3. the hypothesis that the networks are interrelated (as in the Oedipus interrelation).

The theory of the transference consists of:

4. the hypothesis that unconscious networks of ideas influence the associations given to the analyst;
5. that a train of contiguous associations (a) have a meaningful interrelation and (b) have a fundamental reference to the analyst;

6. that the mutual relationships of the network of ideas are reproduced closely in the complex relationship between the patient and the analyst.

Of hypothesis (1) he says:

'No support for analytic theory comes from showing that there exists an unconscious so hidden that no ordinary means will give access to it. What would be relevant, however, would be to examine whether the hypothesis that there is an unconscious that displays itself in various guises, can explain our ideas and behaviour' (1956, p. 16).

He describes the short-term technological aim of psychoanalysis as being 'to enable the patient to perceive certain relationships between himself and people in his environment through understanding his relationship to the analyst; ... the patient's understanding of his relationship to the analyst is the quintessence of understanding himself' (ibid., p. 19).

It is interesting to compare this last remark with what Ezriel (1956-7) describes as 'the essence of psychoanalytic therapy', namely, 'a process of reality testing'. They are clearly not incompatible, but there is a difference of emphasis: Wisdom stresses the increase of understanding, while Ezriel stresses the reduction of fear or anxiety when an expected calamity does not materialize. In discussing the tape-recorded extract from a psychoanalytic session quoted in his article, he points out that Mrs X was *consciously aware* of the forbidden word which was causing anxiety ('fart'), and that the interpretation gave her the courage to say it and so to receive the reassurance that the expected calamity did not occur.

Successful therapy causes both reduction of anxiety and increase of understanding, but the relative importance of each factor varies greatly with the individual, and both factors may frequently be obscured when the patient becomes temporarily more anxious and more obtuse, as deeply buried fears become conscious. In a patient who uses 'intellectualization' as a highly developed defence technique, a considerable increase of understanding may for a long time be accompanied by a relatively slight capacity to change the pattern of behaviour which he understands; while, in an unintellectual patient, a dramatic remission of symptoms and reduction of anxiety may be accompanied by no more than a slight increase of understanding.

Wisdom makes a further fourfold distinction which is of great methodological importance: between

'(i) unifying or explanatory theories (which Freud called metapsychology)'	such as the death instinct, the quantity theory of psychic energy, the theory that the function of dreams is to

'(ii) theories with technological counterparts' such as 'that part of libido theory that concerns the erotogenic zones', 'internalized parent figure as superego' — preserve sleep, that the more developed the ego the more it encroaches on the id wish-fulfilment, and so on

'(iii) theories consisting of hypotheses about mechanisms' — such as fixation at the phallic phase

'(iv) the basic theory about mental structure and function'

Of (ii) and (iii) he says, 'these two types of theories govern the contents selected by the analyst in giving the day-to-day interpretations' (p. 21).

'To say that a statement is an interpretation is to say (i) that the analyst sees in the associations a relationship between networks of ideas, which (ii) is governed by one or other of the component theories.' This elucidation of the term 'interpretation' may suggest a procedure more systematic than it really is. When Freud abandoned hypnotism for the interpretation of free association, his 'practical' theories, as we may call (ii) and (iii) for convenience, were derived from his successful interpretations just as much as the interpretations were derived from the theories. When Melanie Klein introduced her play technique in the analysis of young children, the Freudian 'practical' theories were an indispensable guide but could not be said to 'govern' her interpretations in any strict sense of the term. The modifications she proposed in the practical theories were derived from successful interpretations, which were in turn derived from the interrelations between 'networks of ideas' as she understood them.

I would suggest, therefore, that an interpretation might be described as an original intervention in the patient–analyst relationship, consisting of guesses as to the connections between contiguous items of behaviour, feeling, and thought, and between such items and unconscious impulses, guesses both partly derived from and contributing to the analyst's 'practical' theories; that its dynamic efficacy is due to the patient's discovery that the analyst is not afraid of the connections he detects and that therefore the patient need not be quite so afraid as he was; and that its theoretical validity is confirmed or disconfirmed by its effect on subsequent behaviour.

REFUTATION AND PREDICTION

Wisdom speaks of 'understanding expressed as an interpretation "confirmed" by alterations in associations or other ways *intelligible in terms of the interpretation* or a *simple extension of it*' (his italics), and adds: '. . . an interpretation is false if the subsequent associations have no bearing on the interpretation'. It would be gratifying if such a straight-forward criterion could be applied, but there are theoretical difficulties about both confirmation and refutation. What if an interpretation is followed by days or weeks of silence? Should we infer that it was false, or that it was too true to be endured? What if an interpretation is premature? Might it not still be true although subsequent associations have no bearing on it? What if it is partly true and partly false? Would what follows have a bearing only on what was true? What if a true interpretation is followed by associations which are related to it in a way no one can detect? And so on.

There is the further difficulty, mentioned by Wisdom, of excluding the possibility of suggestion. Many analysts, knowing the scrupulous empiricism of their technique, take no interest in the common charge that their patients reproduce their own 'fantastic' ideas like gramophone records. Such ill-informed criticism can be ignored. But it is a difficult scientific task to ensure that *no* false interpretations are ever apparently confirmed because of the patient's desire to reproduce the kind of material he thinks the analyst expects of him, or that no true ones are ever apparently refuted because of the patient's desire to frustrate the analyst or reveal his inadequacy. Positive or negative transference is a serious impediment to the testing of interpretations.

The importance of refutation stems from Wisdom's contention that 'Popper's criterion applies to all theories that purport to be scientific: that is, they must be refutable in principle, which means that we must be able to specify what situation, if the theory were false, would show that it were false' (p. 25). Failing that, psychoanalytic theory 'would be in the position of the mechanistic theory of physiology – capable of endless support, yet never established because incapable of refutation should it happen to be false'.

The other test mentioned by Wisdom is prediction, which he holds to constitute a test for scientific theory only if what is predicted is unlikely in relation to the rest of our knowledge; it is specific; and it follows deductively from the theory.

Both these tests are useful when judging the validity of a theory relating to a relatively simple closed system. We must now consider whether they can be applied to complex systems where the isolation of a few factors is impossible. We can predict a total eclipse of the sun visible in Cornwall on 11 August 1999, but as Eddington (1951) has pointed out, the predictability of the configurations of the system comprising the sun, earth, and moon, is not characteristic of natural phenomena in general:

> 'but of those involving great numbers of atoms in action – such that we are concerned not with individual but with average behaviour' (p. 300).
> 'The eclipse in 1999 is as safe as the balance of a life insurance company; the next quantum jump of an atom is as uncertain as your life and mine. . . . For when we ask what is the characteristic of the phenomena that have been successfully predicted, the answer is that they are effects depending on the average configurations of vast numbers of individual entities. But averages are predictable because they are averages, irrespective of the type of the phenomena underlying them.'

and again:

> 'Thus in the structure of the world as formulated in the new quantum theory it is predetermined that of 500 atoms now in State 3, approximately 400 will go on to State 1 and 100 to State 2 – in so far as anything subject to chance fluctuations can be said to be predetermined' (ibid., p. 301).

I have given reasons for doubting whether conclusive refutation of an interpretation is possible, and there are equally cogent reasons for doubting whether precise prediction of the effects of an interpretation is possible. It *is* possible for an analyst to predict that within a specified period (*not* at a specified time) some, out of a large class of responses which would be allowed to be related in a specified way to the interpretation, will supervene, and such predictions are, in fact, very often verified. Such predictions are much more like predictions of the behaviour of atoms than the prediction of the total eclipse of the sun in 1999. This does not diminish the value of the predictions, but to attempt to make the kind of prediction which is possible only when the system studied is either naturally simple – because large quantum numbers are involved – or artificially simple – because the experiment is devised to make it so – would be to set psychoanalysis an impossible task, and so to make it incur an unjustified disqualification as a science.

To demand of a prediction that it should be 'unlikely in relation to the rest of our knowledge, specific, and following deductively from the theory', would be to narrow the concept so as to exclude the possibility of prediction in psychoanalysis, or, for that matter, in most branches of biology and medicine. There is nothing that follows deductively from any psychoanalytic theory, because the main theories have not been systematized in such a way that the terms are related to each other by agreed definitions. The danger of importing such requirements from the mathematized theories is that important hypotheses in many sciences which are not susceptible of mathematical formulation will be judged by inappropriate criteria.

UNLIKELIHOOD AND SPECIFICITY

The other two requirements, unlikelihood and specificity, are open to a different kind of objection. If a student of international affairs were to predict two successful revolutions, the first in Poland between 1 May and 30 June 1991, and the second in Russia between 1 January and 1 April 1993, we would, at the present time, have some difficulty in deciding whether his predictions were likely or not. They might seem likely to some students, unlikely to others. Compared with the eclipse prediction they would be unspecific, but if they were verified, and if he demonstrated that he had had good reasons for his belief, it would be ungenerous to discount his predictions as tests of his theory. We might even concede that they were remarkably specific *in relation to the complexity of the data*. If he went on to make a series of similar predictions, all of which were verified and supported by a well-formulated theory, we might be more and more prepared to regard the predictions as tests of his theory.

The above arguments may seem to conflict with the profoundly important suggestion made by Ezriel and quoted in Chapter 2:

> '. . . It ought to be possible for the analyst to . . . control the antecedent variables by selecting them from the pre-interpretation material and incorporating them in his interpretations, and to make predictions about the patient's responses to these interpretations. . . . Experimentation in the psychoanalytic session therefore depends on the analyst's ability to select the antecedent variables, i.e., to identify the patient's unconscious object relationships which are determining his behaviour towards the analyst.'

As I am convinced that this suggestion is the key to the problem of setting psychoanalysis on a sound scientific foundation, it is necessary to emphasize that nothing in this passage suggests that the predictions would be like predictions of eclipses. Identifying unconscious object relationships is an art for which no rules can be laid down, and predictions about the patient's responses are valuable for the purpose of validation or invalidation of a technique, and of confirmation or disconfirmation of the 'practical' theories underlying the technique. There are at least four kinds of responses: those which, in the opinion of several trained observers, confirm the analyst's guess; those which seem to be neutral to the guess; those which disconfirm it; and silence. It is sometimes possible to guess the meaning of silences, but their meaning is seldom clearly understood – except retrospectively.

PSYCHOANALYTIC PREDICTIONS

Psychoanalytic predictions, then, do not follow 'deductively' (in any strict sense) from a theory; are less specific than *some* laboratory predictions in the mathematized sciences; and are unlikely in relation to the rest of most people's knowledge, and sometimes in relation to another analyst's. They are predictions about the effects of interventions, and – although unique – are comparable with predictions about the effects of other scientific interventions *in different respects*.

They are like pharmacological predictions in the respect that they are based on similarities between people. The more frequently a drug (e.g. penicillin) is administered, and the more scientifically its effects are studied, the more reliable do predictions about its effects become. An anomalous effect, such as a morbid reaction to penicillin, indicates either a mistake in dosage or preparation, or a physiological deviation from the norm, which needs to be accounted for by pharmacological and physiological theory. In the same way, an anomalous effect of an interpretation may indicate a psychological deviation demanding explanation instead of constituting a clear-cut refutation of the interpretation. In this context, an inadequate interpretation is like an injection of a wrongly prepared drug, whereas the unexpected effect of a sound interpretation is like the unexpected effect of a properly (i.e. properly for the norm) prepared drug.

Psychoanalytic predictions are also like pharmacological predictions in that laboratory isolation of variable factors is impossible. A pharmacological intervention is an intervention in the life of a whole, imperfectly understood organism. Hence the possibility of anomalous effects.

They are *unlike* pharmacological predictions in that diagnosis of gross somatic disorders is easier, quicker, and more precise than that of psychological disorders. It is possible, therefore, to select a number of people suffering from the same disease and from them to choose a control group to test relatively long-term predictions about the effects of a drug. It is impossible, before analysis, to give a precise description of the nature and severity of a psychological disorder, and so to establish control groups. Where the gross physiological effects of a drug are less important than the unmeasurable effects (e.g. as with mescaline), the pharmacologist is faced with the same problem. No pharmacologist could give a full account of the total effects of a given dose of mescaline.

PSYCHOANALYTIC THEORIES

To make use of Wisdom's distinctions, the unifying or explanatory theories of psychoanalysis are comparable to the theories of Preformation and Epigenesis in biology, and to the theories of Psychophysical Parallelism and Epiphenomalism in philosophy in the following respects: they are difficult or impossible to confirm or disconfirm, and the changes in the formulations of the theories would have either no effects or only indirect effects on techniques and lower-level hypotheses; they are likely to be reformulated not only in the light of new discoveries, but also in the light of philosophical criticism. The 'death instinct', for example, is thought by some analysts – especially among supporter's of Melanie Klein's theories – to be an important concept, while others regard it as of little or no explanatory value, emphasize that Freud put it forward as a tentative suggestion, and propose that some such term as 'destructive impulses' be substituted for the term 'death instinct'.

Theories which use the 'id–ego–superego' model are not easily classifiable. Analysts such as Melanie Klein and W. R. D. Fairbairn, who have proposed major changes in Freud's model, have given clinical reasons for finding one model more useful than another, so that there is a sense in which such theories have technological counterparts, but it is possible that psychological models will prove comparable to physical models: that they will be thought of as aids to the imagination, which can be progressively modified as the science develops.

The Attempted Wish-fulfilment Theory of dreams and phantasies is like the Principle of Rectilinear Propagation of Light in the following respects: it has immense heuristic value; it can be reconciled with many apparent exceptions – (even a nightmare may fulfil a wish by bringing a loved person back to life); and its heuristic value survives the demonstration of a *real* exception requiring a modification of the theory. It is therefore different from 'model' theories in psychodynamics in much the same way as the Rectilinear Principle is different from 'model' theories in physics. As a corollary it may be suggested that dogmatic adherence to the exact form of heuristically valuable principles or laws may be a bar to progress in psychodynamics as it has been in physics.

The basic theory of unconscious and transference phenomena is comparable to the theory of the continuity of evolution in the following respects: it is considered by analysts to be well established by a mass of evidence, so that they would not be interested in attempts to 'prove' or 'disprove' the theory; there is some disagreement or uncertainty, not about *whether* but about *how* species evolve; and it has a profound and cumulative effect upon what Popper has called 'the horizon of expectations'. From biology we learn that in origin and embryo we are like the mute animals; from psychoanalysis that in our dreams and unconscious phantasies we are like children, primitive savages, and psychotics.

6

Twelve Kinds of Psychoanalytic Hypothesis

I suggest that kinds of psychoanalytic hypothesis should be distinguished according to a scale of direct relevance to immediately observed clinical and social data:

1. Anomaly Hypotheses

One of the ways a judge or jury assesses the reliability of the evidence given by the accused or by a witness is by its internal consistency. So too, in our everyday judgements of people's characters, we attach importance to inconsistencies between this and that statement, this and that item of behaviour, this statement and that performance. Any shrewd comment which questions the face-value of speech or behaviour is an anomaly hypothesis: 'Although he would deny being jealous, that critic's judgement seems to be warped by his jealousy of the writer'; or 'In spite of his rudeness and professed indifference towards her, he behaves as if he were in love with her'. Such guesses assume that people may be unaware of their deeper feelings, but they are psychologically compatible with rejection of all explicit hypotheses relating to unconscious thoughts and feelings. Listening to a patient suffering from an hysterical illness, an analyst may conjecture: 'Although she says she wants to get well, much of what she says and does is consistent with the desire to keep her son with her by remaining ill.' This would be an anomaly hypothesis.

2. Interpretation Hypotheses

Hypotheses used as interpretations are comparable to the comments about the critic, the man in love, and the patient, except that they are said at a chosen time *to* the subject of the guess, and so are *interventions* which may change the situation. Interpretations are also offered outside the clinical situation, but they are less often effective because they are frequently given in anger or with a sadistic aim. If a mother said to a father, 'You resent the trouble I take over the boy because you are jealous of him', it is more likely that her remark, even if true, would be parried as a blow rather than pondered as a conjecture.

3. Retrospective Hypotheses

These are hypotheses *about* interpretations and their effects. The importance of such hypotheses is that they may yield relatively precise predictions which can be objectively tested. The more regularly such hypotheses are confirmed, the stronger their claim to be the basis of a psychological law.

4. Predictive Hypotheses

These are hypotheses about the effects of interpretations.

5. Ahistorical Hypotheses

These are hypotheses about the patient's current unconscious wishes, fears, and assumptions, which are not used as interpretations. These include hypotheses about the transference, such as that the patient's unconscious object relationships are influencing his behaviour towards the analyst.

6. Lawlike Hypotheses

Hypotheses based on 1–5, such as Ezriel's hypotheses quoted above (p. 25).

7. Individual Development Hypotheses

These hypotheses about the patient's physical and psychic development are based on extrapolation from clinical experience. Refutation is possible when there is independent biographical evidence such as diaries, hospital records, etc., but usually such evidence is relevant to only a small part of such hypotheses.

8. Class Development Hypotheses

These hypotheses about the psychic development of classes or communities are based on extrapolation from 7. Some confirmation or refutation is possible for such hypotheses: statistical studies of the effects on infants and young children of life in institutions, for example, may confirm or refute certain hypotheses about the effects of losing a mother's love. Such statistical checks may be misleading, however, as they can make use only of gross data, and ignore less easily detectable effects or effects such as apathy which, though easily observed and sometimes striking, are unsuitable for quantitative representation.

9. Heuristic Hypotheses

General hypotheses of heuristic value may be put into more, or less, dogmatic form. In *The Interpretation of Dreams* (Chapter Four) for example, Freud describes the dream as 'the (disguised) fulfilment of a suppressed or repressed wish (p. 160); in *New Introductory Lectures* (Lecture XXIX), he suggests that 'if you want to take these latter objections into account, you can say nevertheless that a dream is an *attempt* at the fulfilment of a wish' (p. 29). The hypothesis, or rather the heuristic principle, would be even less vulnerable, and perhaps equally useful, in the form: 'Dreams become more and more intelligible when assiduously studied as attempted wish-fulfilments.' There is always a possibility, however, that such a hypothesis or principle may be superseded by a new one. Fairbairn, for example, has asserted that 'dreams are essentially, not wish-fulfilments, but dramatizations or "shorts" . . . of situations existing in inner reality . . . the situations in dreams represent relationships existing between endopsychic structures' (1952, p. 99). This statement is in the form of a challenging hypothesis, which will stand or fall by the test of clinical experience. Hypotheses of the form 'All x's are y' are refutable in a different way from, say, specific predictions. A single exception constitutes a refutation, but the refutation may lead to no more than a minor reformulation of the hypothesis. Certain transference hypotheses, if regarded as primarily heuristic, could be expressed in a more cautious form, e.g.: 'Patients' associations in psychoanalytic sessions become more intelligible when *all* items of speech and other behaviour which are contiguous are assumed to be meaningfully related, and when they are *all* examined for a disguised reference to the analyst.'

10. Interdisciplinary Hypotheses

These are hypotheses relating to other disciplines such as anthropology, criminology, aesthetics, education, etc. These are based on extrapolation from clinical experience and on hypotheses about psychic development. Just as the volcanologist assumes that volcanoes that erupt and volcanoes that merely rumble and smoke are subject to the same laws, so the analyst assumes that the aetiological principles are the same for antisocial impulses, for example, as acted upon by the law-breaker and as confined to the fantasy and dreams of the law-observing patient.

11. 'Model' Hypotheses

These are devised to facilitate explanation. There is something odd about the attempt to *refute* a model hypothesis such as 'Light travels in waves', or 'The ego keeps down the instinctual claims of the id'. Fairbairn, for example, has suggested a revised 'model', consisting of Central Ego, Libidinal Ego, with its Exciting Object, and Internal Saboteur, with its Rejecting Object, putting forward arguments from clinical experience in support of the superior explanatory value of his model (1952, p. 105). If this model were to win acceptance and supersede Freud's model, we should be inclined to say, not that Freud's model hypotheses were false, but that the new model hypotheses were more *useful* because they enabled us to explain a greater range of data in terms of the model.

12. Speculative Hypotheses

It would be difficult or impossible to specify any empirical test for many of these very general speculative hypotheses. This class includes hypotheses relating to the 'death instinct' and 'libido'. Here again it is convenient to refer to Fairbairn, who explains clearly how far he agrees, and how far he disagrees, with Freud. He says, 'What Freud describes under the category of "death instincts" would . . . appear to represent for the most part masochistic (or sadistic) relationships with internalized bad objects' (ibid., p. 79), and he suggests (p. 31) that the classic libido theory should be transformed into *'a theory of development based essentially upon object-relationships'* (his italics). We shall consider later (pp. 148–50) how the issue is decided between rival theories of this kind.

IS THERE ONE HYPOTHESIS OF THE UNCONSCIOUS?

What Wisdom calls the genetic hypothesis (see p. 64 above) and his hypothesis that the childhood networks of ideas are interrelated are included in the development hypotheses class (8). What he calls the guise hypothesis is included in the lawlike class (6). It is more difficult to place what he calls 'the hypothesis of the unconscious'. The phrase is too multivocal to be allocated a definite place in the scheme I have suggested. *A hypothesis cannot be defended or attacked, supported or refuted, unless it is explicitly formulated.* It is often misleading, as we shall see,* to speak of 'the hypothesis of Behaviourism', or 'of hedonism', or 'of inductivism' and so on, because more than one formulation is possible for each.

Let us consider the following hypothesis (G): 'There are many fears, wishes and assumptions, that seldom, and many that never, become conscious, although they may have a major influence on a person's thoughts, feelings, and behaviour.' Let us compare this with the statement: 'Of the whole range of radiation, revealed by instruments as a continuous spectrum of rays from long radio waves to short gamma-rays, only one part in ten thousand million million is perceptible to our eyes'; and with: 'Of the wide range of sounds which can occur in nature, our ears are sensitive only to those whose pitch lies within about ten octaves.'

The philosopher may object that only what can be heard can be called a sound: an unheard sound is a contradiction. The physicist may reply, 'The accident of the differences in sensitivity of the ears and eyes of various animals, including man, is irrelevant to the physical theory of sound and of the spectrum. You may, if you like, limit the use of the word "sound" to the range of vibrations detectable by the human ear, or perhaps by the ear of any animal, so long as you recognize the continuity we have discovered. So long as our discoveries are understood, it is a question of convenience whether the word "sound" is used for ranges of vibrations that we cannot hear.'

Some philosophers have objected that 'unconscious wish' is self-contradictory. The analyst may reply, 'The accident of the differences in self-awareness between individuals is of great importance, because the making conscious of what was unconscious has dynamic effects. Nevertheless, whatever term you wish to substitute for "unconscious wish", it is the continuity we have discovered that interests us.'

Hypothesis G belongs to a different logical class from the twelve we have distinguished. The injunction γνῶθε σεαυτόν ('know yourself')

* See Straw Man Fallacy, defined p. 203.

would be unintelligible without the assumption that we do not know ourselves fully. Should we then regard G as the basic hypothesis of psychoanalysis, or as a jejune platitude? The answer seems to be that it *would* be a platitude but for the fact that A, an intelligent person, can see quite clearly that B, C, and D are blind to their own characters and motives, but is convinced that he, A, is fully aware of his own character and motives. Hence, in a discussion between people who have the insight to recognize the limitations of their self-knowledge, Hypothesis G *would be* a platitude; in all other contexts it is still the basic hypothesis of psychoanalysis.

There are many possible alternatives to G. Here is Hypothesis H, for example: 'The extension of the language projection TFM (called TFME) is a scientific tool which can be used to bring to conscious awareness thoughts, feelings, and motives which were formerly unconscious; it is a language projection which cannot be "reduced to" or transposed into the language of physics.'

One more example, Hypothesis P: 'Accurate and well-timed interpretations in TFME have the effect of reducing the fear of impulses which were formerly unconscious, increasing the understanding of them, and hence increasing conscious control over them.'

Hypotheses G, H, and P, have been formulated merely to show that there is no single 'hypothesis of the unconscious' to be defended or attacked, supported or refuted.

The problem of testing would be less formidable than it is if the scale of direct relevance to immediately observed data corresponded to a scale from perfect to diminishing reliability, but this is clearly not so. The first class, anomaly hypotheses, are the starting-point of dynamic, as opposed to classificatory, psychology. Yet these hypotheses, like the hypotheses of gravitation, do not inevitably occur to any observer of the 'data'. The first class, anomaly hypotheses, and the second class, interpretation hypotheses, are influenced by the third (retrospective hypotheses), the fifth (transference hypotheses), the sixth (lawlike hypotheses), the seventh (individual development hypotheses), the eighth (class development hypotheses), and the ninth (heuristic hypotheses). They may also be influenced indirectly by the eleventh, model hypotheses, and the twelfth, speculative hypotheses. The general principle, that we observe what we have learnt to observe, applies to psychoanalytic as to any other theory. A biology student has to learn to see what the instructor sees under a microscope or on an X-ray plate. The 'data' are so far from being unequivocally 'given' that the little Latin word hides a major philosophical problem.

Nevertheless, it is at the level of interpretation and transference hypotheses, as we may call classes 1–6, that the insight and originality of the empirical analyst has most scope, and that inadequate hypotheses or models are most likely to be modified. Lawlike hypotheses, when established by rigorous tests of their scope, and agreed upon by many independent observers, will be the foundation of scientific psychology, and, like laws established in the laboratory, will have extensive applications outside the testing situation.

7

Testability and Falsifiability

SEVEN PHILOSOPHICAL FALLACIES

With the distinctions made in Chapter 6 in mind, we can now attempt to answer the question: is there a criterion by which we can distinguish between valid and invalid hypotheses in psychoanalysis? The question will, I believe, prove to be at the same time philosophical and scientific.

As an approach to this question we may examine Popper's contention that 'falsifiability, or refutability, is a criterion of the scientific status of a theory'. Popper's criticism of psychoanalysis is worthy of careful study because so many of his arguments in other contexts are extremely cogent.

Speaking of 'the problem of demarcation' he says:

'... Wittgenstein's criterion of demarcation ... is verifiability, or deducibility from observation statements. But it excludes from science practically everything that is, in fact, characteristic of it. . . . No scientific theory can ever be deduced from observation statements, or be described as a truth-function of observation statements' (1965, p. 40).

I think that most philosophers and scientists today would agree with this criticism. Popper has what seems to be a clear and decisive solution:

'The criterion of falsifiability is a solution to this problem of demarcation, for it says that, in order to be ranked as scientific, statements or systems of statements must be capable of conflicting with possible, or conceivable, observations' (ibid., p. 39).

He exposes, in my opinion justly, seven major philosophical fallacies: the Wittgensteinian Fallacy just mentioned, a Humean Fallacy, a Kantian Fallacy, and the fallacies of Operationalism, Behaviourism, Phenomenalism, and Instrumentalism. Anyone who wields a hammer so deftly that he hits seven nails on the head in one article can intimidate, if not stun, all but the toughest reader.

In answer to Hume's doctrine that our habit of believing in laws is the product of frequent repetition, Popper maintains that

'there must always be a point of view – such as a system of expectations, anticipations, assumptions or interests – before there can be any repetition; which point of view, consequently, cannot be merely the result of repetition' (pp. 44–5).

We have to recognize or interpret a situation as a repetition of another. He points out that

'"similarity-for-us" is the product of a response involving interpretations (which may be inadequate) and anticipations or expectations (which may never be fulfilled)' (p. 45).

He agrees with Kant's dictum that 'Our intellect does not draw its laws from nature but imposes its laws upon nature', adding

'But in thinking that these laws are necessarily true, or that we necessarily succeed in imposing them upon nature, he was wrong' (p. 48).

We try to find regularities in our experience, and

'events which don't yield to these attempts we are inclined to treat as a kind of "background noise" . . . this dogmatism allows us to approach a good theory in stages, by way of approximations' (p. 49).

He describes Behaviourism as

'the doctrine that, since all test-statements describe behaviour, our theories too must be stated in terms of possible behaviour. But the inference is as invalid as the phenomenalist doctrine which asserts that since all test-statements are observational, theories too must be stated in terms of possible observations. All these doctrines are forms of the verifiability theory of meaning; that is to say, of inductivism' (p. 62).

It is not quite clear how large a class of thinkers incur the charge of 'inductivism' – one suspects that it is very large – and it is far from clear that they should all be condemned, but the inferences here mentioned are certainly fallacious.

He pinpoints the fallacy underlying Operationalism when he says that '*measurements presuppose theories*' and that there is 'no operation which can be satisfactorily described in non-theoretical terms' (p. 62).

His view of intellectual development is that the critical attitude, which may be identified with the scientific attitude, 'is not so much opposed to the dogmatic attitude as superimposed upon it' (p. 50).

'I am inclined to suggest that most neuroses may be due to a partially arrested development of the critical attitude; to an arrested rather than a natural dogmatism; to a resistance against demands for the modification and adjustment of certain schematic interpretations and responses' (p. 49).

POPPER'S CRITIQUE OF PSYCHOANALYSIS

Popper's view of neurosis reads like a brief summary of part of the theory of Freud, who said: 'Neurotics turn away from reality because they find it unbearable – either the whole or parts of it' (1911a, p. 218); and 'There is no doubt that persons whom we call neurotic remain infantile in their attitude towards danger, and have not grown out of antiquated conditions for anxiety'. This was Freud's starting-point, and he set himself the task, not merely of describing in vague outline how an infantile pattern of responses interferes with adaptation to new circumstances, but of investigating in minute detail how specific infantile and childish wishes, fears, and assumptions limit and pervert the adult's view of the world and his attempts to find a place in it.

The views so far quoted are all such as could consistently be held by an empirical psychoanalyst. Let us now examine Popper's reasons for denying the scientific status of psychoanalysis. He tells an anecdote which suggests that Adler was unscientific; from this an incautious reader could make the following *non causa pro causa* inference: Adler and Freud were both psychologists; Adler seemed to be unscientific; therefore Freud was probably unscientific. Recalling the eclipse observation 'which in 1919 brought the first important confirmation of Einstein's theory of gravitation', Popper later describes how he was prompted to ask, 'What is wrong with Marxism, psychoanalysis and individual psychology?' He decided that they resembled astrology rather than astronomy. Whereas Einstein's theory was 'incompatible with certain possible results of observation', he could not think of any conceivable instance of human behaviour which could not be interpreted in terms of either Freud's theory or Adler's.

A comparison with astrology is harsh condemnation from a cautious philosopher of science. Marx certainly made great mistakes, and Adler was not comparable in stature to Freud, but both deserve better than this. As to Freud, such a judgement suggests an attitude far from dispassionate. Nevertheless the criticism should be carefully examined.

'"Clinical observations"', he writes (1965, p. 38, n. 3), ' . . . are *interpretations in the light of theories . . . criteria of refutation* have to be laid down beforehand. . . . But what kind of clinical responses would refute, to the satisfaction of the analyst, not merely a particular diagnosis but psychoanalysis itself?' This is the crux of his criticism and to discover what kind of question he is asking I shall propose some comparable questions. What kind of observations would refute, to the satisfaction of the endocrinologist, not merely a particular hypothesis but endocrinology itself? Or archaeology? Or meteorology? Or economics? Or biophysics? Or bionomics? How would we set about refuting radiology? Or anthropology? Or the theory of evolution?

Let us suppose that some critic of archaeology were to produce incontestable evidence that all historical conclusions based on archaeological finds were false. Would he have refuted archaeology? He would have refuted many hypotheses within the discipline, and a great deal of archaeology would have to be rewritten. What would *not* have been refuted is the vast store of data which need to be explained, and the general hypothesis that the individual descriptions of uncovered remains can be linked by a series of interconnected historical postulates. The groundwork and the method would remain; only certain historical assumptions would have to be *modified*. The critic would not have refuted archaeology.

CAN A DISCIPLINE BE REFUTED?

I suggest that Popper has confused a *discipline* with a major hypothesis or system of hypotheses of that discipline. Hypotheses may be refuted, though we have yet to see whether *all* hypotheses can be refuted; disciplines, or branches of knowledge which involve systematic research, can not be refuted. Even alchemy and astrology, to the extent that they are disciplines which made a systematic study of metals and the stars, are not refutable: only hypotheses of those disciplines (in astrology most, if not all, of its hypotheses) are refutable. There is good reason for this: all genuine observations of the stars made by astrologers have been incorporated in astronomy, as all genuine discoveries made by alchemists have been incorporated in chemistry and physics.

Psychoanalysis is a discipline which has already made and recorded a large number of discoveries about the behaviour of adults and children in special conditions. Even if many of its hypotheses were found to be inadequate, those discoveries would still need explanation. Any revision of the hypotheses would itself be psychoanalysis, just as any revision of genetic hypotheses would be genetics. To speak of refuting a discipline which is steadily accumulating fresh observational data, or a theory which comprises many heterogeneous classes of hypotheses, is to make a *philosophical* mistake.

FALSIFIABILITY IN THE PHYSICAL SCIENCES

Nevertheless, there is sometimes a single hypothesis which is so central to a discipline that such a mistake would be relatively unimportant. 'There is a causal relationship between the movements of the stars and the life-histories of men' is a hypothesis whose conclusive refutation could be innocuously, even if inaccurately, described as a 'refutation' of the pseudo-discipline of astrology.

If an astrologer made a series of precise predictions of the events of people's lives, would they be scientific? They would certainly be falsifiable; so that if they are denied scientific status there must be some other criterion, apart from falsifiability, necessary to a satisfactory demarcation. Let us suppose that this further criterion is deducibility from a theory. Our astrologer claims to have deduced his predictions from a theory which is too complex for anyone else to understand. It is quite conceivable that a scientific theory should be understood by only one man. It is a mere accident of history that Einstein's theories have been understood by several mathematicians. Nevertheless, even if all the astrologer's predictions were confirmed, scientists would suspect that they were not deducible from a valid astrological theory; if all were falsified they would allow that they might be deducible from a theory: an invalid one. According to Popper's criterion this invalid astrological theory would be scientific, because it yields falsifiable predictions.

We have seen that the falsifiability criterion allows scientific status to theories which most scientists would call unscientific. Let us now apply it to statements and theories which they would call scientific. Experimental work in modern physics, designed to discover the paths of individual photons, has shown that a series of experiments that are, so far as the physicist can tell, precisely identical, will give different results. If solitary photons, for example, are shot one after another at the same point of a half-silvered mirror, half of them will pass through and half will not. Which photon will and which will not does not depend on any detectable variation in the conditions of the experiment. This fact has led some scientists to discard the principle of the uniformity of nature: that like causes produce like effects.

Describing Dirac's formal theory, which includes the theories of Heisenberg, de Broglie and Schrödinger as special cases, Sir James Jeans (1942, p. 172) suggests that we should picture the world as consisting of three parts: substratum, phenomenal world, and observer. He describes as an essential feature of Dirac's theory 'that events in the phenomenal world are not uniquely associated with events in the substratum; different events in the substratum may result in phenomena which are precisely similar, at least to our observation'.

Is the statement quoted falsifiable or not? Is it capable of conflicting with possible, or conceivable, observations? The answer seems to depend on what A, B, C, and D can, or cannot, conceive. The question is, in fact, a disguised psychological question. If A can conceive a physiological change in the human organism, such that 'events in the substratum' could be directly observed, or at least detected by as yet unimagined instruments, while B finds such a development inconceivable, who is to settle the issue between them? The same question can be asked of a dispute between the religious scientist C, who finds life after death conceivable and claims that 'I shall find the answer to this problem in my next life' is a falsifiable, scientific statement, and the scientist D, who holds that the statement is not capable of conflicting with possible, or conceivable, observations.

A modern physicist may be uneasy about discussing the falsifiability of any *statement* or system of statements in physics. He may agree with Martin Johnson, who describes the later view of physics as 'pattern without demand to know of what THING we discover the structure' (1948, p. 30). He later maintains that recent criticism has left surviving 'the essentials of Measurement, Abstraction and Transformation, and the construction of FORMS and STRUCTURES for expressing functional dependence, without retention of any demand for the meaning of the symbols or for models in the mechanical sense' (p. 89).

If we accept this view of physics it would be fairer to consider Dirac's 'forms and structures for expressing functional dependence' rather than any non-mathematical statement. The question is now whether we can describe the patterns of symbols to which no precise *meanings* can be ascribed as falsifiable or refutable. Jeans has stated (1942, p. 200) that 'the physical theory of relativity has now shown that electric and magnetic forces are not real at all; they are merely mental constructs of our own, resulting from our rather misguided efforts to understand the motions of the particles. It is the same with the Newtonian force of gravitation, and with energy, momentum, and other concepts which were introduced to help us understand the activities of the world – all prove to be mere mental constructs, and do not even pass the test of objectivity.'

Does this mean that the Newtonian theory of gravitation has been 'refuted', and that all statements using the terms 'energy', 'momentum', etc. have been falsified? This would be a misleading description of the developments of modern physics. Most of the functional dependences expressed in terms of the Newtonian theory, of electric and magnetic forces, energy, or momentum, were not liable to outright refutation, but were revisable. The models and assumptions which proved unnecessary or inadequate were discarded but much of the structure of the theory was maintained. Patterns are not falsifiable, only statements. Perhaps equations may be said to be statements, but Einstein's mass-energy equation, $E = MC^2$, is not falsifiable in the same sense that 'Planet P will appear to Observer O at space-time st' is falsifiable. If a prediction deduced from $E = MC^2$ is falsified, the scope of the equation is limited, but the equation is not shown to be 'false' or 'refuted'. It remains applicable to the range of phenomena from which it has been abstracted, just as much of Newtonian physics is still valid for 'macroscopic' phenomena.

FALSIFIABILITY IN PSYCHOANALYSIS

Similar arguments apply to psychoanalysis. It is probable, though some hagiologists might deny it, that what Popper calls 'Freud's epic of the Egos, the Superegos and the Ids' will prove to correspond to the electric and magnetic forces of physics, the forces which Jeans calls 'mental constructs'. It is possible, too, that some psychoanalytic concept will be shown to correspond to 'the luminiferous ether', which, in the words of Jeans (ibid., p. 86), 'became established in scientific thought as "the nominative of the verb *to undulate*", and misled physics for over a century'. Yet, as the modern physicist looks down from the heights of relativity and quantum theory on Newton's 'epic of Gravitation, Energy and Momentum', he will reflect that remarkable progress was made in the eighteenth and nineteenth centuries, in spite of, or perhaps even because of, what have proved to be mere mental constructs.

THE FACT-FINDING FALLACY

Popper's criticism of Freud's 'epic' is that 'These theories describe some facts, but in the manner of myths. They contain some interesting psychological suggestions, but not in a testable form' (1957, p. 161).

This criticism brings us back to the problem of the term 'fact'. In a letter to Bentley, Newton wrote:

> 'That gravity should be innate, inherent and essential to matter, so that one body may act upon another at a distance, through a vacuum, without the mediation of anything else by and through which their action may be conveyed from one to another, is to me so great an absurdity that I believe no man, who has in philosophical matters a competent faculty of thinking, can ever fall into it.'

Yet there was no alternative to this 'absurdity' until the 'myth' of absolute time and a three-dimensional space was destroyed by Einstein's General Theory of Relativity in 1915. All the motions of all gravitating bodies were then explained as being the straightest lines that are consistent with the curvature of the four-dimensional space-time continuum; in other words, a moving object or a ray of light moves along a geodesic. This relativity theory of gravitation is said to be in complete agreement with 'the facts', including the 'facts' described by Newton. Now, Newton's 'facts' were described in terms of the 'myth' of absolute time and three-dimensional space, using locutions such as 'one body acting upon another'. Newton believed that 'Gravity must be caused by some agent acting constantly according to certain laws; but whether this agent be material or immaterial I have left to the consideration of my readers' (*Letters to Bentley*). There is a temptation, when the mythological account is rewritten in terms of relativity theory, to suppose that modern scientists are accounting for 'facts', mystically immutable throughout the changes in physical theory, which were misleadingly described by pre-relativity physicists. This is an example of the Fact-finding Fallacy. Einstein's 'facts' are different from Newton's. The exposure of the myth has changed the 'facts'.

Very general statements such as 'The sun acts upon the earth' are more vulnerable to attacks on the presuppositions and 'myths' of a theory than are lawlike hypotheses abstracted from a limited range of data. When a comprehensive theory is said to be in agreement with the facts, it is the observation-statements and the specific lawlike hypotheses of the theory which are thought of as 'factual'. If we tried to describe in Newtonian terms the 'fact' that, in Eddington's words, 'Light-waves in passing a massive body such as the sun are deflected through a small angle' (1951, p. 122), we should have to say something like this: 'Light-waves are deflected by the force of gravity, which is caused by some material or immaterial agent.' The form of an observation-statement, or a statement based on observations, is not independent of

the theory, and the 'fact' is not independent of the form of the statement. Even Eddington's statement may suggest, by the term 'deflected',
an agency which pushes or pulls.

Speaking of the philosophical consequences of the theory of relativity
Bertrand Russell wrote:

'One thing that emerges is that physics tells us much less about the physical
world than we thought it did. Almost all the "great principles" of traditional physics turn out to be like the "great law" that there are always three
feet to a yard; others turn out to be downright false. The conservation of mass
may serve to illustrate both these misfortunes to which a "law" is liable'
(1925, p. 220).

He then maintains that one interpretation of the 'law' is a truism; the
other is false.

'It is a curious fact – of which relativity is not the only illustration – that,
as reasoning improves, its claims to the power of proving facts grow less
and less' (p. 224).

'Abstraction, difficult as it is, is the source of practical power. A financier
whose dealings with the world are more abstract than those of any other
"practical" man, is also more powerful than any other practical man. He
can deal in wheat or cotton without needing ever to have seen either: all
he needs to know is whether they will go up or down. This is abstract
mathematical knowledge, at least as compared to the knowledge of the
agriculturalist. Similarly the physicist, who knows nothing of matter except
certain laws of its movements, nevertheless knows enough to enable him to
manipulate it. After working through whole strings of equations, in which
the symbols stand for things whose intrinsic nature can never be known to
us, he arrives at last at a result which can be interpreted in terms of our
perceptions, and utilized to bring about desired effects in our own lives'
(p. 230).

Physics, then, is a discipline which until recently had an elaborate
'mythology' which is being progressively discarded. It now consists
largely in the manipulating of abstract mathematical symbols. Can it be
regarded as a system of falsifiable hypotheses? At this point we may
recall Toulmin's distinction between four classes of scientific statement:
abstract statements of a law or principle; historical reports about the
discovered scope of a law; applications of a law to particular cases; and
conclusions of inferences drawn in accordance with a law (see p. 24
above). Only the reports and the applications, in his opinion, can be
called empirical statements. We may now add that only the reports and
the applications are sometimes clearly falsifiable or refutable. And even

these may be *revisable* rather than refutable. If reports and predictions are confirmed, the important question remains whether the methods of representation and the techniques by which inferences can be drawn are sound or unsound.

8

Are Psychoanalytic Hypotheses Falsifiable?

OBJECTIVITY AND NON–INTERFERENCE

In the light of what has been said about modern developments in physics, we can now ask whether any psychoanalytic hypotheses are falsifiable. We have seen that anomaly hypotheses are not essentially different from shrewd guesses about people's characters in social life. There *is* a difference, however, in the technique of falsification. If an analyst guesses that a patient's boastful, selfconfident speech and behaviour is a façade which conceals an unconscious conviction of impotence and a need to be dependent, he may predict that as a result of his interpretations the conviction and need will become manifest. At this point Popper might ask how he can be sure that apparent confirmation is not due to what he calls the 'Oedipus effect' – 'the influence of a theory, or expectation, or prediction, *upon the effect which it predicts* or describes'. How can the analyst know that his interpretations will not act like suggestions on a hypnotized patient, so that his constant reiteration of the patient's conviction of impotence does in time produce the conviction?

The answer is that the conscious conviction *will* be the effect of the interpretations, so that in this sense there *is* an 'Oedipus effect' in analysis. Not only will the patient, if the analysis is successful, become aware of a need to be dependent; he will become *in fact* almost as dependent on the analyst as he was on his mother when a child. In his emotional life he will *become* a child. Does not this fact invalidate the prediction?

This criticism is based on the mistaken assumption that a person's character can or should be objectively studied in analysis without being changed. This is impossible. The assumption is due to a confusion between objectivity and non-interference. Once more, physics provides an instructive parallel. Jeans has pointed out that

'in the exact sciences, and above all in physics, subject and object were supposed to be entirely distinct, so that a description of any selected part of the universe could be prepared which would be entirely independent of the observer as well as of the special circumstances surrounding him. The theory of relativity (1905) first showed that this cannot be entirely so; the picture which each observer makes of the world is in some degree subjective. Even if the different observers all make their pictures at the same instant of time and from the same point of space, these pictures will be different unless the observers are all moving together at the same speed; then, and then only, they will be identical. Otherwise, the picture depends both on what an observer sees, and on how fast he is moving when he sees it.

The theory of quanta carries us further along the same road. For every observation involves the passage of a complete quantum from the observed object to the observing subject, and a complete quantum constitutes a not negligible coupling between the observer and the observed. We can no longer make a sharp division between the two; to try to do so would involve making an arbitrary decision as to the exact point at which the division should be made. Complete objectivity can only be regained by treating observer and observed as parts of a single system; these must now be supposed to constitute an indivisible whole, which we must now identify with nature, the object of our studies. It now appears that this does not consist of something we perceive, but of our perceptions; it is not the object of the subject–object relation, but the relation itself' (1942, p. 143).

In psychoanalysis also, the picture which each observer makes of the world is in some degree subjective. How much an analyst can understand of the verbal and other behaviour of a patient, a group of patients, or, by extrapolation, of people in general, depends (a) on the breadth and depth of his own experiences; (b) on the depth and success of his own analysis; (c) on his capacity for empathy; (d) on the adequacy of the theoretical framework with which he works, and (e) on his readiness and capacity for the empirical modification of his initial presumptions. Agreement between trained observers – when studying the tape-recorded sessions of an analysis – as to the effectiveness or otherwise of the interpretations and as to the confirmation or falsification of specific predictions, represents an important step towards objectivity.

PSYCHOLOGICAL INTERACTION

The analogue of the theory of quanta is the theory of *psychological interaction*. Although the strict adherent to the classical method of psychoanalysis reduces interaction to a minimum by abstaining from asking or answering questions, giving or taking advice or help, in short from doing anything except interpret, there can be no sharp division between the observed object and the observing subject: between the patient and the analyst. Adherence to the rules corresponds to the physicist's attempt to eliminate the irrelevant factors from an experiment; in both physics and psychoanalysis interaction is sometimes negligible, sometimes important, but never absent. Just as the cytologist or biochemist cannot study individual living cells or fragments of living tissue without interfering with the original organization of cells, so the analyst cannot understand mental processes without interfering with them. 'Objectivity can only be regained by treating observer and observed as parts of a single system.' *The object of psychoanalysis is not the object of the subject-object relation, but the relation itself.* The analyst cannot make a detailed, controlled study of the spontaneous neurosis; he can only study the transference neurosis which develops when interpretations have interfered with the pre-analytic equilibrium. As the transference neurosis develops it is necessarily different from the spontaneous neurosis as it would have developed without analysis. The spontaneous neurosis must remain a subject for speculation even when massive evidence is available (as in the cases of, say, Dostoevsky, Nietzsche, or Hitler) of a person's life or thought or both. And such speculation is not to be judged by the standards of scientific rigour appropriate to the investigation of a transference neurosis.

The study of the counter-transference, the effect of the patient's behaviour on the analyst, is a partial recognition of the fact that psychoanalysis studies the relation or interaction between analyst and patient rather than the patient himself. The patient may arouse other feelings in the analyst than scientific curiosity, and these feelings may modify his 'objectivity' – in a slightly different sense of the term. In a scientific study of recorded sessions, such manifestations of the counter-transference are material just as important as the more obvious reactions to interpretations of the patient.

THE OEDIPUS EFFECT

The 'Oedipus effect' then, should not be discounted. It helps to explain the tendency of some trainees to adopt (sometimes uncritically) the theoretical assumptions of the training analyst. It cannot, however, be used as a criticism of lawlike hypotheses about the analyst-patient interaction, unless they are formulated in terms which suggest what I shall call 'trainee-dogmatism'. It would be just as unreasonable to describe the analyst's intervention in the situation he is studying as unscientific, as to call the bombarding of atoms with neutrons unscientific. In both cases, however, the theoretical description of the process is a very difficult task.

ARE INTERPRETATIONS ENACTIVE?

Let us suppose that an analyst has been studying the free associations of a patient suffering from an hysterical paralysis. After a few months he makes the conjecture that 'Her symptom has probably more than one function. It serves to ease her unconscious sense of guilt for a crime she has committed in phantasy, to make herself harmless so that she cannot carry out dangerous impulses, and to force people to stay with her, look after her, and show her sympathy.' Is such a hypothesis refutable? Before we can answer this question we must consider in what ways it could be modified or abandoned.

First, further evidence may cause the analyst to change his mind. He may decide that his preliminary conjecture was based on the study of case-histories which were in broad outline similar to, but in certain essential respects different from, the case-history of the present patient. Second, he may find that interpretations based on his initial conjecture, although they evoke associations which seem to confirm it, fail to remove the symptom. A colleague then suggests an alternative hypothesis, and interpretations based on the new hypothesis prove successful. Could either of these two possibilities be called 'refutation of the hypothesis'?

'Refutation' suggests public tests. It may seem an illegitimate extension of 'refutation' to apply it to the private discarding of one hypothesis in favour of another. And the second? Effectiveness is certainly used by analysts as a rough-and-ready criterion of the truth of interpretations and the conjectures on which they are based. Yet it is theoretically possible for interpretations and their underlying assumptions to be effective though false, or formulated in terms of an invalid theory. We find, then, that some of the successful methods by which analysts advance their theory do not make use of conclusive refutation, although a scientific analyst will always be prepared to abandon a hypothesis if it *is* refuted.

The question may now be asked: 'If an interpretation is an intervention which may have a profound effect on the person concerned, can it at the same time be a falsifiable hypothesis?' Philosophers may think of situations where statements are interventions: where they are *enactive*:* 'Guilty', when said by the foreman of a jury, or 'Your eyelids are getting heavier and heavier', when said by a hypnotist. These are not falsifiable hypotheses. The single word 'Guilty' *can* be used to make a falsifiable statement: if, for example, in a discussion about the result of a trial, someone asks a witness 'Did the jury find the accused Guilty or not Guilty?' and the witness answers 'Guilty'. When, however, in answer to the judge's question 'Do you find the prisoner Guilty or Not Guilty?' the Foreman replies 'Guilty', his reply is informative only in part, and therefore falsifiable *to that extent*. One of the jurors may not have found the accused guilty and may have been coerced, so that the implication that the finding was unanimous may be deceptive. But the utterance of the word 'Guilty', if it goes unchallenged, is an enactive utterance which cannot be called the utterance of a falsifiable hypothesis.

If the reiterated suggestion, 'Your eyelids are getting heavier and heavier' is unsuccessful, it may provoke the sharp protest, 'No they're not!' It would be misleading to say that the hypnotist's hypothesis has been refuted, and accurate to say that his suggestion has failed. Similarly for suggestions in the future tense. 'You will detest alcohol and tobacco when you wake up' is more accurately described as a successful or unsuccessful suggestion than as a verified or falsified prediction. 'Shell shares are going to fall to half their value' would be a pure prediction if I said it, but an enactive pseudo-prediction if said in public by the Chancellor of the Exchequer. His words might cause a rush to sell and so bring about what they 'predicted'.

Are interpretations enactive like verdicts and suggestions? The answer to this question is not a simple one. Let us suppose that a disinterested friend says to a man who has for a long time been suffering from a vague malaise: 'If you were honest with yourself you would admit that you are bored with your job and unhappy with your wife, and that you stick in the rut out of habit and fear of change.' This remark comes at a time when it is sufficient to make his dissatisfaction specific and fully conscious. He sells up and goes off to a tropical island to write poetry. Perhaps we could call the remark the 'precipitating cause' of his voluntary exile. Could we also call it 'enactive' rather than 'informative'?

Another example: the relationship between a man and his wife has deteriorated to the point of mutual hatred. He is suffering from acute

* See p. 16 footnote.

depressions and has twice tried to kill himself. During one of his depressions they quarrel violently. Knowing the highly probable effect of her words she says, 'The child is not *yours*'. Soon afterwards he kills himself. This remark was a straightforward, factual, informative, falsifiable statement. It is the *timing* which makes it almost equivalent to murder, and therefore enactive.

FOCUSING UTTERANCES

These examples suffice to show that 'informative' and 'enactive' do not distinguish mutually exclusive categories, but are used to stress the relative importance of various functions of language which may coexist. This is true also of other functions, such as the normative, pre-scriptive, appraising, claim-staking (etc.) functions of language. In the example of the voluntary exile the term 'descriptive' applies, but 'informative' seems inappropriate. In one sense of 'know' he had known for a long time what his friend put into words. We are considering a use of language which has not been described by philosophers: *the putting into unambiguous words and making conscious something which has been vaguely 'known', suspected, or 'felt', or something which is just outside the 'focus-range' of consciousness.* For this use I suggest the term 'focusing'.

We can imagine the exile-to-be saying in response to his friend's remark, 'Of course! Why didn't I see it before?' It *does* make sense to ask of a focusing remark whether it is true or false. In this particular example it is unlikely that the friend's remark would have been *effective*, that is, effectively enactive, if it had been false. But if it had been ineffective it would not follow that it was false. In other words, in some situations truth is a necessary but not a sufficient condition of the effectiveness of *focusing utterances*.

An interpretation, then, is a would-be focusing utterance, which must be for the most part both true and timely to be effective. Although it is about the behaviour, feelings, attitudes, and thoughts of the person to whom it is addressed, rejection or denial by that person does not constitute refutation; it may merely be a manifestation of resistance. One of the remarkable phenomena of analysis is the interpretation which, although consciously rejected or even excluded by sleep, mishearing, misunderstanding, or some other defence technique, brings about a symptomatic change in the patient. *The effectiveness of a focusing remark is compatible with rejection, exclusion, or misunderstanding.*

TRANSFERENCE AND HYPNOTISM

This last statement may call to mind the hypnotic suggestion, whose effectiveness is compatible with sleep and subsequent forgetting ('You will remember nothing of what I have just said'). It is because of the resemblance between the state of transference and the hypnotic state that I made the qualification 'for the most part' in the preceding paragraph. The reason why a hypnotic suggestion is effective is that it by-passes (to put it crudely) the critical, discriminating conscious–preconscious which is immobilized by sleep. It is for this same reason, the by-passing of the conscious–preconscious, that hypnotism is inadequate as a technique for effecting a far-reaching change in the dynamic relationship between conscious–preconscious and unconscious thought processes.

Now a hypnotic suggestion does not have to be true to be effective. If the sentence 'Your eyelids are getting heavier and heavier' is uttered, say, six times, the first utterance may be purely suggestive (and untrue), and the sixth may be purely descriptive (and true), because the first five utterances have been effective. The closer the resemblance, then, between the state of transference (the transferring of strong, primitive feelings from their original objects to the analyst), and the hypnotic state, the less the effectiveness of interpretations will depend on their truth.

The analyst who adheres strictly to the classical nothing-but-interpretation technique does not use hypnotism, and does not include in his interpretations anything which he believes to be – *at the time of speaking* – false. Nevertheless his interpretations, if effective, will arouse primitive feelings appropriate to early childhood, and he will become, even to a highly critical adult, a feared, loved, hated, authority.* The inadequacies of his interpretations, whether psychological or philosophical, will, like those of the works of Aristotle, be difficult to detect in proportion to the uncritical acceptance of the analyst as an authority.

This is not a criticism of psychoanalytic method; the success of the method depends upon the establishment of the transference. But the above arguments suggest that although interpretations are testable, there is no simple method of falsifying them. Progress in technique and

---

* Freud has pointed out (1940, Chapter 6) that 'therapeutic successes that occurred under the sway of the positive transference are open to the suspicion of being of a *suggestive* nature. If the negative transference gains the upper hand, they are blown away like chaff before the wind.'

theory depends on two factors: the individual analyst's ability to modify his assumptions in the light of new evidence, and the criticism by trained observers of recorded interpretations. Freud's amazing achievement in the course of one lifetime was accomplished almost entirely by the progressive *modification* of his own hypotheses, but the second factor, with its advantage of increased objectivity, is likely to become more and more important.

TESTING PSYCHOANALYTICAL HYPOTHESES

If the analyst, in the course of a tape-recorded analysis, puts forward predictive hypotheses about his interpretations and their effects, and if several observers, studying the sessions retrospectively, agree about which predictions have been verified and which falsified, their conclusions can be made the basis of the objective science of *the interaction between analyst and patient or group*.

Lawlike hypotheses abstracted from this study have a similar status to those of other sciences. They are not, like predictions, conclusively falsifiable, but they are subject to modification and restriction of scope.

Hypotheses about the psychic development of individuals, groups, and communities, are based on extrapolation from the basic hypotheses.

Heuristic hypotheses, when expressed, not in the form 'All Xs are Y' but in the form 'Xs become more intelligible when assumed to be Y', are more like suggested rules for procedure than falsifiable hypotheses. They are less likely to be conclusively refuted than to be superseded by more fruitful heuristic hypotheses.

Hypotheses relating to other disciplines are of many logical classes. Some belong to the class of falsifiable statements, others do not. The hypothesis (H_1): 'If the first of two groups of homogeneous lawbreakers is given six years' psychotherapeutic treatment, confined but in tolerable conditions, while the second is given six years' hard labour in an old-fashioned prison, there will be a significantly higher proportion of recidivists in the second group than in the first' is a falsifiable predictive hypothesis, but the practical difficulties of arranging experiments to test such sociological hypotheses are formidable. As in attempts to assess the relative efficiency of various psychotherapeutic methods, the difficulty lies in the lack of reliable criteria of homogeneity, and in the statistically inadequate numbers involved. The hypothesis (H_2): 'Criminals do not constitute a distinct nosological or characterological class' is not falsifiable in the same way. It is partly descriptive, and based on clinical findings, and partly normative, with the implication, 'Classification by acts is less scientifically satisfactory than classification by character or by disease'.

Hypotheses of the class H1, if they survive adequate tests, are much more impressive to the layman than those of class H2, but both kinds play an important part in the development of the sciences and in the gradual modification of social attitudes.

PROBABILITY

Model hypotheses, as we have seen, are seldom if ever conclusively refuted; they are modified or abandoned either in the light of new data or in the light of a new theory. Popper, when attacking what he calls 'a characteristic development of verificationism', namely that we are interested in '*highly probable* theories', maintains that 'the probability of a statement (or set of statements) is always the greater the less the statement says: it is inverse to the content or the deductive power of the statement, and thus to its explanatory power. Accordingly, every interesting and powerful statement will have a low probability; . . . *as scientists we do not seek highly probable theories but explanations, which is to say, powerful and improbable theories...*'

This view I find very difficult to accept. What would it mean to say that Newton's theory of gravitation, Darwin's theory of evolution, Mendel's hypothesis of unitary hereditary factors, and Einstein's theory of relativity, which most scientists would call powerful theories, are improbable theories?

Popper is using the term 'improbable', as he uses 'scientific', in a way which does not conform with ordinary or scientific usage. The question is, therefore, not whether he is right or wrong, but whether there is good reason to follow him. By an improbable theory he means a theory from which a large number of falsifiable hypotheses can be deduced. If we follow him, we will use 'probable' and 'improbable' to indicate a supposed formal relationship between hypotheses which is independent of the knowledge or intentions of the speaker, writer, hearer, or reader. If we follow normal usage, we will use those terms to make guarded statements, predictions, promises: guarded either because our information is inadequate for definite statements or predictions, or because our theory is not fully established, or because we calculate mathematically or statistically the chance of something happening, or because we do not want to commit ourselves to a definite promise, and so on.

According to the view I am putting forward, 'Psychoanalysis is a probable theory' and 'Psychoanalysis is an improbable theory' are both equally bizarre statements, whether they are intended as compliments or insults. It makes sense to say, 'People's lives are probably influenced by the forgotten experiences of infancy', or 'All observable changes are probably due to unobservable atomic changes'; these are guarded statements which manifest scientific (or philosophical) caution. But 'Physics is a probable (or improbable) theory' is a puzzling collocation of words. In brief, *the terms 'probable' and 'improbable' are appropriate in the context of specific hypotheses or promises, and inappropriate to theories which comprise a large class of heterogeneous hypotheses: descriptive, predictive, lawlike, and speculative; and to high-level explanatory hypotheses or formulae, such as $E = MC^2$.*

It would be reasonable to say that most psychoanalytic hypotheses seem improbable to most people at the present time; and to say that the hypotheses of Quantum Theory seemed improbable to most scientists when they were first put forward. Quantum hypotheses conflicted with existing physical models, and psychoanalytic hypotheses conflict with models – theological, philosophical or psychological – which most people want to retain. The scientific criticism of modern physicists and modern empirical analysts seeks to revise existing physical and psychological models, and this can be done only by close study of current theory.

SPECULATIVE HYPOTHESES

It is only the last class of psychoanalytic hypotheses I have distinguished, the very general speculative hypotheses, such as those relating to the 'death instinct', which might be vulnerable to philosophical, as opposed to psychological criticism. If an analyst who maintained such hypotheses were unable to specify or imagine any evidence which would cause him to modify them, they would be open to the suspicion of being dogmatic and 'metaphysical'. Even here we have no clear-cut 'demarcation' such as Popper claims. There are many relatively undogmatic scientists who would probably be unable to specify or imagine any evidence which would cause them to abandon the hypothesis, 'The death of each individual terminates his thought processes'.* Yet we might hesitate to infer that their belief was dogmatic and metaphysical. This hypothesis is neither testable nor refutable, unless we allow claims to communication with spirits as relevant evidence; and it is difficult to imagine how the possibility of

* This hypothesis will later be referred to as 'Hypothesis D'.

alternative explanations of such 'communication' could be excluded. I would suggest, as a reason why such a belief may be held firmly in the absence of any supporting or refuting evidence, that the hypothesis is, not *deduced* from, but a derivative of, a complex of scientific theories, beliefs, and expectations, which is incompatible with the strong desire for some kind of survival, however tenuous.

DERIVATIVE ASSUMPTIONS

If my argument is sound, it follows that *hypotheses and unformulated assumptions which are derived from, and not formally deducible from, theories and high-level hypotheses play a very important part in determining attitudes and expectations.* Good judgement consists partly in having, in the main, *sound, untestable derivative assumptions*, and bad judgement in having unsound derivative assumptions.

THE FALSIFIABILITY OF PSYCHOANALYTIC HYPOTHESES

We can now summarize the answer to the question: are psycho-analytic hypotheses falsifiable? Some are; some are not, and to show which are falsifiable we need to use the distinctions made in Chapter 6 between classes of psychoanalytic hypotheses.

1. Anomaly hypotheses, a class which is meant to include all guesses about discrepancies, logical inconsistencies and inconsistencies between attitudes and behaviour, thought and feeling, and so on, are such as occur to all good judges of people. Although they may not be recognized as such, they are the starting-point of psychodynamics. They are testable only in the sense that several observers may be asked whether they agree that p is inconsistent with q, and they are not conclusively falsifiable.

2. Interpretations are descriptive but not informative in the usual sense of the term. They are conscious-making, *focusing* statements, enabling what is unconsciously 'known' or suspected to be consciously known or at least clearly formulated. As they are also *enactive* (having effects on behaviour), and sometimes suggestive (inducing beliefs which might not otherwise take that form), they are not always conclusively falsi-fiable; but they are frequently confirmed – as when a shrewd guess provokes the admission of consciously withheld secrets – and sometimes shown to be inadequate or mistaken. In short, they are indirectly testable and modifiable.

3. Retrospective hypotheses about interpretations and their effects *are* falsifiable, in the sense that a number of observers may uphold or reject the claim that a prediction has been confirmed or that interpretations have had certain specific effects.

4. Predictions of all kinds are the most promising candidates for falsifiability. Even lawlike descriptions ('salt is soluble in water') and laws ('water boils at 100°C') are tested by testing predictions derived from them. This holds for psychodynamic predictions. A prediction is not conclusively falsifiable unless it is sufficiently specific, but we have seen (p. 69) that specificity has to be assessed in relation to the complexity of the data. The most specific predictions a psychoanalyst could make to a scientific observer are of the form: 'Interpretations $p, q, r, \ldots$ will be followed within 24 hours by changes $a, b, c, \ldots$ in the analysand's behaviour.' The more precisely $a, b, c, \ldots$ can be described, the more conclusively falsifiable and the more scientifically valuable the predictions will be. But it is just as impossible to predict exactly what words will follow the interpretations as it is to predict which individual photons will penetrate a half-silvered mirror.

5. Ahistorical hypotheses about the subject's current unconscious wishes and fears are not directly falsifiable, but the failure of interpretations based on those hypotheses forces the analyst to try to revise them. They are modifiable and indirectly falsifiable.

6. Psychodynamic lawlike hypotheses are modifiable in the same ways as any scientific laws. They can be indirectly tested by directly testing predictions derived from them. If, for example, the hypothesis 'Obsessional symptoms are a defence against phobias' yields the prediction 'As the obsessional symptoms disappear during analysis the phobias will appear', the appearance or non-appearance of the phobias constitutes a test of both hypotheses: a direct test of the second, an indirect test of the first.

7. Hypotheses about the patient's physical and psychic development are derived from lawlike assumptions and what is known about his present condition. For example, analytic findings may be correlated with direct study of children to produce the lawlike assumption 'Phobias precede obsessional symptoms', and this assumption, combined with a knowledge of the patient's present symptoms, may yield the guess 'He probably suffered from phobias $r, s, t, \ldots$ in his second and third

years'. Such guesses may be confirmed or refuted by biographical evidence, and the reappearance of those phobias would be further confirmation. Most historical hypotheses, however, are mere speculation, with little chance of decisive test. It is a legitimate criticism of some psychoanalytic work that the transition from well-established findings to tentative speculation is made without sufficiently clear warning signals, sometimes even without its being noticed that the boundary has been crossed.

8. Similar comments apply *a fortiori* to hypotheses about classes or communities. Let us consider the hypothesis that there is, in any large modern community, a class of people whose unconscious aggressive impulses, whether directed against themselves or against others, make them prone to accidents. Let us suppose that a comprehensive statistical survey is made to determine to what extent the distribution of road and factory accidents among road-users and factory-workers deviates from 'random distribution', in the sense that the distribution of Premium Bonds by electronic computor is claimed to be random. If the survey led to the conclusion that a small proportion of road-users and factory-workers were responsible for or involved in a large proportion of accidents, would this conclusion be a confirmation of the psychoanalytic hypothesis?

It would be a *prima facie* confirmation of the hypothesis that some people are accident-prone. If the experiment were made of withdrawing the licences of all vehicle-drivers who had been involved in more than two accidents, and transferring all factory-workers so involved to relatively accident-proof jobs, and if the number of accidents suddenly dropped, the result would be a further *prima facie* confirmation. Neither of the findings, however, would confirm the *explanatory* hypothesis that people are accident-prone because of their unconscious aggressive impulses, and neither the survey nor the experiment would be a conclusive *test* even of the theory that some people are accident-prone. (The determined sceptic could object that deviation from random is not conclusive *proof* of any theory.)

This is an unusually clear example of a hypothesis which is not directly or conclusively testable or falsifiable, but is of such theoretical and practical importance that *prima facie* statistical or experimental confirmation would be a genuine scientific advance. Psychoanalytical, as opposed to sociological, confirmation of the hypothesis would be provided in the consulting-room, if a patient became aware of specific self-destructive or aggressive impulses, formerly unconscious, which coincided with certain accidents.

9. Heuristic hypotheses are not conclusively falsifiable. Let us examine one of the most fruitful of such hypotheses, that associations in analysis become more intelligible if all contiguous remarks and actions are assumed to be meaningfully related. An example will bring out some of the problems of scientific testing. In a first interview with an analyst a man discussed his emotional problems in a way that suggested a conflict over homosexual impulses. He then went on to discuss his son's forthcoming marriage, without expressing any positive feelings about it. Next he mentioned a dream he had had the night before, but said he could remember nothing about it except the name 'Lindberg'. The interview took place at the time when the kidnapping of the Lindberg baby was headline news. The analyst then asked him whether his son was going to marry someone older than himself and the man, greatly amazed, confirmed this guess. The analyst, assuming that the apparently disjointed remarks were connected, and knowing the part played by puns in unconscious thought, had made the link: 'Kidnapping – babysnatching – jealousy – resentment.' Now the fact that the wife-to-be *was* older than the son might have been coincidental; it did not establish beyond doubt the truth of the analyst's unspoken interpretation.

Fluctuating Rigour

Would its truth be established if in a subsequent analysis the patient revealed a strong resentment of his son's future wife? The answer is that the sympathetic critic would regard the further evidence as *prima facie* confirmation; the hostile critic would deny that it was confirmation at all because the real or apparent resentment could have been 'suggested' to the man by the analyst's interpretations. (*The sophisticated technique which enables scientists and philosophers to maintain the appearance of impartiality while giving subtle expression to prejudices for or against theories, hypotheses, or individuals, by lowering or raising the required standard of evidence or 'proof', so as to include the required or welcome beliefs and to exclude the inimical, I shall henceforward term the Technique of Fluctuating Rigour.* An example of the technique follows in section 10, below and an attempt to link it with a psychological technique will be made in Chapter 10, p. 128.)

The *contiguity hypothesis* is now so well established that an analyst, when he fails to see the connection between associations, is more inclined to attribute the failure to the ingenuity of the patient's defensive disguising, or to the inadequacy of his own ingenuity, than to the absence of any such connection. He assumes that there is a pattern which will, sooner or later, 'click' in his mind. Yet this assumption is not falsifiable: it cannot be tested in a way that would satisfy the rigid experimentalist.

10. Hypotheses relating to other disciplines, which for convenience I shall call interdisciplinary hypotheses, are of many kinds – some directly falsifiable, some indirectly falsifiable, others not falsifiable at all. The impact of psychoanalysis on other disciplines, however, has taken the form not so much of specific hypotheses – which are often provided by critics who want something to refute – as of changes in attitude, expectations, and methods of inquiry, and of the introduction of new concepts. An example of the resulting 'scientific' debate is provided by a letter to the *New Statesman*, 19 October 1957, by Professor H. J. Eysenck, attacking an article which he says 'states categorically that the criminal psychopath can be cured'. 'The truth of the matter', Eysenck continues, 'is (a) that agreement on whether a given criminal or patient is or is not a psychopath is so low when the diagnosis is made by experienced and highly qualified psychiatrists, that no responsible person would be willing to take action on the basis of such a diagnosis, and (b) there is no proper evidence to suggest that any form of psychotherapy or psychiatric treatment produces any effect whatsoever on psychopaths.'

Eysenck offers constructive as well as destructive criticism: 'What is required clearly is a properly set up experimental or clinical trial containing a treated group and an untreated control group; these would then have to be followed up over a period of many years to ascertain any possible effects of the treatment.'

This example of the Fluctuating Rigour Technique is less subtle than most. The argument seems to be as follows: even experts have no agreed method of diagnosis by which a class of psychopaths can be distinguished. No responsible person would take action on the basis of their attempts at diagnosis. We should set up two groups (of what?) of psychopaths (chosen by whom?), chosen by experts (on the basis of what?), on the basis of a psychiatric diagnosis; one of them should be treated (by whom?), by the experts who cannot agree about what a psychopath is, and the other not. We should then wait a period 'of many years'. If both groups commit crimes in roughly equal numbers, the 'properly set up trial' will have shown either (a) that the treatment was useless, or (b) that the diagnosis was unreliable. If the treated group commits fewer crimes we can conclude either (a) that the treatment had some effect, or more probably (b) that the diagnosis was unreliable. If the treated group commits more crimes we can infer either (a) that the treatment made them worse, or (b) that the diagnosis was unreliable, or (c) both!

The above is an important as well as an amusing example of the Fluctuating Rigour Fallacy. When considering whether psychoanalysts' recommendations should be acted upon, the standard of rigour for diagnosis is raised to the point where such recommendations are useless. When considering a 'properly set up trial' the standard of rigour is tacitly lowered to enable the 'tough-minded' scientist to get on with his experiment. This philosophical criticism is quite independent of the facts of the dispute. It is highly improbable that psychoanalysts would claim a technique of diagnosis by which they could definitely distinguish a nosological class of psychopaths, or, if this were possible, that they would confidently claim to be able to cure them. For this very reason they would not be interested in a 'controlled' experiment based upon the impossible pairing-off of equally ill and equally danger-ous psychopaths, one to be sent to the 'cure' group, the other to the 'control'. What 'highly qualified psychiatrists' would claim it is more difficult to say, since psychiatrists form a heterogeneous class which includes psychoanalysts with long experience of psychotherapy and hospital staffs with little or none.

Hypotheses and Ideas

The important contributions of psychoanalysis to other disciplines have been in the form of *ideas*, and these ideas do not always naturally take the form of hypotheses. Once the idea of the unconscious need for punishment has been grasped, for example, several social problems such as juvenile delinquency and certain kinds of crime appear in a different light. The hypothesis, 'Many criminals, delinquents, neurotic patients, and patients suffering from "stress" diseases are suffering from an un-conscious need for punishment' is not falsifiable except by the evidence of psychoanalytic sessions, but the *idea* can throw light on social phenomena formerly inexplicable. The idea that there is *some* connec-tion between methods of suckling, weaning, sphincter-training, etc., etc., and the character and mythology of primitive tribes, rather than specific hypotheses about the connection, is having a revolutionary effect on anthropological investigation, and the discovery made by Freud of the resemblance between infantile thought, adult dreams, myths, and the thought of psychotics, has enabled the knowledge of each subject to be applied to the others. It would be artificial to phrase this discovery in the form of a hypothesis; *we have to add to the inadequacy of the falsifiability criterion the inadequacy of the reduction of a science to a collection of hypotheses.* (Those writers who have produced sweeping social hypotheses on the basis of Freud's insights are justly accused of being unscientific.)

11. We have already seen that 'model' hypotheses are not falsifiable. They are aids to the imagination which may be superseded when they are no longer adequate to the complexity of the data. Yet they may easily be underestimated. Could Newton have achieved his physical discoveries without the model of gravitational pulls?

12. The very general speculative hypotheses are not directly falsifiable; more important, it may be suspected that they are not directly *modifiable*, as all the other classes are. There is a serious theoretical difficulty in the way of defending or attacking a hypothesis which is suspected of being 'metaphysical'. In every analysis a 'constitutional factor' must be postulated to explain differences in reaction to environmental influences. This factor is assumed but unknown: (X). If A attributes to X some factor (e.g. destructive impulses) which B attributes to a reaction to environmental influence, how can the dispute be settled? It cannot be settled by controlled variation of environmental influences, as some of these influences (e.g. unconscious rejection of the infant by the mother) cannot be quantitatively assessed. I am inclined to think that any attempt to *prove* to a serious clinical psychologist that some of his hypotheses are metaphysical would be futile. Yet the question, 'Can you imagine any evidence, clinical, sociological, anthropological . . . which would lead you to modify this belief?' is a valuable question which might induce a scientist to suspect that if the answer is 'No', the belief may be a metaphysical speculation.

LOGIC

One of the major philosophical implications of developments in psychoanalysis is that there is a fundamental mistake in the belief (explicitly or implicitly held by most philosophers) that there is a right way and a wrong way to use language, and that the study of logic enables one to find the right way. Every major theoretical innovation creates an entirely new logical problem: the problem, that is, of preserving all the discoveries for which the unconventional terminology was introduced, while establishing a progressively greater degree of consistency within the new terminology, and reconciling that terminology with those of adjacent disciplines. The problem is further complicated by the fact that the new use of language is not static, and that neither philosophy nor science are *necessarily* of any help in deciding which proposed innovations in any new theory will be the most fertile.

9

Judgement

Falsifiability, I suggest, fails as a criterion to distinguish between scientific and unscientific hypotheses for the following reasons:

1. There are many hypotheses which nearly all scientists and philosophers would call scientific but which, although susceptible of modification and revision, are not conclusively testable or falsifiable.

2. There are many hypotheses which are falsifiable, and derived from a theory, such as the many predictions that the world will come to an end at such-and-such a date, but which most scientists would, with good reason, call unscientific.

3. There are powerful explanatory theories, such as Darwin's theory of evolution, which are generally (though not universally) agreed to be scientific, but from which many general expectations but few, if any, specific falsifiable hypotheses can be deduced. Where there is disagreement over the definition of scientific terms there can be no agreed method of deduction from general hypotheses; descriptive and predictive statements can be *derived* from the theory, in the sense that they could not be made without the understanding gained from the explanatory theory. Even *derivable* predictions play a relatively minor part in evolutionary theory.

Anyone can, of course, decide to give the term 'scientific' a new definition, and apply it to forecasts of the end of the world while withholding it from the theory of evolution. Language can always be forced to fit the Procrustes bed of an arbitrary theory.

Popper's general theory, of which the falsifiability criterion is an important conclusion, stands or falls by the account he gives of his 'basic statements' in *The Logic of Scientific Discovery*. Let us bring together his main comments on this topic.

'The system of basic statements . . . is to include . . . *all self-consistent singular statements* of a certain logical form – all conceivable singular statements of fact, as it were' (1959, p. 84).

'. . . basic statements have the form of singular existential statements' (p. 102). 'Basic statements are . . . statements asserting that an observable event is occurring in a certain individual region of space and time' (p. 103).

'From a logical point of view, the testing of a theory depends upon basic statements whose acceptance or rejection, in its turn, depends upon our *decisions*. Thus it is *decisions* which settle the fate of theories' (p. 108).

Later he says (1965):

'Basic statements state (truly or falsely) the existence of observable facts (occurrences) within some sufficiently narrow spatio-temporal region' (p. 386).

Now let us consider the class of potential falsifiers of a hypothesis about the effects of interpretations on a patient in analysis. There is no doubt that the problem of formulating a hypothesis relating to the effects of interpretations is as much a scientific problem as that of explaining the effects of penicillin. We have seen, further, that in Popper's view a theory is falsifiable if the class of its potential falsifiers, which are basic statements, is not empty. We have also seen that the acceptance of basic statements is part of the application of a theoretical system.

We can now apply Popper's requirements to Ezriel's second lawlike hypothesis (see p. 25 above):

'If the analyst gives a here-and-now interpretation – that is, points out the hidden dynamics of the patient-analyst relationship in terms of the three object relations (the required, the avoided, and the calamity) and their connection, by means of a "because" clause – the subsequent material produced by the patient will contain the avoided relationship in a clearer, i.e. less repressed, form.'

The potential falsifiers of this hypothesis will be self-consistent singular existential statements asserting that an observable event is occurring in a certain individual region of space and time. If, for example, the analyst identifies certain initial conditions which in conjunction with his lawlike hypothesis enable him to predict that interpretation (I) will have effect (E) – (E) being a verbal attack – at time (T), on the analyst or some substitute for the analyst, the basic statement which will serve as a falsifier is the statement uttered at time (T): 'The patient is not making a verbal attack on the analyst or some substitute.'

So far, so good. But at this point there is a complication. Suppose that the analyst maintains that the patient *is* making a verbal attack at time (T) – not on the analyst but on his employer, who is in this context a substitute for the analyst. As the patient has never before dared to attack an authoritative male figure, his present attack shows the avoided relationship in a less repressed form. The dispute now turns on the *form* of the basic statement. Just as the layman is asked to take on trust the physicist's description: 'This is the path of an electron', so is he asked to take on trust, failing a detailed study of the case-history, the analyst's description: 'In this context his employer is a substitute for the analyst.' In both examples the layman may refuse; we can whole-heartedly agree with Popper that he makes a *decision*, and that his decision is like that of a jury; and that the verdict of the jury never justifies, or gives grounds for, the truth of what it asserts. ('The verdict has to be found in a procedure that conforms to, and thus applies, part of the general legal code.')

When jurors who have listened to the same 'facts' and the same exposition of the relevant section of the legal code cannot agree on the answer to a question of fact (*quid facti*), it is reasonable to look for a psychological explanation and to investigate their conscious or unconscious attitudes, motives or prejudices. *Fluctuating Rigour* does not apply only to philosophical criticism. If the majority of a white jury condemns a coloured man on what seems to the dissenters and to most disinterested observers to be patently inadequate evidence, it is reasonable to suspect racial prejudice. How then does Popper maintain his sharp distinction between the logic of knowledge and the psychology of knowledge?

He vehemently and repeatedly rejects 'psychologism', but it is not always clear what is meant by that term. Perhaps it always refers to 'the doctrine that statements can be justified not only by statements but also by perceptual experience'. In the context of Fries's trilemma, Popper rightly points out that 'experiences can *motivate a decision*, and hence an acceptance or rejection of a statement, but a basic statement cannot be *justified* by them—no more than by thumping the table'. But this does not solve the problem of the relation between psychology and logic, because he maintains that basic statements are not *justified* at all, but merely decided upon.

We have now come to the central flaw running through Popper's theory of demarcation. If it is *decisions* which settle the fate of theories – and I believe that he is right in thinking so – then the investigation of scientific method leads directly to the question, 'Why do people make the decisions they do?' This is a psychological question, to which only a psychological answer is possible. On Popper's own premises, therefore, the theory of scientific method, with which he maintains that epistemology should be identified, is a superstructure on the foundation of psychology.

LOGIC AND DECISIONS

Popper frequently comes near to a recognition of the inextricable intertwining of the logic and the psychology of knowledge and, then recoils from it. The attempt to equate the psychology of knowledge with the theory of 'mental acts' or with the study of 'the process of conceiving a new idea', or with the theory of the 'justification of basic statements by experiences' or by perception, has the effect of throwing a smoke-screen across the whole area of the dispute. Such an attempt is an example of what I shall call the Straw Man Fallacy:* an indefensible version of the 'psychology of knowledge' is presented, and when that version is exploded the reader is left to assume, unless he is exceptionally acute, that the same arguments would apply to any other version. If we avoid falling into this trap we shall see that the interesting epistemological questions which are also psychological are as follows:

1. Why do some observers accept, and others reject, the presuppositions, the terminology, the theoretical system, the experimental set-up, etc., without which a prediction cannot (a) be regarded as scientific, or (b) sometimes even be shown to be verified or falsified? This question is relevant to the dispute over 'acquired characteristics'. Some biologists have accepted *by decision* certain basic statements (i.e. reports of experiments) which falsify some scientific hypothesis that prohibits inheritable changes produced by environmental influences; others have by decision rejected them. (The precise form of the hypothesis is here, as always, of the highest importance.) Why is this? Each side will hold that the hypothesis is intersubjectively testable, and there seems to be no reason to suppose that it is not. It would be too easy to say that one camp is scientific and the other not; the problem of demarcation is that of deciding, as in the case of the jury, who has motives for misreading the evidence.

* For definition see p. 203.

2. If we make the *decision* to accept the basic statements, and hence the theoretical presuppositions and terminology, of the psychoanalysts whom we *judge* to be scientific, is it legitimate to apply their understanding of motives to the criticism of beliefs? And if so, when?

3. How is the descriptive psychology of belief – that is, the account of the conceptual schemes of individuals and groups and of the hypotheses accepted by them as corroborated – related to logic and epistemology?

HOW DO WE DECIDE?

At this point I intend to answer only the first two questions, and it may be that the argument will lead us to surprising conclusions. Let us begin with the traditional philosophical view that the epistemologist has to guard against a particularly insidious form of the *Genetic Fallacy*: the supposition that the psychological origin of an item of knowledge prejudices, whether favourably or unfavourably, its cognitive validity. This is one interpretation of 'psychologism' as a pejorative term. If 'psychologism' is a philosophical sin, it is one which every rational person commits when judging a case of extreme paranoia. If a patient confidentially reveals to us that all the waiters in all the restaurants in London have been bribed to put poison in his food, we do not investigate the charge in the same way as we would investigate a credible accusation by a responsible person against a blackmailer. Even if we look for evidence to exonerate some of the London waiters we do so not to allay any doubts of our own but in order to meet the patient on his own ground. Even prior to investigation *we do not believe him*. The two possible reasons for incredulity are not exclusive: they are the extravagance of the charge, and our knowledge of the excessive and irrational fear of persecution which is one of the patient's symptoms. These two reasons are complementary. If his claim is fantastic enough we may doubt the rationality of a hitherto rational person; if we are fully convinced that a person is suffering from delusions of persecution, we may doubt an otherwise credible complaint of persecution.

LOGIC AND PRAGMATICS

1. We can now attempt to answer the first question. People become committed to certain theoretical systems, with their distinctive presuppositions and terminologies, for psychological reasons, conscious or

unconscious, rational or irrational. The question whether a belief is true or false is independent of the question *why* X believes it, and to fail to see this is to fall victim to a fallacy which could be called 'psychologistic'. But whenever X decides that *q* is true he is associating himself with a certain way of thinking and talking, and he is running the inescapable risk involved in committing himself. Y can say, 'X believes *q* but *q* is false', but if X says 'I believe *q* but *q* is false' he is uttering a self-stultifying remark (in most contexts). The remark need not be self-contradictory, and is not even self-stultifying if he is referring to an unconscious belief; he can infer his belief from his behaviour and reject the belief at the conscious level. ('I suppose I must believe deep down that everyone is plotting against me, although intellectually I recognize how absurd that is.')

When a man joins a political party, Conservative, Labour, Communist, Nazi, Fascist, or any other, there is a psychological pressure on him, of which he may or may not be consciously aware, to believe more and more of what is accepted by the group. He objects and makes a stand only if the required beliefs conflict with some passionately held conviction. Further, the differences *between* such groups are not only differences of beliefs in special propositions but differences in language projections. The language projections which are comprehensible to the average English Conservative intellectual are so incompatible with those of, say, a Russian Communist intellectual, that for the one to say of the other that he believes many propositions to be true which are in fact false would be an absurdly inadequate way of judging an alien point of view. It would not be much less absurd than for a Frenchman to believe that the English could not measure accurately because the conversion of metres into yards, feet, and inches is usually only approximate.

There seems *prima facie* to be an important difference between '*q* is false' and 'I disagree with *q*'; between '*q* is logically impossible' and 'I do not find *q* conceivable'. There is a real difference, however, only if we assume '*q* is false' to be uttered by an omniscient being who is never semantically confused, never conceptually out of date, never ambiguous, and immune to self-deception from unconscious motives. If we consider the utterances in context, uttered by fallible human beings, at the pragmatic level (the cash-value level), i.e. at the *psychological* level of semiotic, '*q* is false' has the same cash-value as 'I disagree with *q*'; and '*q* is logically impossible' as 'I do not find *q* conceivable'.

This last statement will at first be unacceptable to most philosophers. Not only does it seem to be false: it seems to threaten the autonomy of philosophy as a method of inquiry. 'If a statement is true', it will be objected, 'it is true whether anyone believes it or not; if a proposition is true, it is true even if it has never been formulated.' If challenged to give an account of the notion of an unformulated proposition, the objector may give examples: 'The number of fish in the Pacific Ocean is such-and-such'; 'The number of stars in the Milky Way is such-and-such'; 'The next President of the United States will die in such-and-such a year'. In the first two examples the number may never be known, but we feel that there *is* a determinate number of fish and of stars, and that if someone were to make a lucky guess he would be making a true statement, a statement expressing a true proposition.

RISKLESS UTTERANCES

There is a sense, which I shall call the non-cash-value, or blank-cheque, or *riskless* sense, in which a person who went on murmuring 'The number of fish in the Pacific ocean is five million, the number of fish in the Pacific Ocean is five million and one,' and so on indefinitely, would almost inevitably make a true statement sooner or later *without knowing that he was doing so*. His success would be as impressive as the success of the student of geography who made a true statement by saying successively, 'Berlin is bigger than Moscow', 'Berlin is smaller than Moscow', and 'Berlin is the same size as Moscow'. From the point of view of formal or 'pure' logic abstracted from psychology, there is no difference between the true statement 'Berlin is smaller than Moscow' as uttered by the risk-avoiding student* who interposes the statement between the only two alternatives, and the same statement as uttered by a risk-taking student answering the question in an examination. If we ignore the psychology of the utterances we will call the statement a true empirical statement; if we contrast the utterances psychologically, we have to make a distinction between a risk-utterance and an utterance which has no more cash-value than a tautology. The *riskless* utterance is a pseudo-empirical utterance which has neither empirical nor analytic force, as contrasted with the risk-utterance, which has empirical force, and with the utterance of the analytic statement, 'Berlin is bigger than, smaller than, or the same size as, Moscow'. This last statement may have point in teaching the use of the words.

I suggest that 'The number of fish in the Pacific Ocean is such-and-such' (unspecified), is a riskless statement, and that 'The number of

---

* Like the U.S. student who scored full marks in a machine-marked questionnaire examination by ticking all alternative answers!

fish in the Pacific Ocean is 220, 536, 829,' if put forward by a person who has no reason to believe that that particular number is a better guess than any other, is also a riskless, pseudo-empirical utterance, even if the statement happens to be true. I suggest that the floating, feet-off-the ground feeling that pervades a large part of philosophical discussion is due in part to the tendency of some philosophers to move imperceptibly from risk-utterances to riskless utterances and back again, to the failure to distinguish between the two classes of utterances, and to their consequent false belief that statements or propositions can be classified according to their logical *form*, without reference to current live disputes between individuals or groups.

WISH-FULFILMENT AND FEAR-FULFILMENT BELIEFS

2. We can now try to answer the second question: when, if ever, is it legitimate to apply the psychoanalytic understanding of motives to the criticism of beliefs? We need first to distinguish between motives for inquiry and motives for distortion. The fact that a scientist's passionate interest in rocket-propulsion, or a doctor's in gynaecology, may have developed from some intense frustrated curiosity in early childhood is irrelevant to the assessment of his knowledge and skill, *unless* there are anomalies or inhibitions in his work which invite explanation. Curiosity itself is a motive for inquiry but not for distortion. There are motives, however, which conflict with curiosity or the passion for inquiry, and which are for the most part motives for distortion. Any belief which coincides with the fulfilment of a wish or the fulfilment of a talion fear which is linked with a guilty wish, is *prima facie* suspect, and to be examined for motives for distortion.

Examples of wish-fulfilment beliefs are the belief that one has special, mysterious powers, that one is an exception, outside moral rules, that one belongs to a special race, that one can dispense with scientific knowledge when giving an account of the universe, and so on. There is no discontinuity between the extreme forms of such beliefs, easily recognized for example in the manic phase of manic-depression, and the subtle and sophisticated forms, well under control and hard to detect, which can be found in the work of writers such as Nietzsche.

Examples of talion-fear-fulfilment beliefs are the belief in Hell, the belief that one is unworthy of any good fortune, that any exceptional period of luck or happiness will be counterbalanced by a period of exceptional misfortune, that one will be deserted or found out as a contemptible person by the people one loves. Such beliefs may be conscious or unconscious. We are now face to face with a difficult question* which cannot be answered here: 'How do we distinguish between unwelcome beliefs which originate in talion fear, and unwelcome beliefs which have been forced upon us by the ascendancy of our need for rationality over our indulgence in wish fantasy?'

APPROPRIATENESS OF METHOD

Can any criterion be found as an alternative to falsifiability? There seems to be no short cut. The only satisfactory way of distinguishing between the scientific and the unscientific is to make a detailed study of both the hypotheses and the *methods* of each discipline: a task which cannot, of course, be carried out by any one person. We judge end-of-the-world hypotheses to be unscientific, not by ascribing them to any logical *class* of hypotheses, but by rejecting *the methods or the motives* of those who hold the beliefs.

This point can be established by contrasting the prediction, 'The earth will be destroyed on 5 June 2091', as uttered by an interpreter of biblical prophecies, with the same statement as uttered by a reputable astronomer who claimed to have calculated that the paths of the earth and another large body would meet at that date. Both are utterances of a prediction, falsifiable in the same way (whether they are utterances of the same statement in all senses of the term, and whether the statement has the same *meaning* in both instances of its use, are distinct philosophical questions), but one utterance would generally be deemed unscientific and would have negligible effects, while the other would be thought scientific and would have considerable effects. In this example the criterion of demarcation is *appropriateness of method*.

THE AUTONOMY OF LOGIC FALLACY

Let us suppose that both the scientific and the unscientific utterance of the same predictive statement are made by deduction from internally consistent theories. Then according to Popper's contention, they both have the same logical status. This example brings out clearly, not only the inadequacy of the falsifiability criterion, but also a much more pervasive fallacy which I shall call the Autonomy of Logic Fallacy.† It is the fallacious assumption *that statements, including scientific hypotheses, can be examined and assigned logical status without reference to particular*

* See General Testing Principle, pp. 236-8.   † See also p. 204.

utterances by particular individuals in particular contexts and situations. In other words, it is the assumption that syntactics is not only abstractable from but *independent* of semantics, or that semantics is independent of pragmatics.

MOTIVES FOR DISTORTION

If a Presidential candidate on the eve of an election, or a heavy-weight boxer on the eve of a championship fight, were to predict, 'I shall win', we should hesitate to say that he had made a purely scientific prediction, *even if his evidence and his ostensible methods* of deriving the predictions were the same as those of a disinterested student of form. We should hesitate partly because the predictions may have an enactive element, like authoritative predictions of a slump. The confidence of the contestant may influence the voter or intimidate the opponent. The other reason for hesitation is the suspicion of a *motive for distortion*, which would not be removed by denial *however honest* we believed the denial to be. This is a further illustration of a point discussed before, that the rejection of the *theory* of unconscious motives is compatible with some *understanding* of unconscious motives. In this example the criteria of demarcation are *freedom from the enactive element and freedom from conscious or unconscious motives for distortion*. (It may be added that if either the candidate or the boxer lost the contest we should say that his prediction, although not purely scientific, had been falsified; though if he won we might hesitate to say that a prediction had been verified. We might prefer to say that his confidence had been justified.)

CRITERIA OF SCIENTIFIC STATUS

We have already travelled so far from the delightful simplicity of the falsifiability criterion that it will be useful to summarize the alternative criteria. I suggest that a discussion about demarcation is more fruitful when applied to people than to theories. There may, for all I know, be scientific Marxists who have refused to make the 'conventionalist twist' by which people who predict often wriggle out of the obligation to modify their theories when their predictions are falsified. There may be Marxists who admit Marx's mistakes, and who have modified his theory in the light of twentieth-century events. They would not be very influential, as their influence would be in inverse proportion to their safety, so it would not be surprising if they remained unknown. One of the reasons why it is difficult for a Marxist leader (or for that matter any leader) to be purely scientific, is that many of his statements are enactive as well as descriptive.

Falsifiability has to be abandoned even as one of the criteria, but the element of value in the principle should be retained in a theory of demarcation applied to people: *a person is scientific to the extent that (i) he is prepared to modify, reformulate, or abandon his beliefs, either in the light of new evidence or in the light of philosophical criticism; (ii) he uses appropriate methods to form his hypotheses; (iii) his predictions are not enactive in such a way that they change the situation they describe or predict; and (iv) he is free from motives for distortion.*

JUDGEMENT

This formulation is open to many criticisms. The philosopher may object that the criteria are not logical but psychological, and so do not help us to distinguish scientific from unscientific *theories*. I would reply that logical principles are abstracted from speech or writing that is judged to be valid or successful (or invalid or unsuccessful) and therefore cannot be used without modification to judge the validity or success of new ways of talking or writing. Logical principles may help us to detect inconsistencies in the writings of biologists, economists, or psychologists, but do not by themselves enable us to rewrite them, or even to decide whether or not they are worth rewriting. *In order to revise a theory, a detailed knowledge or the purpose and method of the theorist is necessary.*

The second criticism is that 'appropriate methods' introduces a new problem. How do we know that the astronomer's methods are sound and the astrologer's unsound? My answer would be that there is no simple criterion. We *judge* that certain methods are unsound, often without being able to demonstrate that they are. More than this, we have to judge that certain methods are not worth investigating. Otherwise a lifetime would be consumed with the futile investigation of nonsense. Such judgement is a psychological capacity, whose analysis would be psychological.

Freud's major error of judgement is instructive in this context. He wasted valuable time in the investigation of Fliess's theory of periodicity. His unconscious motive was probably the preservation of a friendship with a then sympathetic colleague, a friendship whose value at the time may have outweighed the claims of dispassionate scientific judgement.

This example is relevant to a third criticism: how can I tell whether

I or you or he has motives for distortion? You may be philosophically more astute than I, so that I cannot point to the weak links in your arguments though I vaguely feel that there are some – or vice versa. This is both a philosophical and a psychological problem. The detection, exposure, and classification of false steps in reasoning is a philosophical task; the explanation of the motives for reaching false conclusions is a psychological task.

10

Motives for Distortion

Some unconscious motives for distortion can be clearly understood by anyone who *stands outside the motive-producing situation*. He 'sees through' the employer who believes that his workers 'would not know what to do with the money' if they received better wages; the colonial administrator who believes that the colony will be 'ripe for independence' three hundred years hence; the rigid party member who believes that a popular revolt has been organized by foreign agents; the politician who believes that the occupation of foreign territory thousands of miles from home is 'essential for defence'; the man who begins to believe, shortly after the death of someone he loves, that the dead can communicate with the living; the theologian who believes that evidence of evolution has been put on earth to test our faith.

Other motives for distortion produce much more subtle forms of rationalization, and some motives can be discovered only in analysis. It is doubtful whether anyone is free from motives for distortion; the 'rational' man is the man who is relatively free. The assumption underlying recourse to arbitration, that neither disputant is as well qualified to judge a dispute as an arbitrator because each has something to gain or lose from the settlement, has a much wider application in analysis: the stronger the hope or fear associated with a belief or attitude the greater the likelihood of distortion.

The term 'distortion' suggests intellectual inconsistency, and this is one of the forms of anomaly which the analyst finds a useful clue to the underlying conflict. Another important clue, which may or may not produce detectable inconsistencies, is what Anna Freud calls 'isolation' – the severance of links between associations, and the isolation of ideas from affects. The split between thought and feeling and between thought and action has been well described in her book *The Ego and the Mechanisms of Defence*:

'When the pre-pubertal period begins, a tendency for the concrete interests of the latency period to give place to abstractions becomes more and more marked. In particular, adolescents of the type which Bernfeld describes as characterized by 'prolonged puberty' have an insatiable desire to think about abstract subjects, to turn them over in their minds and to talk about them.... They will argue a case for free love or marriage and family life, a free-lance existence or the adoption of a profession, roving or settling down, or discuss philosophical problems such as religion or free thought, or different political theories such as revolution versus submission to an authority, or friendship itself in all its forms . . . we are not only amazed at the wide and unfettered sweep of their thought, but impressed by the degree of empathy and understanding manifested, by their apparent superiority to more mature thinkers and sometimes even by the wisdom which they display in the handling of the most difficult problems.

We revise our opinion when we turn from the examination of the adolescent's intellectual processes themselves to consider how they fit into the general picture of his life. We are surprised to discover that this fine intellectual performance makes little or no difference to his actual behaviour. His empathy into the mental processes of other people does not prevent him from displaying the most outrageous lack of consideration towards those nearest to him. His lofty view of love and of the obligations of a lover does not mitigate the infidelity and callousness of which he is repeatedly guilty in his various love affairs' (1949, p. 174).

Anna Freud goes on to explain this split by pointing out that asceticism, with its prohibition of instinctual impulses, does not, by itself, solve the adolescent's problem: how to deal with the danger situation created by the intensification of those impulses. The *thinking-over* or intellectualization of the instinctual conflict is an attempt to surmount the conflict.

'The philosophy of life which they construct – it may be their demand for revolution in the outside world – is really their response to the perception of the new instinctual demands of their own id, which threaten to revolutionize their whole lives. Their ideals of friendship and undying loyalty are simply a reflection of the disquietude of the ego when it perceives the evanescence of all its new and passionate object-relations. The longing for guidance and support in the often hopeless battle against their own powerful instincts may be transformed into ingenious arguments about man's inability to arrive at independent political decisions. We see then that instinctual processes are translated into terms of intellect' (ibid., p. 177).

'If it is true that an increase in libidinal cathexis invariably has the automatic effect of causing the ego to redouble its efforts to work over the instinctual processes intellectually, this would explain the fact that instinctual danger makes human beings intelligent. In periods of calm in the instinctual life, when there is no danger, the individual can permit himself a certain degree of stupidity. In this respect instinctual anxiety has the familiar effect of objective anxiety. Objective danger and deprivations spur men on to intellectual feats and ingenious attempts to solve their difficulties, while objective security and superfluity tend to make them comfortably stupid. The focussing of the intellect on instinctual processes is analogous to the alertness which the human ego has found to be necessary in face of the objective dangers which surround it' (ibid., p. 179).

It would be easy to point to exceptions to the processes described above: those of congenitally subnormal intelligence whom instinctual danger does not make intelligent, and those of potentially high intelligence for whom the instinctual danger is so terrifying that it paralyses rather than stimulates their intellectual life. But these exceptions can easily be accommodated in a more cautious formulation of the theory (cutting out such terms as 'invariably' and 'automatic', for example) and do not invalidate the insight of these passages. It is possible to extend the analogy with objective danger. In men and animals, fear, rage, or fear–rage may manifest itself in fight (or constructive attempts to solve the problem), flight, or paralysis, according to the nature of the danger or frustration, the character of the individual, and his current psychological state. Deprivations may spur him on or weaken him to the point of apathy. Analogously, instinctual danger may provoke intellectual 'flight' (asceticism?), constructive struggles (the endeavour to master instinctual impulses by means of thought?), or paralysis of the intellect. The analogy is imperfect, however, as the three intellectual reactions are not incompatible, and may (perhaps usually do) occur in one person alternately or simultaneously. To be more specific, a person who is in danger of being overwhelmed by instinctual impulses (in adolescence for example), may shrink from thinking clearly about immediate sexual problems ('flight'), brood and struggle over problems which are their remote and abstract intellectual substitutes ('fight'), and suffer from temporary phases of partial intellectual paralysis.

At this point we are face to face with a clear divergence of approach between philosophers and psychoanalysts. Both groups are interested in intellectual inconsistencies, but for different reasons. The philosopher is interested in the truth, falsity, implications, entailments, etc. of statements, and in finding and classifying fallacies. The psychoanalyst sees inconsistencies as clues to unconscious conflicts, and tries to combat the technique of isolation by interpretations which relate isolated ideas to each other and to feelings and actions; to show the patient in detail how his abstract thinking is an attempt to deal with an unconscious conflict.

It is well known that professional preoccupations tend to produce professional attitudes. There may be some analysts who are tempted to dismiss philosophy as a compulsive–obsessional symptom; some philosophers who regard psychoanalysis as a psychiatric technique which is irrelevant to philosophy. With full awareness of the risk I am running of alienating both philosophers and analysts, I shall maintain that *all* abstract thought, including philosophy, is subtly influenced by unconscious thought processes, and that *all* abstract thought, including psychoanalysis, is subject to philosophical criticism; and that there is some connection, which it is a philosophico-psychological problem to elucidate, between the mechanisms of defence discovered by analysts and the fallacies discovered by philosophers.

In *The Ego and the Mechanisms of Defence*, first published in German as long ago as 1936, Anna Freud listed nine methods of defence: regression, repression, reaction-formation, isolation, undoing, projection, introjection, turning against the self, reversal, and 'a tenth, which pertains rather to the study of the normal than to that of neurosis: sublimation, or displacement of instinctual aims' (ibid., p. 47). She gives an example which illustrates *turning against the self*, *projection*, and a defence mechanism which for some reason she does not list above, *displacement*.

'I will take as an illustration the case of a young woman employed in an institution for children. She was the middle child of a number of brothers and sisters. Throughout childhood she suffered from passionate penis-envy relating to her elder and her younger brother, and from jealousy, which was repeatedly excited by her mother's successive pregnancies. Finally, envy and jealousy combined in a fierce hostility to her mother. But, since the child's love-fixation was no less strong than her hatred, a violent defensive conflict with her negative impulses succeeded an initial period of uninhibited unruliness and naughtiness. She dreaded lest the manifestation of her hate should cause her to lose her mother's love, of which she could not bear to be deprived. She also dreaded that her mother would punish her and she criticized herself most severely for her prohibited longings for revenge. As she entered upon the period of the latency, this anxiety situation and conflict of conscience became more and more acute and her ego tried to master her impulses in various ways. In order to solve the problem of ambivalence she displaced outwards one side of her ambivalent feeling. Her mother continued to be a love-object, but from that time on there was always in the girl's life a second important person of the female sex, whom she hated violently. This eased matters: her hatred of the more remote object was not visited with the sense of guilt so mercilessly as was her hatred of her mother. But even the displaced hatred was a source of much suffering. As time went on it was plain that this first displacement was inadequate as a means of mastering the situation.

The little girls' ego now resorted to a second mechanism. It turned inwards the hatred which hitherto had related exclusively to other people. The child tortured herself with self-accusations and feelings of inferiority and, throughout childhood and adolescence right into adult life, she did everything she could to put herself at a disadvantage and injure her interests, always surrendering her own interests to the demands made on her by others. To all outward appearance she had become masochistic since adopting this method of defence.

But this measure, too, proved inadequate as a means of mastering the situation. The patient then entered on a process of projection. The hatred which she felt for female love-objects or their substitutes was transformed into the conviction that she herself was hated, slighted or persecuted by them. Her ego thus found relief from the sense of guilt. The naughty child, who cherished wicked feelings against the people around her, underwent metamorphosis into the victim of cruelty, neglect and persecution. But the use of this mechanism left upon her character a permanent paranoid imprint, which was a source of very great difficulty to her both in youth and adult years' (ibid., pp. 48–9).

(The above case is interesting for its moral implications as well as for the light it throws on the defences, the subject we are concerned with here.)

As it stands, the above passage could be misleading to someone with no direct experience of clinical work. It might appear that displacement, turning against the self, and projection were datable processes (she displaced her hatred at the beginning of the latency period), whereas Anna Freud is describing *economic* changes which cause one defence to predominate over other, concurrent, defences. The above condensed account is mainly in terms of feelings, but such transformations as those described are invariably accompanied by changes in beliefs and attitudes. It is hatred which is displaced, turned inwards, and projected, but each shift coincides with shifts in judgement which seem to be 'objective': 'I am worthless', 'They hate and despise me', 'She is cruel', 'Life is pointless', and so on.

Further, feelings of curiosity, love, hatred, etc. can be displaced not only on to people but also to theories, subjects, activities. In the course of analysis a patient came to realize that the repressed hatred and fear he had once felt for a dictatorial headmaster, whose admiration he longed to win, was *displaced* to the subject he represented, Classics. His *reaction-formation* against the repressed hostility to a near-sadistic teacher took the form of extreme obedience and submission. His devotion to Latin and Greek verse was a form of *sublimation* which enabled him to harness his curiosity to an attempt at *reparation*, the *undoing* of the damage he had done in phantasy, by careful reconstruction in the shape of conscientious compositions. The compulsive nature of this work was shown by its *perfectionism*, the horror of making mistakes or falling short of a high standard. Yet there was clear evidence of the technique of *compromise*. In examinations he would regularly forget some very common Greek or Latin word (say, the equivalent of 'wood' or 'chair'), so that the whole passage had to be ingeniously reformulated to avoid using the word. This probably served the double purpose of punishing him for the unconscious impulses associated with his work, and attacking the teacher by demonstrating that his teaching was unsuccessful. The ingenious and anxious reformulation was an instance of *camouflage;* the forgetting was attended by disproportionately strong feelings of anxiety and guilt, and so it had to be covered up by clever stratagems.

The real problems and difficulties I have described were dealt with by the technique of *denial*: in his phantasy he merely had to choose whether to become a great classical scholar, poet, philosopher, actor, or Prime Minister. The fact that the difficulties resulting from his ambivalence would preclude a career as a classical scholar was simply denied. After passing the scholarship examination with a significant compromise (doing well in some papers and missing two altogether), he left both school and headmaster, and with them the hope of reparation and the fear of rejection. The *repressed* hostility to Latin and Greek became more and more conscious at the university, but was *rationalized* as a shift of interest to other subjects and activities. The technique of *isolation* enabled him to contemplate his increasing inability to *take in* (incorporate) the lectures with *conscious* indifference; in other words, the knowledge of his failure was isolated (*split off*) from the appropriate feelings. This splitting-off became to a certain extent a *character defence*, pervading diverse situations. The hostility to the headmaster was *displaced* to the lecturers who were forcing unwanted intellectual 'food' down his throat. The problem had a pseudo-solution when he was able to turn his back on Latin and Greek (withdraw cathexis).

The above condensed illustration of several defence mechanisms might be dismissed, by anyone unfamiliar with psychoanalysis, as 'abnormal', especially since it is deliberately expressed in technical terms. Yet the techniques described are all 'normal' techniques: more difficult to *detect* if there is little conscious conflict. As I have mentioned more mechanisms* than the ten listed by Anna Freud, it is necessary to examine briefly the most important techniques before trying to trace their effects on abstract thought.

Anna Freud uses the case of Little Hans† (Freud's 'Analysis of a Phobia in a Five-Year-Old Boy') to illustrate displacement, reversal, regression, and denial. (Little Hans was analysed by his father, under Freud's guidance, for a phobic inability to leave the house because of his fear of horses).

'He loved his mother and out of jealousy adopted an aggressive attitude towards his father which, secondarily, came into conflict with his tender affection for him. These aggressive impulses roused his castration-anxiety – which he experienced as objective anxiety – and so the various mechanisms of defence against the instincts were set in motion. The methods employed by his neurosis were *displacement* – from his father to the anxiety-animal – and *reversal* of his own threat to his father, that is to say, its transformation into anxiety lest he himself should be threatened by his father. Finally, to complete the distortion of the real picture, there was *regression* to the oral level: the idea of being bitten. The mechanisms employed fulfilled perfectly their purpose of warding off the instinctual impulses; the prohibited libidinal love for his mother and the dangerous aggressiveness towards his father vanished from consciousness. His castration-anxiety in relation to his father was bound in the symptom of a fear of horses, but, in accordance with the mechanism of phobia, anxiety-attacks were avoided by means of a neurotic inhibition – Little Hans gave up going out of doors. 'In the analysis of Little Hans these defence mechanisms had to be reversed. His instinctual impulses were freed from distortion and his anxiety was dissociated from the idea of horses and traced back to its real object – his father, after which it was discussed, allayed, and shown to be without objective foundation. His tender attachment to his mother was then free to revive and to be given some expression in conscious behaviour, for, now that his castration-anxiety had disappeared, his feeling for her was no longer dangerous. Moreover, that anxiety dispelled, there was no need for the regression to which it had driven him, and he was able once more to attain to the phallic level of libidinal development. The child's neurosis was cured' (1949, pp. 75–6).

Anna Freud then illustrates the *denial of reality by means of phantasy*, a technique in which conscious insight into the inevitable plays no part:

* See Index under 'Mechanisms, Psychological'.   † See p. 51 above.

'At the end of his analysis Hans related two day-dreams: the fantasy of having a number of children whom he looked after and cleansed in the water-closet, and, directly afterwards, the fantasy of the plumber who took away Hans' buttocks and penis with a pair of pincers, so as to give him larger and finer ones. The analyst (who was Hans' father) had no difficulty in recognizing in these fantasies the fulfilment of the two wishes which had never been fulfilled in reality. Hans now had – at least in imagination – a genital organ like that of his father and also children with whom he could do what his mother did with his little sister' (ibid., cont'd).

The language of such abbreviated case-histories is a kind of shorthand, which traces an outline pattern through the complex interplay of psychological factors. The patterns are analogous to the numbers, made up of coloured dots, in the colour-blindness test. These are distinguishable by people of normal colour-vision; indistinguishable by the colour-blind. There is nothing to differentiate the dots which make up the pattern from the surrounding dots except 'being more yellowish' or 'being more bluish'. Are the patterns 'really there'? I am not sure that this question makes sense. If it means anything to say that the patterns are 'really there' it probably means no more than that people whose visual discrimination ranges from p to x regularly discern the figures when they look at the cards. To the question, 'Do the processes called displacement, sublimation, etc. *really* occur?' the appropriate answer would be, 'Here is the transcript of a recorded analysis; you may or you may not see certain patterns in the course of events; if you do see them, you may or may not agree to describe them in these terms.' The possibility of alternative descriptions, like the possibility of alternative geometries, is an important fact, whose recognition is essential for the progress of psychoanalysis.

Some of the defence techniques I have mentioned overlap in a rather confusing way. Isolation, splitting, and displacement, for example, are not clearly distinct. We all, philosophers, psychologists, entomologists, and rodent-operatives, 'normal' and 'abnormal', split our feelings of love and hatred, affection and dislike, in such a way as to maintain some sort of equilibrium. The distribution is constantly changing, and each change involves some degree of displacement. I can maintain a predominantly affectionate relationship with A because I split off some of my feelings of hostility and displace them to D, E, and F, who matter less to me. Next year the unfortunate substitutes may be G, H, and I. If, in spite of obvious connections or resemblances, I cannot see that they are substitutes, I am using the technique of isolation; to some degree I am using it all the time. By the same token, if I succeed in maintaining a predominantly affectionate (if ambivalent) interest in philosophy, it is by splitting ideas or philosophers into two main camps: friends whom I defend and enemies whom I attack. However this situation may be complicated by a scrupulous attempt to be fair and just, the *emotional* bifurcation is inevitable; ideas are accepted or rejected, supported or refuted. For 'philosophy' could be substituted 'psychoanalysis' and for 'I' could be substituted 'we'.

PHILOSOPHICAL ANALOGUES OF DEFENCE MECHANISMS

Fluctuating Rigour

The Fluctuating Rigour Fallacy (described on p. 103) is a *philosophical* aberration which is closely connected with the *psychological* technique of splitting. Hostility to a subject can be subtly evinced by unconsciously raising the required standard of evidence, confirmation, and so on. The 'mental constructs' of an 'accepted' subject are thought of as legitimate concepts (gravitation, energy, momentum, . . .) even when they are being superseded; those of a 'rejected' subject are described as 'myths'.

Fluctuating Scepticism

The Fluctuating Scepticism Fallacy, on the other hand, though it may sometimes serve a similar unconscious purpose, requires further explanation. The 'other minds problem' is partly a genuine philosophical problem arising out of the logical differences between statements in the first person ('I am in pain') and statements in the second or third person ('He is in pain'). But there is more to it than that. The answer to the question 'How do we come to be satisfied that he is in pain although we never *feel* his pain?' does not dissolve the philosophic anxiety. The balloon of scepticism is blown a little bigger, and the question now becomes 'How can we *ever* really *know* that he is in pain?' The doubt has been inflated to the point where even *cogito* is uncertain.

In order to explain this most pervasive and incorrigible philosophical tendency, let us consider the childhood conflict that provides a possible explanation for inflated scepticism. It seems reasonable to suppose that the child needs to feel *certain* (not merely to believe that it is highly probable) that he is so unconditionally loved that he will not be abandoned whatever he thinks and does. On the other hand, there is ample evidence from analyses that he *projects* his own feelings, including violently aggressive feelings, on to those nearest to him (normally mother, father, brothers, and sisters). It may be, therefore, that he also needs to feel *certain* that other people do *not* feel as he does when he is so angry that he wishes his mother dead.

His problem is never fully resolved. If other people are like him, if they are as potentially destructive as he is, it is dangerous to make contact with them. But if they are *not* like him, if they do not see and hear and think and feel as he does, then he is alone, isolated, condemned to live in a nightmare, solipsistic world. There is a conflict between the need to find something certain and the need to doubt the dangerous repercussions of something both certain and terrifying. Philosophical argument has two antithetical tendencies: first, an usually obstinate, even perverse, attempt to establish certain favoured propositions as certain; and, second, the inflation of sceptical doubts beyond the point required by scientific caution. The first is exemplified by the quasi-mathematical 'proof' of empirical hypotheses, adopted by Spinoza, for example; by the theory of 'sense-data'; and by Popper's 'basic statements'. The second is exemplified by the obsessional philosophical worrying over such questions as 'How can I know he is in pain?'

The Sophistication of Magical Thinking

The tendency to fluctuating scepticism and the insistence on divorcing philosophy from 'matters of fact' (including psychological hypotheses) are the two factors mainly responsible for the sterility of *part* of the philosophical discussion of recent years. The clue to these factors is what I shall call *the sophistication of magical thinking*.* The child is reluctant to give up the consolation of magical thinking, and in fact he does not completely give it up throughout his life. In adult life it persists in the form of superstition, night and day dreams, fiction (where it is relatively innocuous because split off from realistic thinking), and subtle distortions of serious thought. The Kantian fallacy that the forms imposed upon experience by the mind are necessarily valid is an example of sophisticated magical thinking. The whole of *The Critique of Practical Reason* is vitiated by Kant's uncritical acceptance of the Categorical Imperative ('Act on maxims which can at the same time have as their object themselves as universal laws of nature'). Apart from the philosophical criticism that Kant overlooked the logical difference between a maxim, such as 'Always keep promises', and a law of nature, and the psychological criticism that maxims are of little or no value when serious decisions have to be made ('Should I tell him

* For definition see pp. 211–12.

the truth about his cancer?'; 'Should we drop an atom bomb on Hiroshima?'), the psychoanalyst would be most struck by the *futility* of exhorting someone whose behaviour is irrational to behave rationally, to act on maxims, to 'pull himself together'. It is not for nothing that exhortation has been excluded from 'classical' psychoanalysis.

Nietzsche, another philosopher whose life was largely insulated from the morally bewildering complex of social and sexual intercourse, achieved an unusual degree of sophistication of magical thinking. His *Thus Spake Zarathustra* and his more discursive writings are a beautiful illustration of several techniques explored by psychoanalysis: beautiful in the double sense of aesthetically and intellectually exciting. Perhaps the most obvious is the technique of *denial*. By identifying himself with the Superman of the future he magically denied his social inadequacies, and by inviting his readers to a similar identification he compensated for his weaknesses by becoming the prophet of would-be supermen. His violent revolt against the professed 'humility' of Christians was an *intellectualization* of the conflict between sadistic and masochistic impulses. His sadism is revealed by many passages which contemplate the 'necessary' but rather exciting torture in war of the 'bungled and botched' who constitute the vast majority of mankind. 'The object is to attain that enormous *energy of greatness* which can model the man of the future by means of discipline and also by means of the annihilation of millions of the bungled and botched, and which can yet avoid *going to ruin* at the sight of the suffering created thereby, the like of which has never been seen before.' His famous aphorism, 'Thou goest to woman? Do not forget thy whip', reveals his fear and hatred of 'woman', and suggests suffering and humiliation suffered at 'her' hands. There is evidence, however, of complementary masochism: the great man with whom he identifies himself must suffer even greater torment than the despicable masses. 'I test the *power of a will* according to the amount of resistance it can offer and the amount of pain and torture it can endure and know how to turn to its own advantage.' It may be guessed that the 'pain and torture' of the superman are in part a punishment for the torture he inflicts, and in part transferred by identification from Nietzsche's own suffering as a chronic invalid. His ill health forced him to retire from his professorship at the age of thirty-five, and for twelve years, from the age of forty-four until his death, he was mad. His contempt for women and their 'pedantry, superficiality, schoolmasterliness, petty presumption, unbridledness and indiscretion' is clearly a *rationalization* of his fear and hatred rather than a reason for them, since his experience of women was negligible. He may conceivably have been generalizing from one or two instances, since the only women he knew intimately were his mother and his sister.

More interesting and harder to explain are his attacks on Spinoza, Pascal, and Dostoevsky. The virulence of his vituperation suggests stronger feelings than philosophical antipathy, and it is excess in combination with minor *anomalies* which often serves as the analytic clue to *projection* and *reaction-formation*. In his outcry against Spinoza, 'How much of personal timidity and vulnerability does this masquerade of a sickly recluse betray!', it is the phrase 'sickly recluse' which catches the eye. It is more appropriate to Nietzsche than to Spinoza. He says of Christianity that '. . . it aims at destroying the strong, at breaking their spirit, at exploiting their moments of weariness and debility, at converting their proud assurance into anxiety and conscience-trouble; that it knows how to poison the noblest instincts and to infect them with disease, until their strength, their will to power, turns inwards, against themselves – until the strong perish through their excessive self-contempt and self-immolation: that gruesome way of perishing, of which Pascal is the most famous example.' Here it is the phrase 'turns inwards against themselves' which merits attention, as it foreshadows Freud's explanation of the extreme sense of guilt, conscious or unconscious, found in neurosis and (in a purer form) in psychosis: in melancholia and in the depressive phase of manic-depression. He explains it as the turning against the self of repressed aggression.

Does this description indicate insight on Nietzsche's part into his own problem? If so, we may guess that his theoretical Will to Power and superhuman ruthlessness are a reaction-formation against his self-contempt, his opinion of himself as a 'sickly recluse', personally timid and vulnerable. He finds in Spinoza, Pascal, and Dostoevsky a *projection* of his self-contempt (or rather, in Spinoza's case at least, he projects a degree of self-contempt which Spinoza may not have felt), and attacks it with revealing ferocity. His anger is *displaced* from unconscious factors in himself (Fairbairn might say 'from internal objects') which may have been threatening his sanity. His phantasy, as revealed in his writings, is *isolated* from the rest of his life in the sense that there is a notable disparity between the Napoleonic quality of his work and the quietude of his career.

So much for speculation. I feel on surer ground when I speak of the temporary exhilaration I experienced when reading Nietzsche's works. For a little while *I* was the Superman: in Russell's shrewd phrase, 'very like Siegfried, except that he knows Greek'. I despised the 'bungled and botched' and was prepared to annihilate them by the million. I felt a Napoleonic Will to Power, without taking a single step towards acquiring any power. I displaced my hatred of my sense of guilt and inadequacy, which at that time was entirely unconscious, to that 'poisoner of the noblest of instincts' – Christianity; I was relieved to discover that my adolescent sufferings were the sufferings of a superior being, intellectually and artistically remote from the uncomprehending and expendable rabble. My virtues were Nietzsche's virtues, 'pride, pathos of distance, great responsibility, exuberant spirits, splendid animalism, the instincts of war and of conquest, the deification of passion, revenge, anger, voluptuousness, adventure, knowledge'. I longed to take a whip to woman, but unfortunately (or fortunately) neither whip nor woman was to hand. My career as a Superman Outsider lasted little longer than the time of reading, but long enough to give me insight into the appeal of the Nazi and Fascist parties, the fascination of Alexander, Caesar, and Napoleon, and (in retrospect) into the techniques responsible for the exhilaration.

Relevance of Psychological Techniques to Philosophy

Without attempting to make an inclusive list, it is time to bring together some of the most important psychological techniques and to inquire whether they have any bearing on philosophical problems. The descriptions of defence mechanisms in psychoanalytic literature raise many philosophical problems which lie outside the scope of this work. Some methods of warding off anxiety, for example, such as Little Hans's refusal to leave the house (phobia), or the obsessional's need to perform rituals (frequent hand-washing, keeping books in a special order, etc.), are not usually described as defence mechanisms although they have this in common with them: any interference with the method provokes extreme anxiety. Should sublimation be described as a defence mechanism? What is the precise meaning of 'reversal'? In some of the examples given by Anna Freud in *The Ego and the Mechanisms of Defence*, it refers to the conversion of anxiety into aggressiveness, of love into hate, of envy into over-insistence on magical powers. In another example it refers to the transformation in phantasy of a dreaded father into protective beasts: an ideational rather than an affective change. In yet another example 'reversal' refers to the transformation of Hans's own threat to his father into his father's threat to him. This we would now call projection. There are clearly three techniques here, which should be distinguished by three different names.

I propose now to give a list of recognized techniques, and then pick out those which are germane to the present discussion. In addition to the nine listed by Anna Freud (regression, repression, reaction-formation, isolation, undoing, projection, introjection, turning against the self, and reversal) there are the techniques of displacement,

denial, compromise, character defence, camouflage, and rationalization. Anna Freud also describes the technique of *restriction of the ego*, a
withdrawal from some activity as a defence against painful external
stimuli: to be distinguished from *inhibition*, which she describes as a
defence against inner processes. Giving up games or dancing after
unsuccessful competition would be an example of restriction of the
ego, while writer's cramp, singer's throat, and the partial paralysis
which sometimes afflicts violinists, pianists, public speakers, and so on,
are examples of inhibition: the desire to write, play, sing, remains, in
spite of the painful struggle with the inhibition.

Of the techniques discussed, the ones which may prove to be the
most important for the understanding of abstract thought are: projection, projective identification, introjection, repression, displacement, denial, compromise, isolation, undoing, reaction-formation, and
rationalization. The question whether they are *defence* mechanisms can
here be ignored. I exclude 'reversal' because I suspect that it may be
equivocal, and that all the phenomena so described may be explicable
in terms of projection, projective identification, introjection, camouflage, denial, and displacement. In the case of Little Hans quoted in the
previous chapter, for example, as we have seen, the 'reversal of his
own threat to his father, that is to say, its transformation into anxiety
lest he himself should be threatened by his father', could have been
described as his projection on to his father of his own hostility. The
projected hostility was then displaced to horses.

THE FALLACY OF NON CAUSA PRO CAUSA

Let us consider an example of the philosophical fallacy of *non causa pro
causa*. ('Misleading technique of argument' would be better than
'fallacy' but 'fallacy' is the accepted term.) The fallacy consists in
discussing several assumptions simultaneously, say p, q, and r; reducing
one to absurdity, say p, and inferring that q or r has been refuted, when
p could have been refuted without reference to q or r. I shall first discuss
some of Ryle's arguments, which offer few vulnerably definite opinions, and then show how an incautious reader could fall into the
fallacy of *non causa pro causa*.

In the sixth chapter of *The Concept of Mind* ('Self-Knowledge'),
Ryle sets out to refute the theory of 'Privileged Access'.

'The questions "What knowledge does a person get of the workings of his
own mind?" and "How does he get it?" by their very wording suggest
absurd answers. They suggest that, for a person to know that he is lazy, or

has done a sum carefully, he must have taken a peep into a windowless chamber, illuminated by a very peculiar sort of light, and one to which only he has access. And when the question is construed in this sort of way, the parallel questions, "What knowledge can one person get of the workings of another person's mind?" and "How does he get it?" by their very wording seem to preclude any answer at all; for they suggest that one person could only know that another person was lazy or had done a sum carefully, by peering into another secret chamber to which, *ex hypothesi*, he has no access. In fact, the problem is not one of this sort. It is simply the methodological question, how we establish, and how we apply, certain sorts of law-like propositions about the overt and silent behaviour of persons' (1949, p. 169).

I suggest that the problem is far from being simply a methodological question. It is a complex problem with a methodological, a semantic, and a psychological aspect. Ryle seems to be synchronously discussing several questions:

1. 'Is a person constantly aware of his current thoughts and feelings?'
2. 'Can a person deliberately scrutinize his thoughts and feelings?';
3. 'Has a person "privileged access" (in the sense of being in the best position to know) to his current thoughts, feelings, sensations, memories, images, and so on?'
4. 'Has a person "privileged access" (in the same sense) to the understanding of his own beliefs, motives, character traits, and so on?'
5. 'Are "What knowledge can a person get of the workings of his own mind?" and "How does he get it?" intelligible questions?'
6. 'If a person has some kind of "privileged access" to his thoughts and feelings is the information so derived infallible?' Without suggesting that Ryle would assent to this reformulation of the questions, I shall show how his argument could lure his readers into the fallacy of *non causa pro causa* and hence into the fallacy of Behaviourism.

   1. 'Is a person constantly aware of his current thoughts and feelings?' The answer is 'No'. I can be intent on solving a problem, absorbed in a game of chess, or 'carried away' by a string quartet, and be quite oblivious of my thoughts and feelings.

   2. 'Can a person deliberately scrutinize his thoughts, feelings, or memories?' The answer is 'Yes', in the sense that I can 'search' for a name or a telephone number; 'ask myself' whether I am angry or afraid; try to 'form a clearer picture' of someone I met some weeks ago; try to 'locate' a pain when the doctor asks me to do so; 'ask myself' whether I am ashamed of something I have done; 'look back on' my behaviour and try to decide whether I have been consistent; 'examine' my motives and try to be 'honest with myself'. The visual metaphors

K

in these examples point to a well-recognized analogy between 'scrutinizing' someone else's face or conduct and 'scrutinizing' one's own thoughts, feelings, or motives. But of course there is an important difference between the two kinds of scrutiny. Perhaps Ryle might object that all the cited forms of 'looking inwards' are what he calls 'silent behaviour', 'silent soliloquy', and 'silent colloquy' throughout his book. But these terms beg the question. Silent, inaccessible, secret thinking does not cease to be so when it is called 'silent colloquy'.

3. 'Has a person 'privileged access' to his current and habitual thoughts and sensations? The answer is 'Yes', in the sense that only I know if I have committed a murder and am worrying about it at this moment; only I know that my right foot is itching; only I know that I find her attractive and exciting and am carefully and successfully concealing my feelings from her and from everyone else because she is indifferent to me.

4. 'Has a person "privileged access" to the understanding of his own beliefs, motives, character traits, and so on?' This is more difficult. The most common situation is that A has more data relevant to an understanding of A's beliefs and character than B, C, or D, but is in a less favourable position to *colligate* the data and *focus* the picture than B, who knows quite a lot about A; is on a level with C, whose lack of knowledge or empathic understanding prevents him from getting a better picture; and is in a better position than D, who is too ignorant or too unperceptive. If B is a psychoanalyst, he will for a long time understand A much better than A understands himself, but if the analysis is successful A will begin to catch up. He may even overtake B in time, because some of the data are for ever inaccessible to B. *A has privileged access to them.*

5. 'Are "What knowledge can a person get of the workings of his own mind?" and "How does he get it?" intelligible questions?' Yes, provided that 'mind' is not taken to refer to an *object*. Answers to the second question would be: by thinking about his dreams when he wakes up; by noticing whether difficult problems are ever solved on waking (this would suggest that he does unconscious work on his problems); by noticing how often he forgets certain names and correlating the degree of amnesia with the degree of fear or guilt or hostility; by trying to find out whether his friends think he is lazy, forgetful, witty, suspicious . . .; and, if he wants to do the job thoroughly, by submitting to psychoanalysis.

6. 'Is the information derived from "privileged access" infallible?' The closer I get to a minimum risk-taking statement in the first person present tense, the closer I get to infallibility. 'I seem to be hitting a

typewriter'; 'My right foot seems to be itching'. The reward of caution is confidence; its price vacuity. Otherwise *no* information, whether privileged or handicapped, is infallible.

Ryle's argument shows that questions 1 and 6 should both be answered with a 'No'. The fallacy of *equivocation* could be made to support the fallacy of *non causa pro causa*. Sometimes the belief in 'privileged access' is assumed to involve the belief that it is 'exempt from error'; sometimes, as in the phrase 'a windowless chamber . . . to which only he has access', what is being criticized is the legitimate belief that A is often in a better position to know what A is thinking than anyone else. His argument disposes of the false assumptions that 'conscious' means 'consciously aware of one's current thoughts and feelings', and that we cannot make mistakes when we 'scrutinize' our own thoughts, sensations, and beliefs. His argument might well suggest to the incautious reader that questions 2, 3, 4, and 5 should also be answered in the negative, whereas 2, 3, and 5 should be answered with a (guarded) 'Yes', while 4 cannot be answered 'Yes' or 'No'. Herein would lie the fallacy of *non causa pro causa*, which would at least open the door to the fallacy of Behaviourism.

Finally, Ryle allows 'retrospection' and disallows 'introspection'. It is difficult to see why one should be compatible with the rejection of 'privileged access' and not the other. I can 'scrutinize' my memory of the terrifying firework display on the French landing beaches on 6 June 1944, and decide how much it has 'faded'; and I can 'scrutinize' my after-image after looking at the sun, and decide what colour it is. Both experiences are private, in the double sense that no-one else can perform the scrutiny and that I need not report them. The *facts* that I remember the Normandy landing, and see an after-image of the sun, can be made public if I decide to report them.

THE FALLACY OF BEHAVIOURISM

Such philosophical analysis may seem irksome and pettifogging to any reader who is not a philosopher. But it is necessary to disclose the possible fallacy before attempting to trace the psychological origin of the fallacy of Behaviourism.

A possible clue to its origin is an apparent contradiction. On p. 158 Ryle points out that

'a person may pay sharp heed to very faint sensations; when, for instance, he is scared of appendicitis, he will be acutely conscious, in this sense, of stomachic twinges which are not at all acute. In this sense, too, a person may be keenly conscious, hardly conscious, or quite unconscious, of feelings like twinges of anxiety or qualms of doubt.'

On p. 160 he describes as a 'misinterpretation' that he is arguing

'that mental processes are, in some mortifying sense, unconscious, perhaps in the sort of way in which I often cannot tell of my own habitual and reflex movements.'

This *need* not be a contradiction. He could argue that twinges of anxiety and qualms of doubt are not mental processes; or alternatively that they are not unconscious in a mortifying sense. But this is what Freud meant by 'unconscious processes': processes which play a very similar part in a person's life-history to their conscious equivalents, except that he is not aware of them. Just as he may not be aware of his digestive processes except when something goes wrong, so he may not be aware of his fear, guilt, or jealousy except when they become acute or when a *focusing* remark disrupts his successful repressions.

I would guess that the *psychological* technique underlying the *philosophical* fallacy of Behaviourism is what I shall call *reinforcement of repression*. The term 'mortifying' is the *mot juste* for the discovery that we know very little about our own motives, and that an expert may be constantly one step ahead in analysing the personal problems we try so hard to solve. Most people who have submitted to an analysis would describe it as a mortifying experience. The belittling of all conscious and unconscious mental processes which do not consist in intelligent and purposeful performances serves to reinforce the repression and rationalization which is necessary to preserve our equilibrium.

'Overt intelligent performances are not clues to the workings of minds; they are those workings. Boswell described Johnson's mind when he described how he wrote, talked, ate, fidgeted and fumed. His description was, of course, incomplete, since there were notoriously some thoughts which Johnson kept carefully to himself and there must have been many dreams, daydreams and silent babblings which only Johnson could have recorded and only a James Joyce would have wished him to have recorded' (ibid., pp. 58–9).

Only a James Joyce or an analyst! All the details of Boswell's *Life* are data for the understanding of the man Johnson; but if Johnson had kept a diary of his dreams, day-dreams, and 'silent babblings' (to which only he had access), there would be material for a more profound understanding of his life and character.

Should we agree that 'overt intelligent performances are not clues . . .'? Intelligent tennis-playing or car-driving is not a clue to clever theorizing. Ryle has inflicted on the Intellectualist Fallacy what we may hope is a fatal wound. He has effectively reduced to absurdity the theory that 'for an operation to be intelligent it must be steered by a prior intellectual operation' (p. 32). But intelligent chess-playing *is* a clue to what the player is thinking while he is playing. At the end of the game we can ask him, 'When you moved your knight to threaten the king and queen simultaneously, had you considered and rejected alternatives *p, q,* and *r*?' He may reply, 'I rejected *p* and *q*, but I didn't think of *r*.' A chess-player, watching a friend of roughly equal competence to himself playing a well-matched opponent, cannot *predict* what his friend will do, but he can, using each move as a clue, make very good guesses as to what he has just been thinking: 'If I do this, he can do that; if I do that . . .' and so on.

We have seen that a single word can be a clue to complex thought processes which may or may not be conscious.* Sometimes an analyst uses what is said as a clue to conscious thoughts that are deliberately being concealed, and that are subsequently admitted when he guesses them correctly. At other times he uses 'intelligent' speech as a clue to unconscious thought processes, which are subsequently made conscious by a focusing interpretation. Every intelligent person uses other people's conversation as a clue to what they are thinking; only very young children and very naïve adults say everything that 'comes into their heads'.

'In making sense of what you say, in appreciating your jokes, in unmasking your chess-stratagems, in following your arguments and hearing you pick holes in my arguments, I am not inferring to the workings of your mind, I am following them. Of course, I am not merely hearing the noises that you make, or merely seeing the movements that you perform. I am understanding what I hear and see. But this understanding is not inferring to occult causes. It is appreciating how the operations are conducted' (ibid., p. 61).

The term 'occult causes' serves to ridicule the not so ridiculous idea that I *do* use your jokes, chess-stratagems, and arguments as clues to your less obvious thoughts, beliefs, and attitudes. You may be thinking while you are talking to me, and quite consciously thinking, 'What a crashing bore that man is!'; you are polite enough and subtle enough to conceal this opinion from me, perhaps for the whole of our acquaint-anceship. In sophisticated societies people are genuinely and under-standably worried about what is going on beneath the deceptively

* See p. 103: 'Lindberg'.

lifelike masks of their friends and acquaintances: even of their husbands or wives. When the mask slips in analysis the worry becomes fully comprehensible. It is hardly an exaggeration to say that analysis is a long and painful undoing of the long and painful attempt of up-bringing and education to conceal, deny, disguise, and divert a person's antisocial tendencies and impulses: undoing, not in the sense of making him antisocial, but in the sense of making him aware of those impulses in relation to a single, all-important person – the analyst. The rejection of the valid 'clue hypothesis' is an example of the technique of *reinforcement of repression*.

What do we mean by 'unconscious thought processes'? The only confirmation for hypotheses about 'unconscious thought processes' comes from the effects of consciously expressed interpretations, from conscious memories of dreams, forgotten feelings . . ., and from 'as if' hypotheses about patterns of behaviour: 'Her conscious attitude to him is almost consistently affectionate, and yet she behaves as if she wanted to wreck everything he undertakes.' If in the course of analysis she becomes conscious, perhaps with a shock, of a desire to frustrate him and make him miserable, the conscious desire seems to be confirmation that there was formerly a corresponding repressed, unconscious desire, which 'explains' the pattern of behaviour. Is this like the explanation of cracks in the earth's crust by a volcanological hypothesis in terms of the expansion of unseen gases and molten rock? Or like the explanation of changes of temperature at the surface of an ocean in terms of unseen currents? Or like the explanation of a colour change in a fluid in terms of chemical changes, which are in turn explained in terms of atomic theory? Or like finding the key to unintelligible enemy messages by 'breaking' the code?

Like and unlike. We assume that deeper ocean currents are like surface currents, unseen molten rock like molten rock that erupts; but not that dreams are like conscious thinking, not that unconscious are like conscious processes. Psychoanalytic theory is like physico-chemical theory in that the unfamiliar helps us to explain the familiar, and undetectable processes are postulated to explain the observed, but we cannot describe those processes in terms of measurable units; we are obliged to describe them either in terms of 'systems' or 'institutions' or in terms derived by analogy from conscious processes. Analysis resembles decoding, but there is no unequivocal prescramble message with which to compare the unscrambled interpretation. Psychoanalytic explanation is *sui generis*, and 'unconscious thought (or mental) processes' is legiti-mate only as a technical term in the science; these processes may be as unlike conscious thinking as transmitted electrical waves are unlike the ensuing television picture.

THE FALLACY OF REDUCTIONISM

Ryle has ably exposed one form of the prevalent fallacy of *Reductionism*:

'. . . there is no contradiction in saying that one and the same process, such as the move of a bishop, is in accordance with two principles of completely different types and such that neither is 'reducible' to the other, though one of them presupposes the other.

Hence there derive two quite different sorts of "explanation" of the moves, neither of which is incompatible with the other. Indeed the explanation in terms of tactical canons presupposes that in terms of the rules of chess, but it is not deducible from those rules. . . .

A spectator might ask, in one sense of "why", why the bishop always ends a move on a square of the same colour as that on which it began the game; he would be answered by being referred to the rules of chess, including those prescribing the design of the board. He might then ask, in another sense of "why", why a player at a certain stage of the game moved one of his bishops (and not some other piece) to one square (and not to another); he might be answered that it was to force the opposing queen to cease to threaten the player's king' (ibid., p. 78).

The argument could be carried further. The quite different question may be asked: 'What does he always make a disastrous and uncharacteristic move, when he is in an overwhelmingly superior position, in every game he plays with his father?' The answer may be a simple one: 'He knows how it enrages his father to lose, so he deliberately throws the game away.' If the inept move is not deliberate, the answer is far from simple. He may become aware of his tendency to throw away games of chess, not because he consciously wanted to, but because of a 'blind spot (another visual metaphor) which prevented his 'seeing' the obvious danger. He may be able to link up this tendency with the throwing away of other games of many kinds, with attempts to ruin his chances in examinations, and with the neglect of opportunities in many spheres or the failure to follow them up. These various tendencies once linked together, seem to suggest a common cause. *Why* did he throw away those games?

The answer to this question is a psychological answer; it presupposes both the tactical canons and the rules of chess, but is not 'reducible' to either principle. Ryle rightly criticizes (p. 81) the question 'What makes

my hand do what my mind tells it to do?', but the perversity of this
question should not blind us to the legitimacy of the question 'What
prevents my hand from doing what my mind tells it to do?' This might
be a cry of despair from a violinist, who feels that in some sense he has
lost neither his skill nor his conscious desire to execute this skill, but finds
that his hand will not perform the movements which were formerly
an intrinsic element of his skill. Again, the question is legitimate
provided that 'my mind' is not taken to refer to a *thing*. At least two
different kinds of answer are possible, the physiological and the
psychological, and neither is 'reducible' to the other.

THE ICONOCLASTIC FALLACY

A further fallacy, related to the Reductionist Fallacy analysed by Ryle,
is what I shall call the Iconoclastic Fallacy. A naïve form of this fallacy is
the popular belief that psychoanalysis 'reduces everything to sex', or
that Darwin held that we were 'nothing but animals'. More sophisticated was Keats's disgust that physicists should 'explain' the rainbow:
its beauty depended on its mystery. His intellectual descendants complain that the analyst tries to destroy the nobility of *Hamlet* by explaining it; a great dramatic poem is exposed as the sordid story of a man
who could not kill his uncle and so avenge his murdered father,
because he himself had unconsciously desired to commit the crime: to
murder his father and marry his mother. They complain that the
surgeon's skill with the knife or the dentist's with the drill is represented
as 'nothing but' sublimated sadism, philanthropy nothing but a reaction
formation against sadism, altruism nothing but identification and
vicarious satisfaction, painting nothing but sublimated coprophilia,
friendship nothing but sublimated homosexuality, love nothing but
mutual interest in a 'sexual object' combined with dependence on a
mother, father, or child 'substitute', and so on.

Such complaints are understandable, for science is inevitably iconoclastic whenever its hypotheses conflict with comforting delusions.
Scientific progress is often progressive disillusionment. Perhaps every
modern student of Greek literature feels a nostalgic regret that while
understanding the Greek myths he can never *believe* in them. Perhaps
both the rainbow and Mount Olympus were more beautiful when their
beauty was enhanced by awe of magic and myth. Perhaps man felt
more secure when he believed that he stood on a fixed, flat earth at the
centre of a universe created for his benefit – so long as he was free from
the fear of hell-fire. A manic-depressive's description (Custance, 1951)

of his recovery from the illness could be fancifully applied to a people's loss of Heaven and Hell: life became rather humdrum! Progressive disillusionment is an inevitable part of a person's, as of a people's, development towards maturity.

Yet there is an important distinction between reaction to, and adjustment to, disillusionment. I have now recovered from the intense distress I suffered when Father Christmas faded into a myth. I am beginning to accept – and this is a much more difficult adjustment – the survival within myself and within my friends of a savage, ruthless, helpless, fearful infant.

The Iconoclastic Fallacy is evidence of *reaction* rather than *adjustment* to disillusionment. The man who discovers to his horror that repressed homosexuality plays an important part in his friendships is like a person who would be horrified to learn that silk was the secretion of worms. Similarly, the naïve reaction to the discovery that it is possible to give a psychological explanation of Nietzsche's philosophy is the rejection of his writings as valueless. It is possible to admit that the effect of his writings on politicians whose neuroses were compatible with the acquisition of power may have been extremely pernicious, without denying the unusual aesthetic and intellectual merit of those writings. It is possible to accept the shrinking to molehills of metaphysical mountains by modern philosophical and psychological criticism without swinging to disillusioned condemnation of modern philosophy as 'nothing but' verbal quibbling and hair-splitting.

VALIDITY OF JUDGEMENTS

We can now try to answer a question implicit in an earlier discussion. If my attitude to philosophy is ambivalent, and if attitudes to other subjects and people have been displaced to philosophy, how can my judgement be sound and unprejudiced? How do I know that I am not trying, like Nietzsche, to deal with my emotional problems by intellectualizing them, by using the techniques of projection and rationalization? The answer is that I do not know. I can do no more than try to analyse, and have analysed for me, my unconscious tendencies, and listen carefully to criticism. Yet there are more general clues. The young child asks of the characters in a book, play, or film, 'Is he a good man or a bad man?'; 'Is she a good woman or a bad woman?' and is dissatisfied with the answer 'Neither good nor bad'. The appeal of melodrama is due to the survival of this primitive splitting technique. There is a double satisfaction in finding the 'good' men and women easily distinguishable from the 'bad', and finding that vice is punished and virtue rewarded. We may suspect therefore that the wholesale rejection, without careful study, of the ideas of a thinker who has had a wide and lasting influence may be due to primitive bifurcation. Marx and Freud are the two thinkers of the last century whose influence on the 'human' disciplines has been widest and deepest; to use the mistakes of either as an excuse for dismissing him altogether is like saying, 'He's a *bad* man!' The most effective criticism of Marx would be a profound social analysis that avoided his mistakes and took into account not only all the facts he attempted to explain but also relevant events, since he wrote *Das Kapital*, which have confirmed, disconfirmed, or refuted his hypotheses. The most effective criticism of Freud would be the psychological correlate of Einstein's revision of Newton's theory. The hard truth – which many theorists find it difficult to accept – that such a task could be undertaken only by someone who has undergone a personal analysis, can easily be explained. Only direct experience of the multifarious and bewildering physical and mental effects of interpretations enables the theorist to give scientific explanations or predictions of these effects. Yet the effects are checkable scientific data, which any adequate psychological theory must attempt to explain.

DISTORTION

We are now in a position to add something to the earlier account of intellectual judgement. I suggested that there were many motives for distortion, conscious and unconscious, rational and irrational. The decision of a political leader that the exposure of a myth has gone too far for safety and that the true situation has to be clouded again, is an example of a conscious, rational motive for distortion. Here the term 'distortion' has undergone a semantic shift; the leader may be honest with himself, so that there is no distortion in his own private thinking, but only in his *representation* of the situation. On the other hand, a leader may deceive himself from the unconscious need to deceive others. The employer's tendency to believe that the workers would be made miserable and discontented by higher wages is due to a *situational* motive for distortion, partly conscious, partly unconscious; his opinions on the subject may not be entirely irrational, but merely biased. The bereaved man's need to believe in communication with the dead is an example of an unconscious motive: *unconscious because the belief itself would be jeopardized by the recognition of the need for the belief.*

We can now add a further motive for distortion: *love, hate, or fear of the author or representative of a theory or work of art.* Self-love should not be excluded, for an author may be no more dispassionate about his brainchild than a mother about the child of her womb. The reason why a scientific approach to Marx and Freud is so much more difficult than to Newton or Einstein is that Marx and Freud are primarily objects of love, hate, or fear, conscious or unconscious. To most of the world's inhabitants Marx's ideas represent either the hope of gaining or the fear of losing a better way of life. To those for whom Freud is more than a name he represents either the fear of recognizing or the hope of escaping (through psychoanalysis) 'the tyranny of the unconscious'. The pseudo-scientific style of modern writing about Freud is often an elaborate camouflage to conceal the desire to defend or attack, or the fear of attacking, or a mixture of these motives.

The most formidable criticism of psychoanalysis as a science is that the necessary qualification of an analyst, personal analysis, may also be a partial disqualification: the student may fall victim to trainee-dogmatism, that is, to the tendency to uncritical acceptance of the beliefs of the training analyst.

Criticism of a theory is seldom *mere* criticism of a theory. To give a psychological explanation of theoretical defects in Freud's writings, or in the writings of the critic's own analyst, is *felt* by both critic and readers as an obnoxious personal attack. It is as if a physicist could not make certain steps forward in his scientific work without writing a letter to *The Times* exposing certain secrets in his professor's private life.

This inherent difficulty in the subject is a useful stick for those who want to beat it, and it has been used eagerly, often, and hard. I believe, however, that other disciplines are faced, to a lesser degree, with the same difficulty, and that it is not insuperable. I have found (perhaps by introspection) that I have to overcome a certain reluctance to criticize the more sacrosanct of Freud's writings, and I suspect that this reluctance is due to an unconscious fear of an omnipotent, vengeful father–mother figure. It requires little ingenuity to link up this reluctance, rightly or wrongly, with the reluctance of 'orthodox' psychoanalytic writers to criticize any of Freud's formulations except those which were tentative or later revised, and with the strong feelings which even the most sympathetic revision arouses.

PROGRESSIVE AFFECTIVE DISCRIMINATION

If it is true that the techniques of splitting and displacement are normal and universal and underlie all abstract thinking, so that ambivalent feelings towards the parents are displaced to the analyst and thence to the theory, how is it possible to have a genuinely scientific approach to the theory? I suggest that the solution lies in what I shall call *progressive affective discrimination*. This is the discursive counterpart of the development of literary taste, in an individual or in a society, from melodrama to psychological realism. By realism I do not mean merely naturalistic dialogue in the modern style, but the attempt to portray the complexity of human character. We feel that the terms 'good' and 'bad' are quite inadequate to describe Hamlet, Lear, Othello, Raskolnikov, or Anna Karenina; analogously the terms 'right' and 'wrong', 'true' and 'false', 'valid' and 'invalid', 'scientific' and 'unscientific', and other sharp dichotomies are inadequate to describe certain complex and original theories.

I shall try to illustrate the concept 'progressive affective discrimination'. Authors who have a profound influence often create in the reader, for a considerable time, a state of extreme excitement and almost uncritical enthusiasm. This stage, the 'devouring' stage, represents the displacement to the author of almost pure 'love', the 'hatred' being split off and distributed among other objects. The period of uncritical acceptance is often followed by a period of doubt and partial disillusionment. The third stage is the stage of critical re-examination, reassessment, and conscientious discrimination: I shall call it *the achievement of sustained intellectual ambivalence* towards an author, a theory, a hypothesis, or an idea. Such *discriminating ambivalence* is to be contrasted with four other kinds of ambivalence: the first, ambivalence to science-in-general, takes the form of splitting *disciplines* into 'good' and 'bad' (often disguised as 'scientific' and 'unscientific'); the second takes the form of splitting *writers or theories within a discipline*, without adequate study, into 'sound' and 'unsound'; the third of splitting *hypotheses* into 'good' or 'bad', by applying a single criterion, and totally rejecting those which do not satisfy it; the fourth of oscillating between uncritical acceptance and uncritical rejection of writers, theories, or hypotheses.

The process of progressive affective discrimination is a continuation of the process which Winnicott (1958), following Melanie Klein, calls 'the *achievement* of the depressive position' by infants or by patients in analysis. The infant is assumed to begin life by oscillating between 'total' acceptance of the 'good' and 'total' rejection of the 'bad'. The gradual recognition that the 'good' and the 'bad' are really the same thing or the same person (the mother) sets the infant the difficult problem of emotional adjustment to an object, and later a person, who is 'good', 'bad', and indispensable. The 'working-through' the inevitable depression caused by this problem is the *sine qua non* of mature relationships.

Progressive affective discrimination, then, *is a gradual change of attitude from one of total acceptance or total rejection or oscillating ambivalence towards a thing, person, country, race, author, discipline, theory, hypothesis, idea, form of art, artist, or work of art, to one of acceptance of those elements in each which seem valid or valuable and rejection of those which do not.* A person may, of course, achieve a high degree of discrimination in one sphere and a low degree in another. He may be emancipated from colour-prejudice, for example, while remaining violently anti-German, anti-Russian, anti-American, or anti-Jew. Ignorance gives greater scope to primitive splitting techniques, but when increasing knowledge in any sphere is not accompanied by increasing affective discrimination it is reasonable to assume a powerful unconscious need to find 'good' and 'bad' objects for the techniques of projection and displacement.

12

Reductionism and Overextensionism

Progressive affective discrimination is exemplified in R.L. Munroe's study *Schools of Psychoanalytic Thought*. Without condemning any of the theorists she examines, she has a sharp eye for the weaknesses as well as the merits of their theories. Before considering her criticism of 'Reductionism' in her own special sense, I shall illustrate the strength and weakness of her judgement by quoting her remarks on Jung and Melanie Klein.

She describes (1957, p. 566) how she partially overcame an antipathy to Jungian material, and found one aspect of Jung's theory, a psychology of symbols, 'worthy of very careful consideration and esteem', in spite of her criticism of the other aspect, the psychology of types:

> 'Since the psychic entities Jung proposes are systems of profound importance, since he is sensitively alert to their interaction, and since he calls upon intuition to penetrate the disguises they assume, it sounds like a foolish paradox to say that his theory leads towards a static intellectualism. Nevertheless I think that this is the ultimate fate of any theory that does not find its psychological roots in the genetic process' (ibid., p. 569).

There seems to me to be only one serious defect of judgement in Munroe's sympathetic and scholarly work. Although she gives a fair and well-balanced summary of the theoretical position of Melanie Klein, I suspect that she underestimates, in common with many American psychologists, the theoretical and practical importance of Klein's theory of the 'superego'. She writes:

> 'Her tendency to equate very primitive mechanisms of projection and introjection with the superego leads to blurring or actual misunderstanding of aspects of Freudian doctrine and therapy which depend on a sharp perception of the development and function of *Freud's* superego' (p. 610).

This remark seems to miss the point. The important question is not whether the 'very primitive mechanisms' should be 'equated with the superego' but whether the phenomena discovered and described in the analysis of very young children (whatever umbrella term may or may not be used to refer to these phenomena) are connected with the phenomena discovered in long and deep analysis and can throw light on them: whether the fear of persecution and irrational sense of guilt discovered in the one-, two-, or three-year-old has any genetic relationship with the fear of persecution and irrational sense of guilt discovered in the later stages of a deep adult analysis.

The point of Melanie Klein's insistence that the superego develops within the first year is that the key to the young child's difficulties, as to the adult's, is excessive fear and guilt which are due to his own aggressive impulses. In *Psychoanalysis Today*, she writes:

'The vicious circle that is thus set up, in which the child's anxiety impels it to destroy its object, results in an increase of its own anxiety, and this once again urges it on against its object, and constitutes a psychological mechanism which, in my view, is at the bottom of asocial and criminal tendencies in the individual. Thus, we must assume that it is the excessive severity and overpowering cruelty of the superego, not the weakness or want of it as is usually supposed, which is responsible for the behaviour of asocial and criminal persons' (1948c, p. 67).

'. . . so long as the function of the superego is mainly to arouse anxiety it will call out those violent defensive mechanisms in the ego which we have described above, and which are unethical and asocial in their nature. But as soon as the child's sadism is diminished and the character and function of its superego changed so that it arouses less anxiety and more sense of guilt, those defensive mechanisms which form the basis of a moral and ethical attitude are activated, and the child begins to have consideration for its objects, and to be amenable to social feelings' (p. 68).

'When, in our analytic work, we are always seeing how the resolution of early infantile anxiety not only lessens and modifies the child's aggressive impulses, but leads to a more valuable employment and gratification of them from a social point of view; how the child shows an ever-growing, deeply-rooted desire to be loved and to love, and to be at peace with the world about it; and how much pleasure and benefit, and what a lessening of anxiety it derives from the fulfilment of this desire – when we see all this, we are ready to believe that what would now seem a Utopian state of things may well come true in those distant days when, as I hope, child-analysis will become as much a part of every person's upbringing as school-education is now' (p. 74).

I interpret her remarks as implying that a modified and tolerable sense of guilt is a constructive factor which underlies successful sublimations, successful attempts at reparation, successful creative work in art and science; while an excessive sense of guilt and excessive anxiety, whether conscious or unconscious, are destructive and disintegrative factors that hinder or prevent sublimation and reparation. This view coincides with Ezriel's opinion quoted earlier that reality-testing and *reduction of fear* are the essence of psychoanalytic therapy. Self-knowledge is an adjunct, which may play a much less important part in child than in adult analysis.

The dispute about the superego is an instructive example of the interaction of theory and clinical practice. According to the epistemological approach I have been advocating, discussion about the term 'superego' is at the level of 'model' hypotheses (p. 76), whereas discussion about the relationship between the effects of interpretations in child analysis and the effects of interpretations in adult analysis is at the epistemologically prior level of 'retrospective' hypotheses (p. 74). From this point of view the importance of Melanie Klein's insistence on the early development of the superego lies in her determination to link up the methods and findings of the analysis of very young children with the methods and findings of those stages of adult analysis where very primitive emotions and attitudes reappear. As in the dispute about 'mind', so in the dispute about 'superego', what may seem to be a quibble about a word is really an attempt to deal with an authentic problem: 'Which of many ways of colligating and organizing data is most scientifically valuable?'. There is no point in adhering to Freud's use of the term 'superego' if, as Melanie Klein holds, there is genetic continuity in the attempts to deal with the problems of fear, rage, and guilt from early infancy into adult life. These remarks leave open the possibility of further progress in the theoretical organization of the clinical data of psychoanalysis.

DEFINITIONS OF 'REDUCTIONISM'

The philosophical fallacy which appears most frequently in Munroe's criticism of the schools of psychoanalytic thought is the fallacy of 'Reductionism'. Before examining this fallacy we must draw a distinction between the usual philosophical sense of 'Reductionism' and the sense in which the term is used throughout her book. In philosophy, to 'reduce' sentence a to sentence x, or the set of sentences a, b, c, to the set of sentences x, y, z, is to substitute x for a, or x, y, z, for a, b, c, for some philosophical purpose (usually for the purpose of clarification or simplification), with the intention that the substituted sentences should express all that was valid in the original sentences but in a less misleading, less complex, less abstract . . . (etc.), form, without including a certain term or terms occurring in the original. The fallacy of 'Reductionism' in its philosophical sense, therefore, is either (1) illegitimate substitution of this kind, or (2) the tacit assumption that such substitution is possible.

R. L. Munroe uses the term 'Reductionism' in a different sense:

'– the process of overextension from basic principles by logical deduction' (1957, p. 601).

She writes:

'As a fellow theorizer, I have tried to present a *view of systems* as a philosophical solvent for school variations. This view . . . avers that scientific truth lies in the progressive recognition of dynamic systems of different types and degrees of inclusiveness' (ibid., p. 601).

Munroe points out the 'Reductionism' in the theories of Jung, Adler, Horney, Fromm, and Sullivan. She regards a large part of Jung's theory (excluding the psychology of symbols) as being

'. . . rooted in a logico-philosophical approach conceived as universal in principle and hence reductionist' (ibid., p. 570).

Of Adler she says that an

'. . . important aspect of human experience, the helplessness of the infant, is used as an abstract principle which is then applied generally in all situations' (ibid., p. 363).

Of Karen Horney,

'. . . the *need for security* becomes a kind of universal which supplies the dynamic theme upon which the variations in personality development are constructed' (ibid., p. 364).

Of Erich Fromm she writes that he, too, seems to feel the need for an underlying psychological universal.

'He finds it in the process of individuation – an evolutionary event, the corollary of which is the psychological conflict between growing independence and dependence on primary ties. . . . In practice, the fear of being alone and insignificant becomes in Fromm's writings a sort of primary drive hardly different from the need for security (Horney) and for superiority (Adler)' (ibid., p. 397).

Of Sullivan she writes:

L

'The concept of the pursuit of security tends to become as reductionist as the theories of the other non-libido writers, because it is not kept in sufficiently close relationship to the pursuit of satisfaction.

This reductionism does not seem to me at all a necessary part of Sullivan's theory. . . . The theoretical analysis of drives as existing only in relation to the living complex of an organism in its milieu is a very healthy corrective to the tendency to think of instincts as existing somehow in themselves and as identifiable apart from the environment within which they function. But such analysis should not go so far as to ignore the organismic systems through which the child perceives his environment. Exaggeration of the cultural side of this living complex is quite as objectionable according to Sullivan's own theory as an over-emphasis on the drive-systems ("instincts")' (ibid., pp. 492–3).

When discussing 'Reductionism' she incidentally exposes a Teleological Fallacy:

'Selye and others have demonstrated that widespread neurochemical connections exist between organ systems which until recently have been considered relatively independent of one another. Eventually theories about the content of the "id" may be profoundly modified by extension of knowledge about human physiology. Nevertheless the undeniable fact that the individual perishes when integrative functions fail does *not* imply a positive organismic or psychological urge towards integration *as such*.

The distinction . . . becomes of crucial importance when *de facto* integrative phenomena observable in the organism and in cultural history are turned into tight dynamic systems by the sleight of hand of theory, and when the theoretically derived system is applied reductively to concrete events. It cannot be too strongly emphasized that recognizing a measure of integration as the *sine qua non* of survival is *not* the same as taking integration as a biological goal, or as a need for wholeness in the Rankian sense, or as a "real self" in Horney's theory' (ibid., pp. 607–8).

Finally she says of Freud:

'As a very great mind, Freud was able to observe freshly and to integrate his observations at many levels. He was never as reductive in approach as many of his followers and opponents. Thus, if I firmly reject a naïvely "energic" view of instinctual drives and the libido, I do not feel that I am going *against* Freud. Instead I am assuming that he meant very earnestly the modest caution with which he presented such generalization.' (ibid., p. 616).

She suggests that

'. . . instead of thinking in terms of instincts, or even instinctual drives or needs, we think in terms of the major *systematizations* of the organism as a biological unit' (ibid., p. 617).

'For some of the most important drive systems, notably the sexual systems, Freud's analysis of the source, aim and object aspects of the "instinct" seems to me valid and brilliantly implemented. It seems to me possible to retain all of the Freudian work and thought on these systems, including the inte-grating concept of the libido – save only the exclusiveness and tendency towards theoretical reductionism based on these particular systems, con-sidered either as *the* systems of psychology or as disposing of a fixed quantum of "energy"' (ibid., p. 620).

She puts forward a cogent argument, which cannot be fully presented here, for the view

'. . . that what is currently called "aggression" is not a *unitary* drive system and that much confusion in Freudian theory could be avoided if the concept of *an* instinctual drive opposed to Eros were given up' (ibid., p. 624).

She suggests that the constructive aspects of 'aggression' should be subsumed under the neutral heading of 'nonsexual drive systems',

'. . . with emphasis on the inborn motility patterns. These patterns may *in fact* be "destructive", because the baby does not properly distinguish between valuable *objets d'art* and the objects he is permitted to bang around in baby fashion' (ibid., p. 624).

As regards the operation of the nonsexual drive systems, 'aggression' in any hostile sense of the term is

'. . . a matter of social interpretation of essentially neutral behavior, or a reactive hostility to situations created by the essentially neutral behavior, or a by-product of the effort to establish an effective idea of the self. Doubtless more "or's" could be added' (ibid., p. 635).

To sum up, Munroe makes out a strong case for an element of 'Reductionism', in the sense of overextension from basic principles, in all the writers she discusses. There seems to be no good reason to associate such overextension with any single psychological technique. Why then, a philosopher might ask, bring psychology into philo-sophical discussion at all? If philosophical fallacies can be exposed by philosophical techniques, what need is there to correlate them with psychological mechanisms?

REDUCTIONISM AND OVEREXTENSIONISM

In order to answer this question we need to differentiate kinds of fallacy. The fallacies I have called Fluctuating Rigour and Fluctuating Scepti-cism are non-specific, in the sense that they cannot be pinned down in a glass case, and put into a museum once and for all. They are techniques rather than fallacies, which can be used at any time by a clever disputant *without his being aware that he is using them*. They are techniques which may make use of the more specific fallacies hitherto recognized by philosophers, such as amphiboly, equivocation, *ignoratio elenchi*, many questions, *non causa pro causa*, *non sequitur*, *petitio principii*, *post hoc ergo propter hoc*, and so on.

To put it another way, they are general unconscious tendencies rather than particular slips. This distinction is analogous to the distinction between the unconscious tendencies studied by analysts, and the symptoms, slips of the tongue, blind spots, and so on, which serve as clues to those tendencies. This analogy can be extended. Wittgenstein claimed that his philosophizing had a therapeutic purpose, directed against the perennial temptation to ask senseless questions in philosophy. This purpose accords with my thesis that philosophical analysis and psychoanalysis are complementary; that the recognized fallacies are clues to underlying philosophical tendencies, just as symptoms are clues to underlying psychological tendencies. I suggest that the recognition and naming of such tendencies as Fluctuating Rigour and Fluctuating Scepticism, though unlikely to have any decisive *therapeutic* effect, is a major step towards putting the student of philosophy on his guard, and rendering the techniques ineffective and innocuous.

While Fluctuating Rigour is a philosophical tendency which invariably vitiates theoretical argument, and Reductionism in the sense of Overextension from Basic Principles – which I propose should be renamed 'Overextensionism' to prevent confusion – is a failure to recognize the complexity of a theoretical problem, Reductionism in the sense of 'attempting to clarify by eliminating the mythical' may be either a retrogressive or a progressive tendency, according to the intellectual judgement of the reductionist.

Behaviourism is an example of illegitimate Reductionism. 'He is angry' is not reducible to 'He is flushed', 'He is trembling', 'He is shouting', and the rest of the behavioural story. On the other hand, the elimination of 'the luminiferous ether', 'energy', 'force', 'gravitation', 'space', and 'time' in theoretical physics; the disappearance of 'faculties', 'volitions', and 'soul substance' in psychology; and the discrediting of reified 'being', 'essence', substance', 'the absolute', 'non-natural properties', 'absolute truth', and other mythical entities in philosophy, have marked an important advance in those disciplines.

We can now define 'Reductionism' and distinguish it from 'Overextensionism'. Sound Reductionism is the ability to eliminate concepts in a theory without reducing the explanatory power of that theory. The Fallacy of Reductionism is the restriction of the explanatory power of a theory by rejecting some of its concepts and hypotheses without finding some adequate alternative method of accounting for the phenomena. An outstanding instance of this fallacy is Behaviourism.

Overextensionism is the selection from a complex theory of one or more principles, such as attempted compensation for inferiority (Adler), the search for security (Horney), or the need for and fear of individuation (Fromm) to perform an explanatory task to which they are not adequate. Overextensionism is a form of oversimplification.

13

Incompatible Points of View

LIMITS OF THE HYPOTHETICO-DEDUCTIVE METHOD

Philosophical fallacies may be thought of either as mistakes or as tendencies. Although any given *instance* of amphiboly, equivocation, and the other classified philosophical fallacies is a particular mistake, and therefore corrigible, amphiboly and equivocation regarded as *liabilities* or *risks* are general tendencies rather than particular fallacies, and are therefore difficult to detect and to eradicate. This point has been ably clarified by R. Crawshay-Williams. His methodological study, *Methods and Criteria of Reasoning*, deals with two major fallacies which he calls the Universal Context assumption and the Universal Meaning assumption. He points out that

'. . . many philosophical theories and systems derive from misinterpreting disguised methodological statements as either factual or logical, and then placing them in the Universal Context' (1957, p. 87).

The Universal Context assumption is

'that the correctness of an empirical statement is in no way related to the purpose for which its subject is being paid attention to' (p. 63).

The Universal Meaning assumption is that 'a (disputed) informal implication may be valid', which is

'in the logical field a counterpart of the Universal Context assumption in the empirical field; . . . whenever we defend an informal implication against attack we are in effect assuming that the usage from which we have derived the implication is the only legitimate usage' (p. 185).

Crawshay-Williams's thesis is relevant to the general risk of equivocation:

'If we wish to find testable answers to interesting philosophical questions, it is no use treating them as logical. The grounds for this recommendation are as follows: if a proposition which is asserted as analytic is disputed in any given company for longer than it would take to work out a short deductive sequence, then this is *prima facie* evidence that the statement is (to be treated as) underdefined in the sense that the definition of at least one word in the statement, though precise enough for some purposes, is not precise enough for the purpose of settling the present dispute. Moreover, this *prima facie* evidence can be decisively tested by a process of so to speak tracing the disagreement backwards through the deductive sequence and seeing whether the necessary premisses are in fact agreed' (p. 180).

The philosophical reader will notice the relevance of this paragraph to my criticism of Popper's version of Peirce's theory that scientific method is 'hypothetico-deductive'. Deduction is possible in mathematics and symbolic logic, and deductive inference is successful in applied mathematics,

'because all we need to know in order to determine the mathematical context is what is being treated as the unit; and in practice we take good care to specify this unit unambiguously' (p. 199).

'. . . any system which cannot be built up mechanically from its axioms is not (to be treated as) testable by appeal solely to logical considerations' (p. 201).

'. . . we cannot assume the validity of a deductive sequence containing different instances of (say) the word 'event' unless we can also assume that all these instances have the same designatum' (p. 28).

'. . . what I am throwing out of the window is not logic but the assumption that logical considerations have the force of law in certain empirical linguistic fields' (p. 29).

The theory that scientific method is hypothetico-deductive, I suggest, is an illegitimate generalization based on the sound observation that *the use of applied mathematics in exploratory scientific research is hypothetico-deductive*. It has the merit of emphasizing that a hypothesis is a guess which needs to be tested and not a mere generalization from particular instances; it has the serious demerit of setting a rigid and arbitrary frame round a section of the total field of scientific work, and attempting to discredit and disqualify everything that is done outside that frame.

In his *Collected Papers* (Vol. 3, p. 554), C. S. Peirce maintains that

'the mathematician does two very different things: namely, he first frames a pure hypothesis stripped of all features which do not concern the drawing of consequences from it, and this he does without inquiring or caring whether it agrees with the actual facts or not, and, secondly, he proceeds to draw necessary consequences from that hypothesis.'

In another place he says

'. . . every hypothesis that merits attention is subjected to severe but fair examination, and only after the predictions to which it leads have been remarkably borne out by experience is trusted at all, and even then only provisionally. . . .' (Vol. 5, p. 412).

We have seen that many generalizations about scientific method tend to overemphasize certain methods of certain scientists at the expense of others. The important point here is that original scientists who need to invent new concepts and a new terminology to explain their discoveries cannot make indisputable deductions from their hypotheses if their hypotheses are not susceptible of mathematical formulation. *If there is any science outside mathematical physics, it is misleading to call such science hypothetico-deductive without any qualification.*

After revealing (in my opinion convincingly) the disguised ambiguity of the expression 'infinite series' in Kant's antinomy about time, and so demonstrating that Kant's argument is invalid, Crawshay-Williams goes on:

'As in all cases of disguised equivocation, the meanings which are to be interchanged and combined must be held far enough below articulate consciousness for the jerk which takes place when changing step from one to the other to be felt on the surface (if at all) as merely a sort of logical hesitation – as a sign, not that two meanings are involved, but that some logical step has been nearly tripped over' (1957, p. 281).

NEUTRAL FACTS

Let us now consider the central thesis of his book, and inquire whether it is completely or only partially in accord with the methodological recommendations I have put forward:

'Since the correctness of the description expressed by an empirical statement depends both upon the neutral facts about its subject and upon the purpose for which they are being paid attention to, we may treat empirical discourse as a sort of function of three variables: the neutral facts about the subject (S), the description (D), and the purpose or context (C). Thus the form (for this purpose) of an empirical statement is "S is D in C". And the thesis of this book is that each of the variables is a function of the other two taken together; for example, the correctness of a description (D) cannot be tested unless we appeal to both of the other variables as criteria; that is, not only to the single objective criterion traditionally adopted (S) but to the contextual criterion (C) as well. . . . The *general* recommendation is therefore that an empirical statement is (to be treated as) indeterminate unless all three variables are adequately determined. . . . Thus, if we are given a context and a description, we can enquire as to what subjects are correctly so described in that context. (Given C and D, what is S?). This happens when we ask, for instance, "What does a psychoanalyst mean by the word 'sexual'?"; that is to say "What things (mental events, types of behaviour, etc.) does a psychoanalyst find he needs to treat, for his therapeutic purposes, in the same way as things normally called sexual?". The answer to this question can be discovered by empirical enquiry. Note however that there would be no answer if the question were simply "What mental events or types of behavior are fundamentally sexual in origin?" (Given D, what is S?)' (ibid., p. 238).

The example seems to me to be particularly well chosen. It is widely assumed that Freud's extension of the concept 'sexual' was arbitrary and perverse, whereas it was due to the scientific discovery that the core of a neurosis (as opposed to its superficies) can best be modified by the therapist who treats the symptoms 'in the same way as things normally called sexual'. But this is merely the technological aspect. It is necessary to add that for the purpose of *understanding the origin* of neurotic symptoms, as well as for therapeutic purposes, the analyst needs to treat them in the same way as things normally called sexual. This is the context of pure science, and it is here that the Universal Context assumption is a more prevalent hazard, since the pure scientist is widely assumed to be describing things *as they really are*. But we have seen that even for the purposes of pure science the physicist needs to treat light as 'photons' in some contexts, 'waves' in others; he has (I think) given up asking what light 'really is' (in the Universal Context).

Once more we are faced with the puzzle about 'facts'. What are 'the neutral facts about the subject (S)'? Clearly some 'facts' are more 'neutral' than others, in the sense that some *descriptions* are more generally acceptable than others. A physicist shows a photograph to a layman and says, 'Do you see that white line? That's the path of an electron'. The layman, if his sight is normal, will agree that there is a white line, and if he is deferential to the physicist (as most laymen are) he will accept the 'fact' that it is the path of an electron. Of the two 'facts' the second is less neutral than the first, because the statement is meaningful only in relation to the physicist's complex theory. In fact, if the layman is an unabashed sceptic he may may say, 'We used to take your word for your mythological "energy", "momentum", "forces", "gravitational pulls", and so on, and now we have to accept your "electrons", "protons", "neutrons", and "mesons" (which are said to have a half-life of a few micro-seconds). But how do we know that you won't revise your theory in fifty years' time? Is it really a *fact* that this is the path of an electron?'

By analogy, if a psychoanalyst were prepared to flout the rules of professional discretion, he could play a recording of an analytic session and explain, 'You will notice that as soon as I finish talking Miss X bursts into tears. This is a reaction to a distressing interpretation.' The sceptic might agree that there were sounds of sobbing, but object, 'How do we know that this is a reaction? How do we know that it is *propter hoc* and not merely *post hoc*?'

As usual, there is no answer to the thoroughgoing sceptic except 'Be reasonable!' or 'You are guilty of the Fluctuating Rigour Fallacy!' Both physical theory and psychoanalytic theory will almost certainly change and develop within the next fifty years, but this is not a sufficient reason for refusing to profit from the successes and insights of both theories *at their present stage of development*. Further progress is in the hands not of the extreme sceptic but of the physicist, the psychoanalyst, and the philosopher who understand the purposes, methods, and language of the scientist.

Let us now turn to Crawshay-Williams's treatment of 'neutral facts':

'. . . when a statement is highly self-determinate, we can usually treat it, *qua* statement-type, as testable by appeal solely to the objective criterion – to the objective structure of events. . . . Nevertheless, for the special purpose of understanding how factual and methodological statements function, we do need to distinguish . . . "factual statements" . . . and . . ."neutral facts". . . . And we can epitomize the distinction by saying, for instance, "The neutral facts about the substance ordinarily called 'arsenic' are such that the sentence 'Arsenic is poison' expresses a correct factual statement in an axiomatically understood everyday context, while the sentence 'Arsenic is a tonic' may express a correct factual statement in certain axiomatically understood medical contexts"' (ibid., pp. 72–3).

'Since, given a collection of neutral facts called "A", we can correctly say of them for one purpose "A is B" and for another purpose "A is not B", it follows that we may sometimes correctly say "A is B" and then subsequently say (also correctly) "A is not B" without thereby indicating any change in the actual pattern of A – in the structure of the neutral facts' (ibid., p. 168).

This distinction between 'factual statements' and 'neutral facts' may be adequate for the disputes Crawshay-Williams has in mind, and in situations where there is no dispute (both doctors and laymen would agree that arsenic is a tonic in very small doses and a poison in large doses); but in physics and psychoanalysis, where description involves interpretation in terms of a theory, it may be impossible to 'appeal solely to the objective structure of events': in other words to point rather than to explain. The white line and the sound of sobbing are relatively 'neutral facts'; the 'path of an electron' and the 'reaction to an interpretation' have to be taken on trust. Both the physicist and the psychoanalyst have to say, 'If you take the trouble to learn my language and undergo a difficult training I will be able to offer you a partial explanation of these puzzling events. You may then be able to point out to me that there is something wrong with the language I am using and help to improve it.'

The above examples suggest that we are moving in the direction of 'neutrality' when we substitute for a description in terms of a theory or 'coloured language' that is currently disputed or conceivably disputable a description which any 'sane' person would agree to apply. Instead of saying 'The rioting mob illegally broke into the embassy and assaulted the ambassador', or 'The fighters for freedom demonstrated their spontaneous indignation against the enemy agent by entering his spy-centre and forcibly restraining him', we say 'Twenty-three men entered the embassy and four of them tied the ambassador to a chair'. This is called 'factual reporting'. Instead of saying of a woman, 'She is a criminal because she has committed fifty-five acts of larceny', or 'She is in need of treatment because she is suffering from a compulsion which has caused her to steal fifty-five things for which she has no practical need and which she could easily have paid for', we say, 'She has taken fifty-five articles from stores without paying for them'.

These two examples show that several antitheses'* have to be distinguished. In the first example the antithesis is *factual-tendentious*; factual reporting leaves the reader to make up his mind what attitude to take to the events. In the second example the antithesis is *factual-explanatory*. If we want to be more explicit we can speak of two antitheses: *factual-legal* and *factual-psychological*. The 'criminal' statement is tendentious only if made before her trial; if made after she has been found guilty it is a true factual statement *from the legal point of view*. The psychological statement is *descriptive-explanatory*; it says a little more than the 'neutral' statement because it implies a distinction between kinds of stealing. The 'neutral' statement is merely a starting-point, and the legal and psychological statements, although both

* See Index for 'Fact Antitheses'.

'descriptive' in form, point beyond the 'factual' statement in different directions, one towards prison, the other towards the consulting-room.

These remarks may seem to confirm Crawshay-Williams's thesis: the neutral fact is that she took the articles; for the purposes of the law she is a criminal; for the purposes of therapy she is suffering from an illness. All three statements may be true and compatible. I hope to show, however, that two statements may be true factual statements and yet in an important sense incompatible. Let us suppose that before being charged, tried, and sentenced to six months' imprisonment, the shoplifter was in analysis. It is difficult to imagine the analyst saying, 'She is ill. One of her symptoms is a compulsion to steal. Now that she has been found guilty she is a criminal.' The last two statements may both be strictly true; the incongruity of their juxtaposition derives not from a muddling of contexts but from the fusion of *incompatible points of view*. It is akin to the macabre incongruity of saving a man's life by an operation the week before he is due to be hanged.

It is different from the incongruity of 'A plank is not solid'. Crawshay-Williams criticizes, in my opinion justly, the 'fluid' picture of matter propounded by Eddington in *The Nature of the Physical World*, which was set in the everyday context with the implication that the physicist's description of matter 'is somehow more correct, because more detailed and precise, than the everyday description' (Crawshay-Williams, 1957, p. 148). He maintains that 'the statement "A plank is not solid" is . . . false, however strictly we are speaking, because it is false in the context which it self-determines' (ibid., p. 148). The incongruity in my example comes from this: to call someone a criminal or a felon is *to associate oneself with a legal judgement* in a way that is impossible if the mode of judging is rejected. To put it another way, the question 'Is she or is she not a felon?' is not adequately answered by appeal to the 'neutral facts', to the agreed definition of 'felon' and to the purpose or context. The question (or the statement 'She is a felon') may be disputed not because the 'neutral facts', the definition, or the context are disputed, but because we want to redescribe the 'neutral facts' in non-neutral, explanatory terms. In order to justify the re-description it may be necessary to refer to a complex theory.

My argument can be summed up in the following thesis: 'Neutral fact' is a misleading expression. We can communicate by pointing, screaming, smiling, and other non-discursive signs, but such communication is never unequivocal (unless it answers a question expressed in a language), and is an efficient way of expressing facts. When we communicate by means of some form of language we inevitably select from our experience what we have been taught to name, indicate, or describe, and for many years we imitate more expert 'fact-staters' in making 'factual statements'. Some of our early experiments ('Daddy, the moon's turned yellow. It's got jaundice.') may be laughed at and abandoned; if all the expert fact-staters we meet are unanimous we accept certain statements (such as 'The earth is flat') as the foundation of a body of knowledge: as 'factual statements'. If we are rebels we begin to question authority and emulate the eccentrics such as Socrates, Galileo, Newton, Einstein, and Freud, who cast doubt upon well-established 'factual statements' and introduced new ways of describing events. While such descriptions are fresh they are not allowed as 'factual'; they are 'paradoxical' or 'speculative'. *They become 'factual' when they are stale.*

DISPUTED DESCRIPTIONS

Although descriptions are never neutral, since words are part of a language and a language, like a map-projection, expresses a way of looking at things, a way of colligating and assimilating, *descriptions are less or more neutral* in the sense that they are less or more denuded of controversial theory, of value judgements, of recommendatory, explanatory, performative, and enactive elements, and so on. For the most part, the more neutral a description, the less enlightening. The most neutral descriptions are those which no person would dispute; they are either the starting-point from which we go on to say something interesting, or the solid ground under people's feet ('The earth is flat') which is taken for granted until the innovator dissolves it. Just as we found that the road to certainty was the road to sterility, so now we find that the road to descriptive neutrality is the road to banality. If we want to *find out* something new and important about the atom, the acorn, the human embryo, the Ice Age, the Milky Way, kleptomania, paranoid delusions, genetic risks from radiation, or any other phenomena, we have to put our money on some prancing erratic horse of a theory, and risk losing it.

In my opinion, therefore, Crawshay-Williams's thesis is vitiated by what I have called the 'Fact-Finding Fallacy'. But how serious is this? Perhaps it can be saved by some minor revision. His thesis is that each of the variables—the neutral facts, the description, and the context—is a function of the other two taken together; the correctness of a description cannot be tested unless we appeal to both the other variables as criteria. Let us now substitute for 'neutral facts' 'undisputed description' and for 'description' 'disputed description'. We can now apply his thesis to my 'compulsion' example. The undisputed description is 'woman who has taken fifty-five articles from stores without paying for them'; the disputed descriptions are 'criminal' and 'woman suffering from a compulsion'; the disputants are a lawyer and a psychoanalyst discussing the case after she has been sentenced. What is the context? How can the context be adequately determined? The answer seems to be that both disputants will come to see that for the purposes of the law (or in a legal context) she is a criminal; while for the purposes of therapy (or in a therapeutic context) she is suffering from a compulsion. With a sigh of relief they shake hands and congratulate each other on their philosophical acuity. They have brought up to date an old solution of an old problem: for the purposes of the seventeenth-century church (in an ecclesiastical context) a woman could be judged to be a witch and burned alive; for everyday purposes (in a common-sense context) she was a harmless eccentric. But *should* they be shaking hands?

At this point the philosopher may object that my example is badly chosen. The analyst is against the term 'criminal', not because it is a disputed description, but because it is not a purely descriptive term; it has pejorative emotive overtones. If 'criminal' were given its purely descriptive use, he may maintain, the dispute would not be about the appropriateness of the term; it would be about the proper attitude to take towards the 'criminal'.

To find out what kind of dispute we are dealing with, let us consider the question 'She has been found guilty after a fair trial, but is she really a criminal?' This question may be roughly equivalent to:

1 'Did the jury bring in a bad verdict?'

or to

2 'Should legal theory and practice be revised in the light of psychological theory?'

or to

3 'Has the term "criminal" an agreed definition in law, and if so does it apply to the innocent who are found guilty and not to the guilty who evade capture or the guilty who are acquitted?'

or to

4 'Is she really to blame?'

Question 1 introduces a discussion in which the judgement is being judged; the *execution* of the law is being evaluated. The discussion might go on to the question 'Is a jury of non-specialists capable of judging whether she is suffering from a compulsion?' This would be an attempt to evaluate a legal *method*.

Question 2 suggests that the technical use of terms in a specialist discipline may be challenged, shown to be inconsistent, or shown to be intellectually anachronistic. In the ensuing discussion an appeal to a legal definition of the term 'criminal' (i.e. to the current use by the majority of a group of specialists) would be out of place.

Question 3 demands clarification of current usage without implying that it could be challenged.

Question 4 introduces a moral discussion in which non-legal as well as legal uses of the term 'criminal' are in order.

We can now see that even if we ban question 4 and treat 'criminal' as a purely descriptive term, it is possible *to challenge any proposed definition, to question the methods of a discipline, the internal consistency of its theory, and its consistency with relevant advances in other disciplines, and to reject the point of view which is manifested in a certain way of using language.*

THE TECHNIQUE OF NON-COMMITMENT

To return to the 'witch' example: the term 'witch' certainly had pejorative overtones in the seventeenth-century in Salem: it was not a purely descriptive term. Yet the question 'Is X a witch or is she not?' was assumed to be a factual question which could be answered by expert demonologists whose impartiality and 'scientific' training enabled them to ignore emotive overtones. The dramatic power of Arthur Miller's reconstruction of the 1692 witchcraft trials in Salem (*The Crucible*) stems in part from the pathos of the intellectual impotence of reasonable, uneducated men when confronted with the expert reasoning of well-educated specialists with ecclesiastical authority. As the play unfolds, the spectator experiences sympathetic anxiety, and asks himself how he could defend *his* beliefs against a madness that is organized and authoritative.

I suggest that a certain class of scientific dispute may be clarified or even settled by 'determining the purpose or context', but that the examples I have given are members of a very large class that cannot be settled in this way. To indicate the boundary between the classes, I need to introduce a concept which I shall call the 'Technique of Non-commitment'. If I do not care whether X is called, regarded as, and treated as, a criminal or as a patient, I can use the non-committal, clarificatory technique: 'There is a valid use of the term "criminal" according to which X is a criminal, and there is a valid use of the term "patient" according to which X is a patient.' If, however, I am *committed to a certain point of view*, which conflicts with some other point of view, I shall reject not only the positive expression of the rival point of view but also the noncommittal eirenicon. I shall do this, not because either 'X is a criminal' or 'There is a valid use . . .' is a false statement, but because I want to dissociate myself both from the tacit promotion *and from the tacit condonation* of a certain way of talking, thinking, and acting. My position then becomes: 'X is not a criminal; the definition of the term by which she can be so called is derived from an out-of-date conceptual system, and the procedure by which she can be so treated is an out-of-date procedure.' The three conflicting statements, 'X is a criminal', 'There is a valid use . . .', and 'X is not a criminal', are all tacitly recommendatory, and it is interesting to notice that, while the first two can also be called *true* statements, the third, if we apply the bifurcation at all, *must be called a false statement if we accept current usage*. I choose the *false* statement. Adopting a fresh point of view and a fresh usage means consistently making 'false' statements and *making* them 'true'.

Perhaps we have hit upon a clue to one of the reasons for the common dissatisfaction, among philosophers and laymen, with some forms of philosophical debate. I have maintained that the techniques and theories of philosophy and of the sciences, including psychology, are changing *pari passu*; that the evolutionary and psychoanalytic theories can be more fruitfully thought of as *shifts to a genetic point of view* than as collections or systems of testable hypotheses, although many hypotheses can be and should be rigorously tested. I now suggest that the psychoanalytic point of view is incompatible with the 'commonsense' point of view as regards the explanation of human behaviour; that the incompatibility is relevant to philosophical debate because the philosopher is interested in making, defending, or attacking general abstract statements; he attacks some by putting forward counterexamples, and defends others by trying to accommodate to them the counter-examples of his opponent. The examples are usually chosen for their 'strength', that is, their acceptability to the company, and are therefore drawn from common sense or from uncontroversial science. The definitions of terms upon which the appeal to logical criteria depends are mainly dictionary definitions, and the usage which the philosopher refers to when demonstrating that out-of-date philosophy is out-of-date is 'ordinary educated usage'.

The technique of testing general statements by inventing relevant examples, and of appealing to ordinary usage to expose false presuppositions derived from grammatical analogy, has made and will continue to make important contributions to the progress of philosophy. *It is only when 'ordinary educated usage' conflicts with scientific usage or with that of an original writer that the onus rests on the philosopher to justify his choice of the common-sense point of view.* He will not be able to do so unless he understands the reasons *why* the scientist or any other original theorist thinks, talks, and writes as he does.

TOWARDS A TESTING PRINCIPLE

We can now try to formulate a very general principle which will be valid for both science and philosophy. *Whenever possible, an assertion or an assumption should be tested by scientific experiments, and/or by real or invented examples, all designed to show that it should be either abandoned or reformulated.* Sometimes both the philosophical and the scientific techniques will be applicable; sometimes only one or the other. When direct testing is impossible, a statement may be indirectly supported or undermined by relevant evidence and examples (e.g. indirect biological evidence supports but does not conclusively establish 'Every man's thought processes come to an end at his death').

Two forms of description which are apparently incompatible are genuinely incompatible only if they are appropriate to the same context (e.g. 'The table is solid' is not incompatible with the physicist's description of the table; the psychoanalyst's description of hysterical paralysis is not incompatible with the neurologist's). Forms of description which are correct according to current educated usage may at any time be rendered invalid by progress in science or philosophy.

M

14

'The Will'

An area of thought where the assumptions of common sense and the assumptions of psychoanalysis can be shown partly to coincide and partly to diverge is the group of problems relating to 'the will'.

The following attempt to distinguish, in the light of psychoanalytic discoveries, between the sound and the unsound assumptions underlying 'ordinary educated usage' as it relates to 'the will' serves as an illustration of the technique I am advocating: the application of philosophical analysis to psychological problems *with clear recognition of the methods and motives of the theorists who introduce new language projections*.

If we write down the reflexive expressions in everyday speech which are related to problems of decision and self-control, we will find an interesting pattern emerging. 'I found myself going there in spite of my resolution'; 'I caught myself boasting about it'; 'I didn't want to start a quarrel but I couldn't stop myself'; 'I didn't want to be cruel but I couldn't help myself'; 'I knew it would be better from every point of view to break off the affair but I couldn't tear myself away from her'; 'After a struggle I managed to wrench myself away'.

These examples have an element in common: they suggest instinctual impulses getting out of control. Whose control? It seems to be some organized and organizing part of the self.

Here is a second group: 'I dreaded the task I had set myself, but I forced myself to go through with it'; 'I knew that if I didn't cut off the gangrenous finger I would lose my hand, but I couldn't force myself to do it'; 'I had to screw myself up to ask for a rise'; 'I made myself eat the disgusting mess for fear of offending my hostess'; 'I whipped myself into a final spurt when he began overtaking me'; 'I hardened myself to go through with the operation in spite of her screams'. The common element here is coercion of instinctual or reflex impulses and reinforcement or encouragement of the organizing part of the self.

A third group: 'I decided to treat myself to three weeks' idleness'; 'I felt like indulging myself that evening and being wildly extravagant'; 'He was so sympathetic that I unburdened myself of my secret anxieties'; 'I threw myself into the work with a feeling of relief'; 'I abandoned myself to sensual enjoyment'; 'I flung myself into a round of pleasures and engagements so that I should have no time to think'. The common element is release of control, or active encouragement, of impulses usually held in check. The last example also suggests that one is keeping at bay some other part of the self which has not hitherto appeared: the punishing or tormenting part, which is the central element of the fifth group.

Consider a fourth group: 'I denied myself the pleasure of making a witty remark because I knew how wounding it would be'; 'I could have replied to his attack with a much more devastating interpretation, but I held myself back because he wasn't strong enough to take it'; 'I felt myself slipping into one of my disastrous rages but I managed to control myself just in time'; 'I felt myself sinking into one of my periodic fits of depression but I pulled myself together and went for a long, brisk walk'; 'I restrained myself from talking about my problems because I felt it would embarrass him'. The common element is restraint of impulses by the organizing part of the self.

Here is a fifth group: 'I punished myself for shirking work for so long by cancelling all engagements and shutting myself up in my room'; 'I kept torturing myself by visualizing her mutilated body and telling myself that it was I who had killed her'; 'I submitted myself to a humiliating self-examination'; 'I realized that all my life I had been defeating myself by stopping short whenever I was close to any kind of success'; 'I sentenced myself to six months' abstinence from drinking and smoking'; 'I was so disgusted with myself that I deliberately condemned myself to lifelong fidelity'; 'I lacerated myself by reconstructing all the incidents in my life I was ashamed of'. The common element in these examples is the suggestion of one part of the self punishing or hurting another.

Consider a sixth group: 'I steeled myself to sack him although I knew how he and his family would suffer'; 'I hardened myself against my feelings of sympathy and pity and sentenced her to the maximum penalty'; 'I forced myself to take the money in spite of my qualms of conscience'; 'I made myself join in with the lynching although I was filled with disgust and self-loathing'. Here the common element is the suppression by one part of the self of another, usually inhibiting part, sometimes called conscience, sometimes pity or sympathy. Where the inhibiting part is dominant we may say, 'I felt like breaking it off but could not bring myself to do it'.

Here is a seventh group: 'That was so unlike me that when I did it I must have been beside myself with rage'; 'I was annoyed with myself for taking her casual remark so much to heart'; 'I surprised myself planning a very mean kind of revenge'; 'I had not realized how jealous I was, but caught myself out when he invited her to dinner'; 'I despised myself for being so ineffectual when I really wanted to hit back'; 'When I came to myself I realized that I had killed him'; 'I tricked myself into working by starting on something only remotely connected with the task'; 'I shocked myself when I noticed how fascinated I was by the description of the tortures'; 'I saw through myself when I was posing as a sympathetic observer'. These examples have in common the tendency to treat as foreign, to disown, or to exclude from the organizing self, impulses which are either unconscious or only intermittently conscious.

We now come to the eighth and last group: 'I lost myself in the novel and when I came to myself I found that three hours had passed'; 'I sank myself in the music and was oblivious of everything else'; 'I gave myself up to a reverie'; 'I submitted myself to a hypnotist's suggestions and was soon lost in a a trance'. Here the common element is the absence of conflict, or the fusion of the habitually warring parts of the self, the abdication of control by the organizing part and of interference by the inhibiting, criticizing, and punishing part.*

The foregoing examples are, I think, a fairly exhaustive representation of the English idioms in which there is a transitive relation relevant to the 'will' between the personal pronoun and the corresponding reflexive pronoun. I have refrained from using psychoanalytic terms, but it is remarkable how closely the three warring parts of the self presupposed by ordinary language correspond to the id (the reflex and instinctual impulses), the ego (the organized and organizing part of the self), and the superego (the inhibiting and punishing part). These terms, however, have the disadvantage of being singular nouns, thereby encouraging the tendency to reification.

To recapitulate the classes of examples: the first suggest instinctual

---

* 'I wrestled with myself' may refer to a conflict between the organizing part of the self and an impulse, or between the organizing part and the critical or punishing part.

impulses getting out of control of the ego; the second suggest coercion of instinctual or reflex impulses and reinforcement or encouragement of the ego; the third imply release of control or active encouragement of impulses usually held in check; the fourth, restraint of impulses by the ego; the fifth, one part of the self punishing or hurting another; the sixth, suppression of feelings of pity, sympathy, or conscience; the seventh, the disowning or exclusion from the ego of unconscious or intermittently conscious impulses or actions; and the eighth, the fusion of conflicting parts of the self and the loss of self-awareness. The idioms, when analysed, reveal that the layman's unformulated understanding of the organization of mental processes coincides surprisingly closely with one of the model hypotheses of psychoanalysis.

At this point the hostile critic could object that Freud, far from making a discovery which coincides with the implicit understanding of common sense, has merely formulated suspect common-sense assumptions and elevated them to the rank of scientific hypotheses. We are once more faced with the problem of Fluctuating Scepticism. It is a matter of individual intellectual judgement to decide whether the complex psychological material which is organized and explained by psychoanalysis can be *equally well explained* without postulating the tripartite organization of the personality. It should be remembered, moreover, that the superego, to choose the most difficult psychoanalytic concept, was a relatively late addition to Freud's intellectual scheme, that it has been developed and fundamentally changed as a result of Melanie Klein's work with children, and that it is so far from coinciding with the conscience, or any other common-sense concept, that the modern theory of the superego, as distinct from the implicit presuppositions of ordinary language, appears both incomprehensible and repugnant to common sense.

AMBIGUITY OF THE PERSONAL PRONOUN

The interesting philosophical problem is the unsystematic ambiguity of the personal pronoun. Consider the example: 'I must have lost consciousness, and when I came to myself I realized that I had killed him.' The 'I-losing-consciousness' suggests the inhibition of the conscious ego; the 'I-coming-to-myself' suggests the renewed functioning of the conscious ego; the 'I-realizing' suggests the awareness of the continuing personality (a part of the ego); and the 'I-killing-him' suggests the innervation of the motor-system of the body by an unconscious impulse. While it is difficult or impossible to suggest

precisely what the first 'I', the second 'I', the 'myself', the third 'I', and
the fourth 'I' *refer** to, it is clear that the differences in their use are both
bewildering and philosophically important.

In the example 'I made myself join in with the lynching although I
was filled with self-loathing', the first 'I' seems to refer to the organizing ego and the second to the critical conscience. In the example 'I
shocked myself when I noticed how fascinated I was by the description
of the tortures', the first 'I' seems to refer to the part of the self which is
usually unconscious, probably the sadistic impulses; 'myself' to the
ego, or possibly to the superego; the second 'I' to a more comprehensive 'self' which includes that which shocked and that which was
shocked; and the third 'I' to the conscious ego.

The examples prompt the question, 'Is the attribution to the body, to
various impulses, to the ego, to the correlating self, to the superego,
and to various split-off sections of the ego, of the pronouns 'I', 'me',
'myself', 'you', 'yourself', 'he', 'him', 'himself', etc., a purely arbitrary
attribution? The term 'overcame' is instructive in this context. In the
examples 'I overcame the temptation to go to the cinema instead of
working' and 'I overcame the impulse to make a scathing remark', we
find the same transitive relation as in the fourth class I have distinguished
('I restrained myself from talking about my problems'): the restraint of
impulses by the ego. In the examples, 'I was overcome by the temptation', 'I was overcome by the impulse', 'The temptation overcame me',
the relation is as in the first class ('I couldn't help myself'): the over-
whelming of the ego by instinctual impulses. In the examples, 'I
overcame my qualms of conscience and stole the money', 'I overcame
my scruples and accepted the job', we find the same kind of relation
as in the sixth class ('I forced myself to take the money'): the suppression of the conscience by the ego. In all these examples the pronoun
refers to the ego, whether in its relations with impulses which can or
cannot be controlled, or in its relations with the conscience.

We may conclude, therefore, that although the pronouns are
unsystematically ambiguous, there is a tendency to identify the 'willing
self' with the ego, and to apply the pronoun in its 'willing' use to the
ego. The character adjectives, whether approbatory, such as 'self-
controlled', 'determined', 'resolute', 'strong-willed', 'forceful', 'purposeful', 'steadfast' and 'decisive'; or pejorative, such as 'wilful',
'self-willed', 'obstinate', 'impervious', 'intractable', 'unruly', 'incor-

---

* Some philosophers hold that pronouns do not 'refer' or designate at all. I find it
useful and innocuous to speak of the pronouns 'referring' or 'indicating' provided it is
understood that instances of 'referring' are as heterogeneous as instances of 'describing'.

rigible', 'inflexible', 'ungovernable', 'refractory', 'recalcitrant', 'head-strong', 'stubborn', and 'obdurate', are all applicable to children or adults who have strong, well-organized egos.* The only difference between the first class of adjectives and the second is that the first are applied to strong egos which evoke approval, and the second to strong egos which evoke disapproval in the speaker.

The Alexanders, Caesars, and Napoleons, in whom the ego is unusually strong, seem to evoke the admiration and envy, overt or covert, of multifarious individuals, including many intellectuals, who tend, as a class, to have egos which are painfully counterbalanced by the system of inhibitions. Just as it is difficult for the normal observer to believe that the hypnotized subject, in holding a weight at right angles to his body for twenty minutes, is making no *effort*, so it is difficult for the intellectual who is tormented by the choice between porterhouse steak and roast duck to believe that decisions involving thousands of lives can be made in a few seconds *without effort*.

SITUATIONS OF CONFLICT

The only situations which are philosophically interesting for the student of the 'will' are situations of conflict. Sometimes two conflicting impulses are conscious; sometimes the feeling of resistance to a consciously intended performance is unspecific and incomprehensible. A person may have the ability to write, the opportunity to write, many strong motives for writing, a feeling of exhilaration when he succeeds in writing, and the ability to work hard at any other task, and yet be unable to write except intermittently at long intervals. If he has a theory of Free Will† he will say that he has a weak will, and that from time to time he makes a tremendous effort and overcomes his inertia. If he believes that Free Will – in the sense of some factor to which scientific explanation is inapplicable – is an illusion, he will say that his conscious desire to write is counterbalanced by an unconscious fear of what writing signifies, that the desire and the fear fluctuate, and that whenever the fear is for any reason reduced it becomes possible for him to write.

All philosophers agree that the subjective feeling of 'free will' is

---

* Except when terms like 'unruly' and 'incorrigible' refer to strong impulses which cannot be controlled by external *or* internal (i.e. ego) discipline.

† 'Free Will' will henceforward be written with capitals to indicate the *illusory* concept; 'free will' indicates the *legitimate* commonsense concept as explained on pp. 179–80, paragraphs 1, 2, and 3.

sometimes illusory: the feeling, that is, that one contributes something different *in kind* to the interplay of competing impulses when one makes a decision. When the causal factor is known to the observer but not to the subject (e.g. a hypnotic suggestion), whatever reason is offered by the subject for the so-called 'deliberate decision' can be exposed as a rationalization. The regular resolutions or 'decisions' of the drug-addict to give up the drug can be exposed as self-deception if from a certain date to the end of his life he did not once give up the drug. If a compulsion, say the compulsion to terminate with a violent quarrel any relationship which reaches a certain degree of intimacy, is clearly recognized and described, then the multifarious reasons offered for the final break will be exposed as rationalizations. When it is realized that unconscious impulses act like hypnotic suggestions, and are carried into action in a similar variety of ways, sometimes as conscious acts with the feeling of compulsion, sometimes as conscious acts with the feeling of deliberate decision attended by ingenious rationalizations, sometimes as acts performed when the subject is unconscious, sometimes as acts in the form of accidents, or acts carried out in moments of inattention or fatigue, it becomes clear that the class of 'acts of Free Will' is coterminous with the class of 'acts not yet scientifically explained'.

RESPONSIBILITY

The relationship between scientific psychodynamics and 'acts of Free Will' is parallel to the relationship between physics and miracles. Some people believe that whatever science can or will explain, miracles will remain a subject for a different kind of comprehension. Others have a point of view which excludes miracles, even though they admit that the most advanced sciences cannot, and will never be able to, explain everything. The two parallel debates will continue indefinitely.

I do not wish to maintain that ordinary language is always so confused as to need rewriting. The eight classes of reflexive idioms mentioned above seem remarkably perspicacious when the systemic outline of mental processes is grasped. Only where common sense conflicts with clinical experience and understanding is it necessary to make explicit and to question the presuppositions of everyday language. One example must suffice. It is a presupposition of the law and of common sense that acts which are deliberate, intentional, premeditated, calculated, or planned (such as the legal 'malice aforethought') are *ipso facto* 'responsible'; this is a widely held belief although it is known even

to laymen that psychotics (schizophrenics, paran
depressives), if they are intelligent, are capable of
intentions, of devising elaborate plans, of arguing w
uity than their doctors, and of performing intrica
'responsible' person is not a person who can plan an
person who can form stable attachments which modify the re
the ego, the instinctual impulses, and the system of (som
inhibitions.

Nor do I wish to maintain that the illusion of Free Will is one that can be decisively dispelled by philosophical argument: the belief in the freedom of the Will, like the belief in miracles,* can be retained by sophisticated as well as by naïve thinkers. The illusion of Free Will is like a mirage: the better one understands its origin the less likely one is to be deceived by it. In the minds of many people it also resembles a mirage in that, even when the phenomenon has been explained and the *belief* in Free Will dispelled, the *illusory sensation* remains. The parallel is not perfect, however, as it is possible in the case of Free Will, and not in the case of the mirage, for both the belief *and* the illusory sensation to be totally dispelled: there are some people who are able to choose or decide after deliberation without experiencing the illusion of Free Will. Even if a writer does not know WHY he has used capitals rather than italics, for example, he may not even *feel* that his choice was magically undetermined.

What I do wish to maintain is that mental processes are amenable to scientific explanation, and that a very large number of previously inexplicable psychological anomalies and paradoxes have been explained by detailed psychoanalytic investigation during the past seventy years. Nevertheless a philosophical paradox remains which we can now try to solve. Let us assume for the moment that psychodynamic problems can be approached in the same scientific spirit as physical problems, and that the subjective conviction that 'the will' is free – that there are 'acts of Free Will' which occasionally intervene in the interplay of impulses, and are *alteri generis*, having no postulated physiological counterparts – is a delusion which is due to the identification of the self with those mental processes which include the winning impulse. Why, then, are punishment, reward, encouragement, praise, blame, censure, approval, disapproval, incentives, deterrents, etc., often effective in modifying character and influencing behaviour? If Free

---

* The erudite forms of both beliefs are examples of the Sophistication of Magical Thinking; the belief in Free Will originates, to use Freud's concept, in Omnipotence of Thought.

is an illusion, it seems to follow that everyone *has* to do what he in fact does, cannot *help* doing what he does, and is not 'responsible' for moral or legal transgressions in the sense that he can be fairly and justly blamed or punished for them. If this is so, why is there an important difference between such terms as 'wicked', 'evil', 'sinful', 'virtuous', 'chaste' . . . which have today dropped out of the language projection of science, are gradually disappearing from common-sense talk, and are self-consciously retained by a minority, and such terms as 'responsible', 'irresponsible', 'amenable' 'incorrigible' . . . which are all natural, intelligible, and indispensable elements of the language, and not the defiant vocabulary of a conservative rearguard?

The answer will, I believe, seem obvious when stated. If we accept something like Freud's threefold division of mental processes, the problem can be solved; if we do not, it cannot. The ego is the organization which corresponds to the part of the common-sense 'self' which tries to control and organize impulses; it is partly conscious, partly unconscious. The superego, for the most part unconscious, is the inhibiting and tormenting part of the common-sense 'self'. If a child or an adult has an intimate relationship with a person whose love he needs and does not want to lose, he will pay the price for that love, if it is demanded, of consciously controlling (ego) or inhibiting (superego) impulses which the loved person discourages. If his development produces an ego which is strong in relation to both unorganized impulses and the superego, he will be strong-willed, resolute, decisive and responsible; if it produces an ego which is weak in relation to his impulses, he will be self-destructively mercurial, impetuous, and irresponsible; if it produces an ego which is weak in relation to the superego, he will be indecisive, self-questioning, self-doubting, over-conscientious, and conscience-ridden; if it produces an ego which is exceptionally weak, he will be psychotic.

We can now see both why the terms 'responsible' and 'irresponsible' are intelligible and why the common-sense and legal conception of the function of praise, blame, reward, and punishment is mistaken. A responsible person is one who forms strong positive attachments to people, groups, or ideas; attachments which are so valuable to him that he is prepared to sacrifice gratifications for their sake. The strongest attachment may, in adult life, be not to a human, but to an ideal being, such as God. Because the responsible person is prepared to make sacrifices he is amenable to praise and blame. Impersonal punishment by a stranger, however, someone who is neither loved nor admired, cannot increase the strength of the ego – though it may increase fear and circumspection – and can never have a stabilizing effect on anyone's character. Therefore imprisonment without therapy or rehabilitation, and supervision by guards or warders who inspire neither affection nor respect, do not protect society from the recidivism, often predictable, which results from increased fear and resentment combined with diminished occupational opportunity. Such imprisonment is primarily a ritual revenge.

The paradox has now dissolved. The expression 'responsible', like 'free will', has a legitimate and an illegitimate use. When used to mean 'liable to be called to account' or 'capable of giving up gratifications for the sake of a relationship or a goal', it expresses a legitimate concept; when used to mean 'deserving blame or punishment because he could have done otherwise' it expresses an illegitimate concept derived from the illusion of Free Will. Provided that no disaster in infancy has destroyed the capacity for strong and lasting attachments to human beings, anything that tends to strengthen the ego at the expense of the id and the superego, including praise, blame, reward, punishment, encouragement, discouragement, by loved or respected individuals or groups, will tend to produce a strong, decisive character, to which the approbatory adjectives ('resolute', etc.) will be applied by those who approve of the direction it takes, and the pejorative adjectives ('headstrong', etc.) by those who disapprove.

THE AMBIGUITY OF 'CONSCIOUS'

We have not yet found the key to the psychological difference between those who believe that 'the will is free' and those who regard this belief as a delusion. Here too, I think, the explanation will seem obvious when stated. Those who are familiar either by systematic introspection or through psychoanalysis with the details of psychodynamic explanation must necessarily observe, over and over again, first, that the subjective feeling of Free Will occurs when two incompatible impulses appear simultaneously to consciousness, or when an alternative course of action, 'equally likely', is provided as an afterthought, and when the 'self' is identified with those mental processes which include the winning impulse; second, that the attribution of the 'self' to the winning or to the losing impulse is often arbitrary; and third, and in my opinion conclusively, that the question whether either or both of the imcompatible impulses is conscious at the moment of the decisive supremacy of one of them is irrelevant to the scientific explanation of the conflict and its resolution. To put it another way, the transitory pinpoint of consciousness – the momentary awareness which will not endure from the beginning to the end of this sentence – is irrelevant to the scientific explanation of the interplay of id, ego, and superego impulses.

An example may make this point clearer. If a man is suffering from a compulsion to kill, there are three possibilities, each of which may be instantiated on successive occasions. First, he may be fully aware of a conflict between incompatible impulses which lasts up to the moment of the act, and he feels that he has been overwhelmed by the impulse to kill: he could not stop himself. Second, he may be fully aware of the conflict but feel that he *decides* to give in to the impulse. Third, he may be aware of the conflict up to a few seconds before the killing, lose consciousness, and come to consciousness a few seconds after the act of killing, having made no decision and having had no sensation of being overwhelmed. These variations, although themselves a problem for psychoanalytic study, may be irrelevant to the scientific explanation of the three successive failures of the ego to control the obsessional impulse.

The term 'irrelevant' suggests a paradox. Consciousness is clearly seen in analysis to be, as Freud described it, 'a transient quality which attaches to a psychical process only in passing (*Moses and Monotheism*, 1939, p. 96), and 'a quality of the psychical, which may be present in addition to other qualities or may be absent' (*The Ego and the Id*, 1923a, Chapter 1). The paradox is this: if psychoanalysis strengthens the ego in relation to the id and the superego by making conscious what was formerly unconscious, how can the fact of being conscious be irrelevant to the control by the ego of obsessional impulses?

The answer to this question is linked with the philosophical problem of the personal pronoun. Some philosophers object to the term 'ambiguity', whether systematic or unsystematic, as applied to the pronoun, on the grounds that it does not 'refer', as descriptive nouns refer, and so it cannot refer ambiguously. Yet however the problem is stated there *is* a philosophical problem concerning the use of the personal pronoun in such sentences as 'I dreaded the task I had set myself, but I forced myself to go through with it'. The key to both problems is the ambiguity of 'being conscious' and 'making conscious'. The strengthening of the ego is achieved by extending the *system* 'ego', which is partly unconscious, partly conscious. The term 'conscious' in the last sentence is equivalent to 'preconscious', or 'capable of entering consciousness', and this is distinct from 'conscious' in the senses of 'momentarily experienced' and 'momentarily aware'. An impulse which is not under the control of the ego may enter consciousness, and part of the ego may become unconscious; the problem of such variations is distinct from the problem of the dispositional interrelations of the system 'ego' with the id and the superego. The relative freedom of the id and the superego during sleep is normally conditional upon the immobilization of the motor system of the body. If an obsessional impulse to kill can be carried into action, there is a *dispositional* disturbance of the equilibrium of the id, ego, and superego, whatever impulse may, or may not, be momentarily accessible to consciousness.

REFERENTS OF THE PERSONAL PRONOUN

We are now in a position to solve the problem of the pronoun. *The personal pronoun can be used to indicate*:

1. the ego as a whole;
2. the split-off element of the ego which is felt as the continuing personality: in some sense 'the same' in spite of growth, development and decay, and in spite of changes of state such as sleeping and waking, health and sickness;
3. any *phase* element of the ego, which can be split in an indefinite number of ways, as it is constituted at a given point of time;
4. the id as a whole;
5. any id impulse or its agent (e.g. part of the body);
6. the superego as a whole;
7. any superego impulse;
8. the total personality (the fused id, ego, and superego);
9. the body, whether at a time of consciousness or unconsciousness.

In the example, 'I dreaded the task I had set myself but I forced myself to go through with it', the subject of 'dreaded' is a split-off part of the ego; the subject of 'had set' is the ego; 'myself' is the whole personality; the subject of 'forced' is the ego; and the object of 'forced' ('myself') is the whole personality.

The 'grasshopper' behaviour of the pronoun is the key to the problem of 'free will'. The solution falls into four parts:

1. There are no decisions or acts that are 'free' in the sense that it would be unreasonable to look for explanations in terms of conscious or unconscious motives and to attempt to relate them to foregoing or similar decisions or actions. This conviction, like the parallel conviction that unexplained physical phenomena are to be studied *by the same general method* as those which have already been explained, grows with every successful explanation, but cannot be proved to the sceptic.

2. The kind of action to which the description 'act of free will' is used to apply is the act which satisfies the following three conditions:

(a) It is either preceded by deliberation and choice – that is, by contemplation of alternative modes of behaviour, and the decision to carry out one of the alternatives – or is subsequently provided with a *retrospective* alternative mode of behaviour (see footnote on p. 184);

(b) It is carried out by a person whose ego is, at the time of acting, strong, so that his action, in common with most of his behaviour, is relatively ego-syntonic, and not the effect of an ego-dystonic, irrational impulse;

(c) It is relatively free from external constraint or coercion, whether physical or moral.

The person who acts 'of his own free will' in this sense would give an account of his motives similar to that of a disinterested observer. Far from being inaccessible to psychological explanation, this kind of behaviour will usually be the easiest to explain. Further, *it is possible to use all the idioms in which the phrase 'free will' occurs in this sense without having the illusion of Free Will.*

3. Where there is lacking any one of the above three factors – deliberation, ego strength, and freedom from constraint – we may reasonably hesitate to call an action an 'act of free will'. For example:

(a) We do not customarily call our unnoticed blinking, our spontaneous laughter or weeping, our 'instinctive' leap to the safety of the pavement, even our beautifully timed winning stroke in the tennis match . . . 'acts of free will'. We do not, even if we have strong egos and are unconstrained, because we have not deliberated before doing these things.

(b) The premeditated crime or futile action of a paranoic or other psychotic should not be called an 'act of free will', even though there is deliberation and freedom from constraint; and this holds for premeditated heavy drinking, drug-taking, and sexual crimes. He is lacking in ego strength.

(c) We may hesitate to call the payment of money to a blackmailer an 'act of free will', even though the victim is normal, has a strong ego, and has made a voluntary decision after deliberation. He is not free from constraint.

In each of these three examples one factor only is absent. Where two or all three factors are lacking we do not hesitate to say 'He did not do it of his own free will'.

4. The illusion of Free Will is due in part to the bewildering convention of the personal pronoun. It may arise (i) from the confusion of

the split-off element of the ego which is felt as the continuing personality (the enduring, *non-phase* element, p. 179, paragraph 2) with a transitory element of the ego as it is constituted at a given point of time (the *phase* element, p. 179, paragraph 3).

'*I could have passed the examination*' may be *either* an honest conditional which can be expanded: 'I would have passed if I had worked harder' or '. . . if I had not had unconscious self-punishing impulses'; OR a disingenuous conditional, not to be expanded, which confuses the enduring *non-phase* 'I', embracing all the potentialities I believe I possess at my best, with the limited, transitory, *phase* 'I' who actually took the examination.

It may arise (ii) from the confusion of two different, transitory phase elements of the ego, a confusion which is facilitated by the additional, distinct, but concurrent use of the pronoun for the continuing personality.

Here is an example: '*I hesitated until the waiter became impatient and then I chose roast duck.*' The 'I' that hesitated is and is not the 'I' that chose. The transitory phase element, the hesitating 'I', embraced both inclinations, the inclination to eat steak and the inclination to eat duck, the winning and the losing inclination; the transitory phase 'I' that *chose* duck embraced only the winning inclination, and dissociated itself from the losing; the enduring, non-phase 'I' of the continuing personality remained unchanged. If the first transitory phase element, the hesitating 'I', is confused with the second transitory phase element, the 'I' that has chosen – the confusion being facilitated by the use of 'I' for the continuing personality – it becomes possible to say 'I could have chosen steak' without providing a protasis, without, that is, providing an imaginative reformulation of the initial conditions.

The ego associates itself with the winning inclination when the winning inclination 'feels' ego-syntonic, reasonable, acceptable. If the choice were between nut steak and duck, however, and the chooser a vegetarian, the inclination to eat duck would be ego-dystonic, unacceptable, and if it won he might say, 'When the waiter became impatient I found myself ordering roast duck.' The locution 'I found myself' is a means of dissociating the ego from the winning inclination, the 'I' referring to the ego or part of it, and 'myself' to the agent of the disowned impulse.

DELIBERATION AND DECISION

Deliberation, then, or hesitation between inclinations or impulses, may be resolved in different ways.

First: where two or more inclinations are equally ego-syntonic, and there seems to be no reason for preferring one to another, the ego associates itself with the winning inclination the moment the decision is made, and the illusion of Free Will arises from mistaken identification of two different, transitory phase elements of the ego. The transitory phase 'I' that has irrevocably chosen is thought and *felt* to be *identical* with the past, transitory phase 'I' that still had alternatives to choose from. The identification is facilitated by the additional, different, but concurrent use of 'I' for the split-off, non-phase element of the ego which is experienced as the enduring personality. Hence 'I could have chosen steak' is felt to mean more than 'I would have chosen steak if . . . (I had known how tough the duck was, etc.)'. The conditional with the explicit protasis is an honest conditional, and the 'I' refers back imaginatively to the undecided chooser in changed conditions; the conditional with the suppressed protasis *may* be disingenuous, and the 'I' that has chosen may be magically identified with the 'I' that still had a choice to make, *while keeping the initial conditions unchanged.* If, in an imaginative reconstruction of the past, the initial conditions are kept unchanged, then everything must occur in the reconstruction as it *did* occur in reality. ('I could *not* have chosen steak'). *If in the reconstruction the initial conditions are changed, then the change should be susceptible of explicit formulation in the protasis of the past unfulfilled conditional sentence.*

'*You could have given up smoking*', for example, may have any of a number of implications. It may mean: 'You would have given up smoking if you had been treated with a drug which causes acute nausea whenever you puff a cigarette.' Here the initial conditions have been imaginatively changed, and the change has been explicitly formulated in the 'if' clause. This is an honest conditional.

It may be an indirect reproach: 'Why didn't you give up smoking (if you were so hard up that you couldn't pay the grocery bills)?' The explicit reformulation might be: 'You would have given up smoking if you had been concerned enough about your debts to sacrifice some gratification.' This conditional is intelligible and honest, and does not presuppose Free Will.

It may, however, be intended to mean: 'Even if all the initial conditions, including your circumstances, your character traits, your state of mind, your motives, etc., had been exactly as they were, you *could* have given up smoking by an act of Free Will, and therefore you are to blame.' This is a disingenuous conditional, because no protasis except a vacuous* one can be provided for a 'would have' conditional sentence.

---

* Neither this statement nor any other, of course, can decisively terminate the dispute, because the believer in Free Will can assert that 'You could have given up smoking' is

Every honest 'could have' conditional is analysable in terms of a 'would have' conditional with an explicit protasis.

Second: the decision may represent itself as 'dictated' by facts or arguments, as when a juryman decides that the accused is guilty after he has 'weighed all the evidence'. A conscientious juryman would not naturally speak of deciding 'of his own free will', because a decision opposed to his judgement would be ego-dystonic, and so there are for him no genuine alternatives. Only an unscrupulous juryman, who deliberately voted against his judgement, would feel that he had a genuine choice and was acting of his own free will; an unscrupulous person, we may note in passing, is one in whom inclinations which are generally regarded as immoral are ego-syntonic.

Third: there may be a conflict between two inclinations, one acceptable and the other unacceptable to the ego, and the unacceptable, ego-dystonic inclination may be chosen ('I hoped I would have the strength to refuse, but when the time came I accepted the invitation'). Such decisions are intermediate between the feeling of being overwhelmed by an irresistible impulse and the feeling of choosing freely; although there is a choice the choice is usually not felt to be free. In such cases ego strength is diminished, but not to the point of utter helplessness; hence their intermediate status.

Fourth: if an ego-syntonic inclination triumphs over one that is ego-dystonic, not only does the ego associate itself with the winning inclination, but there may also be a feeling of exhilaration or depression: exhilaration if the demonstration of ego strength is felt to manifest the strength of the whole personality; depression if the suppressed inclination is felt to be an important need which is being denied, with consequent impoverishment of the personality. The successful decision to give up smoking, for example, may, if the craving ceases entirely, produce a feeling of exhilaration, whereas the decision not to accept an interesting job with rich opportunities, for fear of endangering the family, may cause a deep depression.

Fifth: if a period of indecision ('wrestling with oneself') is terminated by the involuntary execution of an uncontrollable impulse, the ego disowns the impulse, and there is no subjective feeling of choice even if the impulse is conscious at the time it is carried out.

Sixth: if a period of vacillation is ended by a decision for which no

---

analysable as 'You would have given up smoking if you had exercised your Free Will', just as the believer in miracles can say 'The eclipse would not have occurred if a miracle had taken place'. In both cases it can be denied that the protasis is vacuous or question-begging.

good reasons can be given, as when a girl makes the unreluctant decision to marry a man who seems to everyone else to be unsuitable, there are at least two possibilities. A phantasy conception of the situation destined to ensue upon the course which is chosen may make that course seem so desirable that doubt is dispelled; or an intuitive, inarticulate insight into strong unconscious needs may cause a temporary fusion of id, ego, and superego: may, that is, for a time eliminate the habitual conflict between instinctual impulses, the organizing, planning part of the self, and the inhibiting, criticizing, and punishing part of the self. Whichever explanation is appropriate, the person may say either 'I made up my mind and acted of my own free will' or 'The decision seemed to be made for me, and I found myself wholeheartedly agreeing to everything'. The person may even say 'I made up my mind and acted of my own free will, but I could not have done otherwise'. Hesitation in the choice of locutions is a sign of a truce between habitually warring parts of the personality.

The difficulty of distinguishing between these two possibilities, first, withdrawal into phantasy, when the fusion of id, ego, and superego is achieved by partial or total exclusion of unwelcome reality, and, second the simultaneous recognition and acceptance of what is important in external *and* internal reality, is reminiscent of the problem of distinguishing between unwelcome beliefs that a person is forced to face by his need for consistency and rationality of thought, and unwelcome beliefs that issue from irrational fear or guilt.

CONDITIONS FOR THE ILLUSION OF FREE WILL

This brief selection of examples of various kinds of deliberation has enabled us to state more precisely the conditions which make possible the illusion of Free Will. The illusion of Free Will is possible in a subclass of the class of situations in which, after a period of concurrent or alternating* awareness of incompatible inclinations or impulses, one impulse alone is felt to be destined for enactment, or is suddenly enacted, and the ego immediately associates itself with that impulse because it is ego-syntonic, and dissociates itself from the alternative impulses. The feeling that the one impulse is destined for enactment

---

* It may also happen that an **alternative** which is subsequently thought of as having been possible at the time of decision may not be conscious *at the time of decision*. For example, if a man says to a friend 'Come and join me in my firm', and the friend immediately agrees, he may subsequently feel that he had a choice and acted of his own free will *because he could have refused*. The alternative course of action, i.e. refusal, is supplied retrospectively, thus providing a choice.

may itself be an illusion, and the subject may be the only person who believes that his 'decisions' and 'resolutions' are more than subjective experiences (e.g. the drug-addict). There is no criterion for distinguishing between illusory and genuine choices, decisions, and resolutions except subsequent enactment, and that is too rigorous. A decision may be genuine, but its enactment may be prevented by a change in the situation.

Of the class of situations described above, the illusion of Free Will is possible only when it is possible to be in doubt as to the reason why that one particular impulse is suddenly felt to be destined for enactment. If a person *feels* that he really has been persuaded by the evidence to vote 'Guilty', he has no illusion of Free Will, whether the evidence is the *real reason* for his decision or a pretext which facilitates rationalization.

The illusion of Free Will is possible if, and only if:

1 there is a period of concurrent or alternating awareness of incompatible inclinations or impulses (or an alternative is supplied retrospectively);

2 one impulse alone is suddenly felt to be destined for enactment, or is suddenly enacted;

3 it is possible to be in doubt as to why it is *that* particular impulse and no other;

4 the ego associates itself with that impulse because it is ego-syntonic; and

5 the ego dissociates itself from the alternative impulses.

PSEUDO–OBJECTIVITY

The argument of this chapter is an example of the philosophical analysis of common-sense idioms and their presuppositions from a psychoanalytic point of view. Most of the common-sense idioms are seen to be compatible with that point of view, but there has occurred at one stage a word which may well have shocked the philosopher and the scientist: the overt recommendatory 'should' (p. 180, 3(b)).

That is the tiny leak that sinks the ship of pseudo-objectivity.* There is a strong temptation for the serious writer to adopt a style (the textbook style) which suggests that he is brushing away the surface soil of confusion to reveal the bedrock of fact. The pronoun 'I' does not appear, except in examples, and the area of conflicting opinions, where

---

* Fallacy of Pseudo-objectivity, defined p. 202.

pseudo-objectivity has to be abandoned in favour of personal commitment to a controversial point of view, is either skilfully circumnavi-
gated or misleadingly represented as an area of established fact. The
word 'should' destroys the illusion of objectivity, and reveals that an
individual writer is putting forward an individual point of view, based
upon his individual intellectual judgement, and that when the point of
view of common sense, of law, or of any other discipline, coincides
with his own, he is recommending that its terminology should be retained, and when it conflicts with his own, he is recommending that its
terminology should be revised.

15

Recapitulation: 'Facts'; Communication; Language Projections; Fallacies and Mechanisms

There are, in the argument of this book, many interwoven strands. Four of these will now be identified and retraced:

A. The examination of the problematic term 'fact';
B. The attempt to distinguish several forms of communication;
C. The introduction of the concept of language projections;
D. The correlation of philosophical fallacies and misleading techniques of argument with psychological mechanisms and techniques.

A. 'FACT'

To begin with the term 'fact': at the end of Chapter 4 I suggested that what we call factual statements are hypotheses which we feel no scientific or philosophical need, at the present time, to question or modify. This is a psychological account which many readers may find inadequate. 'When I say', it may be objected, 'that the *facts* of the world have remained unchanged for millions of years – before man existed, when man could utter sounds but not coherent speech, when he could speak, but only in the language of superstition – when I say that the facts are completely independent of anything man has ever thought or said, I mean that the tides have ebbed and flowed, the trees have burgeoned and shed their leaves, the birds and fish have migrated and returned. . . . All these are *facts*, whatever language you use to describe them.'

A similar objection could be raised to the suggestion that facts cannot be re-allocated (p. 28), or that new ways of talking, writing, and thinking, when tested and established, initiate new facts (p. 41).

'When I speak of re-allocating facts', it may be said, 'I mean that the theories which purport to explain the movements and significance of the stars, or the rise and fall of the tides, may change with the advance of science, but the *fact* that there are stars which exhibit a certain pattern of changing interrelations and the *fact* that the tides ebb and flow at certain intervals have never changed: they are timeless facts, independent even of the existence of human observers or of human language.'

The problem was put in the form of a paradox in Chapter 3: chromosomes, like the blue of the sky or the sourness of lemons, are neither mind-dependent nor mind-independent (p. 41). Is this a paradox that can be resolved? Some modern philosophers give a neat and simple answer: a factual statement is a true empirical statement; a fact is a proposition to which a true empirical statement refers; and there are many facts (true propositions) for which no statements (or sentences) have been formulated.

My objection to this view is threefold: first, the use of 'true' in this context is an instance of what I shall call the *Supra-controversy Fallacy*,* which is widespread in philosophy. If there is a genuine philosophical problem it results from a conflict between incompatible beliefs or points of view: either those of rival schools of thought or those within the mind of an individual person. The conflict is evaded, not resolved, by standing aloof and relating the term 'fact' to the term 'true' without reference to any actual dispute. Part of what we ask when we ask 'Is that really a fact?' is: 'Is that really true?' and: 'Is that an empirical proposition?' – so that to say 'If it is true and if it is an empirical proposition it is a fact' does not solve the problem of 'facts'.

The second objection is to the *Technique of Non-commitment* (p. 165, 'Is X a criminal or a patient?' . . .). A statement may be true according to current English usage, and yet I may refuse to call it a true statement because my point of view conflicts with that of common sense or current scientific convention. To say that a statement is a true statement in ordinary usage, therefore, is not equivalent to *asserting* it.

The third objection is to unformulated propositions. I can assert that the tides ebbed and flowed before the advent of man because I have formulated the assertion, but I cannot maintain that there are facts that have never been formulated† and at the same time adhere to the definition of 'fact' as 'that to which a true statement refers'.

The sky is blue because most of us see it as blue; lemons are sour

* For definition see p. 206.

† Except in the innocuous sense in which we can say that there are questions that have never been formulated.

because they taste sour to most of us; chromosomes are the units of heredity because they are the elements which we can identify in the complex associated with heredity. 'The sky is blue' does not *describe* a relation between the passing of the sun's rays through the atmosphere and our mode of seeing: the statement *reflects* the relationship; 'He is a tall man' does not *describe* the relation of his height to the average height: the statement *reflects* the relation; 'The Pantheon is nearly 2,000 years old' *reflects* our current convention of time measurement; 'I flew from Sydney to Tahiti and arrived at Tahiti at an earlier time than the time I left Sydney' *reflects* the date-line convention; 'This is the path of an electron' does not state a part of the physicist's theory: it *reflects* it; 'That sobbing was a reaction to the interpretations' *reflects* psycho-analytic theory.

The Reflecting Use of Language

We have hit upon yet another important use of language which, like the suggestive use, produces a class of statements that cannot be judged true or false without elaboration. 'I arrived at Tahiti at an earlier time than the time I left Sydney' is no less *true* than 'I arrived at Tahiti nine hours after I left Sydney', said of the same flight. They are true 'factual' statements which *reflect* two different systems of reference. The first reflects the relation of clocks in the various parts of the world; the second reflects the temporal progression as experienced by the traveller. I shall call this the *reflecting use of language* and try to use the concept to throw light on the 'mind-dependence' paradox.

Like the apparently incompatible statements about the flight from Sydney to Tahiti, 'This lemon is sour' and 'This lemon is sweet' can be truly asserted of the same lemon. The first statement *reflects* a comparison with fruit-in-general; the second with lemons-in-general. The description of the sky as blue by a colour-blind man is not anomalous because his description reflects the normal usage, which he has been taught, of the colour-discriminating majority.

The mind-dependence paradox arises for the following reasons: the passing of sunrays through the earth's atmosphere at a certain angle and in certain atmospheric conditions is a necessary* but not a sufficient condition of the sky being called blue by a human observer, and the observer's having normal colour-vision is a necessary but not a sufficient condition of his seeing the sky as blue. Further, the regular passing of sunrays, etc., and the normal colour-vision and condition of

* Unless the language is eccentric or artificial.

most observers, are together a necessary but not a sufficient condition of the language convention which allows the timeless (as well as the episodic) description of the sky as blue. Briefly, 'The sky is blue' *reflects* physical, psychological, and linguistic conditions in a single utterance.

Now, clearly, all utterances in all languages *reflect* conditions, conventions, frames of reference, points of view, and so on. The distinction I wish to make, as in the *focusing* and *enactive* uses elucidated earlier (p. 16, footnote; p. 95) is between situations and contexts in which one use *predominates* over others. We can distinguish, for example, between explicit statements such as 'The sun goes round the earth *if* we take the earth as a fixed point of reference' and *reflecting* statements such as 'The sun goes round the earth' which leave the point of reference implicit. 'We cannot ever know the thoughts of others' is not an incontrovertibly *false* statement, but one which reflects the point of view of Fluctuating or Unrestricted Scepticism, while 'We can know the thoughts of others very much as others know ours, and others often know ours surprisingly well' reflects emancipation from the Fluctuating Scepticism Fallacy.

We have seen that the search for absolutely 'neutral facts' is as futile as the search for certain knowledge. When we have squeezed out all the elements in language which reflect theory, special language projections, points of view, . . . the remaining pulp is poor nutriment. Yet we cannot leave the problem of 'facts' without glancing at the legitimate antithetical uses of the term. Fact–theory, fact–explanation, factual–tendentious (reporting), factual–verbal, factual–analytic, fact–fiction, fact–phantasy, fact–rumour, fact–surmise, fact–illusion, fact–delusion – these are the antitheses that come to mind. To each antithesis there corresponds a distinct nuance of the 'fact' concept. To each nuance the same technique of analysis can be applied. Here the discussion must be confined to the fact–theory and fact–explanation antitheses.

Re-allocation of Facts

If we say that 'facts have been re-allocated', we may mean any one of three things:

1 that what, according to our present beliefs, we are using true and unequivocal factual statements to describe, corresponds in some way with what was formerly described by false, equivocal, or misleading statements; or

2 that we can still use some of the statements which were used by the outmoded theorist, while relating them to a new theory; or

3 that *events* which were formerly misdescribed have been continuing unchanged independently of any theorizing.

Here is an example of (1): What is referred to by our present-day precise descriptions of the orbits of the planets round the sun may be thought to correspond in some way to what was described by the system of Hipparchus. The reason why this belief, or better, feeling, has such a strong hold on common sense is that we think of past events in terms of the current scientific language projection and 'feel' that there was a veridical picture of the world (our picture) in existence in the time of Hipparchus (in other words, 'the facts') which Hipparchus failed to see, or of which he could see only a part. We have only to remember that nineteenth-century scientists 'saw' the past in terms of a different, simpler language projection, which they believed to be veridical with more confidence than modern scientists believe *their* speculations, and we realize at once how probable it is that the current scientific language projection will seem inadequate and misleading to scientists of the twenty-second century. *A fortiori* the simplified projection now available to the layman will be out of date.

The concept 'language projection' may help us to combat the above illusion, although it is only at the acme of our intellectual awareness and self-discipline that we can see our own language projection as one of many alternatives. Imagine a child who has been taught geography with the aid of maps exclusively drawn to Mercator's projection, and who believes that the maps he has studied are *the veridical maps* of the world. He is now told that the lines of longitude need not be parallel, that an *equally veridical map* would show them as meeting at a point at the North Pole and meeting at another point at the South Pole. He is now asked to visualize, without being *shown* an equally veridical map, the shapes of the continents of the world as they would appear on maps of various projections, and to visualize them as those projections are (not exemplified but) *specified*. His task, formidable as it is, is less baffling than our attempts to see our own language projection, with all its conceptual implications, as a projection which will be progressively modified with the advance of scientific and philosophical understanding to the point where our distant descendants will have to make a tolerant effort of the imagination to project themselves back to our antiquated point of view. *The continuity* (however imperceptible) *of the modification of language projections implies continuous rewriting or rethinking of 'the facts'*.

When we compare 'I arrived at Tahiti earlier than I left Sydney' with 'I arrived at Tahiti nine hours after I left Sydney', have we any justification for saying that there is a single fact which has been referred to in two different ways? Or for saying that a fact has been re-allocated? We feel that a single *event* has been referred to in two different, equally valid, alternative ways, and the 'fact' that there is only one event, and that this event can be described by a statement which *reflects* the relativity of the two points of view, tempts us to answer 'Yes' to the question. I can say, for example, 'I arrived at Tahiti nine hours after I left Sydney, when the time, according to international agreement, was earlier than when I left Sydney'. It must be insisted, however, that the 'fact' referred to by the last, explicitly relative, statement, is different from the facts referred to by the alternative, non-relative statements, and that an undescribed event is not a fact. It is misleading, therefore, to speak of re-allocating a fact, or referring to it in two different ways. The precise form of words would be unimportant, as the use of 'The sun is rising' is unimportant, but for two things: the existence of the live, difficult philosophical problem of relating language projections to 'events', and the prevalence of the Fact-finding Fallacy.

We now come to the second possible interpretation of 'facts have been re-allocated' (p. 191, 2): that we can still use some of the statements which were used by the outmoded theorist. We can still say 'There was a total eclipse of the sun visible in Greece on 28 May 585 B.C.', just as Thales, who was credited by the Greeks with the prediction of the eclipse, was able to make that statement in 584 B.C. Similarly, scientists of the thirtieth century A.D. will be able to say 'There was a total eclipse of the sun visible at Land's End, Britain, on 11 August 1999 A.D.', just as some of *us* will be able to make that statement in A.D. 2000. Should we say that the fact referred to by Thales has been re-allocated? There seems to be no justification for this view; the statements do not *reflect* any scientific theory, and are therefore epistemologically uninteresting. The fact has remained the same, and has not been re-allocated, because changes in theory have not necessitated any modification in the translatable *statement* Thales was able to make.

The third possible interpretation (p. 191, 3) is that *events* which were formerly misdescribed have been continuing unchanged independently of any theorizing. When we use the term 'events' we feel that we have disentangled ourselves from the net of language. It has been pointed out (p. 44, 1c) that we have reason to believe that neurological events occur which we cannot describe because of the limitations of scientific techniques. We know, however, what *kind* of description to expect if new techniques are invented. We also have reason to believe that events have occurred and are occurring whose description we cannot even adumbrate; and this belief reinforces our feeling that 'events' are independent of language projections. Even more independent than 'events', which reflect our conception of a time continuum, and 'entities', which reflect our notion of 'things', are 'data' and 'phenomena', which seem to have been invented expressly to reflect as little as possible. The important philosophical question is whether this independence is an illusion.

I suggest that it is legitimate to *postulate* undescribed events but not to apply to them the term 'facts', or any other terms which reflect a language projection or presuppose the true-false antithesis. To apply such terms to them is to fall into the *Supra-controversy Fallacy*: the fallacy, or fallacious technique, of discussing philosophico-scientific problems – problems, that is, which are not purely philosophical – as if we could, or might, achieve a purely philosophical God's-eye-view which is superior to the points of view of those engaged in a *practical* as well as theoretical philosophico-scientific controversy. Corresponding to the supra-controversy point of view is the supra-controversy language projection, a projection created by the philosopher's fiat, and bearing no relation to the underlying scientific problems. Anything that can be described and discussed in a language projection that has *grown*, and not been manufactured, is controversial; about anything that cannot be so described we can say nothing except that *some* events of a certain kind can be postulated.

We can now sum up the analysis of the fact–theory and fact–explanation antithesis. Every factual statement has an underlying element of theory, and *explanation* is the explicit elucidation of the relations between the statement and the (formulated or unformulated) theory. A factual statement seems to be non-theoretical when the underlying theory is either an unrecognized presupposition or a theory which is universally accepted without question at any given stage of history.

We have found no reason to retract the original contention that the only legitimate account of 'true factual statement' *is a psychological account*: what I am prepared to call a true factual statement is a hypothesis which I feel no scientific or philosophical need, at the present time, to question or modify.

B. COMMUNICATION

Chapter 4 was devoted to an attempt to distinguish the main kinds of situations in which events, experiences, sensations, states, moods, dispositions, tendencies . . . are:

1. known or felt but not conveyed or described;
2. conveyed only in non-verbal, non-informative, or non-discursive form;
3. described, conveyed, or indicated in ordinary language or conventional technical language; and
4. described in puzzling, unconventional language.

Within these four main sections we can distinguish situations or conditions where there is:

(i) Common-sense Verbal Communication;
(ii) Technical–Verbal and Symbolic Communication;
(iii) Non-verbal Communication;
(iv) Non-discursive Communication;
(v) Inadequate Knowledge;
(vi) Inadequate Language;
(vii) Situations where Communication is possible but Withheld; and
(viii) Situations where the Language is Unfamiliar, new, or for any reason philosophically puzzling.

We can now apply these distinctions to those already discovered.

1. *Known but not conveyed*

1(a) Experiences of unusual or abnormal mental states, such as elation, heightened perception, and ecstatic love, which cannot be adequately conveyed by any form of communication, are a major problem for the philosopher. If he has known no sensations of this kind he is cut off from an important area of human experience and is to this degree limited as a philosopher; if he has known these things he finds it difficult or impossible to extend his conceptual scheme to embrace this area of experience . . . (vi) . . . (Inadequate Language).

1(b) The philosopher's inability to describe the sound of a clarinet or the aroma of coffee is less frustrating because he can communicate by producing the object . . . (vi) . . . (Inadequate Language).

1(c) Neurological and other physical processes which can be postulated but not described are not in themselves a special philosophical problem, because the scientist knows the *kind* of description that would be appropriate if he could make the necessary discoveries. If such discoveries were made, however, and needed to be correlated with complementary accounts (e.g. psychological) in different language projections, the task of correlation would raise philosophical problems ... (v) ... (Inadequate Knowledge).

1(d) The twinge of toothache which is not mentioned and the murder which no one suspects are known or felt by *someone* but not described ... (vii) ... (Communication Withheld).

2. Conveyed in Non-verbal or Non-discursive Form

2(a) There is an important failure of communication between the musician, to whom the world of music is complete, relatively isolated, and in some sense more *real* than the world of words, and the intellectual whose thought is predominantly verbal. Is the tone-deaf or colour-blind philosopher a limited philosopher? Not necessarily so. Philosophizing, like creative or executive work in music, ballet, painting, sculpture, architecture, and all other non-verbal arts, is a special skill which may or may not be accompanied by skill or appreciative capacity in other spheres ... (iii) ... (Non-verbal Communication).

2(b) We have seen (p. 44 above) that some of the most direct and important modes of communication are neither verbal nor unequivocal. Before acquiring language we communicate by screaming, smiling, pointing, and other movements of the body. The extreme underestimation of the experiences and communication of infancy is due at the superficial level to exaggeration of the role of conscious, articulate thought in children and adults, and at a deeper level to unconscious guilt over the irreparable harm inflicted on infants by excessive frustration of their instinctual needs. Communication by smiling, frowning, tone of voice, nodding and shaking the head, and a wide range of other significant gestures, remains a major part of total communication in adult life, but is not strictly informative except as a form of answer to a question ... (iii) .... (Non-verbal Communication)

2(c) Experiences, thoughts, and events that are conveyed or described in idiosyncratic rather than common-sense or scientific language, are sometimes more, sometimes less, easily distinguishable. Lyric poems and imaginative novels and plays are manifestly non-informative; some novels, however, such as *War and Peace* and Scott's novels, and some plays, such as *Julius Caesar, Antony and Cleopatra*, and *Saint Joan*, are fusions of history and imaginative characterization; and history itself is seldom 'pure' or untendentious ... (iv) ... (Non-discursive Communication).

3. Described in Conventional Language

3(a) Situations in which people describe things and events, give information, directions, instructions, in conventional, unpuzzling commonsense language, without being suspected of telling lies, are philosophically interesting only when the underlying assumptions or *points of view* of the language are questioned or rejected ... (i) ... (Commonsense Verbal Communication).

3(b) Technical language, including the symbols of mathematics and symbolic logic, is a minority language which acquires prestige among the majority when it is demonstrably successful in its practical application. Mistakes, fallacies, and invalid assumptions are the more difficult to detect the greater the prestige of the technical language ... (ii) ... (Technical–Verbal and Symbolic Communication).

3(c) Events described or assumed by interpolation and extrapolation from well-established scientific data in conjunction with well-tested scientific laws are philosophically interesting because such description or assumption is based on the *individual intellectual judgement* of each theorist. This vast area of knowledge and speculation presents the philosophical problem of the Technique of Fluctuating Rigour (pp. 103–5). The good scientist is the one in whom passionate curiosity and a further quality which cannot easily be analysed, intellectual integrity, predominate over unconscious motives for distortion. Sometimes ... (v) ... (Inadequate Knowledge); sometimes ... (viii) ... (Unfamiliar Language).

3(d) Unwitting misdescription includes mistakes due to the fallibility of memory, the influence of false theories on history and current affairs, self-deception, illusion, slips of the tongue, rationalization, and sentimentalizing ... (v) ... (Inadequate Knowledge).

3(e) Lying may or may not be detected; when it is, the clues are: manner of reporting, internal inconsistency of reports, conflicting evidence, and motives for lying. When we cannot find a motive there is a psychoanalytic problem ... (vii) ... (Communication Withheld).

4. Described in Unconventional Language

The fourth class are situations where, in addition to the problems of (3) – the uneliminable possibility of unsuspected false assumptions, fallible judgement, unwitting or deliberate misdescription – there are several sources of semantic bewilderment.

4(a) Bewilderment may be due either to a shift in an existing language projection or to the introduction of a new language projection. Psychoanalysis provides an example of both. An analysis can be conducted from beginning to end without introducing into the interpretations a single technical or unfamiliar expression. Even the term 'unconscious' need not appear. What is new in interpretation can best be described as, first, the introduction of the systematic *focusing* use of language, and, second, *a shift in the language projection of common sense, which represents a shift in point of view*. The technical language of the theory of psychoanalysis, on the other hand, is a new language projection which gives rise to new philosophical problems . . . (viii) . . . (Unfamiliar Language).

4(b) Bewilderment may be due to the need to choose between *alternative* language projections or to the philosophical problems raised by *overlapping* language projections. Complementary descriptions such as the political description and the economic description of a given section of space–time are examples of overlapping language projections. Rival theories, such as the theories of Freud and Jung, are conflicting points of view which are manifested in conflicting, or alternative, language projections. The problems raised by the relations between P (physical language plus common-sense language which is translatable into the physical), TFM (common-sense and literary language in the sphere of thoughts, feelings, motives, etc.) and TFME (the extension of TFM which is used to express the psychoanalytic point of view, both technical and common sense) are problems of overlapping language projections, but of a special kind. Common-sense speech uses P, TFM, and TFME without distinction and usually without noticing the transition from one to another. TFME is an indispensable tool of science because it can change the situation by linking up elements that are dissociated. *The philosophical hypothesis of Chapter 4, pp. 58–9, the need-lack-wish-fear hypothesis, is an index of the vast programme of philosophical work to be undertaken in the sphere of overlapping language projections* . . . (viii) . . . (Unfamiliar Language).

4(c) The attempt to apply rational to irrational thought has been made possible by Freud's elucidation of the connections between the thought of children, primitives, neurotics and psychotics, and the dreams of all human beings, including normal adults. Abstract, scientific understanding is being reinforced by empathic understanding derived from the individual's study, in analysis, of his own underlying thought processes . . . (viii) . . . (Unfamiliar Language).

4(d) The speculations of scientists and philosophers, to be judged by less rigorous standards than laboratory or clinical work, open up new fields for investigation and research. Because they are tentative and precarious they demand a high level of intellectual judgement; because they often use unfamiliar language projections they create philosophical problems; and because they are not susceptible to decisive tests they provide an opening for Fluctuating Scepticism and Fluctuating Rigour . . . (viii and v) . . . (Unfamiliar Language and Inadequate Knowledge).

4(e) Heterogeneous description is the use in one discipline of technical terms adopted from other disciplines ('inhibition', 'energy', 'instinct'). The task of making relatively consistent a heterogeneous language projection, while taking into account *all* that the theorist has attempted to explain, is an important and neglected philosophical undertaking. *There is no better reason for objecting in principle to the adoption of, say, 'inhibition' from neurology into psychology, or of 'instinct' from ethology into psychodynamics, than for objecting in principle to the adoption of, say, 'nucleus' from astronomy or cytology into atomic physics.* The only kind of criticism that would be legitimate is the criticism of those concepts *as they are used as new concepts in the adopting disciplines.* For such criticism a detailed knowledge of the purposes of the new use of the concept is essential . . . (viii) . . . (Unfamiliar Language).

Towards a Testing Principle

In the light of the above distinctions we can extend the general principle of Chapter 13, p. 167, which is valid for both science and philosophy:

When an assertion or an assumption or a theory is in dispute, whether it is an individual utterance (token) or a repeatable statement or hypothesis (type) *which is always based on individual utterances*, then –

1. it should first be precisely formulated, and *not* merely given a name such as 'Positivism' or 'Behaviourism'; and then examined to determine:

(i) whether it is predominantly descriptive, informative, explanatory, directive, lawlike, heuristic, classificatory, emotive, prescriptory, appraisive, performative, suggestive, focusing, enactive, etc., or a heterogeneous theory comprising several such elements;

(ii) whether it is made from a conventional and familiar or from an original or unfamiliar point of view; and

(iii) whether it is expressed in a familiar or an unfamiliar language projection, or in overlapping or heterogeneous language projections –

2. if it is decisively testable it should be tested by scientific experiments and/or by real or invented examples, all designed to demonstrate that it should be either abandoned or reformulated –

3. if it is *not* decisively testable it should *not* be discredited solely for that reason, because some of the most important assumptions are not testable (e.g. Hypothesis D, Chapter 8, p. 99, and its contradictory) and because good judgement consists, in the main, in being able to make sound, untestable assumptions, and bad judgement consists in the reverse; it should be examined for the part it plays in a theory, or traced to the testable assumptions from which it is *derived* (not deduced).

The above is a principle, that is to say a heuristic methodological recommendation. It will later be referred to as the *General Testing Principle*.

C. LANGUAGE PROJECTIONS

The new and difficult concept 'language projection' has been introduced several times without being defined. This omission is deliberate. The concept is too young to be fitted with the armour of a definition; it can best be elucidated by examples of its use.

Natural languages, such as English, Russian, Chinese, French, . . . are language projections. They are *partially translatable*; the more idiosyncratic the form of language, the more difficult, inadequate, or misleading the translation. Hence the difficulty of translating lyric poetry. The more precisely concepts are related to each other by definitions, as in some areas of the mathematicized sciences, the less misleading is translation from one natural language to another. Mathematics, which has grown out of natural languages but which has achieved relative independence, comes closest to universality.* Nevertheless, wherever there are two incompatible systems of mathematics there will be two mathematical language projections.

Mathematics, physics, chemistry, economics, psychoanalysis, the law, . . . are language projections which, like map projections, are only partially translatable into other projections, including the projection of common sense. The concept 'language projection' is considerably

---

* Music, a universal form of communication, is not a language projection because it is not a system of concepts which has to be related to other systems. It does not inform or mislead: it *impinges* on the hearer.

wider than the concept 'map projection' because it embraces more distinctions of purpose. Several maps, designed for several purposes, such as political, population, contour, and rainfall maps, may have the same projection, but the term 'language projection' refers to a system of concepts which reflects a point of view, so that two concept-systems, such as the political and the economic, when applied to a single area of space–time (e.g. the example of the Russian Revolution given in Chapter 4, p. 47) are *overlapping* language projections.

P, TFM, and TFME, explained and illustrated in Chapter 4, pp. 48–54, are overlapping language projections because they are concept-systems which reflect points of view and have areas in common. The technical language of physics is *partially translatable* into the language of common sense, and the concept-system which reflects the point of view of psychoanalysis is partially translatable into common-sense thought, feeling, and motive language. Part of TFME is compatible with TFM, but part is incompatible. In those areas, therefore, where TFME is repugnant to common sense, *TFM and TFME are both overlapping and incompatible language projections.*

A language projection is the verbal or symbolic correlate of a point of view. Where two points of view are incompatible, the corresponding language projections will be incompatible. There may be conflicting language projections, therefore, within a natural language, within a science, within common sense, and within a discipline, such as law, which itself has a distinctive language projection. Incompatible points of view, with their corresponding incompatible language projections, should be distinguished from the conflicting opinions of disputants who use the same language projection. Differences of opinion in matters of taste, concerning, for example, the merits of a painting or a symphony, or in matters of information, concerning, say, historical events, where Fluctuating Rigour may produce differences in the degree of credulity, are compatible with agreement in the use of a language projection. *Language projections are incompatible if and only if the explicit formulation of the corresponding points of view reveals a failure of the disputants to agree upon the use of language* (see Chapter 13, pp. 163 and 165).

D. I. PHILOSOPHICAL TECHNIQUES

The term 'fallacy' has been retained in these pages for such beliefs as Behaviourism, and for such logical slips as *non causa pro causa*, because it has a long philosophical history. Most of the snares in the path of the student of abstract thought, however, are better described as misleading *techniques*, which are responsible for fallacies and mistaken points of view. The most important of such techniques in the sphere of philosophy are Fluctuating Rigour, Fluctuating Scepticism, Unrestricted Scepticism, Pseudo-objectivity, the Straw Man Fallacy, the Fact-finding Fallacy, the Autonomy of Logic Fallacy, the Behaviourist Fallacy, the Supra-controversy Fallacy; the four most important of the recognized fallacious techniques, namely *non causa pro causa*, many questions, amphiboly and equivocation; the four most glaring logical solecisms, namely *ignoratio elenchi*, *non sequitur*, *petitio principii* and *post hoc ergo propter hoc*; and finally Overextensionism.

Fluctuating Rigour

Fluctuating Rigour is the technique of raising the standard of evidence, confirmation or proof required before accepting or acting upon an unwelcome hypothesis, theory, point of view, assumption, project, etc., and lowering the standard for a welcome hypothesis, etc. (see Chapter 8, p. 103).

It is a convenient technique, which is used universally, is difficult to detect, and is even more difficult to confute, because standards of evidence are seldom explicitly formulated. Miracles, life after death, spiritualist phenomena, psychokinesis, flying saucers, astrological predictions, if placed on a scale from certainty through credibility to absurdity, would be very variously assessed by a cross-section of the population of the world. All these subjects lie in the realm beyond proof and disproof where Fluctuating Rigour may release phantasy elements from the custody of scientific judgement. Yet proof itself, from the point of view this argument has reached, must be given a psychological explanation. What is acknowledged a proof is that which convinces the one who acknowledges it: to prove p to X is to convince X of p; to prove a person guilty in a court of law is to convince the jury (or a larger audience) that he is guilty; to prove a theorem is to perform an operation which satisfies mathematicians; to prove a theory is to test it in a manner which convinces all or most of the theorists in that field. *There is no logical technique for excluding shared delusions or for eliminating Fluctuating Rigour*: the classification of psychological techniques offers illuminating clues but no decisive logical weapons.

Fluctuating Scepticism

Fluctuating Scepticism is the technique of using *philosophical* argument as a device for playing with ideas without committing oneself to unwelcome beliefs, for doubting any belief or theory without decisively rejecting it, and for moving alternately towards and away from a definite intellectual position according to changes in the psychic equilibrium. Although it is the philosopher's malady *par excellence*, it tends, like all the other philosophical techniques, to pervade every sphere of abstract thought. The alternating mockery and quasi-belief which is a common posture towards astrology and folk-superstitions is an example of the lowbrow form of Fluctuating Scepticism.

Unrestricted Scepticism

Unrestricted Scepticism is the philosophical correlate of the psychological technique of Non-commitment. It enables the thinker to attack any philosophical or scientific position without risk. It enables him to engage in a perpetual battle, without any fear of losing, and with the hope of winning possession of the deserted battlefield. When used deliberately as a device, by a philosopher who is capable of committing himself to definite beliefs, it is a valuable philosophical tool. As Ayer remarks in *The Problem of Knowledge*: 'Our reward for taking scepticism seriously is that we are brought to distinguish the different levels at which our claims to knowledge stand' (p. 222). If, on the other hand, it is used, not as a heuristic device, but as a mechanism of defence against the dangers of commitment, it is a symptom of obsessional neurosis or of schizoid withdrawal.

Pseudo-objectivity

The Pseudo-objectivity Technique is a sophisticated manœuvre for enlisting the prestige of science or philosophy as a combined reinforcement and disguise for personal prejudices, or for giving mental constructs the status of the 'objectively real'. The terms 'good' and 'evil', or 'virtuous' and 'vicious', are no longer applied to people without embarrassment; they are replaced by pseudo-scientific epithets of approbation and disapprobation, such as 'scientific' and 'unscientific'; 'normal' and 'pathological'; 'productive' and 'antisocial'. The Pseudo-objectivity Technique is a pervasive risk for the abstract theorist. The mental constructs, which are the pioneer thinker's scaffolding for the erection of his theoretical edifice, are thought of, both by him and by his followers, as objectively real things or processes (e.g. 'force', 'energy', 'gravitation', 'phlogiston', 'the ether', etc.).

The Straw Man Fallacy

The Straw Man Fallacy is a method of discrediting a point of view by reducing to absurdity a representation of that point of view which is either the writer's own idiosyncratic misrepresentation or an indefensible version of the point of view, and having or giving the impression that the *reductio ad absurdum* applies equally to a *defensible* version of the point of view. It is possible, for example, to reduce 'psychologism', 'logical positivism', 'Behaviourism', 'psychoanalysis', 'empiricism', 'pragmatism' . . . to absurdity without making clear what writer is being criticized or what formulation of his theory is being confuted.

The Fact-finding Fallacy

The Fact-finding Fallacy is the false assumption that underlying our tentative beliefs and speculations there is a substratum of certain, unalterable 'facts'. If we sketch a mental picture such as would give plausibility to the fallacy we will see that it is not altogether absurd: the substratum of 'facts' is like the substratum of rock underlying earth, water, and air; the rock is reliable, the earth a little less so, and the water and air treacherous; yet in favourable conditions the water is safe enough for sailing and swimming, and the air is the medium for daring pioneer flights which may later be consolidated as routine air services.

Such a mental picture, misleading in this form, could be rectified by a small but important modification. The 'facts' of the world may be likened to the crust of the earth along the earthquake belt, which in part remains relatively stable for thousands of years, and in part undergoes periodic violent disruptions, both seismic and volcanic, as a result of the cumulative subterranean pressure of philosophical and scientific speculation.

The term 'fact' is logically linked with the true–false antithesis; universal agreement that a statement is true (e.g. that the statement 'Julius Caesar was killed in Rome in 44 B.C.' and all accurate translations of that sentence are true statements, or express a true proposition) implies universal agreement upon a 'fact'. The question why there is or is not universal agreement is a socio-psychological question, not a logical one; where there is not universal agreement, to describe a proposition as a 'fact' is to align oneself with those who assent to the proposition. The Fact-finding Fallacy is the supposition that 'the facts of the world' are independent of the consensus of opinion of the population of the world, and independent of the psychological problems relating to the motives for holding, rejecting, or ambivalently oscillating between, assumptions and beliefs.

The Autonomy of Logic Fallacy

The Autonomy of Logic Fallacy is the counterpart in analytic discourse of the Fact-finding Fallacy in empirical discourse. It is the assumption that statements, sentences, or propositions, including scientific hypotheses, can be examined and assigned logical status without reference to particular utterances by particular individuals in particular contexts and situations, or without reference to the special purposes for which unfamiliar locutions are adopted. To discuss the legitimacy or the optimum usage of such phrases as 'motive', 'intention', 'disposition', 'mind', 'consciousness', 'will', 'unconscious wish', 'unconscious fear', 'the need for punishment', 'the principle of indeterminacy' . . . as if the discussion were a purely logical one with no relation to the scientific problems involved is to succumb to the Autonomy of Logic Fallacy.

The Behaviourist Fallacy

Before defending my contention that Behaviourism is a fallacy, I must make clear what I mean by Behaviourism. Failure to do so would be an instance of the Straw Man Fallacy.

A distinction has been made between dogmatic and methodological Behaviourism: the former denying 'consciousness' entirely, and the latter merely advocating the objective study of behaviour without reference to 'consciousness'. We have seen that heuristic or methodological hypotheses are not susceptible of outright refutation, and it may now be added that methodological hypotheses, including any form of methodological Behaviourism, cannot be called fallacies. Dogmatic Behaviourism is a fallacy; methodological Behaviourism is a misguided* heuristic principle.

Nevertheless, any systematic psychological technique is a technique for the study of behaviour. The psychoanalyst studies the behaviour of

---

* i.e. misguided as a general principle, but sometimes valuable as a principle for particular experimental studies.

the patient: his spoken or written words, his smiles, frowns, groans, tears, yawns, his gasping, panting, sweating, shouting. . . . Behaviour, then, is the material of psychoanalysis, and if Behaviourism meant nothing more than the principle that psychology should have as its starting-point the objective and systematic study of behaviour, it would be an unexceptionable point of view. If the term is ever in fact used with this meaning, then such use is exempt from the present criticism.

My objection to Behaviourism as a school of psychology and as a philosophical theory or presupposition is not to its conception of psychology as the study of behaviour but to the arbitrary restrictions it attempts to impose, first, on the *kind* of behaviour to be studied, and, second, on the theoretical concepts to be used in the *explanation* of behaviour. Because our introspection is so often misleading, the argument runs, and because the various accounts of thinking, of the instincts, and of the emotions given by individual philosophers and psychologists on the basis of their introspection are divergent, arbitrary, and untestable, let us abandon introspection altogether, study no behaviour that is not measurable, call thinking 'subvocal speech', call emotion 'implicit visceral reactions', and use no concept, such as 'instinct', 'mind', or 'consciousness', in our *explanation* of behaviour, which would not be appropriate in an *account* of behaviour.

The first restriction, on the *kind* of behaviour to be studied, is as crippling to psychology as it would be crippling to biology to restrict the study of migration to the observation of controlled, experimental migration, or to restrict the study of the mating instinct of the lion to the observation of the mating of lions in controlled, experimental conditions in the Zoo. Pavlov's observations of the behaviour of dogs were observations of the behaviour of imprisoned animals tortured to the point of breakdown by the master to whom they were attached. The strongest had to be castrated before the torture was effective in producing a nervous collapse. As Pavlov himself insisted, his work was physiology, not psychology, but psychological extrapolation from his physiological conclusions provides us with useful speculative insight into the effect of indefinitely prolonged imprisonment, fear, hunger, isolation, uncertainty, conflicting expectations, alternating cruelty and kindness . . . in producing a nervous breakdown in human beings. Similar neurotic symptoms to those of a spontaneous breakdown then appear, and are followed by greatly heightened suggestibility if some hope of escape or rehabilitation, however humiliating the form it may take, is offered by the persecutors. The assumption that the nervous system of the dog is not totally dissimilar to that of the man has been confirmed experimentally by using a similar technique of imprisonment, deprivation, debilitation, and physiological and psychological torture to produce an experimental neurotic breakdown, with subsequent suggestibility and docility: the technique of brainwashing and indoctrination.

Such psychological extrapolation from Pavlov's physiology, however repugnant to humane minds, is genuine psychodynamics; it may fittingly be called the Psychodynamics of Nosopoiesis, and it provides an instructive and repellent inverse to the Psychodynamics of Therapy. The difference, however, is not merely a difference of direction and aim – the former to intensify, the latter to mitigate, both conscious and unconscious fear – but also a fundamental difference of method and point of view. The Pavlovian Psychodynamics of Nosopoiesis originates in artificial experimental conditions, and falls into the fallacy of Overextensionism when it applies its limited theoretical equipment (stimulus–response, the conditioned reflex, etc.) to spontaneous, or to controlled, near-spontaneous relationships. The Freudian Psychodynamics of Therapy originates in experimental conditions which reproduce the important instinctual elements of human relationships in a controlled situation, and is therefore as close to the animal ethology of Lorenz and Tinbergen as the Behaviourist Psychology of man is close to the rat-in-maze psychology of the laboratory.

The Supra-controversy Fallacy

The Supra-controversy Fallacy needs to be distinguished from the Pseudo-objectivity Technique and from the Fact-finding Fallacy. Whereas Pseudo-objectivity is the illegitimate objectification of attitudes or mental constructs, and the Fact-finding Fallacy is the false philosophical assumption that language pictures the 'world of facts', the Supra-controversy Fallacy is an attempt to escape from the arena of conflicting individual points of view based on the fallible intellectual judgement of individuals. The belief that there can be unformulated propositions is a characteristic product of the Supra-controversy Fallacy. For the true statement that people can, at any time, coin new sentences which will be used to express original propositions, is substituted the metaphysical theory that there is a class of propositions which there are no sentences to express. This fallacy is a consequence of divorcing thought from the thinker, a device as indefensible as divorcing the dance from the dancer. Just as choreography is an imaginative foreshadowing of the evocation of the talents of dancers, influenced by experience of their achievements and capacities, so original philosophy is an imaginative foreshadowing of the expansion, coordination or re-focusing of the points of view of theorists, based upon a knowledge of their achievements and their language projections.

One form of the Supra-controversy Fallacy, the invalid assimilation of empirical theorizing to mathematical reasoning and proof, with geometry as the model for philosophical reasoning, has been losing ground, in the twentieth century, to the analytic attack of modern empiricist philosophers. The fallacy still survives, however, in more subtle forms, and the most valuable clue for its detection is the facile 'proof' or 'disproof' of controversial hypotheses.

The Recognized Fallacies

Non causa pro causa, as we have seen, is the fallacy of assuming, when one of several linked assumptions has been reduced to absurdity, that one of the other assumptions has also been shown to be false.

Many Questions is the device of putting a question and requiring a single answer which must be misleading, either because the question involves several questions which should be answered separately, or because it contains an implicit assumption which would seem to be confirmed by an unqualified answer. 'Should such criminals be allowed to escape the consequences of their crime?', for example, cannot be answered by 'Yes' or 'No' without condoning the emotive description of the people discussed.

Amphiboly is an invalid argument arising from the ambiguity of a grammatical construction; *equivocation* is an invalid argument arising from the ambiguity of a word or phrase. The argument in each case would be valid if there were no shift of meaning in its course.

Ignoratio elenchi is an argument which reaches an irrelevant conclusion instead of the proof or the refutation that was intended.

Non sequitur is an argument in which there is no connection between the premisses and the conclusion.

Petitio principii is the fallacy of including among the assumptions of the premisses the conclusion to be proved.

Post hoc ergo propter hoc is the fallacy of assuming that a temporal consequent is *caused* by an antecedent simply because it *is* a temporal consequent.

Overextensionism

Overextensionism, finally, is the use of a single principle or theory to explain a range of phenomena too extensive or too complex to be adequately explained, without distortion, by that principle alone. As every theorist has to specialize, and to ignore large areas even of his own subject, Overextensionism is very common; it can be corrected by a critical synthesis of several related theories, reducing their scope and increasing their explanatory power. Let us suppose, for example, that the theory based on Pavlov's experiments with dogs is the physiological correlate of *part* of the psychoanalytic theory of the production of a neurosis. Let us further suppose that the inverse of the theory of psychoanalytic therapy is the Nosopoietic Theory (the psychological extrapolation from Pavlov's physiological theory), based on the technique of deliberately producing neurosis and pathological suggestibility by the use of terror, uncertainty, and debilitation, and by the exploitation of the transference* situation to increase dependence and fear. Then the synthesis of the two complementary theoretical approaches would enhance the explanatory power of both, and would serve as a corrective to Overextensionism.

II. ASSOCIATED PSYCHOLOGICAL TECHNIQUES

The above philosophical techniques come into play when there are motives for distortion. A brief account must now be given of the psychological techniques with which they are associated.

It should be emphasized that the psychological techniques are not abnormal or pathological, except when they appear in such extreme form that the reality sense is seriously defective in relation to the age of the individual. They are normal tendencies of the mind, operating throughout childhood and into adult life, which are needed to make 'reality' tolerable. Only for short periods, at the diurnal and the developmental acme of our intellectual efficiency, can we oppose to these tendencies a system of coherent, consistent, rational thought,

---

* The brainwashing interrogator has an opportunity to create a transference situation by making his prisoner dependent on him both for relief from solitary confinement, or from chains and handcuffs, and for hope of eventual release.

attitudes, feelings, and behaviour, and even this is achieved only by a minority, who owe their rare capacity for sustained intellectual ambivalence either to exceptional emotional security or to a passion for rational consistency which we have hitherto found unanalysable.

We may use a clue from Anna Freud's *The Ego and the Mechanisms of Defence* to suggest a speculative explanation of the passion for *intellectual* consistency and rationality. According to her theory, the process of sublimation sometimes results in the sexualization of thought, especially in adolescence, so that argument, criticism, and imaginative writing become tinged with the passion we usually associate with instinctual impulses. I would go further and suggest that the threat to the ego from the upsurge of long-repressed erotic and aggressive desires is warded off by an integrative effort at the more manageable level of intellectual activity. Success at that level would serve to mitigate or to counterbalance the relative failure of the adolescent's attempts to introduce order and rational organization at the level of passionate personal attachments.

Intellectual rationality, then, becomes a *need*, comparable in urgency to the more intelligible instinctual needs, so that an area of order can be staked out and defended against emotional chaos. A clear distinction should be made, therefore, between *intellectual* rationality, which is compatible, through the techniques of Restriction of Libido, Isolation, and Denial, with a stunted or chaotic emotional life, and progressive affective discrimination, or the combined affective and intellectual attempt to extend rational organization to the sphere of instinctual tendencies. This is the aspiration of those for whom the problems of the irrational in their own behaviour and emotional attachments have become even more urgent and important than the problems of making consistent their intellectual beliefs and attitudes.

Although the terms 'intellectual' and 'affective', like all other antithetical terms, suggest a crude bifurcation which I do not intend, they are needed to make clear, from a new angle of approach, the complementary functions of philosophy and psychodynamics. The 'area of order' which the intellectual adolescent fences round, cultivates, and weeds, in a corner of the wilderness of his total experience, may, like a garden, be neglected and lose ground, be maintained and hold its ground, or be expanded and gain ground upon the surrounding area. In a complementary fashion, the area of order in feelings and behaviour may increase, remain constant, or diminish. Either intellectual or affective rationality, as it develops, may contribute to the other.

The 'intellectual motive', then, for submitting to an analysis, may be the desire to extend the area of order (or ego-control) beyond the intellectual sphere. The urge of the philosopher to psychoanalyse and the urge of the psychoanalyst to philosophize would be more common and more fruitful if philosophy were more generally recognized as the indispensable art of abstract thought, and if psychoanalysis were recognized as the starting-point of the philosophy of psychodynamics.

The most important unconscious psychodynamic techniques underlying philosophical distortion are: Splitting and Displacement, the Sophistication of Magical Thinking, the Reinforcement of Repression, the Restriction of Libido (Non-commitment), Projection, Projective Identification, Rationalization, Isolation, Denial, Intellectualization, and Reaction-formation.

Splitting and Displacement

The techniques of Splitting and Displacement are closely connected. People can be split into contrasting loved and hated groups, which are called 'good' and 'bad', or, in sophisticated terms, 'superior' and 'inferior', 'sensible' and 'unreasonable', 'scientific' and 'unscientific', 'loyal' and 'disloyal', and so on. In the same way, groups, classes, countries, races, religions, artists, arts, art forms, works of art, scientists, sciences, scientific theories, hypotheses, . . . can also be split into 'good' and 'bad', or the numerous sophisticated modifications of this simple antithesis.

Displacement is the change in emotional attitude which results from a shift in the distribution, among known objects and ideas, of love and hatred, confidence and fear. When Little Hans became aware of his fear of his father he lost his fear of horses; his fear, which had originally been displaced from his father to horses, was now displaced again as a result of the analyst's interpretations, this time from horses back to his father (Chapter 10, p. 126). The transference in analysis is, essentially, displacement. It consists in the cathexes, love, hatred, fear, . . . which are displaced to the analyst from the significant people in the patient's life.

The techniques of Splitting and Displacement are provided with an intellectual disguise by the philosophical techniques of Fluctuating Rigour, Fluctuating Scepticism, Pseudo-objectivity, the Straw Man Fallacy, the Supra-controversy Fallacy, the recognized fallacies (*non causa pro causa*, etc.), and Overextensionism.

The Sophistication of Magical Thinking

The Sophistication of Magical Thinking is the technique of maintaining the appearance of rationality while giving free play to some element of the phantasy life. In Chapter 10 (pp. 129–32) examples of subtle forms of the technique in the writings of Kant and Nietzsche were pointed out and discussed; in modern philosophy the technique reveals itself in the form of passionate preoccupation with theories which have significance for the unconscious phantasy of the philosopher. One example must suffice. The concept of 'the logically possible' is a legitimate notion which is used to indicate ideas that do not involve a contradiction. It is logically possible, it might be said, for a ten-foot-tall man to exist, because no specification of height occurs in the definition of 'man', and so no contradiction is involved in the notion of a man who is ten foot tall. Arguments about what is or is not logically possible sometimes rest upon implicit reference to dictionary definitions, but many arguments are such that they cannot be settled by appeal to a dictionary, either because the dictionary definitions are being called in question, or because no definition can be offered which would provide the needed criterion. If A, who finds a ten-*mile*-tall man 'logically possible' is arguing with B, who rejects the notion as 'logically impossible', what account can we give of the dispute?

Philosophers A and B may say that they are trying to settle a logical question which is independent of psychology. I maintain that the true analysis of the dispute is psychological. A finds the notion of a ten-mile-tall man conceivable: he is prepared to call such a monster a man. B finds the notion inconceivable: he refuses to call the creature a man. Each is trying to persuade the other to share his point of view. The questions *what* a person finds conceivable and *why* he finds it so are psychological questions.

If, then, a philosopher claims to have demonstrated that unconscious wishes, say, are logically possible or logically impossible, or that life after death is logically possible or logically impossible, he is merely evincing his own willingness or unwillingness to include the concepts in his language projection. If his arguments are persuasive he will induce others to share his point of view. The appeal to logical criteria where there are no criteria provided by agreed definitions may be an example of the Sophistication of Magical Thinking. The assertion, for example, that life after death is 'logically possible' may be a pseudo-logical compromise between the wish to believe that life after death is factually certain and the doubt whether there is any reliable evidence for life after death.

The Sophistication of Magical Thinking manifests itself in the following philosophical techniques: Fluctuating Rigour, Fluctuating Scepticism, Pseudo-objectivity, the Fact-finding Fallacy, the Autonomy of Logic Fallacy, the Supra-controversy Fallacy, the recognized fallacies (*non causa pro causa*, etc.), and Overextensionism.

Reinforcement of Repression

Reinforcement of Repression is the technique of excluding from consciousness, or refusing to believe or consider possible, or refusing to take seriously or act upon, any idea or theory which has associations that arouse conscious or unconscious anxiety. To deny that what I have called unconscious motives for distortion, for example, are relevant to philosophical disputes, is an example of reinforcement of repression. Behaviourism is a theory which utilizes the unreliability of introspection in order to renounce introspection, and to support the delusion that an adequate psychological theory is possible without using introspective techniques and without the empathic understanding of the minds of others.

The dogmatic renunciation of introspection provides a further illustration of the all-pervasive technique of Fluctuating Rigour. The required standard of reliability for scientific evidence is raised to exclude a major source of valuable scientific clues. Many important scientific clues are unreliable in the sense that they may be misread or may be used as the basis for doubtful speculative theories. Pioneer astrophysicists, for example, have to work with clues which may mislead, and so have anthropologists, archaeologists, palaeontologists, biophysicists, and all other scientists who are working at the exploratory limits rather than in the consolidated areas of their sciences. In all sciences except Behaviourist psychology the renunciation of any technique which yielded valuable clues would be recognized as timidity rather than legitimate scientific caution.

Reinforcement of Repression is manifested in the following philosophical techniques: Fluctuating Rigour, Fluctuating Scepticism, the Straw Man Fallacy, the Behaviourist Fallacy, and the recognized fallacies (*non causa pro causa*, etc.).

Restriction of Libido and Non-commitment

Restriction of Libido is the inability or unwillingness to feel strongly about, or to attach oneself to, or to commit oneself to, some person

or activity in the environment that could, but for conscious or u̶
conscious fear, be a source of direct or sublimated instinctual satisfaction. It is the affective correlate of repression. Just as repression may
take the form either of forgetting something which was important in
the past or of excluding some new idea from consciousness, so restriction of libido may take the form either of withdrawing from someone
or some activity that formerly had deep emotional significance or of
remaining aloof from some new potential relationship which would
have emotional significance in the present. In other terms, restriction
of libido may be either the withdrawing or the withholding of cathexis. It is not a clearly recognizable neurotic symptom like a phobia
or an obsession; in fact, the people who are most likely to be judged
'normal' by the majority are those whose personalities are restricted to
the sphere of relationships and activities in which they feel emotionally
secure. Restriction of Libido may, however, be an important element
of the syndrome of conscious and unconscious fear.

Restriction of Libido and Non-commitment are associated with the
following philosophical techniques: Fluctuating Scepticism, Unrestricted Scepticism, the Autonomy of Logic Fallacy, and Overextensionism.

Projection

Projection is the attribution to people, or to real or imaginary entities
in the external world, of one's own feelings, impulses, and attitudes.
The infant projects his impulses to bite the breast to the 'being' he later
recognizes as a whole object, the mother, and the paranoid fears of
sadistic persecution originate in the infant's own aggressive phantasies.*
He projects his desire to swallow up, incorporate, and control
the breast, so that it cannot frustrate him, and this impulse too
leads to fears of being swallowed up and controlled by external
entities.

Paranoid fears of persecution, such as fears of being poisoned, are
based on the mechanism of projection. The impulse to attack and
destroy, in the infant and the paranoid adult, produces the talion fear
of being attacked and destroyed.

Projection is associated with the following philosophical techniques:
Fluctuating Rigour, Fluctuating Scepticism, Pseudo-objectivity, the
Fact-finding Fallacy, the Supra-controversy Fallacy, and Overexten-
sionism.

* Illustrated by the paranoic terrors of Dr J (p. 270).

cation

ication, the valuable concept introduced by Melanie
ne case of projection. The source of projection is the
fear that originates when the self and the not-self of
early distinct. The impulse to bite results in the fear
...ten. The impulse to swallow up and incorporate the good
object (introjection), so that it cannot be lost, results in the fear of being
swallowed up. The impulse to force himself into the object, in order
to regain the security of the womb, results in the fear of being invaded
and controlled. As so many of the inevitably frustrated infant's impulses
are hostile and aggressive, the person with whom he identifies himself
becomes a persecutor. In the analysis of schizophrenia the analyst
becomes a persecutor. Rosenfeld (1965) vividly describes how the
patient fears to 'take in' the words of the analyst, who has become, by
projective identification, the persecutor who is trying to force himself
into the patient in order to control her.

Projective identification, then, is the state of confusion which results
from putting one's own impulses into the mind of another and
identifying oneself with the other to such a degree that the border
between self and other becomes blurred.

Rationalization

Rationalization is the invention of specious reasons to explain irrational
thoughts, feelings, attitudes, and behaviour; or the invention or selection of egosyntonic, acceptable reasons to conceal reasons which provoke
anxiety, guilt, or shame. Rationalization can be experimentally induced
by the simple technique of giving someone a hypnotic suggestion
(which he is told to forget) that he should perform some irrational
action, and when he carries it out, asking him why he did it. Provided
that he does not suspect that the true cause was a hypnotic suggestion,
he will probably invent, without hesitation and without doubting its
truth, a plausible but false explanation. Irrationality is so difficult and
painful to admit that although everyone is from time to time irrational
very few can detect or acknowledge their own irrationality. Recognition of irrationality is exacted in two ways: by psychoanalysis; or by
anomalies of behaviour so gross that rationalization is impossible.

The more complex the motives the more subtle the rationalization,
which may take the form of *selection*, rather than invention, of motives.
Let us suppose, for example, that resentment of an insult is a *sufficient*

motive for A to break off a relationship with B. A does not recognize or admit the resentment, however, and postpones the break until a provocation from B (a broken appointment) can be used as the ostensible reason. By the technique of Fluctuating Rigour the standard of required behaviour is raised to justify A's judgement that the broken appointment is *sufficient* reason for terminating the relationship, although it would not be so judged without the unconscious resentment. This oversimplified example illustrates the use of Fluctuating Rigour to facilitate rationalization by selection of motives.

Rationalization is facilitated by: Fluctuating Rigour, Fluctuating Scepticism, Pseudo-objectivity, the Autonomy of Logic Fallacy, the Supra-controversy Fallacy, and the recognized fallacies.

Isolation

Isolation is the dissociation of ideas from feeling or action, the severance of links between associations, or the predominance of indecisive contemplation over progressive affective discrimination. In Chapter 10 we considered three examples of this technique: Anna Freud's example of the adolescent's isolation of his lofty view of love from his actual behaviour, which is fickle and callous (p. 121); the example of the isolation of the student's *knowledge* that he was failing to assimilate the lectures from the *conscious anxiety* which would have been appropriate – although there was unconscious anxiety (p. 125); and the example of the failure to *see the connections* between relationships in which hostility has been displaced (p. 125). The psychological technique of isolation is associated with the following philosophical techniques: Fluctuating Scepticism, Unrestricted Scepticism, and the Autonomy of Logic Fallacy.

Denial

Denial is the psychological technique by which hypotheses for which there is good evidence, but which arouse anxiety, are continuously or intermittently excluded from the system of beliefs that are effective in a person's life. An extreme example is a mother's 'denial' of her son's death. She may, from time to time, achieve intellectual recognition of his death, but her feelings and behaviour are appropriate to the assumption that he is alive and will soon return. Denial manifests itself in the following philosophical techniques: Fluctuating Scepticism, Unrestricted Scepticism, the Straw Man Fallacy, the Fact-finding Fallacy, the Autonomy of Logic Fallacy, the Behaviourist Fallacy, the Supra-controversy Fallacy, *non causa pro causa*, and Overextensionism.

Intellectualization

Intellectualization is the attempt to mitigate or surmount an instinctual conflict by transforming part of the cathexis into a passionate interest in the interplay of ideas which have a symbolic or representational value. Slogans such as 'Ban the Bomb' have a profound significance at the instinctual as well as the intellectual level. In Chapter 10 (p. 122) an analogy was suggested between the physical and the intellectual mechanisms of 'fight', 'flight', and 'paralysis'. Intellectualization is manifested in the following philosophical techniques: Unrestricted Scepticism and Pseudo-objectivity.

Reaction-formation

Reaction-formation is the psychological technique whereby a compensatory feeling, attitude, or system of thought is maintained by the ego in opposition to its antithetical counterpart which is repressed and therefore unconscious. The reaction is against some impulse (e.g. a sexual or aggressive impulse) which once seemed to be leading to an intolerable danger (e.g. loss of a parent's love, or violent retribution). Two illustrations of reaction-formation occur in Chapter 10: extreme conscious obedience and submission, compensating for repressed hostility (p. 125), and Nietzsche's intellectual Will to Power and superhuman ruthlessness, compensating for his unconscious self-hatred and self-contempt (p. 130). The first reaction-formation is manifested in day-by-day behaviour and attitudes, while the second finds expression in near-manic literary exuberance.

Reaction-formation is associated with the following philosophical techniques: Fluctuating Scepticism, Unrestricted Scepticism, the Supra-controversy Fallacy, and Overextensionism.

RELATION BETWEEN PHILOSOPHICAL AND PSYCHOLOGICAL TECHNIQUES

The relations between the philosophical and the psychological techniques are set out in the Chart on page 218. All references to the philosophical techniques and fallacies can be found in the Index under 'Fallacies', and to the psychological techniques and mechanisms under

'Mechanisms'. Not all the fallacies and mechanisms listed in the Index have been included in the Chart. Some of the fallacies, though still prevalent, have been clearly exposed and refuted by other writers, and some of the mechanisms, such as introjection, are not directly correlated with philosophical techniques. Only those fallacies and mechanisms appear in the Chart which are directly related to important and unresolved intellectual problems and confusions.

From these it can be surmised that the philosophical techniques are often related to the psychological, as tics, stammering, stuttering, paraphasias, paraphraxes, and the falls and crashes of the accident-prone are related to the unconscious impulses or tendencies in which they originate.

An ambitious and determined man with a severe stammer may try to overcome his disability by breath-control, by the study of phonetics and elocution, by Yoga techniques, by persistence in public speaking in spite of painful embarrassment, and so on, and may be so successful in his attempt that he becomes a great orator. The unconscious fear and tension in which the stammer originated may manifest itself in various ways. The stammer may be eliminated only from *public* speaking, for example, and may become worse in private conversation. Or other symptoms may appear which are clearly derivative from the stammer, such as *mental*, rather than vocal, hesitation. Stress symptoms may arise whose connection with the stammer may be disputed or denied, such as asthma or bronchitis. The substitute symptom may be less professionally incapacitating than the stammer, and therefore less obnoxious to a passionately ambitious man. If the substitute symptom causes neither professional inconvenience nor acute conscious anxiety, it may be of minor interest to the man who has conquered his stammer. To the scientist who is interested in the explanation of the total neurosis, however, the stammer and its substitute are of equal importance. The elimination of the most conspicuous symptom, the stammer, serves not to cure, but merely to camouflage, the neurosis.

Analogously, a person who makes logical mistakes (and probably there is no one who does *not* make logical mistakes) may try to overcome his disability by the study of logic. He may be so successful that he eliminates all the more easily detectable fallacies from his conversation and writing. The unconscious need to defend those hypotheses which are welcome and to attack those which are unwelcome, according to the unconscious splitting technique, now reveals itself in the more subtle and sophisticated philosophical techniques, such as Fluctuating Rigour and Fluctuating Scepticism, which are much harder to

PHILOSOPH-ICAL TECH-NIQUES AND FALLACIES	SPLITTING (into loved and hated objects) AND DISPLACEMENT	SOPHISTICA-TION OF MAGICAL THINKING	REINFORCE-MENT OF REPRESSION	RESTRICTION OF LIBIDO; NON-COMMITMENT
FLUCTUATING RIGOUR TECHNIQUE	The FRT facilitates splitting and hence displacement. The standard of rigour can be raised to exclude the inimical and lowered to include the required beliefs.	By lowering the standard of rigour, wish-phantasies can be thought of as possibilities.	The FRT reinforces repression by raising the standard of rigour to exclude what is inimical.	
FLUCTUATING SCEPTICISM TECHNIQUE	The FST enables one to believe the 'good' and doubt the 'bad'.	The FST bestows the power to demolish theories and reconstruct them at will.	The FST reinforces repression by extending the area of doubt at will.	The FST enables the thinker to withdraw at will from unwelcome theories or beliefs.
UNRESTRICTED SCEPTICISM TECHNIQUE				The UST is a method of attacking with impunity and refusing to commit oneself to a point of view.
PSEUDO-OBJECTIVITY TECHNIQUE	Descriptive terminology is substituted for evaluative, to make splitting acceptable (e.g. describing disciplines as 'scientific' and 'non-scientific').	Mental constructs are given the status of the objectively real.		
STRAW MAN FALLACY	The SMF is a weapon to be used against hated theories.		The SMF is a weapon against ideas that threaten the defence mechanisms.	
FACT-FINDING FALLACY		By the FFF a solid foundation of unalterable 'facts' is magically created.		

PSYCHOLOGICAL TECHNIQUES AND MECHANISMS

ECTION	RATIONALIZA- TION	ISOLATION	DENIAL	INTELLECTUAL- IZATION	REACTION- FORMATION
g more us stan- for others or oneself es a loop- or pro-	The FRT facilitates rationalization of wishes, fears, love, hatred, and guilt.				
ST facili- belief in bable ptions (e.g. being uted') by ting scepti- o certain of thought.	The FST enables one to *doubt* dangers (e.g. the hostility of others) which would otherwise be deemed certain, and to rationalize these doubts.	The FST enables the thinker to *contemplate* areas of danger without the feelings appropriate to something *believed*.	By using the FST, hypotheses can be denied and admitted alternately in relation to the degree of anxiety.		Theories or projects which compensate for unconscious impulses or convictions of inadequacy are made plausible by lowering the standard of scepticism.
		By the UST ideas and theoretical disputes are isolated from feelings and impulses to act.	By the UST *any* idea can be contemplated and denied.	The interplay of ideas is substituted by the UST for the interplay of needs and demands.	The UST is a reaction-formation from dangerous self-assertion or commitment.
nscious ses are pro- to people ces and d as real.	The POT facilitates the disguise of love, fear and hatred by rationalization: the hated person, race, theory, etc., is thought of as 'really' dangerous.			Primitive impulses are transferred to the intellectual field by means of the POT.	
			The SMF can be used to attack theories which conflict with a needed way of thinking.		
eed for ty produces jective feel- certainty is pro- to the e world in rm of n 'facts'.			The FFF facilitates denial of perpetual change in conceptual systems and of problems of overlapping language projections.		

[*continued*

PHILOSOPHICAL TECHNIQUES AND FALLACIES	PSYCHOLOGICAL TECHNIQUES AND MECHANISMS			
	SPLITTING (into loved and hated objects) AND DISPLACEMENT	SOPHISTICATION OF MAGICAL THINKING	REINFORCEMENT OF REPRESSION	RESTRICTION OF LIBIDO; NON-COMMITMENT
AUTONOMY OF LOGIC FALLACY		The ALF supports the belief that 'pure' thinking can settle logical problems independently of science and other changing disciplines.		The ALF enables the thinker to evade commitment by treating incompatible points of view as equally legitimate.
BEHAVIOURIST FALLACY			The BF may be used to combat mortifying intrusion of unconscious impulses.	
SUPRA-CONTROVERSY FALLACY	Loved or needed theories are felt to be, not justified beliefs, but discovered, non-controversial, objective facts.	What is believed is exempted from the criticism appropriate to a personal and fallible point of view, and elevated to 'self-evident' or *certain* truths.	The SCF reinforces repression of doubt concerning needed beliefs.	
NON CAUSA PRO CAUSA; AMPHIBOLY; MANY QUESTIONS; EQUIVOCATION, ETC.	These fallacies can be used to attack the 'bad' and to defend the 'good' with an illusory semblance of fairness.	Grandiose wish-fulfilments may be based on one or more of these fallacies.	These fallacies may be used to support Behaviourism, and hence reinforcement of repression.	
OVER-EXTENSIONISM	O-E is a consequence of hyper-cathexis (uncritical love) of a theory or principle and hence overestimation of its explanatory powers.	O-E enables the thinker to feel confident that by means of one principle or theory he has intellectual control over a large area of complex and hetero-geneous problems.		There is a withdrawal of libido from the insecure no-man's-land to well-defended positions within the area supposedly covered by the over-extended principle.

	PSYCHOLOGICAL TECHNIQUES AND MECHANISMS				
JECTION	**RATIONALIZA-TION**	**ISOLATION**	**DENIAL**	**INTELLECTUAL-IZATION**	**REACTION-FORMATION**
	Resistance to conceptual change may be rationalized by the ALF	Intellectual attack or defence may be isolated by the ALF from experimentation, decision and action.	The ALF facilitates denial of impingement of difficult scientific controversies on philosophy.		
			The BF may be used to deny unconscious motives and impulses, and the independence of TFM and TFME.		
cious cer-ty, especially jeopardized nconscious t, is pro-d to others: sane person see . . .'	Rationalization is provided with an illusory basis of 'solid fact'.		The SCF facilitates denial of the psychological basis of so-called objective thought.		The SCF if sometimes a reaction against the strain of weighing the rival claims of disputing individuals and schools of thought.
	These fallacies may support any form of rationalization.		*Non causa pro causa* can be used to deny an assumption which is conjoined with a refuted assumption.		
need for nal control unconscious lses is pro-d by O-E to lectual con-over a bewil-ng complex roblems.			Relevant problems which cannot be accommodated to the overextended principle are denied.		O-E is a reaction against the discipline of modifying beliefs and attitudes in the light of new evidence (sustained intellectual ambivalence).

detect. The psychological techniques, as well as the philosophical, may become more and more sophisticated, so that a hypothesis or point of view may be rejected by a philosopher as inimical merely because it is incompatible with a theory with which his name is associated, or upon which his reputation depends. The persistent and ingenious struggle to achieve perfect consistency may make a man an outstanding philosopher, whose unconscious bias is camouflaged with such masterly skill that it can be detected and exposed only by a philosopher of equal ingenuity.

The achievements of the stammering boy who becomes a distinguished orator and that of the anxious boy who becomes a distinguished philosopher are no whit diminished by the recognition of their persistent unconscious conflicts and psychological techniques. Complete freedom from the distortions resulting from the psychological mechanisms is an unattainable ideal. The highest form of rationality to which the human mind can aspire is the sustained intellectual ambivalence which, in favourable circumstances, crowns the delicate and precarious process of progressive affective discrimination.

16

The General Testing Principle

It is reasonable to suppose that the conceptions of logic, proof, facts, objectivity, rationality, consciousness, unconscious needs, the 'will', responsibility . . . which have emerged from the foregoing argument may seem as disturbing as a surveyor's report that the foundations of the house are resting on quicksand. 'Immutable logic' has become the constantly stretching and shrinking network of an imperceptibly changing language projection which is destined to be superseded. The only honest account we can give of 'facts' and 'proof' is a psychological account, whose point of reference is the individual believer, who has no safeguard against shared illusions and delusions, and no access to his own motives for distortion. Not only has the mountain of metaphysics been reduced to a molehill by logical analysis, but the sun of consciousness which illumined the world of knowledge has shrivelled to a flickering point of light, which usually extinguishes itself the moment it reveals a frightening crack in the rock of reassuring beliefs. Responsibility has now become the capacity, determined by heredity and environment, for love and attachment and commitment. 'Absolute' moral standards are products of environmental impingement on the developing infant and child, and are due partly to accident and partly to intentional or blind inculcation. 'Objectivity' has had its pretensions pruned, and has become merely the opportunity for trained observers, who are not immune from *trainee-dogmatism*, to study 'data' which have to be *interpreted* in terms of a constantly changing theory.

Some of the other new concepts which have been introduced in the course of the argument, such as Fluctuating Rigour, motives for distortion, sustained intellectual ambivalence, overlapping language projections, and the enactive, suggestive, riskless, and reflecting uses of language, are also such as to contribute to a disquieting sense of intellectual insecurity. In this they resemble the disturbing shifts in point of view that have been forced upon scientists in every field by the most strikingly successful of all scientific instruments: analysis.

In the sphere of psychology, analysis is of two main kinds: the theoretical analysis which corresponds to philosophical analysis, and which is best described as the making and clarifying of heuristically important distinctions; and *therapeutic* analysis, or the focusing of unconscious fear so that its irrational elements can be clearly discriminated from the rational, and in consequence drained of their virulence. These two kinds are closely connected; the difference between enlightening and trivial distinctions is like the difference between the splitting of hairs and the splitting of threads which are too coarse to go through a needle. The criterion of the value of a new distinction is its usefulness in the weaving of a new theory or in the achievement of a therapeutic effect.

The loss of a comforting illusion needs to be offset by some psychological gain. For the scientist or philosopher the gain may be the thrill of breaking new ground; for the patient it may be the reduction of anxiety or the disappearance of a symptom. It is more difficult to imagine any possible gain for the student of philosophy or psychology that would induce him to assimilate a painful insight at the purely theoretical level. The insights of Darwin and Freud have been absorbed so slowly and incompletely not because of their intrinsic difficulty but because of their affective unacceptability. There is a moral as well as an intellectual barrier between those who feel comfortable in the protective covering of reassuring theories, such as Special Creation, Free Will, life eternal, posthumous reward and punishment, miracles, ethical intuitionism, pure rationality, autonomous logic, absolute truth . . . , and those who feel compelled to confront the certainty of extinction, the irrevocability of cruelty, the finality of tragedy, the uncertainty of beliefs, the pervasive risk of shared delusions, the inaccessibility of motives for distortion, the tyranny of the unconscious, the limitations of the techniques of emancipation from that tyranny, and the instability of illuminating new language projections.

One of the factors which may offset the pain of disillusionment is the exhilaration which for some minds attends each step in the direction of greater honesty. A second factor is the relief experienced by those for whom rationality has become a passion, when a wall between isolated compartments of thought is suddenly breached by an original theorist.

A third factor is the sense of exultation which comes from the acquisition and control of new and powerful intellectual machinery. A fourth possible factor is the feeling of pride, when the crutches which most men have found indispensable throughout history are finally discarded. A fifth is the sense of relief which emanates from the release of psychic energy which has been repressed, or the reconcentration of energy which has been dissipated or misdirected.

THE VERIFICATION PRINCIPLE

A problem was left unsolved in Chapter 11 (pp. 145–7). Why do some ideas or theories act as catalysts on one mind, precipitating the fundamental reorganization of beliefs, attitudes, and aspirations, and as anticatalysts on others, provoking anger and stimulating the defensive marshalling of threatened beliefs and attitudes?

An outstanding catalytic agent in modern philosophy was the work of the Vienna School. The Verification Principle which was clearly and succinctly formulated in Ayer's *Language, Truth, and Logic* is one of the progenitors of the preliminary Testing Principle (valid for science and philosophy) of Chapter 15 (pp. 198–9), which also descends from the hypothetico-deductive hypothesis of Peirce, developed by Popper, with its derivative criterion of falsifiability. The important insights of the three concepts, verification, hypothetico-deduction, and falsifiability, have been retained: first, that one of the most urgent tasks for modern philosophers is the discovery of a method for distinguishing between sense and nonsense; second, that the guess or the hunch comes first, and that science and philosophy do not advance through generalization or induction from 'presented' instances; and, third, that the testing of assumptions is first and foremost the devising of experiments and examples in an attempt to refute the assumptions. Critical reassessment of the Verification Principle, of the hypothetico-deductive theory, and of Popper's criterion of demarcation, has guided my argument towards the first formulation of the General Testing Principle, which must seem less striking and less intellectually satisfying than its precursors because it does not lend itself as an instrument for the Splitting Technique (see p. 210), and because it *reflects* the complexity of the problem. Even the *derivation* assumption, which, in the General Testing Principle, replaces the hypothetico-*deductive* assumption, is less intellectually exciting than its predecessor, which offered the delusory hope that important disputes over the scientific status of theories could be settled by straightforward mathematical or logical techniques. The *derivation* assumption, on the other hand, releases anxiety concerning the fallibility of the observer. Who is to *decide* what particular hypotheses are derivable from what general statements, or when a hypothesis has been falsified? And how are we to preclude the subtle distortions of Fluctuating Rigour and of the unconscious psychological techniques?

I can now begin to explain the impact on philosophy students of *Language, Truth and Logic*. The conflicting theories of metaphysicians had been producing an effect comparable to that of the conflicting stimuli presented to Pavlov's dogs, or to the victims of brainwashing. The high-toned bell signalling the food of insight alternated with the low-toned bell signalling the empty plate of nonsense, and sometimes the bells were brought painfully close to the point of indistinguishability. The elegant clarity of *Language, Truth and Logic* awakened the hope that the criterion it offered would enable the perceptive reader to cultivate a phototropic discrimination of the meaningful. The five factors suggested on pp. 224–5 above also contributed to its impact: the reader felt a challenge to clear his mind of cant; felt relief that intellectual walls were breached; excitement that a powerful technique could be acquired; pride in the spurning of illusions; and exhilaration in the reconcentration of misdirected energy.

Although the Verification Principle has been revised by its originator in the light of meticulous and prolonged critical reassessment, the organization of attitudes which it precipitated has undergone surprisingly little change. The untestable metaphysical assumptions and theories which were discredited by that principle have not been reinstated, and the rehabilitation of 'metaphysics' by modern philosophers, such as Strawson, far from being a reversion to the armchair science of the universe, is the exercise of individual judgement on the basis of a tacit hypothesis made explicit in the Testing Principle: good judgement consists, in the main, in being able to make sound, untestable assumptions, many of which are derived, but not deduced, from testable hypotheses (pp. 157–8). The untestable assumptions may be derived from a hypothesis which is not consciously recognized, but which could be tested if it were formulated and made conscious. Intuitive judgement of character, for example, is probably the unconscious apprehension of minute signs, such as smell, details of expression, conduct and demeanour, and so on, which point to some characteristic which has been unconsciously associated with similar signs in the impact or demeanour of other people. If such an association becomes the subject of a psychodynamic hypothesis ('Obsessional symptoms

$S_1, S_2, S_3, S_4 \ldots$ are associated with thrift, orderliness, independence of thought and obstinacy', for example), a new situation has been created. The pre-scientific, untestable, intuitive judgement can now be explained, the new hypothesis can be tested, and a scientific psycho-dynamic training can increase the capacity for shrewd, intuitive discernment, just as a training in microscopy can augment the capacity for visual discernment.

The important difference between the Verification Principle of *Language, Truth and Logic* and the General Testing Principle towards which we are advancing in this book is the recognition in the latter that the two-storied house of syntactics and semantics rests upon the shifting sands of pragmatics; the recognition that there is no decisive proof, but only indecisive persuasion; no decisive criterion for distinguishing between *consistent* dreaming and consistent waking experience; no decisive criterion for distinguishing between consistent sense and consistent nonsense.

One mechanism which contributed to the impact of the Verification Principle remains to be elucidated by reference to Freud's theory of wit. The intellectual pleasure attending the origination and appreciation of wit is derived from the sudden release of psychic energy which is normally 'bound' by an inhibition. The inhibiting factor is a taboo, and the forms of communication thus proscribed in our community are primarily forms which exhibit certain deprecated attitudes to religion, sex, excretion, and antisocial aggression. The subtlety, deviousness, ingenuity, and humour of the witty remark provide a literary licence which permits a sudden release of aggression, sexual curiosity, religious irreverence . . . or a combination of such prohibited elements.

An interesting example of elements in combination is the witticism quoted by Freud (1905b). Two new-rich businessmen, who had made their fortune by dubious methods, and were determined to gatecrash 'high society' by lavish hospitality, were giving one of their splendid house-parties to the titled, rich, and famous. The climax of the evening was to be the unveiling of two large portraits of themselves, painted by a distinguished artist, and placed one at each end of an enormous wall. An eminent art critic was to pass judgement upon the merit of the paintings. He walked from one to the other and then stood gazing at the bare wall between. 'And where,' he asked, 'is the Saviour?' Here we find a combination of slight irreverence towards the sacrosanct, extreme indirect aggression against the unscrupulous businessmen, and a breach of the social taboo on criticism of a host by his guest.

Freud's theory, I suggest, can be extended beyond the sphere of wit. Part of the intellectual pleasure afforded by the Verification Principle sprang from the newly sanctioned release of aggression against numerous obscure and pretentious but not patently valueless philosophical writings which had kept slipping out of focus under the unwilling eyes of the conscientious student. The taboo on irreverence was broken.

The key to the catalytic efficacy of literature also unlocks the problem of its anticatalytic effects. A theory or word-picture or a work of art may induce either liberating hope or paralysing fear. The hope which revived the victims of the Hell-terror induced by Wesley, for example, was his word-picture of Heaven. The hope which revived some victims of philosophical obfuscation was the criterion of demarcation offered by the Verification Principle. For those whose hope lay in some metaphysical doctrine or theory, however, the Verification Principle was a threat. This explains the principle's anticatalytic effects and the defensive reaction it provoked. The technique of Fluctuating Rigour assumed one of its most devastating forms: the sound logical objections to the early formulations of the Verification Principle were used, not as a first step towards more and more adequate reformulations, but as excuses for rejecting a dangerous instrument. Offensive action against the potent instrument of logical analysis is a means to the defence of cherished beliefs and attitudes. The Straw Man Fallacy may also be put to destructive use: an indefensible version of 'Verificationism' may be persuasively refuted, with the implication that all attempts at verification are misguided.

COMMITMENT

If a clear criterion of demarcation between sense and nonsense, between the meaningful and the meaningless, between the true and the false, between the testable and the untestable, between the scientific and the unscientific, between the veridical and the illusory, between appearance and reality, or any other of the pairs of antithetical concepts which become charged with affective significance – is the quest which sustains the hope of the philosophical crusader, the argument of this book has been continuous discouragement. To assume, for example, that catalytic efficacy can provide a criterion would be to succumb to a naïve form of psychologism. The psychological impact of a work of science, philosophy, literature, or art can never guarantee its merit or validity.

At this point the philosopher may object that I cannot assert the impossibility of precluding shared delusions and at the same time use such terms as 'distortion', 'rationalization', 'fallacies', and so on, which seem to imply that some beliefs are 'objectively' false. I simply reply that I can. When I describe a belief as a fallacy I am committing myself to a point of view which excludes that belief. I do not contradict myself when I go on to say that I have no access to my own motives for distortion and that I cannot preclude the possibility of shared delusions. I feel certain that the area of the moon which is normally invisible from the earth has been photographed from a Russian satellite, but I do not find it inconceivable (though so improbable that the possibility does not now interest me) that the photograph was a fake which has not been detected.

The distinctions, therefore, between the fallacy of Unrestricted Scepticism, the fallacy of Fluctuating Scepticism and the philosophically indispensable technique of *tentative scepticism* are predominantly distinctions of degrees of commitment. If I commit myself to a position of extreme scepticism, and take it seriously, I am a little mad. If I cannot eat any food until it has been tested in my presence because I cannot be sure that it is not poisoned, although I am not, for example, an autocrat surrounded by enemies, then I am suffering from a mental illness. If, on the other hand, I can confidently eat any food that is put before me, I may still admit the possibility that I may, at any time, eat food that has been poisoned (perhaps by a fanatical packer in a hostile country), and at the same time assert that the possibility does not worry me and does not affect my appetite. Similarly, I can confidently assert my philosophical point of view, and at the same time admit that I may, at any time, receive a letter from a reader pointing out a fallacy in my argument which I shall be forced by his reasoning to admit. I may also be forced to admit that the fallacy is due to a motive for distortion he has detected. I commit myself to my point of view and wait to be proved wrong: I wait, that is, to be *persuaded by argument* that I am wrong.

If I do not admit the fallacy, however – if I am not persuaded by the argument – it is still open to an observer to say that I have been proved wrong. His statement would *reflect* his own agreement with the critic. If all trained observers were to agree that I had been proved wrong, and I still refused to accept the criticism, then it could reasonably be said by each of them that I was 'objectively' wrong. But there would nevertheless remain the possibility that I was right and they were wrong, although they could reasonably refuse to take that possibility

seriously. In other words, they could confidently commit themselves
to the majority belief.

When I say that there would remain the possibility that I was right,
what do I mean by 'right'? Am I claiming that I might be objectively
right in some different sense of 'objectively' from 'according to the
unanimous or majority opinion of trained observers'? We can all
imagine the situation where a fact is denied by all human beings and
yet is true. We can say that it was 'objectively' true that the earth was
spheroid when everyone believed it was flat. The term 'objectively'
reflects our present confident and unanimous conviction that the earth
is spheroid. It would be eccentric of me to speak or otherwise behave
as if I seriously doubted whether the earth was spheroid, because I
have no reason to do so. Yet I can admit the possibility that advances
in the theory of the structure of 'the universe' might render suspect or
even obsolete our present conception of spheroid objects moving in
orbits. To admit the possibility of changes in beliefs and changes in
language projections is neither to withhold belief from any particular
hypothesis which is universally accepted as true by present-day
scientists nor to refuse to use the current language projections which
today seem most adequate. It would have been unreasonable for a
contemporary of Newton's to refuse to use the terms 'momentum'
and 'energy' on the ground that Newton's theory would almost certainly be revised or superseded by later theorists. It would be equally
unreasonable for me to refuse, on similar grounds, to use 'neutron' or
'proton'.

To refuse to commit oneself to any *particular* hypothesis of a new
theory, without having any *particular* ground for rejecting it, and
without having an alternative hypothesis to suggest, on the *general*
ground that *no* theory has survived in the form that was first proposed,
is just as unreasonable as to refuse to entertain the *general* hypothesis
that *any* current theory may be revised with the advance of science and
philosophy. It is reasonable to refuse to commit myself to a hypothesis
only if I now genuinely believe some rival hypothesis with roughly
the same explanatory powers and the same range of application, or if
my intellectual judgement causes me to reject the methods or the
motives of the theorist.

I could, therefore, consistently maintain some belief which I
uniquely held, asserting that no one else had sufficient insight to share
my point of view, *and* assert the general proposition that there was a
possibility that *any* belief I now held might be mistaken. *Just as to
admit the general possibility that my food may be poisoned does not necessarily*

imply mistrust of any of the food I eat, so to admit the general possibility of error does not necessarily imply a failure of commitment to any particular belief.

THE MEANING OF 'BELIEF'

If I say that a particular belief is true, therefore, I am accepting the language projection in which the belief is formulated and evincing my confidence that the evidence for the belief outweighs the evidence against it. I would hesitate to say that the following beliefs are true: (1) that the ego has developed out of the cortical layers of the id; (2) that the universe is expanding at tremendous speed; and (3) that Tokyo is the biggest city in the world; and for different reasons. I hesitate about the first belief, not because I think Freud was definitely wrong, or because the belief does not contain an important insight, but because I find this particular use of a heterogeneous language projection somewhat bewildering. I hesitate about the second because I do not understand how it is possible for us to know what is happening to 'the universe'; in fact, I personally cannot form a clear conception of 'the universe'. The third seems doubtful to me because I do not know either how the citizens of Tokyo have been counted or how the limits of Tokyo and London are defined for purposes of comparison; in short, I am not sure that the evidence for the belief outweighs the evidence against, though I might be able to find out.

To say that a proposition is true is usually taken to imply that it is timelessly true, and from this it might be inferred that future generations, if they are rational and honest and have access to the relevant data, will assent to that proposition as now formulated. When this implication is made explicit it immediately becomes dubious. Why should we suppose that the shifts in language projections which have rendered earlier theories untenable in their original form should come to a sudden stop in our generation? Some of our current 'factual statements' will be described as true by our descendants of the twenty-fifth century; some will be called false; and others will have come to seem half-true or misleading as a result of shifts in point of view and language projection. If we try to assess the stability of our beliefs, we may judge correctly about a large proportion of them, but over a wide range we cannot be sure.

The argument has now reached a point where we must reject the pseudo-objective and timeless interpretations of 'This belief is true' in favour of a psychological interpretation. If I assert 'This belief is true'

I evince my agreement with the belief and imply (1) that I am convinced that it is expressed in terms which conform to what *I* consider
to be the most up-to-date and consistent language projection relating
to the topic; (2) that I am convinced that the available evidence in
favour of the belief outweighs the evidence against it; and (3) that I
have no reason to suspect that the methods or the motives of the
believer are producing some distortion in his thought which renders
the belief suspect, whether or not I can expose the distortion. This
third implication needs clarification. I may describe as true some belief
expressed by X – say, 'My method of checking the evidence is more
efficient than yours', even though I am aware that X is biased and
that, since he has not thoroughly compared his method with mine, he
has formed a true opinion on inadequate grounds. If, however, I
deprecate X's motives or the method by which he arrived at the belief,
and have no independent source of evidence, I will not say 'This belief
is true' (see p. 117).

If a fortune-teller makes a prediction that a man with red hair, say,
is going to play an important part in a girl's life, and if the girl is subsequently attracted to a man with red hair and marries him, we would
hesitate to say that the fortune-teller's belief was true if we reject her
method of arriving at the predictive belief, or if we think that her use
of language was predominantly suggestive rather than informative, so
that the girl became interested in men with red hair after the fortune-
teller's prediction.

This analysis leaves open the question whether the belief has or has
not any determining effect upon my expectations, dispositions, sets, or
attitudes; whether it has or not depends on the degrees of three scales;
the immediacy–remoteness scale, the relevance–irrelevance scale, and
the scale of rigour. If, for example, the statistical prediction that about
700 people will be killed or injured on roads in Britain during the
Easter holiday causes X to stay indoors to avoid the risk, the observer
can draw the pragmatic inference that X understands the prediction as
immediately relevant to his expectations, and that the risk appears to
him – perhaps because the fear of death or injury is reinforced by a
phantasy fear – much greater than it appears to most road-users. X and
Y, each of whom believes the statement 'About 700 people will be
killed or injured' (p), and each of whom believes of himself 'One of
the casualties may be me' (q), may be said, if we abstract from pragmatics, to have the same beliefs concerning the extent of the risk and
the possibility of being killed or injured. Yet the difference in behaviour
between X, who stays indoors, and Y, who cheerfully sets out on the

crowded roads, is more important than the resemblance in assertion and conscious belief. If the difference is not reflected in a logic, that logic is defective. In other words, it has to be recognized that in this context 'X believes p and q' and 'Y believes p and q' may be statements which have different entailments.

CONFIDENCE IN JUDGEMENT

Judgement, though precarious, can be confident. The skilful canoeist is quick to notice the slightest sign that the current he is riding may be carrying him towards unnavigable rapids or towards the rocks, and quick to act on the warnings of an observer who is better placed to study his mistakes. On the other hand, if he is experienced, he will trust himself to the current with confidence when neither he nor the observer can detect any sign of danger. Similarly, the skilful theorist is quick to notice any paradox, anomaly, or inconsistency which serves as a sign that his stream of conscious–unconscious thought is carrying him towards fallacies or distortions, and quick to act on the warnings of a critic who is better placed to study his mistakes because he has not the same motives for distortion. On the other hand he would be misguided if he did not trust his thought – although a great part of it originates in unconscious phantasy – when neither he nor his critic can detect any fault in the reasoning of an argument, or any defect in the structure of a work of art.

MOTIVES UNDERLYING BELIEFS

We may now assemble scattered clues in the hope of discovering something more enduring, if less gratifying, than a clear-cut criterion: a *method* for distinguishing honesty and rationality. The first clue appears in Chapter 11 (p. 144): 'The bereaved man's need to believe in communication with the dead is . . . unconscious because the belief itself would be jeopardized by the recognition of the need for the belief.' In the same vein we may add: the hypnotized man's rationalization – the false motive he invents *ad hoc* to dissimulate the irrationality of his compulsive execution of the hypnotist's suggestion – would be jeopardized by the knowledge that he had been given just that command while in a state of trance. The belief held by the patient or the student that the analyst has magical powers would be jeopardized by the interpretation that he needs to believe in a God-like magician who can control his emerging aggression. On the other hand, the psychotic's paranoid belief that he is being systematically persecuted may be immune to interpretations, because the irrational conviction is embedded in the relatively inaccessible stratum of the psyche which was formed in the first few months of life.

It follows that the investigation of motives, reasons, and needs for holding certain beliefs is an indispensable factor in the quest for honesty and rationality. The investigation may be limited by two formidable barriers: the inaccessibility of the source of the belief; and the inexorability of the need to believe when there can be no adequate compensation for the loss of the conviction. The philosopher has no reason to despise a pragmatic clue to the second of these barriers: the man who needs to maintain an irrational belief is no more tolerant of scientific investigation into his need than the man who pretends that his glass eye is real. He would resist it with fear or anger or both. Fear or anger evoked by a critical investigation of a belief, then, is *prima facie* evidence (but no more) of a need to maintain a dishonest or irrational belief.

There is a further clue on pp. 144–5: one of the motives for distortion is love, hate, or fear of the author or representative of a theory or work of art. In analysis neither the exaggeration nor the belittling of his powers deceives the analyst, because he expects to be both over- and under-estimated in the positive and negative phases of the analysis. The only delusions which can *totally* escape the scientific investigation of the need to believe are those which are shared by both subject and investigator. Trainee-dogmatism, therefore, whether in psychoanalysis or in any other branch of science, marks the limit of the detachment of the expert: his failure to push the investigation of the need to believe to its conclusion.

Let us now turn to the clue provided by the Need Hypothesis of Chapter 4 (p. 58). The term 'phantasy' may suggest the obviously phantastical, such as illusions, delusions, or day-dreams, but it is intended to comprise everything that is unrealistic or irrational in the thought of any human being. Lack-, wish-, and fear-fulfilment, then, are pervasive elements, not only of dreams, but also of the conscious, would-be-rational thinking of all theorists. The clearest example of an interpersonal wish-phantasy is Heaven (or Elysium or Valhalla); of an interpersonal fear-phantasy, Hell; of an interpersonal lack-phantasy, the jealous and irascible Father–God of the Old Testament, who may reward or punish, who is the object of both hope and fear, and who, when the real father is found wanting, fulfils the *lack* of an omnipotent and omniscient flesh-and-blood father.

The Need Hypothesis reveals that philosophy merges with psychology at the point where the philosopher's interest shifts from the exposure of irrationality to the investigation of the *need* to preserve phantasy elements in the language projection. The original philosopher is an artist who devises a new language projection which he believes to be more consistent and comprehensive than its predecessors, and who seeks to persuade his readers to adopt it. It follows, therefore, that psychological acumen is as indispensable in philosophy as logical skill. To expose fallacies without tracking them to their source is like killing ants without trying to find the nest. The method for distinguishing honesty and rationality is the negative method of stripping away their opposites. It is the analytical investigation of

1 *situational* motives for distortion – the meeting-point of philosophy, psychology, politics, economics, and social science (p. 120);

2 convictions, attitudes, and prejudices inculcated by 'authorities' at the pre-critical stage of the child's development; and

3 phantasy lacks, wishes, and fears originating in unconscious needs.

As this investigation progresses beyond the scope of common sense it becomes psychoanalysis. By the application of psychoanalytical techniques more and more kinds of rationalization, self-deception, hypocrisy, suggestion, and irrational hope, fear, hatred, or guilt can be recognized, named, and stripped of their disguises. The detailed differential study of the effects of interpretations in the clinical situation can provide, step by step, the *scientific* criteria for distinguishing between the rejection of a defective interpretation (falsification of a hypothesis) and the rejection of a true one (resistance); between the acceptance of a true interpretation (insight) and the acceptance of a false or inadequate one (suggestion or trainee-dogmatism); between the rebuttal of a mistaken interpretation of unconscious need and the indignant refusal to admit the accurately diagnosed need to believe, when the admission would jeopardize the belief. By extrapolation from such interaction between analyst and patient or student, or between analyst and group, a differential study can be made of the effects, in other situations, of utterances which exemplify the same uses of language, or of statements which threaten beliefs that are psychologically significant.

Why choose honesty as the cornerstone of the moral edifice? It may be argued that insulatory illusions and delusions are often innocuous, that they mitigate the suffering of mankind, or even that they are a necessary bulwark against moral anarchy. It must be emphasized that the term 'honesty' is here used in an an extended sense comprising psychoanalytic insight and self-knowledge. A choice among values cannot be decisively justified, but it can be defended. Realistic insight into unconscious motives and into potentialities and limitations of character facilitates realistic expectations and demands, and hence realistic relationships, negotiations, concessions, adjustments, and agreements. Unrealistic demands upon human nature and the exaggeration of the differences between those who keep and those who lose a socially acceptable equilibrium tend to produce intolerance, fear, hypocrisy, guilt, and cruelty. The promulgation of impracticable moral imperatives imposes a burden of guilt or despair or hypocrisy on both precept-maker and precept-breaker. It is difficult for the man who has insight into his unconscious impulses to see himself as incomparably superior to the thief, the liar, the murderer, the rapist, or the pervert. It may be better for a man to admit quite freely that he loves himself very much more than his neighbour and that he covets his neighbour's wife, than to spend his life either trying not to notice these psychological facts or suffering acutely from guilt because they have forced themselves on his attention. The man who is not afraid of his desires and his weaknesses may prove to be less likely to fall victim to the compulsive enactment of disastrous impulses than the man who suppresses them until they reach dam-bursting force.

THE GENERAL TESTING PRINCIPLE

The discussion can now be summed-up in the final version of the General Testing Principle, valid for both science and philosophy:

When an assertion or an assumption or a theory or any other kind of proposition is in dispute, whether it is an individual utterance (token) or a repeatable statement or hypothesis (type) *which is always based on individual utterances*, then –

1 it should first be precisely formulated, and *not* merely given a name, such as 'positivism' or 'Behaviourism' or 'pragmatism' or 'verificationism' or 'inductionism' or 'empiricism' or 'psychologism';

2 it should be analysed, and if possible split up into its component logical elements;

3 each of these elements should be examined to determine:

(i) whether it is *predominantly* analytic or synthetic, and whether it is predominantly assertive, descriptive, informative, explanatory, directive, classificatory, recommendatory, performative, prescriptive, appraisive, emotive, suggestive, normative, evaluative, ascriptive, claim-staking, guarded ('probably'), tendentious, coloured, riskless or risk-taking, enactive, focusing, reflective, etc.;

(ii) whether it is made from a conventional and familiar or from an original and unfamiliar point of view; and

(iii) whether it is expressed in a familiar or an unfamiliar language projection, or in overlapping or heterogeneous language projections;

4 if it is decisively testable it should be tested by scientific experiments and/or by real or invented examples, all designed to demonstrate that it should be either abandoned or reformulated;

5 if it is *not* decisively testable it should *not* be discredited solely for that reason, because some of the most important assumptions are not testable, and because good judgement consists, in the main, in being able to make sound, untestable assumptions, and bad judgement consists in the reverse; it should be examined for the part it plays in a theory, or traced to the testable assumptions from which it is *derived* (not deduced);

6 if it is not decisively testable the reason or motive for asserting or assuming it can be investigated; there may be:

(i) a *situational motive:* the holding of the belief may bring some financial, political, social, or psychological gain which can be detected by an observer standing outside the motive-producing situation;

(ii) a *patent genetic reason*, such as the inculcation of convictions or attitudes by 'authorities' (parents, teachers, priests, etc.) at the precritical stage of the child's development: convictions which go on operating like hypnotic suggestions throughout his life; or

(iii) a *disguised psychodynamic reason*, such as a phantasy lack, wish, or fear, originating in unconscious needs, which can be interpreted with the aid of the Need Hypothesis (p. 58) and the theory of Unconscious Psychological Techniques (pp. 210–22);

7 if it is not decisively testable, fear or anger attending the investigation of the reason or motive for holding it is *prima facie* evidence both that the belief is dishonest or irrational and that it is insecure;

8 if a hypothesis, principle, theory, work of art, word-picture, etc., acts as a *catalyst*, precipitating a new organization or orientation of thought, its catalytic impact requires a rigorous psychodynamic analysis; hence the *Catalytic Efficacy Hypothesis:*

The catalytic efficacy of a theory, work of art, word-picture, etc., like the catalytic efficacy of psychologically or physiologically induced excitement or shock, is due to its *affective* impact; this impact may be caused by:

(i) the sudden increase of suggestibility following upon fear or uncertainty or exhaustion;

(ii) the appeasement or satisfaction of the need for punishment;

(iii) the release of phantasy wishes, hopes, fears, or guilt;

(iv) the sophistication of magical thinking;

(v) identification with a powerful or admired figure, real or conceptual (Julius Caesar, the Superman, the Outsider, etc.);

(vi) the release of repressed or suppressed aggression, especially against authority or against imposed ideals;

(vii) the release of psychic energy which has been bound by a social taboo or by personal inhibitions;

(viii) the redirection of dissipated or misdirected energy;

(ix) the relief which comes from the fusion of segregated spheres of thought;

(x) the sense of power emanating from the acquisition of new intellectual techniques or new language projections;

(xi) the pride of dispensing with illusions or delusions;

(xii) the exhilaration of progress towards emotional and intellectual integration;

9 if any of the factors of (8) are seen to contribute to the catalysis, meticulous analysis of those factors may be required to determine whether the psychodynamic gain is real or delusory; and there is no infallible method of precluding shared delusions;

10 the loss of psychodynamically important (e.g. comforting) beliefs or assumptions needs to be compensated by some equivalent psychodynamic gain (see p. 267).

17

The Science and Philosophy of Psychodynamics

LANGUAGE PROJECTIONS AND PSYCHODYNAMICS

It remains to set the foregoing argument in perspective. The point of view has emerged that the essential difference between the science of psychodynamics and other sciences is based, not on any philosophical distinction between mind and matter, but on a difference of language projection, of direction of interest, and of gaining insight. The science of psychodynamics is the science which throws light on processes in the human being and on the interrelations between him and his environment which are described in the language projections TFM and TFME, and which cannot be adequately described in the language projections of the physical sciences with their common-sense counterparts (P), or in the projections of other sciences that study human relationships, such as economics and the social sciences. Many fields of research have contributed to the science of psychodynamics, including valuable work by psychologists who call themselves Behaviourists. The fallacy of Behaviourism does not necessarily vitiate a programme of research. On the contrary, the value of an experimental or statistical study may be enhanced by the precise redefinition (in P) of TFM terms such as 'intelligence', for the specific purpose of the investigation. There is a danger, however, that tests of 'intelligence' (P), for example, will be mistaken for tests of intelligence (TFM).

The science of psychodynamics includes research which *can* be described, wholly or in part, in the language projection P, when such research throws light on mental phenomena: i.e. on phenomena which can *not* be adequately described in P. Of the data which are provided, for example, by brain physiology, endocrinology, pharmacology, Pavlovian animal physiology, intelligence and aptitude testing, Rorschach testing, genetics, research into environmental influences on identical twins, child psychology, educational psychology, social psychology, ethology, etc., much may be written in a language projection from which TFM and TFME are excluded, and yet when these findings are *interpreted*, with the use of TFM or TFME, they constitute important contributions to the science of psychodynamics. The terms 'intelligence', 'personality', 'emotion', 'pain' . . . may be redefined to exclude TFM, and so transferred to the language projection P; but if conclusions about such redefined concepts in P are to throw light on intelligence, personality, emotion, pain . . . in the customary TFM senses of the words, they have to be interpreted, and *the interpretation is impossible without the use of TFM or TFME.*

It is a mistake to believe, therefore, as some behaviouristic experimental psychologists do, that the dolorimeter, for example, measures pain (in the ordinary TFM sense of the term). The dolorimeter does *not* measure pain. It measures certain observable and measurable *symptoms* of pain.

PSYCHODYNAMICS AND CONVERGING DISCIPLINES

The disciplines mentioned above raise few philosophical problems apart from the central problem of the relationship between P, TFM, and TFME. The interaction of the overlapping and *partly* incompatible language projections of behaviouristic psychology and psychodynamics needs clarification. There are two psychodynamic hypotheses, for example, which are clearly relevant to behaviouristic studies of 'memory' (learning, retention, recall, recognition): first, that repressed 'memories' can be revived, which has been established experimentally by hypnotic techniques and by the use of drugs such as LSD 25 (lysergic acid diethylamide), and second, that forgetting and remembering are systematically related to fluctuations in the conflict between unconscious impulses. Any findings experimentally established by behaviouristic techniques or by psychiatric research into the effects of abreactive drugs such as LSD *can be incorporated into psychodynamic theory without modifying the language projection, which includes P, TFM, and TFME.* Most of the findings experimentally established in psychoanalytic sessions, however, *cannot be incorporated into any behaviouristic theory which excludes TFME, or,* a fortiori, *TFM.*

The philosophy of psychodynamics is the application of philosophical techniques to the common-sense language projection TFM, to the science of psychodynamics in general, and to psychoanalysis in particular. There are two reasons why psychoanalysis sets the major problems for the future philosophy of psychodynamics: first, because it has provided the experimental technique and the language projection from which most of the major psychological discoveries have flowed, and will probably continue to flow; and, second, because most of the important philosophical problems in the sphere of psychodynamics are raised by the new language projection of psychoanalysis. The mountain of work facing philosophers of psychodynamics is glimpsed in every chapter of this exploratory study.

The key to the rapid acceleration in the progress of the physical sciences, of philosophy, and of psychology is the technique of analysis. Analysis is the most potent of all scientific instruments because it is the precursor of re-synthesis. It has taken widely dissimilar forms in chemistry, physics, biophysics, biology, ethology, philosophy, and psychoanalysis, but a common element, conceptual analysis, can be distinguished. Chemical analysis consists of four main kinds of identification and estimation: of chemical individuals in a mixture; of elements in a compound; of types of substances in complex mixtures; and of isotopes in an 'element'. Physical analysis has yielded the complex and constantly changing theory of nuclear configurations, and biophysics is the application of physical theory to biological phenomena. Biological analysis has distinguished cells, chromosomes – the units of chromatin, or stainable tissue – and genes, distributed along the chromosomes, which are assumed to be physiological elements associated with distinguishable hereditary characteristics. Ethological analysis provides distinctions between those elements in the environment which provoke an innate instinctual response from an animal, and those elements which are irrelevant even if the animal's sense organs can receive them: that is, between 'sign stimuli' and neutral environmental elements. Tinbergen suggests as 'the question upon which the scientific study of behaviour, or ethology, is based: Why does the animal behave as it does?' (1951, p. 1).

If we make a minor change as a concession to human vanity and substitute 'organism' for 'animal', this is precisely the question upon which, according to the point of view of this book, scientific psychodynamics is based: Why does the organism (here the human being) behave as it does in the conditions under investigation? As ethology and psychodynamics are parallel disciplines, therefore, the findings of ethology are of special interest to the student of psychodynamics. The reason why the subjects appear so different that it may surprise many readers to find that their key questions are identical is that the *verbal* behaviour of human adults is so complex that it constitutes a large part of the material of psychoanalysis. If ethological analysis and the analysis of the play of very young children are compared, however, the similarity is more readily apparent.

We can now obtain a commanding view of a broad stream of inquiry; we can discern a single discipline with two aspects: the science and philosophy of psychodynamics. The central current is the science of psychoanalysis with the philosophy of that science (i.e. the art of the abstract thought of psychoanalysis). Running parallel and contributing a more and more precise theory of instinct is the science of ethology.

The *psychological* theory of instinct has been shown, by Ronald Fletcher's valuable work of analysis and re-synthesis, *Instinct in Man*, to be a progressive cumulation of insights. The concept of instinct, which underwent a period of scientific opprobrium, has been decisively reinstated by that work. Fletcher has demonstrated that none of the components into which instinctive activity has been dissected by conceptual analysis, such as 'need', 'drive', 'behaviour-pattern', 'reflexes', and so on, is a satisfactory substitute for the concept of instinct as a whole. The insights of Darwin, William James (e.g. the Law of Transitoriness, which anticipated the Critical Period Hypothesis), C. Lloyd Morgan, L. T. Hobhouse, William McDougall, James Drever, etc. have been disentangled from irrelevancies and inconsistencies and related to the work of modern ethologists and to psychoanalysis. Fletcher points out that '... the earliest and most fundamental "learning processes" of the human individual (the earliest and most important ways in which he accommodates himself to the complex social environment) are predominantly *affective* in nature, and occur during a *critical period* of development: during the first four or five years of the child's life, and in the context of the family situation (1957, p. 256), and suggests that Freud's system comprises a better 'learning theory' for the purpose of social psychology than any of the orthodox learning theories in psychology.

A quite different concatenation of inquiries which contribute to the science and philosophy of psychodynamics is revealed by William Sargant's *Battle for the Mind*. Although the point of view from which the book is written is alien to that of the present work, and is vitiated, according to my thesis, by a misunderstanding of the distinction between psychology and physiology, the analysis and re-synthesis which have enabled the author to link together apparently unconnected phenomena have made an important contribution to psychology, and potentially to philosophy as well.

A full discussion of the philosophical disagreement between the two points of view would require a chapter to itself; there is space here only for a dogmatic assertion of a rival theory. With stimulating insight, Sargant has related part of Pavlov's *physiological* theory to such *psychological* phenomena as religious conversion, brainwashing and indoctrination, and the eliciting of confessions by police interrogators. The relevant parts of Pavlov's theory are the three distinct and progressive stages of 'transmarginal' inhibition in dogs: first, the *equivalent* stage, when all stimuli produced the same amounts of saliva; second, the *paradoxical* stage, when weak stimuli produced livelier responses than stronger stimuli; and, third, the *ultra-paradoxical* stage, when positive conditioned responses suddenly switched to negative ones, and vice versa. Because these stages can be related to the experiences of the victims of Hell-fire intimidation, brain-washing, and police interrogation, there is a temptation to infer that both lines of inquiry belong to the same discipline. Whereas Eysenck supposed that the Pavlovian hypotheses were psychological, although Pavlov himself insisted that they were physiological, Sargant makes the converse supposition that the theory of brainwashing and conversion is physiological. He says, for example, 'The degree of physiological [*sic*] "co-operation" or "transference" that can be established between the police examiner and the citizen under questioning, or the preacher and his congregation, or the political speaker and his audience, is vital to the problem. Whoever can be roused either to fear or to anger by politician, priest or policeman, is more easily led to accept the desired pattern of "co-operation", even though this may violate his normal judgment' (1957, p. 208).

When incorporating the valuable insight of Sargant's thesis into the philosophy of psychodynamics, we can avoid the confusion of psychology with physiology if we make use of the concept of language projections. Transference is *not* physiological, for the conclusive reason that it cannot be explained or even described in the language projection of physiology. We cannot even transpose a simple sentence such as 'He terrified them by his vivid description of the torments of Hell' into physiological terminology. For such a statement *the language projection TFM is indispensable.*

All the examples related to each other in *Battle for the Mind* are important material for the science of psychodynamics, and the philosophical and religious presuppositions of the author, as well as the sets of phenomena requiring conceptual analysis and re-synthesis are material for the philosophy of psychodynamics. Nevertheless, *Battle for the Mind* is merely a starting-point. There are important differences and resemblances between the scientific torturing of dogs, the symptoms of combat exhaustion, the effects on patients of psychoanalytic treatment, the forms of abreaction produced by drugs or hypnosis, the effects of electric or insulin shock treatment, the phenomena of modern revivalist meetings, the evidence provided by leucotomy, the impact of John Wesley's terrifying eloquence, the conversions described by Arthur Koestler in his autobiographical studies, *Arrow in the Blue* and *The Invisible Writing*, the electroencephalographic evidence that the brain is sensitive to rhythmic stimulation by percussion and flashing lights, the techniques by which confessions are extorted, and the effects of voodoo drums, of the bull-roarer, of the Welsh hwyl, and of medieval orgiastic dancing.

The fascinating problem of elucidating those resemblances and differences requires much more rigorous analysis than appears in Sargant's exposition. We discover, for example, that although Sargant disapproves of the techniques of brainwashing and indoctrination as used by foreign powers, he admires Wesley's 'great success' with methods he finds very similar, because they were good for England! 'It is now generally admitted that he made great numbers of ordinary English people think less about their material well-being than their spiritual salvation, thus fortifying them, at a critical period of the French Revolution, against dangerous materialistic teachings of Tom Paine' (1957, p. 82). 'Must a new concentration on brain physiology and brain mechanics weaken religious faith and beliefs? On the contrary, a better understanding of the means of creating and consolidating faith will enable religious bodies to expand much more rapidly' (ibid., p. 213).

From the point of view of the present thesis, there is only one way of interpreting Sargant's moral recommendation: It is legitimate to subject people to violent shocks or to intimidate them to the point of nervous collapse in order to make them more suggestible, *provided* you then inculcate beliefs that coincide with Dr Sargant's beliefs, or beliefs that he thinks are socially or psychologically expedient.

We are reminded of one of the crucial conclusions of this book. In *Battle for the Mind* conceptual analysis is carried to the point where it becomes clear that any profound reorientation of thought, such as conversion to or from a religion or a political ideology, is not purely intellectual, but has an affective basis which requires a psychodynamic explanation. This hypothesis is comprised in the Catalytic Efficacy

Hypothesis of p. 237, Section 8. The analytic achievement enables the author to effect his philosophically valuable re-synthesis, which itself has the catalytic effect of breaching the conceptual barriers between apparently disparate sets of phenomena. The analysis is not, however, carried to the point where it is possible to undertake a differential explanation of the various kinds of psychic reorganization: the sort of explanation which is briefly indicated in the Catalytic Efficacy Hypothesis. If the General Testing Principle were applied to the material of *Battle for the Mind* it would be impossible to assimilate indoctrination, whether religious, political, or any other, to the interpretations of scientific psychoanalysis, and the differences between the multifarious phenomena would be shown to be as philosophically important as the common factor.

The concept of overlapping language projections could then be used to eradicate the physiology–psychology confusions. Sargant asserts, for example, that 'religious feelings in man may be destroyed if *too extensive* an operation is performed in the frontal lobes' (1957, p. 77). A Salvation Army worker who complained for months that she had committed sins against the Holy Ghost was operated on by the Swedish psychiatrist Rylander (1948) ,who relates: 'After the dressing had been taken off, I asked her, "How are you now? What about the Holy Ghost?" Smiling, she answered, "Oh, the Holy Ghost; there is no Holy Ghost."' 'However,' Sargant remarks, 'using more modern types of operations, and much more limited cuts in the frontal lobes, symptoms of anxiety and obsessional rumination can be lessened without producing too many undesirable effects on ordinary religious beliefs.'

Leaving the implications of this remarkable statement unanalysed, we should note that an account of personality changes caused by frontal lobotomy has to move from TFM to P and back to TFM:

She believed she had committed sins against the Holy Ghost TFM d*
I made an incision of *x* dimensions in area *Y* of the frontal lobes P e†
After recovery she no longer believed in the Holy Ghost   TFM d

When describing the operation in private the doctor might say, 'I excised her belief in the Holy Ghost with a scalpel', but this would be a macabre joke rather than a serious psychological or physiological assertion. A complete explanation of the change in beliefs effected by the incision is at present impossible, because no one knows either how physiological events or states (i.e. those described in the language

* Dispositional.   † Episodic.

projection of physiology or physics) are related to psychodynamic events or states (i.e. those described in the language projection TFM or TFME). Any account or explanation of such a change in beliefs brought about by physiological intervention could *only* be given in a combination of TFM and P, which are then overlapping language projections. It could not be given in a purely physiological or physical language projection.

The above brief comments on the material of *Battle for the Mind* are not, of course, intended as an analysis, but only as an outline of a small part of the programme for the science and philosophy of psychodynamics. The broad stream includes philosophical, as well as psychological, physiological, and ethological writings. The theory of warranted assertability, for example, as propounded by John Dewey in his *Logic: the Theory of Inquiry*, is almost totally compatible with the theses of this book, and although he is concerned only with conscious-level phenomena, his remarks on Social Inquiry as a form of scientific investigation (1938, pp. 487–512) could be applied, with minor modifications, to psychodynamics. Similarly, the theory of symbolic transformation which appears in Susanne Langer's *Philosophy in a New Key* is completely compatible with the present theory of communication.

SPECIALTY DISTORTION

Considering that so much of the material to be studied is correctly called psychological, it may seem arbitrary to describe the discipline which concerns us, not as psychology, but as the science and philosophy of psychodynamics. There is a good reason, however, and that is that a large part of academic psychology is vitiated by what I shall call *specialty distortion*. One of the many motives for distortion which have not found room in this argument is the desire to appropriate a niche in the vast and intimidating laboratory of science where it seems possible to obtain decisive results from precise experiments. Weismann's experiment, for example, is still quoted with approval in some textbooks of general psychology, perhaps because of its symbolic appeal. He cut off the tails of twenty-two generations of mice, and discovered that the tails of the twenty-third generation were just as long as those of the first. Bernard Shaw pointed out that he could have told Dr Weismann the result of this experiment before he started. Shaw would have been able to do so because although he had some intellectual blind spots they did not include this solemn misinterpretation of 'environmental influence on heredity'.

Intellectual judgement, or the capacity to make sound untestable assumptions, is of crucial importance in *selecting*, among the manifold possibilities of research, those which are most likely to provide important new evidence or new techniques to advance our understanding of mental processes. The student of psychology may be fascinated by the problem 'How do the Chinese achieve their successes in the conversion and indoctrination of prisoners from an alien culture?' and by the problem 'What is the effect of vitamin deficiency in the diet of rats on the learning curve based on the number of errors they make when running through a standardized maze?' There may be both an intellectual and a practical motive for devoting the most productive years of his life to the second problem in preference to the first. His intellectual preference may be for the limited, decisively soluble problem, settled by a graph relating the learning curve of the stunted, vitamin-starved rats to the learning curve of a control group of rats which have had a carefully balanced diet. The practical motive may be much more weighty. A worthy scientific paper on the second problem, which is recognized by all universities as a problem in experimental psychology, will be a successful step in an academic career, whereas the time and energy devoted to the first problem may go completely unrewarded.

University life constitutes a motive-producing situation. If the ideas of, say, John Dewey, Bertrand Russell, and Wittgenstein – to confine our attention to the moderns – are deemed to be of sufficient philosophical importance to find a place in the philosophy curriculum, and those of, say, the Indian and the Marxist philosophers are not, the students will have a strong motive for bringing their talent for conceptual analysis to bear on the works of the former writers; and any time and energy they devote to a serious, as opposed to a recreational, study of the latter must be diverted from their careers. It is therefore possible for the philosophy students of half the world's universities to be almost completely ignorant of what is being discussed by their counterparts in the other half. The class of lens-grinding philosophers is a class of one (Spinoza), and as the class of leisured thinkers continues to shrink, the practical, administrative problem becomes more and more nearly coterminous with the theoretical problem of the future of the science and philosophy of psychodynamics.

The problem is not only one of selection; it is also one of definition. If 'the philosophy of mind' is so defined as to exclude the writings of Freud, for example, generations of students will be able to call themselves philosophers of mind without suffering a pang of conscious guilt about their ignorance of the language projection TFME. If the

R

definition 'the art of conceptual organization in all spheres related to the language projections TFM and TFME' is accepted, however, acquaintance with the art of the abstract thought relating to mental processes will be deemed indispensable.

Specialty distortion, then, is a symptom of the form of intellectual myopia which issues from motive-producing situations in society. It is closely connected with the Technique of Fluctuating Rigour. The question 'How important must the expected insight be, to justify the time, labour, and expense of this research project?' clearly offers considerable scope for tenuous justification, obtained by reducing the standard of rigour. The rat experiment mentioned above, for example, showed that the stunted rats surpassed the control rats in the maze performance. The conclusion may have implications for the science of the human mind, but if they exist they are less than impressive. Failure to make a periodic searchlight sweep of the swiftly changing intellectual scene, and to undertake an adjustment of the limited supply of time and talent to the theoretical demands of philosophy and science, is a failure of intellectual judgement which has a direct effect on pure science and pure philosophy. The essential qualification for the student of the science and philosophy of mind is a practical training in psychodynamics. A training in philosophical techniques is also needed for the philosophical work. It follows from this that the systematic development of the discipline demands close cooperation between the medical and the academic branches of inquiry.

PROGRAMME FOR THE SCIENCE OF PSYCHODYNAMICS

We are now in a position to outline the programme for *the science of psychodynamics*. It comprises, first and foremost, the pure science of psychoanalysis. As psychodynamics cannot be adequately studied, like history, from books, the outline of the discipline must begin with the kind of experience which is a prerequisite for the study of the science.

The insight necessary to embark on the theoretical aspect of psychodynamics can be acquired either by individual psychoanalysis or by group analysis. The distinction between 'therapeutic' and 'training' analysis is less important than the result of the analysis, whose minimal duration should be one thousand hours.

The result may be a reduction of conscious and unconscious fear to the point where the student is qualified to become a group conductor or an individual analyst. This result, however, is not automatic. The student who still has serious problems in interpersonal relations is not qualified to undertake the training of others, but may make valuable contributions to the theory of psychodynamics, or apply his insight in a variety of related fields, such as medicine, education, the social sciences, or philosophy. To use an analogy from current university practice, the student of economics who gets first-class honours may be offered a lectureship at his university and teach economics. The student who gets a Second may fail to get a university post and become Chancellor of the Exchequer instead.

Individual and group analysis have only one essential rule. The material for interpretation is provided *only* by free association, or in the case of a group by free discussion, and the analyst does *nothing* but interpret. It follows that he never asks or answers questions or gives advice or direct assistance. The moment he becomes a flesh-and-blood *person* to the student, his role in the student's phantasy life goes out of focus and cannot be scientifically interpreted.

The theoretical study of psychodynamics which follows upon a minimum period of individual or group analysis (100 hours) and continues with the analysis, comprises the case-histories, technique, and theory of psychoanalysis, with special reference to the psychoanalysis of psychotics; the case histories, techniques, and theory of group analysis; the case-histories, techniques, and theory of Kleinian child analysis; and the case-histories of psycholytic drug therapy. This study, in conjunction with practical experience of analysis, provides insight into the development of instinct-feeling-thought processes (affective-intellectual processes) in the infant, child, and adult; into the origin of moral attitudes and convictions and their comparative study; the origin of intellectual inhibitions in contrast to the successful sublimation of curiosity; the origin of schizoid-paranoid mechanisms, of phobias, avoidances, compulsions, obsessions . . . and the therapeutic techniques for their resolution; and the influence of unconscious psychodynamic techniques (mechanisms) on behaviour, thought, and attitudes.

The *theory* of psychodynamics also comprises the systematic investigation of:

– the deliberate induction of neuroses and breakdowns (the psychodynamics of nosopoiesis), including brain-washing, systematic conversion and indoctrination, the eliciting of confessions (true or false), and techniques for indurating potential victims against such hazards;

– the relationship between physiological changes and psychological changes (due, for example, to surgical intervention);

– unusual mental states and changes in mental organization, such as spontaneous conversion, the catalytic effect of theories and works of art, and the ecstasy and trance produced by eloquent speakers, rhythmic drumming, and rhythmically flashing lights;

– those ethological studies of instinctive behaviour in animals which throw light on instinct in man, and those ethological techniques and concepts which are applicable to the play analysis of very young children;

– the various testing techniques, such as intelligence, Rorschach, aptitude, thematic apperception, characterological questionaire, testing . . ., which provide clues (and no more) to ability, psychic organization, and future behaviour; and

– those findings and methods of orthodox psychology which offer genuine insight into human motives.

The field of studies outlined above is extensive. The student who specializes in one aspect of psychodynamics needs no more than an intelligent understanding of the other aspects.

A serious doubt may now occur to the reader. If the future of the science and philosophy of psychodynamics is so closely linked with the future of psychoanalysis, it may seem that the progress of the disciplines must be slow and their influence limited, for the practical reasons that therapy is usually slow, expensive, and unpredictable, and that the theoretical conclusions and implications cannot, like those of other sciences, be adequately transmitted through the literature alone. Although these two obstacles are real, they may not be as formidable as they seem. The therapeutic analysis of an adult is comparable to the treatment of a physical illness in an advanced stage. The most impressive progress in physical medicine has resulted from prophylactic techniques such as immunization and hygienic control of epidemics, the medical education of communities, early diagnosis, and early treatment. The application of similar methods in the treatment of neurosis would result not only in the reduction of recognizable neurotic illness but also in the lessening of the need for irrational psychological techniques among 'normal' people, and the diminution of resistance to their recognition. If the origin of neurosis in infancy were generally understood, and gross mistakes in child-care avoided, by a psychodynamically educated community, and if early diagnosis and treatment lost their stigma, the main obstacle to the progress of the science and philosophy of psychodynamics, psychological resistance, would lose some of its force. Strange though the conclusion may seem, therefore, the prerequisite of a major advance of the disciplines is the general recognition and affective acceptance of psychodynamic diagnosis and prophylaxis or treatment within the first few years of life.

This is the long-term programme; for the immediate future progress will depend on the linking of psychodynamic training with university courses. The method is described in Chapter 20.

The philosophy of psychodynamics is first and foremost the art of the conceptual organization of psychoanalysis. As this book is intended as an exploratory study in the philosophy and science of psychodynamics, it is necessary to refer briefly to those areas of research which have not been given sufficient prominence.

A major task for the philosopher of psychodynamics is the conceptual analysis of the works of Freud and his followers in the light of subsequent psychoanalytical discoveries. Such a task clearly requires not only exceptional philosophical and psychological acumen but also the rare intellectual judgement exemplified by Ernest Jones (1953-7, 1961, 1964), whose appreciation of the discoveries, techniques, and insight of both Freud and Melanie Klein was prompt, discriminating, and unwavering, and who had the courage, ability, and energy to build the basic structure of the science and philosophy of psychodynamics in the English-speaking world. No special training can ensure that a student of philosophy will be able to recognize and seize upon the most fertile ideas and techniques, but a new conception of philosophy could lift the periscope of research above the surface of the traditional ebb and flow of speculation. Freud was a philosopher as well as a psychologist; he was an artist who began to work with new material: with the language projection which gradually emerged from his scientific discoveries. Hence the opportunity for the philosopher whose talent lies in the conceptual reorganization of presented theories.

It follows from the new definition of the subject that the philosophy of psychodynamics includes the conceptual analysis and re-synthesis of any part of the theory of the science of psychodynamics. The scope of the discipline, therefore, extends beyond psychoanalysis. It extends even beyond the science of psychodynamics, because not all insight is derived from systematic investigation. The metaphysics of psychodynamics is the formulation of an original point of view based on assumptions which are not decisively testable. There is no reason why metaphysics should be a splendid cathedral in the sky, formed of the cloud-vapour of phantastic thought. Modern metaphysics must have science as its foundation, but it can extend its edifice beyond the competence of the test-restricted experimental scientist.

The present definition changes the image of the relative development of science and philosophy. As the tree of science has grown, flourished, and blossomed it has overshadowed and starved the neighbouring parent tree of philosophy, whose sapling, modern philosophy, has been ridiculed as unworthy of the vast, half-withered trunk to which it clings. Science flourished at the expense of philosophy because its roots could draw upon the nutriment of experimental and conceptual analysis. The image is now changed. We can now see modern philosophy, not only as a sapling springing from a great but dying tree, but also as the topmost branches of the tree of science. The scientist who undertakes the conceptual organization of the theory of his science is also a philosopher, and the philosopher whose subject-matter overlaps with scientific findings is obliged to investigate their source.

Freud disclaimed any original world-view for psychoanalysis, maintaining that it was a branch of biology and shared the world-view of science. From the present point of view he under-emphasized the philosophical implications of his discoveries. It is true that pure psychoanalysis is a pure science, and that it is of the utmost importance for the future of the science that no extraneous preoccupations or value-judgements should distract the investigator from the most unbiased formulation of hypotheses and laws of which he is capable. Psychoanalysis shares the method and aim of pure science: the method of conceptual analysis and re-synthesis, and the aim of disinterested and controlled intervention, investigation, description, prediction, and explanation. The philosophy of psychodynamics is more, however, than the conceptual organization of scientific findings, and Freud laid the foundations, not only of a pure science and a therapeutic technique, but also of the philosophy of psychodynamics. He introduced a new language projection which does not coincide with that of biology; it creates for the modern theorist a multitude of specifically philosophical problems, many of which fall within the spheres whose links with science are the most difficult to discern: the spheres of ethics and politics.

Just as the world-view of the early physical scientists came into conflict with traditional metaphysics, so the moral world-view of the science of psychodynamics is fundamentally incompatible with traditional moral philosophy. The world-view of psychoanalysis does coincide with the world-view of science, but as the pure scientist, *qua* scientist, cannot make a moral or aesthetic choice among values, the difference in orientation between the psychoanalytic view of motives and behaviour and that of traditional ethics needs to be explicitly stated.

The recognition of unconscious motives adds a new dimension to ethical theory which throws the traditional picture completely out of focus. 'Goodness', as we can see from Anna Freud's example quoted above (p. 123), may be moral masochism or covertly resentful timidity, and the convenience of dealing with a moral masochist does not conceal from the perspicacious observer that he is taking profit from an illness. Conversely, aggressiveness may be an inconvenient step in the direction of a healthy moral balance, a step which may even be welcomed, not only by the analyst, but also by the enlightened teacher, parent, or friend. If the focal psychoanalytic criterion of moral excellence is honesty (in its extended sense) combined with health of instinct and its usual concomitants, courage and generosity, then it is incompatible with the focal criterion of traditional moral philosophy: the observance of prescientific moral rules. This remains true even if the class of the rule-observing happens to include the class of the healthy.

If moral philosophy is to escape the obsolescence of pseudo-scientific metaphysics, it has to add the language projection TFME to its theoretical equipment. In other words, it has to take account of the new dimension of unconscious motives and impulses, and shift its focal point. The task facing philosophers of psychodynamics in the sphere of ethics is comparable to that which was forced on 'natural philosophers' by the rapid advance of physics and biology.

The relevance of pure physics to the practical problems of engineering is clearly understood; the relevance of the science and philosophy of psychodynamics to the practical problems of social organization has hardly been glimpsed, even by original theorists. It is a commonplace that the science of mind has fallen far behind the science of things. The most successful branches of science, such as physics and chemistry, have attracted the major part of the available resources of talent and energy. One of the purposes of this book has been to show that the scientific and philosophical techniques are at hand, if the talent and energy are applied, to redress the balance.

18

Training through Analytic Groups

We saw in the last chapter that the conception of a science held by professors in universities and their choice of questions for that powerful motive-producing situation, the degree examination, may have an increasingly decisive influence on the development of that science as more and more students have to rely on grants for their further education. It would be unrealistic, therefore, to outline a programme for the science and philosophy of psychodynamics without indicating the difficulties which have hitherto excluded that science from the universities.

Psychoanalytic insight has brought about an intellectual revolution, which has transformed psychosomatic medicine, motivation theory, parts of the social sciences, theories of child development, anthropology, criminology, literature, literary criticism, and other subjects, in spite of almost total neglect of the subject in the universities of Europe. This neglect seems inevitable if what psychoanalysts maintain is true: that psychoanalysis cannot be taught in the way history or biology can be taught; understanding of the subject comes from direct experience of the effects of interpretations, and book-knowledge by itself is inevitably superficial.

The key to the solution of this problem lies in analytic group training. Long experience of group analysis has convinced the author that the interpretation of the interaction, in intensive (six to eight hours per week) therapy or training, of a group of eight to ten people, preferably under thirty-five years of age, can be as valuable, both therapeutically and for giving genuine psychological insight, as individual therapy or training, except in the case of very seriously, possibly psychotically, disturbed patients. The method of conducting an analytic group (nothing-but-interpretation) is identical for therapy and training, but the work of the training group is supplemented by theoretical study. We now need to ask whether there is anything which might invalidate analytic training as an educational technique in universities and training colleges.

SUITABILITY FOR TRAINING

The first important problem is that of diagnosis. Is it likely that some would-be students of psychodynamics might be unsuitable for group-analytic therapy-training? The experience of the author as analytic-group conductor suggests that it is likely. In the early stage, at least, of the use of analytic group training as an educational technique, diagnosis by Rorschach, Thematic Apperception, and other tests should aim at excluding those in whom a psychotic breakdown is an appreciable risk. There are also some relatively stable people who seem, at the present time, to be unsuitable for group therapy. Men and women with a well-established and rigid paranoid character structure tend to disrupt a group without gaining insight into their paranoid distortions of reality. To illustrate this tendency, extracts are here taken from notes on groups conducted by the author.

Mrs D

Mrs D consistently behaved towards men in a way which seemed to the other members both heartless and unscrupulous. When describing deception, disingenuousness, and infidelity which shocked some of the members of the group, she showed no sign of shame or guilt, although she was extremely sensitive to criticism from other members. It became clear that the reason for her apparently 'clear conscience' was her conviction that 'men' had treated her so badly that she was fully justified in treating 'them' badly in retaliation. Criticism in the group was identical with persecution. It seemed to her hypocritical and biased against her. The conductor of the group was also a persecutor, because his interpretations seemed to her sadistic, and he did not defend her against the members of the group who were ganging up against her.

Often there seemed to be some substance in her accusations, because some members of the group who were using the splitting technique, and transferring to group members either the idealized, good, non-sexual mother or the bad, sexual whore-mother, tended to transfer to Mrs D the distrust of and hostility towards the bad mother. Some of the women members who sometimes identified themselves with her were particularly shocked and condemnatory when she left her son with her husband to marry another man.

Here we find the special problem of the group member with a rigid, predominantly paranoid, character structure. Such a person is adept at creating the situation which is originally a phantasy. The 'persecution' which is feared and expected may be made real by provocation, and the conductor of the group may be brought to an impasse. If he interprets Mrs D's unconscious guilt, which is projected onto those close to her in order to make them criminals, against whom criminal action is not a crime, then he is, in her eyes, simply allying himself with the persecutors in the group who hypocritically 'condemn' her. He becomes the prejudiced judge whose summing-up can be shrugged off with a sardonic smile. If he interprets the group's need for a scapegoat, and the transference to Mrs D, by some members, of the hostility towards the bad mother, he is merely confirming her belief that the group are condemning and persecuting her unjustly. The most likely issue of such a situation is that the 'victim' will leave the group in disgust, perhaps after driving another member out, still retaining the conviction that society in general and the group in particular are unfairly discriminating against her, and retaining her hatred for the conductor, who has become the bad father (or mother). This is an example of the technique of Fluctuating Scepticism. She is sceptical about any interpretation relating to herself, but quite uncritical of interpretations of other members' hostility.

Mr K

A further example of fluctuating scepticism in the assessment of interpretations is provided by Mr K. His basic problem, fear and hatred of a dominating, scornful, and humiliating father, and fear of himself assuming the responsibilities of a husband and father, soon became evident. His self-assertive, chip-on-the-shoulder manner served as a defence against a constantly expected attack. His hatred and suspicion of his father, from whom he had severed relations, was transferred to his boss, and, at first to a lesser degree, to the conductor of the group. The hatred of the 'authority figure' of the group was largely concealed by compulsive submissiveness, a pattern carried over from his 'homosexual' submission to his intimidating father.

Several factors helped him to create the situation of persecution he expected: foreign origin, the chip on his shoulder, the steady, rather flat and monotonous tone of his defensive self-assertion . . . all these factors tended to make him unpopular with some members of the group. The time came when the conductor interpreted the ganging-up against him, as well as his determined efforts to make persecutors of his boss and of members of the group. Mr K fully accepted all those interpretations relating to hostility to himself. They confirmed his expectations and fears. The interpretations of his own technique, however, although sometimes evoking grudging intellectual assent, had no effect on it whatever. He continued to use factors which in other contexts he admired, such as his wife's loyalty to her father and her father's to her, as evidence of ganging-up against him outside the group which justified his evasion or rejection of elementary responsibilities to a wife, and later to a son. As we have seen, the situation is created, inside and outside the group, which enables the paranoid member to claim: 'Nothing I do against them is wrong, because their crimes against me are infinitely more heinous than anything I could do in retaliation.' This mechanism of defensive framing of others I propose to call 'self-exculpatory incrimination'.

An interesting feature of paranoid character structures in a group is the mutual attraction of members who use the self-exculpatory incrimination technique. For a while one member will identify himself with another and enter into the framing plot, thus forming a sub-group which defends itself against the majority 'gang'. If the two members are of different sexes the alliance may grow into a love-affair. This is likely to be short-lived, since there will be a tug-of-war between the two self-exculpatory incrimination plots, and if the mutual attraction leads to a life-involvement, such as regular meetings, living together or marriage, each partner is likely to become a persecutor to the other, and to be framed by the other.

Experience of paranoid character structures in groups suggests the following conclusions: diagnosis of normal would-be group members (many of whom will have paranoid fears), should aim at the exclusion of members with rigid paranoid characters from nosologically heterogeneous groups, and at the formation of groups of patients in which predominantly paranoid techniques predominate; such groups would need exceptionally skilful handling, and many temporary alliances, followed by disillusionment, disgust, and disentanglement, are to be expected.

THERAPY—TRAINING FOR 'NORMAL' PEOPLE

As this discussion is concerned with the practical difficulties in the way of the establishment of the new science of psychodynamics, it will be limited to therapy-training for normal people. For present purposes 'normal' can be defined as 'not psychotic, able to work, even if the level is far short of the potential, and capable of the social life which is a least acceptable'. In this sense many people are normal who suffer from distressing symptoms, such as headaches, constipation, catarrh, palpitation of the heart, anxiety dreams, insomnia, partial impotence, partial frigidity, periodical depressions, or a tendency to choose an incompatible partner or an unsuitable job. Is there any class of normal people, apart from those with a rigidly paranoid character structure, who would not benefit from group therapy-training? Such training is a form of affective education to parallel intellectual education. As with existing education, although it is important to use experience and judgement in selecting candidates, it is impossible to predict with accuracy which individuals will put most into it and get most out of it.

Mr O'C

Mr O'C, for example, joined a slow-open group conducted by the author, and immediately adopted the role of 'favourite student'. He looked younger than his age, twenty-eight, and revealed signs of a sense of inferiority about his Irish accent, about his sexual competence, about his ability in the profession, electrical engineering, for which he had been trained, and about his failure to get into a university. He compensated for this feeling of inferiority by what I shall call the 'short-cut mechanism'. He gave up direct competition with his coevals and peers ('the rat-race') and tried to achieve relatively quick and decisive pre-eminence by the study of yoga, spiritualism, and, later, Karate. To escape financial pressure he lived in a tiny hut at the bottom of a garden, affected to despise luxury and ostentatious spending, and kept himself alive by part-time jobs which left him many hours free to 'reach a higher spiritual plane'.

His indifference to wealth and notoriety was belied, however, by his dreams, in which he appeared in expensive night-clubs and had his girl-friend stolen from him by Dean Martin, or some other film or top-of-the-pops idol. The short-cut technique was neatly dramatized in one dream, in which he gave up trying to grow mushrooms on the pavement under the eyes of sceptical passers-by, and climbed to the roof of a public library to grow them there. This dream succinctly depicted his secret wish: he would educate himself in solitude until his mental and spiritual powers raised him high above ordinary people, and would produce something astounding, which would grow effortlessly at mushroom speed, far from the gaze of envious and derogatory critics who might question its value.

His lofty aspirations, unmatched by any tangible achievements, had their predictable effect on his relationship with his long-suffering girl-friend. He kept warning her that marriage was out of the question, since it would put an end to all his unworldly aspirations. In this way he achieved a double purpose: by himself consistently rejecting, he was escaping the dreaded danger of being rejected, and by precluding marriage he was escaping not only the rat-race and the feared respon-sibility, but also the sexual test. Once all impediments to love-making were removed there would be no excuse if he failed to satisfy her sex-ually.

At the point where he entered the group, therefore, all his achieve-ments were phantasy achievements, and his consolations phantasy consolations. The impact of the group was in this case dramatic. His need to shine and be the favourite student impelled him to produce so many dreams, often recorded and read to the group, and so many associations to the dreams, that the problem was laid bare with remarkable speed. It was clear to every member except Mr O'C that his aspirations to reach a higher spiritual plane were an escape rather than a step towards sainthood. It seems to the author that the influence of his interpretations in the context of the group probably acted more powerfully and more rapidly than interpretations in individual analysis would have done. Within a few months Mr O'C's life-situation was profoundly changed. He found the courage to face the two challenges he dreaded most: the challenge of competition from his peers in the profession he had studied and neglected, and the challenge of commit-ment to his girl-friend, in the form of engagement, which removed most of the excuses for escaping the sexual test. The sexual problem, *ejaculatio praecox*, alternating with defensive disinclination to make love, was elucidated by a dream, in which a large sea-creature threatened him with its big teeth while he was swimming in deep waters. His fear was gradually revealed as a variation on the classical fear of the *vagina dentata*.

At this point his progress, which was remarkably rapid, consisted in acquiring insight and in facing anxiety-producing situations which constituted a reality test of his easy phantasy superiority. At the same time, his fears were traced back to the excessive expectations of an ambitious mother, whose ambitions were not modified by a realistic assessment of her son's ability and stability. The need to live up to the demand for exceptional achievement, in spite of eleven-plus failure and failure to enter a university, forced the adolescent to abandon competitive struggles, which offered no hope of superman status, in favour of struggles with the self in solitude, where the phantasy element could operate more freely.

The failures in the real world, the world of school and work, were exacerbated by the relative academic and financial success of a younger brother, and the strong feelings of envy, hatred, and expected humiliation which were associated with this brother were subsequently transferred to work rivals, making direct competition even more painful. The group had antithetical effects, puncturing his facile narcissistic pride ('I am exceptional even if I do nothing'), and at the same time giving support and reassurance ('I am better than the others at producing the dreams, associations, and painful self-revelations the group conductor seems to want').

Facing painful competition with his peers was made easier by a technique he had used since the eleven-plus failure. This mechanism I propose to call the 'Anticipatory Excuse'. By putting himself at a disadvantage *before* the testing situation, he provided himself with an excuse in case of failure. Instead of facing the alternatives provided by a true testing situation, namely, 'I have faced a rival in a fair test and lost', and 'I have faced a rival in a fair test and won', he arranged a more comforting pair of alternatives: 'I was at a disadvantage and I lost', and 'I was at a disadvantage and yet I won, so I am exceptional'. The latest instance of this technique, which was used during the first months of group membership, when he gained insight into the spuriousness of his spiritual aspirations, was obtaining, by bluff, jobs so highly paid that only much greater experience would have merited such remuneration. The mechanism of the *anticipatory excuse* provided the less frightening alternatives: 'If I fail to hold this job it will be because I have bluffed my way into a position too highly paid for my experience, so it will not be a real failure'; and 'If I succeed in holding this job although I have missed several years of experience it will prove that I am exceptional'.

The technique of the anticipatory excuse may also have influenced his choice of partner, for he was convinced that his girl-friend had a problem of sexual frigidity at least as serious as his own *ejaculatio praecox*, if not more so. At least he could point to sexual success with a girl, casually encountered on a journey, with whom no serious relationship was contemplated. An anticipatory excuse for sexual failure was thus provided: 'If I fail to satisfy my girl-friend it will be due as much to her frigidity as to my premature ejaculation.'

From the point of view of prognosis, Mr O'C stands at the far end of the scale from Mr K. The paranoid element, through extremely important, has not become rigid and intractable. He can become aware of the fear of the group conductor and of his girl-friend as persecutors, while tolerating a continuing relationship with both of them. The awareness of self-frustrating character defects is sharp and clear. The urgent need to bring about certain changes in personality traits and behaviour patterns is strong and conscious. Even the retrogressive step of escaping from competition into a phantasy world by giving up full-time work indicated moral courage, flexibility, and the desire to take action in the direction of change. In view of the manifest evidence of deep fear of the woman's vagina, the decision to get engaged was a courageous one.

It may be surmised that the contrast in prognostic assessment is due to the contrast in the conception of the self, the residue of infancy and childhood experiences. In spite of all the psychic damage inflicted in infancy and exacerbated by the exaggerated expectations of Mr O'C's mother, the residual conception of the self is of an accepted and potentially exceptional personality, whereas Mr K's residual self-conception is of a rejected, persecuted, and despised personality.

The conclusion I wish to draw is that selection for training in the science of psychodynamics has to be based on diagnosis, in the sense not of judging an illness, though any illness is a relevant datum, but of judging the likely development of the personality. An adequate diagnostic technique would probably have selected Mr O'C for training in spite of an unpromising academic record, and rejected Mr K in view of the significance of the rigid paranoid element in his personality. Shrewd selection for training in this subject is so important for the success of the project, that in addition to the recognized diagnostic tests, such as the Rorschach, the Thematic Apperception, and the diagnostic questionnaires, the therapy-training group itself should be used as a diagnostic tool. Participation in an analytic group for a few weeks would be a valuable pointer to the individual's ability to put something into and get something out of group-analytic work, since the basic character-structure is usually revealed, in an analytic group, with remarkable speed.

SELECTION CRITERIA

The criteria for selection of candidates for training in the science of psychodynamics, in the order of their importance, are as follows:

1 Freedom from serious psychotic indications;
2 Personality structure not rigidly paranoid;
3 Evidence of aptitude from participation in analytic therapy-training group;
4 Performance in IQ tests;
5 Academic record and promise;
6 Performance in Aptitude and Perseverance tests;
7 General evidence from Rorschach, Thematic Apperception, and Questionnaire tests.

THE USE OF INDIVIDUAL SESSIONS

Should group-analytic training be supplemented by individual sessions? The author has come to the conclusion that individual sessions should be granted by the group conductor if time is available, to members of a training group who request them, provided that such arrangements are fully discussed and motives interpreted in the group itself. Individual sessions must, of course, be given by the conductor of the student's group and no one else. Overlapping transference situations make adequate interpretation impossible.

Mrs P

The reason for the above conclusion can best be illustrated by an extract from the author's notes. Mrs P, a highly intelligent and efficient young woman who looked younger than her age, twenty-nine, joined a slow-open group conducted by the author with no presenting symptom whatever. She made no complaint about her health, and indicated that she was happily married, enjoyed making love, did not suffer from frigidity, enjoyed her work as the director of a research laboratory, and gave valuable help to her husband, a heart specialist, in his professional career. When asked why she wanted to join the group, who were concerned with the problems she did not have, she replied that she was interested in the theory and practice of group therapy, and would like to join as a student. She was warned by the author that the group would inevitably resent an observer who had no serious problems, and who might be studying them as specimens, and that her 'superiority' would be challenged, but she felt quite capable of dealing with this situation.

The façade of immunity to the doubts, weaknesses, and shortcomings of ordinary men and women was kept up for several months. The predicted challenge from the group members came, and, unabashed, Mrs P explained that she was interested in group analysis as a student rather than as a participating member. This firm stand was interpreted to the group by the conductor as the need to dissociate herself from people who admitted to weaknesses, because she was afraid that if she failed to maintain her denial of feelings which made her vulnerable those feelings might overwhelm her and disrupt her rationally organized, controlled, and rather 'cerebral' life. In brief, for her head to rule her heart her heart had to be put to sleep.

Although the interpretation seemed to have no immediate effect on Mrs P, it served to placate, to some degree, the other members of the group, who were more inclined to accept the probable truth of the interpretation. They became more tolerant of her apparent superiority and immunity, and waited for signs of the Achilles' heel. Mrs P's unconscious fear became clear to the conductor long before it could be interpreted. She was afraid of allowing herself to be emotionally involved with anyone, and above all with a man with whom she had a sexual relationship, for fear of re-experiencing the dependence which had seemed so disastrous when she was a child, and from which she had broken away with violent rejection and hostility in her adolescence. She was terrified of having a child, because childbirth, at a deep level, symbolized castration, and the loss of all hope of successful competition with men. Her ambivalent attitude to the group conductor, which included unwilling attachment, hatred, and competitive envy, was largely transferred from a similar relationship with her brother, who had been both sought after and hated for having the advantage of possessing a real penis rather than a phantasy one. She had allowed her brother to humiliate her by taking her away from her boy-friends in adolescence and 'practising kissing' on her, leaving her excited and frustrated, and going off to use his expertise on his own girl-friends. The pattern of allowing men (brother-substitutes) to humiliate her had continued in adult life until she underwent what could be called a 'cerebral revolt'. This was not only a denial of her deepest wishes in order to control them, but also an attempted reversal of the original pattern. She now sought to humiliate men by proving herself superior to them, intellectually and in the degree of sexual independence, in revenge for having been humiliated.

Mrs P showed no insight into these mechanisms for several months, but when she asked for an individual session to be arranged, the conductor judged that differences in her attitude in the group and an individual session might be valuably significant. During the session she had a curious *déjà-vu* experience which even now has not been fully explained. She became quite motionless, as if in a deep coma, although she was fully conscious. The conductor interpreted that she was dramatizing her chosen role in life: the Sleeping Beauty. She then exclaimed that she had experienced all this before. Everything that was happening during the session had happened before, down to the smallest detail. The conductor had been sitting behind her head, and had bent down and kissed her on the forehead. In the session she was expecting this to happen again. She then recalled that the 'remembered' experience had been a dream, which she now felt was a predictive dream because it was being re-enacted . . . all except the final kiss.

The conductor interpreted the dream and the 're-enactment' as both a wish and a fear. The conductor was Prince Charming, who was both promising and threatening to bring her to life with a kiss. Bringing her to life meant re-awakening the strong feelings of love, hatred, and envy she had felt for her brother, and, at an earlier and unconscious level, her father; and, at an even earlier and deeply repressed and denied phase, her mother. It meant, and this is what was so greatly feared, reviving her intense longing to be accepted by the parents and brother she had herself rejected, and the need to be loved and to love deeply enough to lose her psychic independence. It also meant what she feared most of all, the conscious recognition of her need to have a child. The idea of having a child aroused such intense dread both because it meant at a very deep level castration and the loss of the competitive phantasy penis, and because it meant at the preconscious level being emotionally attached to a creature which, she felt, would grow up to be a child as cruelly rejecting, hostile, and hurtful as herself.

The conductor who was threatening to bring Sleeping Beauty to life with a kiss represented not only her loved and hated brother, but also, at a deeper level, her mother. The link was a kiss. Her mother appeared in a dream as a witch, dressed in black and trapped in a dungeon, who was pathetically begging her daughter for a kiss. This kiss was felt by Mrs P to be poisonous. She had escaped from emotional involvement with her mother by turning her into a witch (convincing herself that she was evil) and locking her up in the dungeon of her unconscious mind. The kiss would revive all the painful problems, which she was trying to escape, of her 'poisoned' relationships with her family.

The witch was dressed in black, and in another dream Mrs P and an older woman dressed in black were sitting beside an open coffin into which they dared not look, because some disgustingly mutilated body was inside. Mrs P felt that she shared the guilt for the murder with a man, and although the man was in greater danger of being punished if they were caught by the police who were searching for them, she herself was the real criminal. For a long time she resisted the interpretation that the guilt was related to a real 'murder', an abortion during marriage, ostensibly because a child would wreck the plans for two careers. The threat of the internal persecutors (the police) was being directed against the man, but she felt that it was the woman (herself) who consented to an abortion who was really guilty of murder. This interpretation seemed utterly implausible to Mrs P, for two reasons; first, she was convinced that the abortion had had no appreciable psychic effect on her; and, second, she could not believe that real events could play a part in 'symbolic' dreams. She was here using an intellectual theory about dreams to protect herself against a deeper insight into them.

Insight into the need to be loved and into the spuriousness of her psychic independence was precipitated by the coincidence of three events, one in an individual session, one in the group, and one outside. The Sleeping Beauty session convinced her that the group conductor meant more to her than a teacher and a rival; he was a dangerous threat to her coldly and ruthlessly self-imposed psychic equilibrium. The first specifically group interpretation which had an impact on her convinced her that the reason why she was coming back again and again to the group, although she admitted that she had no intention of revealing anything important in the group or interacting with the other members on equal terms, was not because she wanted to study them, but because they represented the family from whom she was standing aloof, and by whom she really longed to be accepted. The third event was outside the group. Her husband admitted that he had 'fallen in love' with a young girl, and suggested a trial separation. Subsequent discussions revealed that he had been unhappy for a long time because he knew that his wife was reluctant to put him, his career, and their possible children before her own studies and interests, and that she resented the time she spent looking after him.

The shock of this announcement was intensified by Mrs P's attitude to the marriage. She felt that she was the boss, and that separation, like other important decisions, would come, if at all, as *her* resolution. Instead of accepting her husband's suggestion, as she felt she would have done before joining the group, she changed her pattern of life to accord better with his wishes. She had suffered her first moral defeat in adult life, and the first serious blow to her pride, fortunately at a time when her insight had increased to the point where she could put the setback to therapeutic advantage.

APPLICATION OF THE NEED HYPOTHESIS

We can now apply to Mrs P's problem the *need hypothesis* of p. 58. The need for *complete* sexual satisfaction takes such a form in unconscious phantasy (intercourse with her brother) that it arouses guilt which is alleviated by the denial, at the conscious level, of a *lack* in sexual satisfaction, and of *lack* of love from her brother and parents. The lack of some element found in her brother but absent in present sexual partners is revealed by behavioural manifestations, such as divorcing sexual intercourse from manifestations of affection.

(i) There is a partial inhibition of the active satisfaction of the need: intermittent and partial frigidity.

(ii) The *lack* of acceptance and love from the brother and parents is manifested by regular attendance in an analytic training group, and in the Sleeping Beauty session and dream, all of which are really attempts to provide the affection she claims not to want. It is also manifested in the dream of the witch-mother begging a poisonous kiss, which is a wish-and-fear fulfilment dream (a *lack-fulfilment* dream.)

(iii) The need for suffering has been appeased by humiliation at the hands of exploiting lovers, and is being appeased by parental rejection which was provoked by herself.

(iv) There are linked wishes and fears: the wish to be awakened by a kiss from Prince Charming, with the fear of arousing the latent love, hate, and envy; the wish to be dependent and to be accepted by the group and the family, with the fear of the vulnerability of admitting the need for love.

(v) The lack of an unconsciously longed-for child, coupled with guilt about the destruction of a child, appears as a percept in the dream of the coffin; the superego fear appears perceptualized as policemen; and the wish (for acceptance and affection) appears as a remembered kiss from the group conductor.

(vi) The lack-, wish-, and fear-elements all reach consciousness as a result of transference phenomena and interpretations in the private and group sessions, and events in the marriage which refute the 'omnipotent control' phantasy.

(vii) The *lack* which originates in the need for love is disguised by the rationalization that the group are being studied psychologically; the *wish* to be kissed by the mother is distorted by repulsion; and the *fear* of being rejected by the mother is distorted by projection and reversal of roles: the mother, in the dream, is begging a kiss and afraid of being rejected.

(viii) No actual experience corresponded, in this case, to the fulfil-ment of a wish that was linked with a talion fear, so there is no trauma. The sexual stimulation caused by her brother's 'practice kissing', however, was near enough to the traumatic fulfilment of a wish-fear to cause a long series of similar dreams about sexual involvement with her brother.

(ix) As lacks and linked wishes and fears are made conscious and related to each other, the direct and and indirect manifestations of irrational fear are gradually reduced. Mrs P can admit her emotional dependence and make herself vulnerable by actively trying to save her marriage. She took a decisive step towards this aim shortly after the threat to her marriage by becoming pregnant and accepting the pregnancy in spite of its disruptive effect on her career.

The above extract is interesting for several reasons. First, the private session provides a dramatization of the conflict which is being concealed from the group. In this session she achieves insight for which she has been prepared by dreams and by group interaction.

Second, if we apply the seven criteria of p. 262 to Mrs P, we conclude that she would be a most promising student of psychodynamics. There are no psychotic indications; her personality structure is not rigidly paranoid; her intelligence, perseverance, and academic achievements are at a very high level, and the only evidence in her disfavour, her superiority pose, aloofness, denial of personal problems, and refusal to reveal herself to the group, would be discounted by an experienced group conductor as a common, and by no means incapacitating, defence mechanism.

Third, the contrast between Mrs P's behaviour in the group, where she consciously and deliberately refused to discuss her own problems, and the dramatization of her conflict in an individual session, when the wish and the fear became manifest, enabled the author to understand and interpret the function of the group: to provide Mrs P with a new family whose rejection of her could be denied because *she* was rejecting *them*.

Fourth, we can apply the final hypothesis of the General Testing Principle (p. 238, No. 10): 'the loss of psychodynamically significant beliefs or assumptions needs to be compensated by some equivalent psychodynamic gain'. What psychodynamic gain compensated Mrs P for the loss of the belief, previously clutched so anxiously, that she was immune to the weakness of emotional dependence, and indifferent whether she was loved or not? The answer is significant for all forms of therapy: the psychodynamic gain which induces a student to give up a comforting belief may be (1) the support (at a deeper level, 'love') of the psychoanalyst or group conductor; (2) the reduction of unconscious fear through the affective recognition that some fear is irrational; and (3) the satisfaction derived from the insight provided by a *focusing* interpretation.

19

LSD Treatment

In *An Outline of Psycho-Analysis*, published in 1940, Freud commented:

'We are here concerned with therapy only insofar as it works by psychological methods: and for the time being we have no other. The future may teach us how to exercise a direct influence by means of particular chemical substances upon the amounts of energy and their distribution in the apparatus of the mind. It may be that there are undreamed-of possibilities of therapy.'

Lysergic acid diethylamide (LSD) in combination with Ritalin is such a remarkable psycholytic agent that it could be described as the microscope of the science of psychodynamics, through which the unconscious memories and phantasies which are pathogenetically important can be directly experienced without loss of consciousness. LSD therapy has serious dangers which have not yet been adequately assessed. The drug should not be taken except under skilled psychiatric supervision, and if the psychological (and possibly physiological) risk cannot be eliminated, its use may have to be confined to selected volunteers. The dangers should not, however, deter the scientist from investigating the invaluable data it has already provided, which have served as striking confirmation of Freud-Klein theory. The following extracts, privately communicated to the author, from notes on supervised LSD sessions, have been chosen to illustrate the various effects of LSD treatment.

Dr J

Dr J, a medical doctor with a practice which involved considerable responsibility, who had spent several years in individual analysis, and was interested in psychotherapy from a theoretical as well as a practical point of view, had one LSD session under supervision. After an initial period of elation, he experienced paranoic phantasies, including the hallucination of being threatened by a mad woman's face, with enormous teeth, which seemed so real and became so terrifying that the 'calm observer' element of the personality, which often remains throughout the most extraordinary LSD sensations, was overwhelmed. For seven days after the session he became intermittently psychotic, suffering from paranoic delusions of oral persecution. He resolved never to take LSD again.

Mrs N

Mrs N had had no psychotherapy of any kind. Her only introduction to psychoanalytic hypotheses was a series of fifty-two LSD-Ritalin sessions. Nevertheless her insight into the influence on her life of her sado-masochistic phantasies, derived from an exceptionally savage sphincter training, and into the compulsively repetitive pattern which forced her to choose married, 'unavailable' men as partners, was of a kind one would expect from a person in, say, the fourth year of intensive psychoanalysis. In her case LSD sessions seem to have operated as a substitute, at best inferior, but probably therapeutic, for psychoanalysis. The effect would almost certainly be greater if LSD treatment had been combined with individual or group psychotherapy.

The insight Mrs N gained, from LSD sessions alone, made her more than usually aware of significant connections between feelings and behaviour patterns. She suspected a connection, for example, between the choice of 'unavailable' partners and the feeling, while she was making love, that 'this is the last time'. This feeling, which seemed to be self-induced, for there was no objective reason for such a belief, coincided with the maximum pleasure in both clitoral and vaginal orgasm. If it is necessary to feel that 'this is the last time' in order to obtain the heightened pleasure which is sought, then a partner who was committed to someone else, she suspected, was preferable to one who was 'free', because it was easier to convince herself that he was going to abandon her. The woman's conviction that the man she loves will frustrate or abandon her is often due to the retention of the childhood expectations about the loved father: 'I love him, and he seems to love me, but it is clear that he will abandon me for his wife.'

This untested hypothesis that the feeling and the pattern are linked would, of course, be more effectively tested in psychotherapy, and, however great the insight and the therapeutic gain derived from

LSD–R alone, large gaps in understanding and achievement are likely to be revealed. These are due to the lack of skilled interpretations by the therapist.

ABREACTIVE USE OF LSD–R

The third extract from a case-history is chosen to reveal the *abreactive efficacy* of LSD–R.

Dr Anglesey

Dr Anglesey joined a closed analytic group and adopted the same defence mechanism as Mrs P, the *pure student* technique, which did not break down until after fourteen months. His physical symptoms were chronic indigestion, constipation, catarrh, intermittent palpitation, and excessive fatigue; his psychological symptoms were periodical deep depression, inability to write, and anxiety about his potency; his characterological symptom was inability to maintain a stable and satisfying relationship with one partner. After a long period of group analysis all these symptoms disappeared, apart from a residual difficulty, much attenuated, in doing the writing he wanted to do. He formed a stable relationship, got married, and had a child. It could reasonably be claimed that group analysis had been successful. The degree of insight and the intensity of the transference to the group-conductor were comparable to that experienced in successful intensive individual psychoanalysis.

Three years after the termination of the group analysis, Dr Anglesey had a series of LSD sessions. They provided vivid confirmation of early childhood anxieties, and revived memories with the appropriate feelings, which at the time were deeply repressed. He saw, for example, over and over again in consecutive sessions, the dead body of his mother shortly before cremation, sometimes accompanied by a clear image of his own dead body lying in a coffin beside her, and the feeling of grief, manifested in childlike sobbing, was now experienced, although there had been no emotional reaction at all when he in fact saw her dead body. This belated mourning was felt as a relief.

Through eight sessions he experienced in great intensity the repressed feelings of love and longing for his mother. During the ninth session, which began with intense fear of being shut in a concentration camp and tortured, his feelings for his mother changed to hatred and rage. He cursed her with loud, obscene curses, and writhed on the bed in an attempt to bite the frustrating breasts. When arranging the tenth session he jokingly remarked, 'Are you nervous? Have you got a gun in case I'm violent? No . . . better than that . . . have a chloroform pad ready!'

For over an hour of the tenth session Dr Anglesey resisted the effect of an increased dose of LSD–R. He spoke rationally of his life-long search for the woman who could not only satisfy his needs for sexual satisfaction and companionship but also fully appreciate his gifts, especially his writing, which was felt as a gift to a woman. Then he lay down and put his hands over his face. His hands became a chloroform pad, and he struggled violently to resist the anaesthetic which was forcing him against his will into deep unconsciousness. 'They tell you you can't feel anything when you're under, but they're bloody liars,' he muttered. His struggling became weaker, and his breathing became slow and deep, as if he were anaesthetized. He recalled an actual experience under gas in a dentist's chair, when he had been convinced that he was dead, that his brain was being rhythmically stretched and released, and that this would continue to eternity. Then he was in a concentration camp, locked in a cell, and the guards were coming in drunk. In an almost inaudible voice he said, 'They go on and on playing with you, and they don't get bored until you're unconscious.' Then he was in an operating theatre, and he could 'see' the bright lights through his eyelids. His breathing became rapid, and he started shouting at the doctors who were about to operate: 'You white-coated bastards! What are you going to do to me? Why didn't you tell me what you were going to do . . . before you put that bloody pad on my face?' His writhing became more and more violent. 'Why didn't you tell me you were going to cut off so many inches of skin?' His movements seemed to be an ineffectual attempt to protect his penis. His breathing became less rapid, but the palpitation of the heart continued.

Suddenly his breathing became very slow and deep, as he pressed his hands more tightly over his face, and then became almost imperceptible. He described later how his hands ceased to be a chloroform pad and became the lips of a vagina. He assumed the foetal position, and non-human noises came from his throat. His curled-up body moved from side to side in a rhythmical rocking movement. He then pushed his head against his hands and squirmed as if being born. With eyes vacant and unfocused like a baby's, he gulped the air as if for the first time, and kicked violently with both legs. The expression on his face was one of infinite delight and exhilaration. He then recovered normal speech and with great wonder exclaimed, 'I've been reborn!'

In this experience in the tenth LSD–R session the abreaction is more important than the gaining of insight. Although the joke when the session was being arranged ('Have a chloroform pad ready!') did not seem significant at the conscious level, it suggests unconscious apprehension about the nature of the session. Although Dr Anglesey did not achieve total recall of the circumcision operation, which was probably interpreted in unconscious phantasy as castration, the abreaction of the fear and the intense hatred of the white-coated doctors served to reduce the unconscious fear of reliving the terrifying experiences which were linked by the common factor, total anaesthesia. The hatred of the doctors was probably linked with the hatred of his mother which appeared in the ninth session. She had not only starved him almost to the point of death, because her breasts did not give adequate milk, but had also betrayed his trust in her by handing him over to the doctor-torturers. Another link which facilitated the transition from the operating-theatre to the maternity ward was the 'chloroform-pad'. Dr Anglesey reported that his mother had been warned not to have a second child because she might not survive the birth, and that she had been given an anaesthetic shortly before the birth. Medical evidence suggests that the anaesthetics used at that time had a direct effect on the baby, so we can surmise that being born meant to Dr Anglesey, at the unconscious level, not only being expelled from foetal symbiosis, but also emerging from deep anaesthesia.

After the tenth session Dr Anglesey reported a step in the session which felt to him like a *decision*: the decision to let himself 'go under the anaesthetic', although he realized it meant facing something horrifying. What induces a man who has been cured of his most distressing symptoms to 'go under'? This is a key question for the science of psychodynamics, because the normal student may not be impelled by the pain of his neurosis to take the step which is a prerequisite for the understanding of that science: facing his own unconscious. The answer must be tentative. Dr Anglesey probably succeeded in 'going under' because group analysis had given him sufficient understanding of the degree of insight and abreaction he had achieved to know that still more precise and detailed insight and still more profound and physiologically direct abreaction would give even greater release of the energy 'bound' in repression. He also knew that direct experience of the repressed traumatic experience may be less terrifying than the phantasy equivalent of the trauma. Phantasy castration is more (unconsciously) terrifying than re-experienced circumcision. This knowledge would not induce him to return to the transference situation once the transference to the group conductor had been successfully resolved, but it would, in conjunction with the knowledge of the properties of LSD–R, provide sufficient hope of a relatively quick break-through to outweigh the fears of the operating-theatre and the maternity ward. There is evidence that this hope was justified, because Dr Anglesey reported, during the LSD–R treatment, a steady reduction in the residual writing inhibition.

At first Dr Anglesey was inclined to congratulate himself that he had 'relived' the birth trauma and abreacted the desperate fear of suffocation which accompanied the birth experience. He expected to go on to the next stage; to re-experience the sensations which were associated with operations under deep anaesthesia, the circumcision operation and the operation on adenoids and tonsils. If these sensations could be brought to consciousness by LSD, the unconscious fears he had been glimpsing in dreams for over thirty years would be reduced to a minimum, and the work of repression would be less burdensome.

Subsequent sessions, however, destroyed this wishful illusion. When he was preparing himself, after the usual dosage of LSD and Ritalin, for the expected lights of an operating theatre, he found himself slipping back into a second reenactment of his birth. This time the struggle was harder and longer. Curled up in the foetal position, he squirmed and writhed for twenty minutes, fighting for air. When the actual moment of birth came, his cry was the tiny, miserable cry of a half-anaesthetized infant. There was no exhilaration at being 'reborn', and when he turned to the breast for what he felt was the reward after a long ordeal, he began to sob in profound despair, saying 'Nothing! Nothing! Nothing!' over and over again. He later expressed the feeling that life, like the struggle to be born, was a series of long and arduous efforts, with illusory goals and illusory, frustrating 'prizes'.

After this session Dr Anglesey concluded that the first re-enactment of his birth was like the cut version of a film, with much of the terror and despair diluted or expurgated. The second was nearer to the original fear of actual asphyxiation and nearer to the original despair when the breast produced nothing. It was now more difficult, however, to convince himself that the original feelings which accompanied a traumatic birth had been re-experienced in their full intensity. He suspected that many re-enactments would be needed in order to abreact the birth trauma, which he now realized to be the mainspring of his adult anxiety. He felt that he even had a partial explanation for the visible but kinaesthetically imperceptible twitchings of nerves in the calves of his legs, which he had noticed while sunbathing. These slight twitchings were probably the neural residues of the violent efforts to escape from the womb.

His suspicion proved sound. Subsequent sessions were re-enactments of his birth, sometimes with, sometimes without, the ecstatic feeling of gulping in 'air' after near-asphyxiation: the feeling of being reborn.

After two more sessions of this kind, when the struggle, accompanied by profuse sweating and half-choked panting, would last up to half an hour, he had a session which was quite different in feeling-tone from any of the others. He lay quite still in the foetal position, relaxed, and with no sign of fear or stress. His breathing was abnormally slow with a quite unusual rhythm. Strange noises came from his throat, which the author had never heard before. After a few seconds it seemed that the breathing and the low, gurgling noises were following the rhythm of ingestion and regurgitation through the umbilical cord. Dr Anglesey later described this sensation as the most blissful experience he had ever had. After about fifteen minutes of this happy 'symbiotic' peace, the regular rhythm of breathing and gurgling was interrupted. Dr Anglesey later described the sensation as a 'blockage in the tube'. At this point the muscular contractions and the writhing of birth began once more, this time ending with the ecstatic gulping in of air and the feeling of being reborn. How do we explain these phenomena? The most likely hypothesis, which accords with Dr Anglesey's later reports of his sensations, is that the anaesthetic administered to his mother disrupted the rhythmical interchange of biochemical substances between the mother and the foetus, producing sensations of asphyxiation in the unborn child which were recorded and preserved so accurately at a deep unconscious level that they could be revived forty-five years later. This hypothesis may seem incredible to anyone who has had no experience of deep analysis or of the effects of psycholytic drugs. What is certain, however, is that the forty-five-year-old man was curled up in the foetal position, breathing and gurgling in a rhythm which is not appropriate to any age after birth, and that his subsequent writhings were appropriate to a severe deprivation of oxygen.

Two sessions later, Dr Anglesey experienced the kind of regressive re-enactment which is familiar to psychiatrists who have used LSD over a long period, but which may seem incredible to others: even to some psychoanalysts. It may be well to keep the P (physical) description separate from the TFM (thought-feeling-motive) report and the attempt at interpretaion.

The P description records what was visible and audible to an observer. Dr Anglesey lay face-downwards on the bed and began to make kicking movements with his legs of the kind used for the breast stroke when swimming. His arms were pressed tightly to his sides, and the overall picture of his kicking and wriggling body was reminiscent of a swimming tadpole. He was breathing hard and began to sweat more and more profusely.

After eight minutes of these movements he arched his back and pressed his head against the pillow, giving a series of rhythmical pushes, and still moving body and legs convulsively. A few minutes later his body began to go limp, starting at the head and neck, then the body, and then the legs. After a few seconds, only his feet were moving, and then they too became limp and still. His breathing rate returned to normal, and his facial muscles relaxed.

After the session Dr Anglesey reported (TFM) that he had felt he was swimming in a race. He had a strong sense of urgency. He felt that he encountered a soft but firm encumbrance which it was important to penetrate. He then felt his whole body going through, starting with his head and finishing with his feet. His whole body was then suffused with a sensation of blissful relaxation, reminiscent of the peace of his earlier 'foetus' session, but with a quite different feeling-tone. He described this feeling as one of great achievement: relaxation and happiness after an arduous and successful effort.

He linked the swimming-struggling sensation with another LSD sensation, the desire to re-enter the mother's womb not as a foetus but as a lover, a desire which had always been frustrated and repressed. He felt there was a link between the effort to get into the womb (conception), the effort to escape from the womb to get air (birth), the effort to re-enter the body as a lover, and substitute efforts, such as cross-country running, which necessitated hard, deep panting and sweating. He recalled the profound satisfaction of the deep, rhythmical panting which came at the 'second wind' on a long-distance run.

How can we account for these puzzling phenomena? It is too simple to say that Dr Anglesey experienced a re-enactment of the part played by the spermatozoon in his own conception. The philosophical problem of giving an account of LSD experiences is the problem of the interplay of abreactive movements and sounds on the one hand, and conscious or unconscious memories, screen-memories, phantasies, and theories on the other. The evidence that there is direct abreaction of *part* of an early experience is the movement of the body, which would be almost inconceivable as a consciously controlled gymnastic exercise.

The movement suggests something repugnant to common sense: that the cell which results from the penetration of the ovum by the spermatozoon carries a 'memory-trace' of the activity of the spermatozoon while swimming towards, reaching, and penetrating the ovum.

In this context it is interesting to note that a woman, Mrs N., describes a very similar subjective experience (TFM) and underwent very similar physical movements during an LSD session. This is less surprising if we bear in mind that the spermatozoon which produces, by penetrating the ovum, a female embryo is active in just the same way as the spermatozoon which produces a male embryo.

The philosophical problem is concerned with what I shall name *retroprojection*. What the subject believes about the past is not irrelevant to the TFM report he will give of his psycholytic drug experiences. Whether his beliefs also influence the movements and sounds described in P by an observer must remain an open question. How would a primitive subject who knows nothing about conception describe the tadpole movements and progressive head-to-foot relaxation of the body? Would a believer in 'transmigration of the soul' have LSD experiences which were modified by retroprojection of his beliefs? Might he have experiences which caused him to question his beliefs?

Such questions point the way to the psycholytic drug research which will be made possible if the risks can be eliminated. Everything in an LSD session that is perceptible to the eye and the ear of the observer should be described in P with the minimum of preconceptions. This description should then be collated with the TFM description of the experimenter, which should be taken seriously, however fantastic it may seem, as a piece of psychic reality. These two descriptions, in P and in TFM, should then be examined in the light of the experimenter's past history, present beliefs, and present wishes, hopes, and fears. In this way students of psychodynamics will add to our store of knowledge about the part played by retroprojection in the re-experiencing of psychodynamically important events in the past.

Although retroprojection almost certainly plays a part in the *description* by the experimenter of LSD experiences, the experiences themselves are often completely unexpected both to experimenter and observer. The programme of research, therefore, should include comparison and contrast of reports by sophisticated and naïve (relatively theory-free) experimenters.

Another important subject of research is the effect of abreaction. Although we know in general that abreaction reduces unconscious fear (probably by modifying the more terrifying phantasy by reliving experiences closer to the less terrifying reality), it is difficult to identify the specific effect of a specific abreactive experience. The reason is that the progress achieved in psychoanalysis, group analysis, or psycholytic drug treatment cannot be assessed until a period of months has passed after the cessation of treatment. *The psychodynamic gain from abreaction cannot be judged until normal repression has been re-established.*

Two sessions after the one recorded above, Dr Anglesey had an experience which caused him to discontinue for a time the regular series of experiments. When discussing the meaning of his experiences with the doctor who had administered the LSD–Ritalin, sitting on the bed where he had many times re-experienced his birth, he found himself slipping into yet another re-enactment of birth *without taking any drug*. He did not resist, but allowed the re-enactment to take its course. He recovered without any sedative, and suffered no un-pleasant after-effects, but felt slightly uneasy upon going to bed the next two nights, in case he might slip involuntarily into a similar regressive experience. Nothing of the kind happened, however, and he continued to sleep normally, without distressing dreams.

  The most likely hypothesis to explain this phenomenon is as follows: the drug many times innervated a neural path, which was compatible with consciousness, from present experience, through the dental opera-tion under total anaesthesia, through the adenoids-tonsils operation, through the circumcision operation, to the experience of birth and the experience of foetal symbiosis. Each time the neural path was inner-vated, the re-enacting and re-experiencing of these events was facili-tated, and each time a closer approach could be made to the original sensations. Finally, the re-enactment occurred by reason of associated stimuli: the room and the bed where the sessions took place, and the presence of the supervising doctor who administered the drugs. The place and the person associated with the effect of the drug became sufficient stimuli to produce the effect without the drug itself.

  We have now seen a *psychodynamic* danger associated with LSD: the danger that experiences which have long been under the control of the experimenter may slip out of his control. The example just given was not seriously disturbing in itself, since Dr Anglesey allowed him-self to regress in a safe situation. What is disturbing is the possibility that such regression might occur in a situation where the experimenter's life was endangered.

  Is there any risk of *physiological* (e.g. cytological) damage to the experimenter? It is too early (1968) to answer that question. Some

LSD TREATMENT 279

experiments have suggested the possibility of damage to the chromosomes (Auerbach & Rugowski, 1967), but they are not decisive. Even
the *possibility* of such risk, however, should be made known to anyone
who wishes to experiment with the drug.

CONTRIBUTION OF PSYCHOLYTIC DRUGS TO PSYCHO-
DYNAMICS

We can now sum up our conclusions about the contribution of
psycholytic drugs to psychodynamics. LSD, the most effective psycholytic drug yet synthesized, provides direct and detailed perceptual and
kinaesthetic confirmation of the continuing availability of significant
experience neurally recorded from foetal to adult life. The case-histories
of patients or experimenters who have taken the drug are worthy of
careful study by all students of psychodynamics. Its value for the science
consists in the possibility of conscious study of phenomena which
normally appear only in dreams, and are therefore normally subject
to distortion and secondary elaboration.

In spite of its exceptional value for theory, and its more problematic
value for the abreaction of traumata, its use by anyone except responsible researchers who have had a long and successful individual or group
analysis, and who are fully aware of the psychodynamic and physiological dangers, is inadvisable and should be discouraged. The student
who has not gained deep insight from some other source may be
seriously discouraged by the magnitude of the problem presented by
the unconscious conflict and by the psychodynamic residue of traumatic experiences which are glimpsed under LSD. Alternatively, he
may try to suck the sugar and leave the pill: to get the exhilaration
while shirking the 'chloroform-pad' fears. If he succeeds, he has no
abreactive benefit and is simply escaping from psychodynamic reality.
Finally, the theory he constructs to make sense of his strange experiences may be based on a wish-phantasy which is not challenged by the
objective interpretations of a trained observer.

There is often a time-lag between the discovery of a potentially
valuable technique of physiological intervention and the elimination
of risks which limit its value. An obvious analogy is the development
of a poliomyelitis vaccine. So long as even a small number of deaths
resulted from the vaccination of healthy subjects, the vaccine could
not be unreservedly recommended. When the vaccine was perfected
by biological research its value could be generally acknowledged.

The development of a safe and effective psycholytic drug may

T

follow a similar course. We know the tool we want for research in psychodynamics, and the biologists, biochemists and chemists may be able to produce it. We want a chemical agent, an *adjunct* to but not a substitute for psychoanalysis or group analysis, which will (a) interfere, under controlled conditions, with the normal mechanism of repression to the degree that deep regressive experiences, including birth, breast-bottle, and early separation, sex, and operation experiences can be abreacted without loss of consciousness; (b) *will not interfere with that mechanism except under controlled conditions*; and (c) *will have no seriously harmful physiological or psychodynamic side-effects*. We already have (a), but not (b), and there is some doubt about (c).

If all three conditions could be satisfied, we would have the valuable chemical aid to psychodynamics which was dreamt of by Freud. It could be used, not as an alternative, but as a supplement, to psychodynamic therapy and training. It could be used by volunteer students when they had gained sufficient insight, after a long period of group or individual analysis, to want and to be able to master the direct *perceptual* experience of the unconscious processes made *conceptually* familiar by their training.

20

The Practical Problem of furthering the Science of Psychodynamics

The ground has now been prepared for analysing the practical problem of furthering the science of psychodynamics which was defined above (pp. 248–53). The problem can be broken down into the following elements:

1 How can suitable students be found to undertake investigations which involve painful insight and painful abreaction, if the incentive of an acute neurosis is absent?

2 How can suitable conductors be found for the programme of analytic group training, if psychoanalysts are split into Anna Freudians, Melanie Kleinians, middle-of-the-roaders, and neo-Freudians; if Jungians turn their backs on the science of psychodynamics unless psychoanalysis is rejected as its basis in favour of analytical psychology; if Adlerians dissociate themselves unless the basis is individual psychology; if all schools and groups unite only to condemn analytic group training as dangerous heresy?

3 How could a Department of the Science of Psychodynamics be tolerated in any university in which there already exists a Department of academic Psychology, with hundreds of rats in cages, and expensive equipment for measuring reaction times?

4 How can the science of psychodynamics have any impact on the spheres where it is most urgently needed, medicine and teaching, if medical schools are physiology-oriented, and teachers are not required to have self-knowledge?

5 How can there be a unified science of psychodynamics if the relevant research is conducted in many disciplines, by scientists who are not familiar with each other's work, and reported in various scientific journals?

1. The first problem is the easiest to solve. The key lies in the suggestion made on p. 247 that university life constitutes a motive-producing situation. We know, for example, that medical students, even if they are sceptical about the value of committing to memory for a few months, and then forgetting, a vast quantity of miscellaneous data which they will subsequently check in reference books, will submit obediently to this initiation ordeal almost to the point of breakdown in order to achieve the goal of qualification. The initiation ordeal for the student of psychodynamics will be quite different. He will be expected to keep abreast of current research and discovery, in any country, in the fields of psychoanalysis, group analysis, pharmaceutical treatment, brain surgery, child development studies of the kind initiated by Piaget, child analysis by the Kleinian play-technique, ethological techniques, concepts, and experiments, and testing techniques, but he will not be required to memorize large chunks of textbook material. For him the ordeal (and the release) will consist in facing, in analytic group training, the unconscious conflicts that have been repressed.

We have seen from the example of Mrs P that a student who does not admit, or even recognize, a characterological problem, and who yet joins a training group, may be an excellent candidate for the science of psychodynamics. The example also indicates that the age-range for students of psychodynamics should be wider (say, eighteen to thirty) than for students of purely academic subjects such as history or biology.

As no specific specialized training is prerequisite to successful participation in an analytic training group, psychodynamics will bridge the gap between the two cultures. Students will be drawn from the sciences and the arts. Their special subjects at school may have been classics, mathematics, biology, history, or any others that have enabled them to acquire the technique of research. The cross-cultural, interdisciplinary nature of psychodynamics has two advantages: it broadens the field for candidates, and it will produce the kind of graduate whose mind is open to originality and discovery in many disciplines.

2. The second problem seems formidable. If university life constitutes a motive-producing situation for students, however, it does so for tutors and professors also. When a chair is created it is seldom impossible to fill it, and this is true of the chair of psychodynamics. The essential qualifications for the professor and tutors are: a successful personal analysis, individual or group, for at least a thousand hours,

experience of leading an analytic group, with the nothing-but-inter-pretation rule, and a sound theoretical grasp of philosophical and psychoanalytic techniques. When the incentive is provided more and more people will be found with these basic qualifications.

The divisions of psychoanalysts into three schools is not an insuper-able obstacle: first, because the schools are drawing closer together; and, second, because dogma must be discouraged if a true science of psychodynamics is to be developed.

This last statement applies *a fortiori* to dogmatic condemnation of new techniques such as group analysis. Any psychoanalyst whose trainee-dogmatism has closed his mind to new scientific possibilities will exclude himself from the science of psychodynamics in its full sense, even if he makes valuable contributions to that science.

3. The third problem can be solved in one of two ways: either Depart-ments of Academic Psychology can abandon the limiting and disas-trous Fallacy of Behaviourism which was refuted above (pp. 204–6), and adapt themselves to embrace psychodynamics; or the science of psychodynamics will develop independently, possibly alongside and in cooperation with, behaviouristic academic psychology.

4. In order to solve the fourth problem, the shift in orientation of medicine and teaching, a clear distinction has to be made between what can, and what cannot, be learnt from books. Everything in psychodynamics can be learnt from books and periodicals except the nosopoietic and nosotherapeutic techniques. It is unlikely, in Britain and the USA at least, that many students will elect to experience the nosopoietic techniques, either as victims or as torturers. Hence the emphasis in this chapter on analytic group training, the key to the practical experience which is needed to open the door to theoretical knowledge. An adequate Department of Psychodynamics in a univer-sity must embrace both practical techniques and theoretical studies. What is needed in medical schools and teachers' training courses, how-ever, is the facility for volunteer medical students and volunteer teachers to join an analytic training group as a supplement to their specialized training; and this is a practical possibility. To achieve their purpose all analytic training groups have to be conducted *in accordance with the nothing-but-interpretation rule*. The only difference in procedure between an analytic therapy group and an analytic training group is that the training group is supplemented by a course of theoretical study.

5. A unified science of psychodynamics is possible only if a Department of Psychodynamics is set up in a university and run by someone who is open-minded enough to recognize the relevance of contributions from the fields outlined on pp. 248–53. The reasons why group analysis, rather than individual psychoanalysis, is the key to the development of psychodynamics are both practical and theoretical. A psychoanalyst who devoted, say, fifteen hours a week to the training, in three analytic training groups, of student group conductors, allowing an equal proportion of fall-outs in both individual and group training, could train eighteen conductors in the time it would take to train three psychoanalysts, and each of the eighteen conductors would be able to provide training for five or six times as many trainees as each of the individual analysts. It is necessary to ask, therefore, whether the advantages of individual psychoanalysis, except for cases which are unsuitable for group analysis, are such as to justify the choice of the slower rate of dissemination of skill and insight. Individual psychoanalytic training is unavoidably expensive, so that the rate of training of individual analysts is limited, not only by the number of hours a training analyst can devote to training, but also by the number of would-be trainees who are both characterologically suitable and financially capable. The problem of suitability creates a cruel *situational motive for distortion*: the conscientious training analyst may have to say to the rich would-be trainee who puts £5,000 on his desk, 'I'm sorry, but you're not the right kind of person.' It must be emphasized that for group training to be as effective as individual training it has to be equally intensive: the minimum period for the full training would be 1,000 hours. Supplementary group training for medical students and teachers, however, could be less intensive: say two two-hour sessions per week.

We can now sum up the advantages for a university Department of Psychodynamics of analytic group training. First, psychoanalytic insight can be diffused at a faster rate, without invidious discrimination in favour of the rich. Second, the transference neurosis and dependency are less likely to be so incapacitating that the student's work is seriously disrupted. Third, the understanding of other people's problems, which is much easier, is a wedge which facilitates insight into one's own. Fourth, the student cannot escape coming to terms with difficult personal relationships that are not of his own choosing. Fifth, there is an opportunity to cultivate interpretative skill, and so develop any psychological flair. Sixth, the group conductor has plenty of time to observe the student in a revealing social situation, and so to decide whether he is a potential group conductor. The author has observed that the basic character and personality structure is revealed, with remarkable clarity, usually within about ten two-hour sessions.

The Psychodynamics course would be, at the minimum, a four-year course, consisting of three elements: a group analysis with one group conductor for the whole period of the course in four two-hour sessions weekly; seminars and tutorials on the Oxford–Cambridge model, with supervision of reading programmes; and finally, during the last year, a training in group leadership under the supervision of an experienced group conductor. The training would have a double purpose: to select those students whose emotional stability and natural talent qualify them for work as group conductors; and to begin the practical training of those students who are going into other fields where an understanding of human relations is essential.

Those who were selected for training as group conductors and who successfully completed the course would have a choice between a career at a university and taking part in analytic group training which would be independent of the university course in Psychodynamics. One important opportunity for group conductors would be the organization and conducting of volunteer groups in conjunction with medical schools and teachers' training courses.

It is fallacious to suppose that value-judgements play little part in the development of science. As in the physical sciences, so in psychodynamics, decisions have to be made which determine the proportion in which resources of money and talent are channelled into techniques of destruction and construction. The nosopoietic torture techniques, such as the experimental induction of neurosis, brainwashing, and indoctrination, correspond to the techniques of nuclear weapon production and of biological warfare. They are likely to be given priority over the nosotherapeutic techniques in those countries where a particular ideological dogma is regarded as a panacea. The ideology, like a religion, is thought to immunize the believer against neurotic difficulties. The danger in countries, like Britain, where no one dogma predominates, is not that nosopoietic techniques will be developed to a menacing degree, but that the whole of psychodynamics, including prophylaxis against neuroses, therapy, training, and induration against indoctrination, will be neglected.

The elements of the science of psychodynamics have been slowly developing, piecemeal, since the beginning of the century, in spite of

istance to all its basic hypotheses. The mainstream of pro-
een the steady, unpretentious clinical and theoretical work
psychoanalysis. Melanie Klein's technique of child analysis,
aluable discoveries about psychic development in infancy,
important contribution to the analysis of schizoid-paranoid
psychoses. Klein's theory of alternating introjection and projection,
with her concept of projective identification, has enabled analysts such
as Rosenfeld (1965) to adhere to the nothing-but-interpretation
method even with patients suffering from acute schizophrenia. In
contrast to some American analysts, Rosenfeld maintains that the
reassurance which the schizophrenic sometimes needs even before he
will eat (I'll make sure you don't eat too much) should be given by
nurses or colleagues and not by the analyst himself.

An understanding of the processes of splitting, introjection, projection, and projective identification is important not only for the analysis
of young children and schizoid-paranoid psychotics, but also for the
training of normal students. A study of psychodynamics is not complete, therefore, without an understanding of the work of such analysts
as Ackerman (1938), Knight (1939, 1940, 1946), Rosen (1946, 1947,
1950), Segal (1950), Heimann (1952), Federn (1953), Bion (1954, 1956,
1962), Fromm-Reichmann (1959), and Rosenfeld (1965). Unfortunately, the study of psychotic states may be disturbing and difficult to
grasp unless the student has had a long and deep analysis, and this part
of psychodynamics, which is the most central and important, should
be left till the later part of the student's course.

The outstanding advances in psychodynamics since Freud have been:
Kleinian child analysis; the analysis of schizoid-paranoid psychoses;
and the technique of analytic (nothing-but-interpretation) group
therapy and group training. The time has come for the integration of
the elements of psychodynamics, for the large-scale extension of
analytic group therapy and training, for the introduction of psychodynamic training groups in medical schools and teachers' training
courses, and the creation of Departments of Psychodynamics in
modern-minded universities, whether old or new.

21

Aggression and Rationality

Many kinds of modern research are beginning to converge. We have already glimpsed the cross-fertilization of modern philosophical analysis, the philosophy of science, psychoanalysis proper, Kleinian play analysis, group analysis, Kurt Lewin's topological psychology, Gestalt psychology, Rorschach and TAT diagnostics, the physiology of pain, hunger, fear, and rage (Cannon), endocrinology, anthropology, and the ethology of Lorenz and Tinbergen. Psychodynamics, which embraces psychoanalysis and group analysis, is an ethological discipline, a form of therapy and a form of training or teaching. The point of view of psychodynamics as described in this book can be summed up in very simple terms.

When we dream, we are mad (psychotic) in the sense that the NEEDS which have not been satisfied by the environment are manifested as phantasy LACK-fulfilment (WISH- and FEAR- fulfilment), logical consistency is abandoned, and the external world is almost completely excluded. Those we call mad or psychotic are those who dare not wake up completely, because they despair of finding good objects in the external world to counteract the bad objects they have internalized.

In 'normal' and neurotic people, repression, though inefficient in distinguishing what it is safe and what it is unsafe to feel, to want, to say, and to remember, is too efficient in keeping the dream world and the external world apart. Conscious life is impoverished because cut off from the source of the strongest feelings, which reappear as a disruptive force. The analyst, the substitute parent, gives the patient or student the courage and insight to bring the two worlds closer together. In an analytic group the boldest tend to impart courage and insight to the more timid.

Contemplation, as practised by the mystic, is a discipline for bringing the two worlds together without the help of an objective interpreter. It is therefore more liable to be vitiated by consoling omnipotent phantasies.

Psycholytic drugs such as LSD bring the two worlds together more abruptly and more disturbingly. If used in large doses outside therapy they are apt either to precipitate a psychotic breakdown or to provoke a reaction into massive repression, because the decrease in total fear (the conscious–unconscious continuum of fear) cannot keep pace with the increase in frightening insight.

Tranquillizing drugs, such as Largactil, act in the reverse direction. They help to keep the two worlds apart by strengthening repression. They tend to make conscious life more bearable and leave the basic fear unresolved. Side-effects are a separate but important and complex subject.

TREATMENT is providing a reliable substitute parent, who understands the dream world, interprets it, and brings it into relation with himself and the external world, thus increasing the sense of reality and reducing total fear. *Scientific* treatment involves the prediction and interpersonal checking of the effects of interpretations. *Control* (the use of restraint in institutions and of tranquillizing drugs) is needed for those phases in treatment when the violence of the dream world is acted out. Apart from this limited use, control, though often misnamed 'treatment', is no more than a substitute for treatment. Psycholytic drugs may, in optimal conditions, be a valuable auxiliary to treatment, especially in the terminal phase, but the danger of side-effects and uncontrolled effects needs detailed investigation. They are a valuable tool of research for those who are prepared to take calculated risks.

The TEACHING of psychodynamics is providing three things: a powerful motive for undergoing the discomfort of bringing the two worlds together (such as the motive of the Final Degree examination or of a professional qualification); a reliable analytic interpreter of the dream world; and access to intellectual understanding of psychodynamics and related disciplines. It provides TIG (see p. 291).

TORTURE is deliberately increasing pain and/or total fear (the conscious–unconscious continuum of fear). Electro-convulsive or insulin shock is sometimes followed, especially in depressed people who need a 'death-sentence' to assuage their guilt, by a temporary remission of symptoms. Shock is a form of torture (even when no conscious pain is felt) in the sense that it increases total fear. It may make subsequent analytic treatment ineffective. Pavlov's systematic torture of the dogs which were attached to him like babies (transference) is a model for the torture of human beings in order to enforce emotional and intellectual submission. Brainwashing (or euphemistically 'thought reform') is the systematic increase of fear and uncertainty, sometimes to the point of breakdown, until false confessions are submissively believed, and an ideology swallowed whole.

Transference, the strong need-fear-love-hate attachment to a person or a group, is the potent instrument of psychodynamics. It can be used for treatment, teaching, or torture.

Part of the science of psychodynamics is the ethology of the inter-action of human beings in a situation where an individual or a group seeks help from an analytic interpreter and enters into a transference relationship with him over a long period.

THOUGHT REFORM

If I had been a resident lecturer in China, had been suspected of hostility to the régime, imprisoned, and kept in chains and manacles until I produced a false confession, which was then rejected, and if I had then been 'struggled' by my more 'advanced' fellow-prisoner cell-mates over a period of, say, two years, I can imagine the kind of 'true' confession I would sign in order to obtain release. After a critical autobiographical study would come something like this:

'In spite of professing vague left-wing sympathies, I was a tool of the capitalists and committed many crimes, wittingly and unwittingly, against the People's Government. I lived the life of an idle, self-indulgent, parasitic capitalist exploiter, profiting from the labours of the true workers, whom I treated as inferiors, without producing any goods or services for the people. Worse than this, by my pseudo-intellectual detachment and so-called scientific attitude I encouraged my students to prostitute their talents in the name of philosophy and psychology, which I misinterpreted as individualistic self-indulgent emotional-intellectual exercises for a tiny minority. In this way I demoralized my students by making them unwilling to take part in the People's glorious and unselfish struggle for freedom and prosperity.

'I am deeply grateful to those representatives of the People's Government who have so earnestly and tirelessly struggled for my conscience, and have succeeded in leading me to sincerity and teaching me the way to expiate my crimes and enter fully into the glorious progressive endeavour of my comrades.'

This confession, if I had been skilfully 'reformed', would not be altogether cynical. There is little doubt that I could be made to half-believe in my crimes and my new orientation. The methods used in thought-reform colleges are more effective, in spite of a fairly high proportion of failures and doubtful results, than any other systematic attempt to bring about a profound psychodynamic change in the individual.

Why are they so potent? First, the Chinese tradition has inculcated a higher level of psychological perspicacity than most other cultures. Second, there is a definite ideology to impart, so that teachers are not impeded by scientific modesty and tentativeness. Third, the group method is used more intensively and devastatingly than in any other society: in the extreme form of disciplinary pressure fellow-prisoners in a cell cannot escape from each other day or night, and the manacled prisoner needs the help of his cell-mates every time he goes to the lavatory.

Fourth, the pressure to conform is linked with a set of incentives. The false confession may obtain at least temporary release from chains and manacles. If it is rejected as unconvincing, the prisoner gradually begins to sense in what direction he has to move when rewriting and rewriting his confessional autobiography. 'Sincerity' is rewarded. Fifth, there are the prerequisites for the growth of transference. Some at least of the cell-leaders and the judges and supervisors of the thought-reform programme are sincere and genuinely concerned with the re-education of the 'deviationist'. A need-fear-love-hate attachment is frequently formed, directly to the cell-leader and indirectly to the judge who controls the prisoner's fate.

Have these techniques any lesson for those who wish to escape from, rather than inculcate, dogmatic ideologies? Analysis facilitates resynthesis. The first factor we have distinguished, psychological acumen, could be acquired by a community only after a change in the intellectual climate from preoccupation with things to preoccupation with people. Such changes are not easily controlled. The second factor, the monolithic ideology, is what the open-minded student rejects, but it is worth careful analysis in order to distinguish those elements which constitute the seductive psychodynamic reward.

PSYCHODYNAMICS AND RE-EDUCATION

The third factor, the intensive group method, is worthy of careful study in conjunction with the fourth, a set of incentives, and the fifth, the prerequisites of transference. The combined use of these three factors has been pioneered in Britain by Mr Lyward (Burn, 1956) in his grammar school for boys who have committed crimes, some of them very serious. When I dined with a group of these boys, who took it in turn to cook their own food, I was surprised to find that the conversation was at a comparable level to that heard at the Scholars' table at an Oxford College. One of the group, a seventeen-year-old, pointed out to me a white-faced, tense-looking boy of fifteen, and said, 'We haven't managed to get him to join us yet, and I'm beginning to wonder whether we ever will. I think he may be psychotic.' In this setting the influence of the group was successfully used for thera-peutic purposes. The teachers were ex-students who co-operated with the less anxious boys to help the new-comers to share the new-found discovery that not all fathers are totally bad. In this school, the transfer-ence to Mr Lyward brought into being a well-integrated intensive therapeutic group, who, after a period of resistance, became amenable to the incentives of higher education and acceptance as respected members of the community. The difficulty of extending this technique of therapy-education is that of finding the necessary cluster of qualities in a single individual: teaching ability, psychological flair, the patience and courage to expose himself to the hatred and (occasionally) violence of parent-hating adolescents, and the devotion to this task needed to spend most of his 'spare time' talking to disturbed boys, arranging grants, persuading the police and magistrates to give them 'one more chance' after a theft in the village, and otherwise 'playing the parent'.

We have seen from this example that transference need not be to psychoanalysts alone. If we analyse further we conclude that the excessive burden carried by Mr Lyward could be distributed, so that potential analyst-headmasters are not deterred from taking up the challenge. The task facing all research workers in the field of penal reform is to distinguish those people and those situations to which the combination of transference, incentives and group interaction (TIG) can be effectively applied.

If, for example, this combination were used in prisons, and release from prison depended in certain cases not, as it does now, on a fixed sentence with remission for 'good conduct' (keeping out of trouble), but upon a change of attitude to the community sufficiently reliable to enable the prisoner to plan realistically for a law-abiding life outside the walls, the group method would then be linked, as in China, with a powerful incentive, and with the transference, and the false 'change of heart' would undoubtedly appear in place of the false confession. That, too, would have to be rejected by people capable of distinguish-ing between genuine and spurious transference developments.

The false 'change of heart' would not be the only problem. The assumption underlying the group method, tacit or explicit, is that the point of view of the group conductor, or (in China) the 'judge' who controls the group method from outside, is 'superior' to that of the group members in the sense that they can learn from him more than he can learn from them. This assumption is not always justified. We have only to imagine a prison group in which some members are trying to 're-educate' the Suffragettes of the group and persuade them to stop breaking the law, in order to see at once the absurdity of supposing that the law-abiding are necessarily more enlightened than the law-breakers. 'Justice' is not always just. In dictatorships laws are the claws of the king of the jungle. If the 'authorities' are to be given the opportunity to 're-educate' offenders, then conscientious offenders, who break the law not for personal gain but to protest against what they deem unjust, should have the opportunity to 're-educate' the legislators. The powerful combination of transference, incentives, and group interaction (TIG) could be used without danger of oppression only if it were applied by people who were impartial and independent of the administration.

PSYCHODYNAMICS AND ETHOLOGY

Such problems are mentioned in passing, not in order to solve them, but merely to indicate the area of research on the borderline between psychodynamics and social science and between psychodynamics and education. We can now indicate more clearly the relationship between psychodynamics, physiology, zoology, and ethology. Zoologists and ethologists have noticed the similarity between the reactions of crying and of 'laughing' in the primates, including the chimpanzee. In the human infant, too, we can evoke the response of laughter by stimulating the initial reactions of fear and producing a signal which means 'No danger'. A mother, for example, can startle her infant by suddenly appearing and saying 'Boo!' and at the same time reassure him by presenting her familiar and trusted face. Only a minor physiological adjustment is needed, in the startled infant, to convert the fear-flight response into the relief-laughter response. A similar, but slightly different, mechanism transmutes rage into laughter.

Custard-pie comedy is funny because the convention of the book or play or film allows the victim to stand paralysed while horrible indignities are being inflicted on him. Wit is funny because the subtlety of the attack on the mocked victim enables the wit to escape punishment or reproach, and his audience to enjoy with impunity vicarious pleasure in the attack. If we see two men insulting and attacking each other, the first phase of the flight or fight response is likely to be initiated in us, because if we identify ourselves with either the stronger or the weaker disputant, we may have to run away from the scene or join in the fight. If, however, we realize that these two men are actors, who are highly paid to tolerate indefinitely the insults, injuries, and accidents which would incapacitate most people, but which leave them unscathed, then our fear-flight or rage-fight response is converted into the relief-laughter response. The audience around us are safe and unthreatening creatures, enjoying the same quasi-sadistic social amusement. The victims are not really suffering, but if they pretend convincingly enough the relief-laughter response is prevented from subsiding into boredom. The more packed the auditorium and the louder the laughter, the greater our quasi-sadistic satisfaction.

Wit is more complex. The businessmen in Freud's story (p. 227 above) who were subtly insulted by the art critic when he asked, 'Where is the Saviour?' were not safe and sound on a stage or in a studio, but were really insulted. Why, then, should anyone laugh? The answer is that the human ape delights in real, as well as simulated, suffering. Although many communities do not have the equivalent of *Schadenfreude* in their languages, they all have the thing. From gladiatorial contests and the mangling of Christians by lions through public burning at the stake, hanging, drawing, and quartering, and guillotine executions, to the shows of naked madmen organized by greedy warders in nineteenth-century Bedlam, the sadism of the crowd of human apes has been amply demonstrated. In Bedlam entertainment, however, the relief-laughter response is not automatic. The idle crowd laughing at the chained, starving, filthy madmen of Bedlam could laugh because other creatures, not themselves, were suffering. If identification becomes too vivid, however, the experience becomes painful and the spectator turns away in horror, disgust, or pity.

In wit, too, the response is not always predictable, because wit often hurts. Sympathy for the vain and vulgar businessmen would inhibit laughter. So would strong feelings about the taboo on jokes with religious associations. So would a strong conviction of the sanctity of the guest-host relationship. So would shocked silence in the rest of the group. In order to laugh heartily at the witticism, a certain ambivalence towards the hosts, towards religious beliefs, and towards guest status, combined with the reassurance provided by the amusement of others, is a prerequisite. Solitary laughter is seldom hearty, and a reputation for wit facilitates wit because the group are predisposed to laughter.

We can now sum up this part of the argument in the following tentative hypothesis:

Humour is the art of initiating the fear-flight or rage-fight response (or both) while providing a form of reassurance which converts it into a relief-laughter response. Wit is the art of breaking a taboo and therefore initiating the fear-flight or rage-fight response in such a way that intellectual inference is needed before the breach is recognized as a breach, so that those who would condemn a crude breach of the taboo are disarmed by the ingenuity, deviousness, and originality of the attack, and the relief-laughter response supervenes.

AGGRESSION

Laughter is frequent and explosive in most well-established analytic groups of normal people. This can be tentatively explained by the relief caused by the frequent breaches of social taboos. The need for a controlling 'authority' to obey or defy leads to the spontaneous setting-up of the group conductor as a father, a mother, a schoolmaster, a judge, or (jokingly) 'God', but the 'authority' is felt to encourage rather than condemn breaches of taboo and etiquette. The combination, therefore, of protection by an authority and permission to break the social rules is clearly conducive to relief and laughter whenever the attitude to the rules is ambivalent and a member has the courage to break a taboo.

Lorenz, in his book *On Aggression* (1966), has suggested that the principal cause of neurosis in man is the lack of outlets for the aggressive drive. This hypothesis is supported by Margolin's (1960) psycho-analytic and anthropological studies of the Ute Indians, formerly a hunting tribe in America, and now the people believed to have the highest incidence in the world of neurosis and car accidents. Several studies have postulated the high positive correlation of accident-proneness and suppressed aggression. Natural selection, even if only for a few centuries, would have favoured the most aggressive Ute warriors, and their culture placed courageous aggressiveness high in the hierarchy of values. It seems that the Ute's only remaining outlet for aggression and for the need to prove his reckless courage is the violence in which the accident-prone can indulge without any conscious decision to attack oneself or others, and so without (conscious) responsibility or guilt.

The clue to the hampering of normal outlets is the occurrence of intention movements, displacement activities, or excessive excitation at an unusual outlet. Lorenz and Tinbergen agree that in the animals they have studied the normal outlet can be hampered by the simultaneous activation of antagonistic drives. In courtship, there is a tension between the sex drive, aggressiveness, and the tendency to escape. In threat, aggressiveness conflicts with the tendency to escape. Tinbergen emphasizes the need of both aggressiveness and sexual behaviour for the maintenance of the species, and since the female, being a member of the same species, provides attack-releasing as well as sex-stimulating sign stimuli, there must always be a conflict between sex and aggression in the male when a female approaches. If the male's aggressiveness were weaker, he could not drive off other males; if his sex drive were too strong, or his escape drive too weak, he would fail to escape from predators. The balance is delicate, and it becomes especially precarious in man, because phylogenetic and ontogenetic inheritance needs to be supplemented by a cultural tradition whose adequacy depends on its continuity. One generation can break the chain.

Two examples from the author's analytic groups will suffice to illustrate excessive excitation at an outlet as a clue to repressed aggression. Mrs P, a woman of dominant personality, interrupted some remarks by Mr R simply by waving her left hand up and down in a deprecating gesture. She succeeded, by this gesture, in switching the group's attention to Mrs S, whom Mrs P admired. We have seen that communication is of many kinds, and that facial expression, tone of voice, gesture, bodily posture, or unconsciously repeated movements may at any time be more significant than verbal communication. Mr R did not comment on this apparently trivial incident until a fortnight later, when he admitted that it had so infuriated him that he prepared and launched a wounding verbal attack on Mrs P. Only when it was clear that the attack had succeeded and that she was hurt did his anger subside.

The second incident was reported by a member of a group whose basic problem was the inability to be fully conscious of aggression and to express it. He could never feel strongly about parents, girl-friends, job, or hobbies, and could never feel angry because in any given situation it would be 'unreasonable' to get angry. One day he reported his surprise at the intensity of his rage when he saw someone smoking in a non-smoking compartment. He was a smoker himself, but because this was one of his 'non-smoking days', and because someone was definitely breaking a rule, he was able to use this apparently minor sign-stimulus to release upon a fellow-passenger he might never see again some of the unexpressed fury which he felt against people who were important to him. In his case, the more intimate and important the relationship, the greater the threat and the stronger the inhibition.

Ethology has discovered, in the few decades of its existence, that the bonds of mating and co-operation are strongest in the most aggressive animals; that intraspecific bonds coincide with extraspecific aggression; that the inhibition against killing a conspecific is reliable only in organisms which can kill near-equals with a single blow; that intra-specific rivalry and selection may favour maladaptive characteristics; that man's ecological and sociological conditions are undergoing a rapidly accelerating deviation from those to which human instinctive behaviour is phylogenetically adapted, so that an unprecedented strain is being placed on responsible morality and social controls.

If man has the endowment of an aggressive carnivorous hunter, but lacks the inhibition against killing conspecifics; if his weapons are not only the most powerful on the planet but also of long-distance kinds which do not arouse sympathetic revulsion; and if his precarious cultures, adapted to local conditions and largely dependent on un-critical acceptance of tradition, which he needs to compensate for his instinctual inadequacy, are colliding with each other and crumbling under the impact of technological change and rational analysis; how can he live peacefully in densely serried and rapidly proliferating packs which are fearful and suspicious of each other, and which have to compete for the progressively more inadequate resources of the planet?

Pessimistic prognoses for mankind are as convincing as optimistic solutions are unconvincing. The freedom of speech and writing which enables the British writer to criticize any religion, any ideology, any president, prime minister, or monarch, may be a luxury which is a freak of history. The monolithic, dogmatic, and forcibly indoctrinated ideology may be the only evolutionary device that will succeed in uniting humans in a pack big enough to eliminate or dominate all other packs. On the other hand, the ideology may prove an inefficient device that results in schisms and 'deviations'.

This is not a problem for psychodynamics, which has to turn its back on sociological speculation, take advantage of the accident of history which gives us free speech and free investigation, and concen-trate on its 'laboratory' work. It is concerned with two basic questions: In the controlled situation in this room, why does this person behave in this way and say these words at this moment? and What will be the effect of this interpretation? Ethology and anthropology are impor-tant to psychodynamics because they provide insights which aid interpretation, but the truly open-minded analyst allows the insights to sink to the deeper levels of the psyche, and dismisses all abstract theories from his mind when he prepares to interpret.

What can we hope may emerge from psychodynamic research? The difficulty of discovering the true needs, lacks, wishes, and fears of an individual or a group is due to the unconscious conviction that what is openly expressed is tantamount to action. At a deep level, openly expressed rage seems equivalent to an attack which destroys the relationship with a needed person; openly expressed sexual desire seems equivalent either to sexual assault or to an invitation to humiliating rejection; openly expressed envy or jealousy seems equivalent to the confession of a wish to devalue, damage, or destroy the envied person or relationship; openly expressed fear, guilt, weakness, abnormality, dependence . . . seem equivalent to an invitation to attack. Before the true needs, lacks, wishes, and fears can be revealed, omnipotent phantasy has to be modified or abandoned, and as omnipotent phantasy is the main consolation of those whose reality satisfactions are inadequate, this step is supremely difficult.

Little by little, with the aid of the transference or with group support, the person becomes more honest and more spontaneous. After each revelation the expected disaster does not occur. Even physical violence (a woman member of one of the author's analytic groups hit a man across the face very hard three times) does not necessarily destroy a needed relationship. It is reasonable to hope, when careful upbringing has been carefully undone, that a new conception of rationality will emerge. It is not rational to deny our phylogenetic, cultural, and ontological inheritance. It is not rational to pretend that we are not clever talking apes but specially created beings who have never torn living flesh with our teeth. It is not rational to believe that if we block every outlet for our phylogenetically determined aggression it will ooze from our pores like sweat. It is not rational to make our children ashamed of the rage and envy and jealousy they sometimes feel towards us and towards each other, or of their natural curiosity about carefully concealed bodies. It is not rational to pretend that children do not infuriate us when they impede our comfort or convenience, and that we are not human enough to get angry. It is not rational to arrest one man for hitting someone on the nose (assault), and pay another man to operate gallows, electric chair, or gas chamber to exterminate a psychotic who was not diagnosed and locked up in time to prevent him from killing someone. It is not rational to make people more desperate and therefore more dangerous to the community by locking them in cells for years, without attempting to find out what makes them unfit for community life, and then releasing them to commit predictable crimes.

It is not rational to pretend that a new generation can cut itself off from its cultural inheritance without psychodynamic loss. Clearly, a man who is 'rational' in the sense that he seeks a high degree of consistency in his beliefs cannot force himself to believe in miracles, or the will of Allah, or the latest version of the Marxist-Leninist theory, just because his father does. Nevertheless, a man who is 'rational' in the sense that he acknowledges his close emotional ties with his parents and the cultural tie with his ancestors will wish to acknowledge, preserve, and integrate every element of his phylogenetic, cultural, and ontogenetic inheritance which is not positively harmful or restrictive. The man who re-enacts his birth as a result of treatment by deep psychoanalysis or by a psychedelic drug is unlikely to pretend that he can reject and cut himself off from his mother. However much he has hated her, he has to accept and modify his relationship with her, whether she is alive or dead. The same is true of his father and his culture.

The new concept of rationality is the recognition of basic instinctual needs and the reconciliation of those needs with intellectual beliefs and attitudes. Rational emotional education is the encouragement of free expression of genuine strong feelings, such as love, hatred, envy, jealousy, rage, within reasonable social limits, combined with the recognition of other people's rights and feelings. Rational intellectual education for the late twentieth century is the encouragement of curiosity and relearning throughout the student and working life, and the inculcation of the necessary skills and techniques to understand most of the articles in the periodicals of a good university library. Open-mindedness is essential, for no one can predict which way the scientific cats will jump. Biologists will almost certainly make 'random' mutation less random through controlled bombardment of the chromosomes. Cloning, the technique of producing exact copies of individuals by implanting the nucleus of the intestinal cell in an unfertilized egg, will be carried out with prize animals, and later, almost inevitably, with men. The power to determine the sex of unborn progeny will force governments to preserve a balance, perhaps by differential taxation.

Psychopharmacology will offer a seductive variety of armchair adventures, some tending towards psychodynamic realism, others towards escapism. Morality may undergo major changes in adaptation to crisis situations. Suicide by those whose lives are miserable and not productive may become a noble rather than a shameful act. It may come to mean leaving to the hungry, when the appetite has failed, the overcrowded and underplenished table.

We are certain to be taken by surprise. The well-trained student of psychodynamics will be equipped and prepared to follow up any clue in any discipline which offers important insight into the thoughts, feelings, and motives of men, and to apply the insight to his laboratory work. He will also keep constantly in mind the central question: With what people and in what situations can constructive use be made of that potent combination, TIG (transference, incentives, and group interaction)?

The author will welcome correspondence from any reader in any part of the world. He will be especially pleased to receive information about articles, books, ideas, experiments, discoveries, methods, or projects that are directly or indirectly related to psychodynamics.

soon
very soon
I shall go into the dark
which will not be dark
lacking memory of light

go into the silence
which will not be silence
lacking memory of sound

go into the cold
which will not be cold
lacking memory of warmth

the warmth of your breasts
the warmth of your womb
the warmth of your love

soon
very soon
I shall go into the dark
without fear
without hope

with regret for the years we had planned
but regret
growing faint as I go
nearer the dark

soon
very soon
I shall lose the desire
the fast fading desire
to live for a while
as a ghost
in your thoughts

as I go to the dark
I am losing the light

as I go to the silence
I am losing the sound

as I go to the cold
I am losing the warmth

soon
very soon
I shall go into the cold

the cold of

not having been

Bibliography

ABRAHAM, K. 1927. *Selected Papers of Karl Abraham*. London: Hogarth.

ACKERMAN, N. W. 1938. Paranoid State with Delusions of Injury by 'Black Magic'. *Bull. Menninger Clinic* **2.**

ALEXANDER, F. 1929. *The Psychoanalysis of the Total Personality*.

—— 1951. Schizophrenic Psychoses: Critical Considerations of the Psychoanalytic Treatment. *Arch. Neurol. Psychiat.* **26.**

—— 1961. *The Scope of Psychoanalysis*. New York: Basic Books.

AUERBACH, R. & RUGOWSKI, J. A. 1967. Lysergic Acid Diethylamide: Effect on Embryos. *Science* (157), 1325–6.

AUSTIN, J. L. 1946. Other Minds. *Supplementary Proceedings of the Aristotelean Society* **20.**

AYER, A. J. 1938. *Language, Truth and Logic*. London: Gollancz, 2nd edn, 1946.

—— 1956. *The Problem of Knowledge*. London: Macmillan.

BACH, G. R. 1954. *Intensive Group Psychotherapy*. New York: Ronald Press.

BAK, R. C. 1946. Masochism in Paranoia. *Psychoanal. Quart.* **15.**

BALINT, M. 1960. Primary Narcissism and Primary Love. *Psychoanal. Quart.* **29.**

—— 1965. *Primary Love and Psycho-Analytic Technique*. London: Tavistock; New York: Liveright. New edition.

BARBARA, D. A. 1944. Positive Transference in Schizophrenia. *Psychiat. Quart.* **18.**

BARKAS, M. R. 1925. Treatment of Psychotic Patients in Institutions in the light of Psycho-analysis. *J. Neurol. Psychopathol.* **5.**

BARNETT, S. A. 1955. *Lancet* 10 Dec., 1203–8.

BERES, D. 1958. Vicissitudes of Superego Functions and Superego Precursors in Childhood. *Psychoanal. Study Child* **13.**

BERKELEY-HILL, O. 1922. A Case of Paranoid Dissociation. *Psychoanal. Rev.* **9.**

BION, W. R. 1954. Notes on the Theory of Schizophrenia. *Int. J. Psycho-Anal.* **35.**

—— 1956. Development of Schizophrenic Thought. *Int. J. Psycho-Anal.* **37.**

—— 1961. *Experiences in Groups.* London: Tavistock; New York: Basic Books.

—— 1962. *Learning from Experience.* London: Heinemann.

—— 1963. *Elements of Psychoanalysis.* London: Heinemann.

—— 1965. *Transformations: Change from Learning to Growth.* London: Heinemann.

BIRD, B. 1957. A Specific Peculiarity of Acting Out. *J. Amer. Psychoanal. Assoc.* **5.**

BOLLMEIER, L. N. 1938. The Paranoid Mechanism in Overt Male Homosexuality. *Psychoanal. Quart.* **7.**

BRILL, A. A. 1911. Psychological Mechanisms of Paranoia. *New York Med. J.* **94.**

BRUNSWICK, R. MACK. 1928. The Analysis of a Case of Paranoia. *J. nerv. ment. Dis.* **70.**

BURN, M. 1956. *Mr Lyward's Answer.* London: Hamish Hamilton; Toronto: Collins.

BYCHOWSKI, G. 1930. A Case of Oral Delusions of Persecution. *Int. J. Psycho-Anal.* **11.**

CANNON, W. B. 1929. *Bodily Changes in Pain, Hunger, Fear and Rage.* New York: Appleton-Century.

CAPLAN, G. 1964. *Principles of Preventive Psychiatry.* New York: Basic Books; London: Tavistock.

CARTWRIGHT, D. & ZANDER, A. (eds.) 1953. *Group Dynamics.* New York: Row Peterson; London: Tavistock; 1954.

—— 1960. *Group Dynamics.* 2nd edn. New York: Harper & Row; London: Tavistock, 1961.

CHOLDEN, LOUIS (ed.). 1956. *LSD and Mescaline in Experimental Psychiatry.* New York: Grune & Stratton.

COHEN, M. M., MARINELLO, M. J. & BACK, N. 1967. Chromosomal Damage in Human Leukocytes induced by Lysergic Acid Diethylamide. *Science* (155): 1417–19.

CRAWSHAY-WILLIAMS, R. 1957. *Methods & Criteria of Reasoning.* London: Routledge & Kegan Paul.
CUSTANCE, JOHN. 1951. *Wisdom, Madness & Folly.* London: Gollancz.

DEUTSCH, H. 1964. *Psychoanalysis of the Neuroses.* London: Hogarth.
—— 1965. *Psychology of Women.* 2 vols. New York: Grune & Stratton.
—— 1966. *Neuroses and Character Types.* London: Hogarth.
DEWEY, JOHN. 1938. *Logic: The Theory of Inquiry.* New York: Henry Holt.

EDDINGTON, SIR A. 1951. *The Nature of the Physical World.* Cambridge: C.U.P.
EZRIEL, HENRY. 1950a. The Psychoanalytic Approach to the Treatment of Patients in Groups. *J. ment. Sci.* **46.**
—— 1950b. The Psychoanalytic Approach to Group Treatment. *Brit. J. med. Psychol.* **23.**
—— 1951. The Psychoanalytic Session as an Experimental Situation. *Brit. J. med. Psychol.* **24.**
—— 1952a. Some Principles of a Psychoanalytic Method of Group Treatment. *Proceedings of the first International Congress of Psychiatry, Paris* 1950.
—— 1952b. Notes on Psychoanalytic Group Therapy: Interpretation and Research. *Psychiatry* **15.**
—— 1956-7. Experimentation within the Psychoanalytic Session. *Brit. J. Philos. Sci.* **7.**

FAIRBAIRN, W. R. D. 1952. *Psychoanalytic Studies of the Personality.* London: Tavistock/Routledge.
FEDERN, P. 1953. *Ego Psychology and the Psychoses.* London: Imago.
FEIGENBAUM, D. 1930. Analysis of a Case of Paranoia Persecutoria. Structure and Cure. *Psychoanal. Rev.* **17.**
—— 1936. On Projection. *Psychoanal. Quart.* **5.**
—— 1937. Depersonalization as a Defence Mechanism. *Psychoanal. Quart.* **6.**
FENICHEL, O. 1934. *Outline of Psychoanalysis.* New York: Norton.
—— 1945. *Psychoanalytic Theory of Neurosis.* New York: Norton.
—— 1954-5. *The Collected Papers of Otto Fenichel.* First and second series. London: Routledge.
FERENCZI, S. 1952. *First Contributions to Psychoanalysis.* London: Hogarth.

FERENCZI, S. 1955a. *Final Contributions to Psychoanalysis*. London: Hogarth.

—— 1955b. Problems and Methods of Psychoanalysis. In: M. Balint (ed.). *Selected Papers*, Vol. 3. London: Hogarth.

—— 1955c. Theory and Technique of Psychoanalysis. In: M. Balint (ed.) *Selected Papers*, Vol. 2. London: Hogarth.

FLETCHER, RONALD. 1957. *Instinct in Man*. London: Allen & Unwin.

FLIESS, R. 1950. *The Psychoanalytic Reader*. London: Hogarth.

FOULKES, S. H. 1964. *Therapeutic Group Analysis*. London: Allen and Unwin.

FOULKES, S. H. & ANTHONY, E. J. 1965. *Group Psychotherapy*. Second revised edition. Harmondsworth: Penguin.

FRAIBERG, S. 1952. A Critical Neurosis in a 2½-year-old Girl. *Psychoanal. Study Child* 7.

FREEMAN, T., CAMERON, J. L. & MCGHIE, A. 1958. *Chronic Schizophrenia*. London: Tavistock; New York: International Universities Press.

——, —— & —— 1965. *Studies on Psychosis*. London: Tavistock; New York: International Universities Press.

FREUD, ANNA. 1949. *The Ego and the Mechanisms of Defence*. London: Hogarth; New York: International Universities Press.

—— 1952. The Role of Bodily Illness in the Mental Life of Children. *Psychoanal. Study Child* 7.

FREUD, S. Unless otherwise stated, references are to *The Standard Edition of the Complete Psychological Works of Sigmund Freud* (24 vols) translated and edited by James Strachey. London: Hogarth Press; New York: Basic Books.

—— 1896. The Nature and Mechanism of Obsessional Neurosis. S.E. 3.

—— 1900. *The Interpretation of Dreams*. Vols I and II. S.E. 4 & 5.

—— 1905a. (*Three Essays on the Theory of Sexuality*) S.E. 7.

—— 1905b. *Jokes and their Relation to the Unconscious*. S.E. 8.

—— 1909. Analysis of a Phobia in a Five-year-old Boy. S.E. 10.

—— 1911a. Formulations on the two Principles of Mental Functioning. S.E.12.

—— 1911b. Psycho-analytic Notes on an Autobiographical Account of a Case of Paranoia (Dementia Paranoides). S.E. 12.

—— 1914. On Narcissism: an Introduction. S.E. 14.

—— 1915. A Case of Paranoia running Counter to the Psycho-analytic Theory of the Disease. S.E. 14.

—— 1916. A Metapsychological Supplement to the Theory of Dreams. S.E. 14.

FREUD, S. 1917. Mourning and Melancholia. S.E. 14.

—— 1918. From the History of an Infantile Neurosis. S.E. 17.

—— 1921. *Group Psychology and the Analysis of the Ego.* S.E. 18.

—— 1922. Some Neurotic Mechanisms in Jealousy, Paranoia, and Homosexuality. S.E. 18.

—— 1923a. *The Ego and the Id.* S.E. 19.

—— 1923b. Two Encyclopaedia Articles. S.E. 18.

—— 1924. Neurosis and Psychosis. S.E. 19.

—— 1926. *Inhibitions, Symptoms, and Anxiety.* S.E. 20.

—— 1927. Humour. S.E. 21.

—— 1931. Female Sexuality. S.E. 21.

—— 1933. *New Introductory Lectures on Psycho-Analysis.* S.E. 22.

—— 1936. *The Problem of Anxiety.* Trans. H. A. Bunker. New York: Psychoanalytic Quarterly Press.

—— 1939. *Moses and Monotheism.* S.E. 23.

—— 1940. *An Outline of Psycho-Analysis.* S.E. 23.

—— 1950. *The Origins of Psycho-Analysis.* (London: Imago.)

FROMM-REICHMANN, F. 1949. Notes on the Development of Treatment of Schizophrenics by Psychoanalysis and Psychotherapy. In: Bullard (ed.), *Psychoanalysis and Psychotherapy. Selected Papers.* Chicago: University of Chicago Press, 1959.

GREENACRE, P. 1953. *Trauma, Growth and Personality.* London: Hogarth; New York: Norton.

GUNTRIP, H. 1961. *Personality Structure and Human Interaction.* London: Hogarth.

HAYWARD, M. L. 1949. Direct Interpretation in the Treatment of a Case of Schizophrenia. *Psychiat. Quart.* **23.**

HEIMANN, P. 1952. Preliminary Notes on Some Defence Mechanisms in Paranoid States. *Int. J. Psycho-Anal.* **33.**

HUXLEY, ALDOUS. 1954. *The Doors of Perception.* London: Chatto & Windus.

JAMES, W. 1890. *Principles of Psychology.* 2 vols. London: Constable; New York: Dover.

JEANS, SIR JAMES. 1942. *Physics and Philosophy.* London: C.U.P.

JOHNSON, J. A. 1963. *Group Therapy.* New York: McGraw-Hill.

JOHNSON, MARTIN. 1948. *Science and the Meanings of Truth.* London: Faber & Faber.

JONES, E. 1953–7. *The Life and Work of Sigmund Freud.* 3 vols. London: Hogarth.

—— 1961. *Papers on Psychoanalysis.* New York: Beacon.

—— 1964. *Essays in Applied Psychoanalysis.* London: Hogarth.

JONES, MAXWELL, et al. 1952. *Social Psychiatry.* London: Tavistock/ Routledge; New York: Basic Books (under the title *The Therapeutic Community*).

JUNG, C. G. 1964. *Man and his Symbols.* London: Aldus.

KADIS, A. L., KRASNER, J. D., WINICK, C., & FOULKES, S. H. 1963. *A Practicum of Group Psychotherapy.* New York: Harper & Row.

KANT, IMMANUEL. 1788. *The Critique of Practical Reason.* Trans. T. K. Abbott. London: Longmans, 1909.

KLEIN, MELANIE. 1932. *The Psycho-Analysis of Children.* London: Hogarth.

—— 1946. Notes on Some Schizoid Mechanisms. In: M. Klein *et al.* (eds.), *Developments in Psycho-Analysis.* London: Hogarth, 1952.

—— 1948a. A Contribution to the Theory of Anxiety and Guilt. *Int. J. Psycho-Anal.* **31.**

—— 1948b. *Contributions to Psycho-Analysis.* London: Hogarth.

—— 1948c. In: S. Lorand (ed.) *Psycho-Analysis Today.* London: Allen & Unwin; New York: International Universities Press.

—— 1952. The Origins of Transference. *Int. J. Psycho-Anal.* **33.**

—— 1957. *Envy and Gratitude.* London: Tavistock; New York: Basic Books.

—— 1963. *Our Adult World and Other Essays.* London: Heinemann.

KLEIN, MELANIE, HEIMANN, PAULA, & MONEY-KYRLE, R. (eds.). 1955. *New Directions in Psycho-Analysis.* London: Tavistock.

KLEIN, MELANIE, & RIVIERE, JOAN. 1962. *Love, Hate and Reparation.* London: Hogarth.

KNIGHT, R. P. 1939. Psychotherapy in Acute Paranoid Schizophrenia with Successful Outcome. *Bull. Menninger Clinic* **3.**

—— 1940. The Relationship of Latent Homosexuality to the Mechanism of Paranoid Delusions. *Bull. Menninger Clinic* **4.**

—— 1946. The Psychotherapy of an Adolescent Schizophrenic with Mutism. *Psychiatry* **9.**

KOESTLER, A. 1952. *Arrow in the Blue.* London: Collins.

—— 1954. *The Invisible Writing.* London: Collins.

LAFORGUE, R. 1936. A Contribution to the Study of Schizophrenia. *Int. J. Psycho-Anal.* **17.**

LANGER, SUSANNE. 1942. *Philosophy in a New Key.* Cambridge, Mass.: Harvard University Press.

LEWIN, KURT. 1936. *Principles of Topological Psychology.* New York: McGraw-Hill.

—— 1951. *Field Theory in Social Science.* ed. D. Cartwright. New York: Harper; London: Tavistock.

LIFTON, R. J. 1961. *Thought Reform and the Psychology of Totalism.* London: Gollancz; Harmondsworth: Penguin, 1967.

LOCKE, N. 1961. *Group Psychoanalysis: Theory and Technique.* New York: International Universities Press.

LODON, L. S. 1931. Mechanism in Paranoia. *Psychoanal. Rev.* **18.**

LORENZ, K. Z. 1952. *King Solomon's Ring.* London: Methuen.

—— 1966. *On Aggression.* London: Methuen.

MARGOLIN, S. 1960. A Consideration of Constitutional Factors in Aggressivity of an Indian Tribe. Paper read at the Menninger School of Psychiatry, Topeka, Kansas.

MAYER-GROSS, W. 1935. On Depersonalization. *Brit. J. med. Psychol.* **15.**

MILLER, ARTHUR. 1956. *The Crucible.* New York: Bantam Books; London: Secker & Warburg.

MORRIS, D. 1967a. *The Naked Ape.* London: Cape.

—— (ed.) 1967b. *Primate Ethology.* London: Weidenfeld & Nicolson.

MORRIS, C. W. 1938. Foundations of the Theory of Signs. *International Encyclopaedia of Unified Science*, Vol. 1, No. 2. Chicago: University of Chicago Press.

MUNROE, R. L. 1957. *Schools of Psychoanalytic Thought.* London: Hutchinson; New York: Dryden Press.

NAPIER, J. & NAPIER, P. 1967. *Primate Biology.* New York: Academic Press.

NEWTON, SIR ISAAC. 1756. *Letters to Bentley.* Published by Cumberland, nephew to Bentley, 1756.

NIETZSCHE, FRIEDRICH. 1883–91. *Thus Spake Zarathustra.* Trans. A. Tille, revised M. M. Bozman, introduction by Roy Pascal. London: Dent, 1950.

NUNBERG, H. 1948. *The Practice and Theory of Psychoanalysis.* New York: Nervous and Mental Diseases Publishing House.

O'MALLEY, M. 1923. Transference and some of its Problems in Psychoses. *Psychoanal. Rev.* **10.**

PEIRCE, C. S. 1931–58. *Collected Papers.* ed. Hartshorne & Weiss. Cambridge, Mass.: Harvard University Press.

PIOUS, W. L. 1949. The Pathogenic Process in Schizophrenia. *Bull. Menninger Clinic* **13.**

POPPER, K. R. 1959. *The Logic of Scientific Discovery.* London: Hutchinson; New York: Basic Books.

—— 1965. *Conjectures and Refutations.* 2nd edn. London: Routledge & Kegan Paul; New York: Basic Books.

REICHENBACH, HANS. 1944. *Philosophic Foundations of Quantum Mechanics.* University of California Press.

RIEFF, PHILIP. 1959. *Freud: the Mind of the Moralist.* London: Gollancz.

RIVIÈRE, J. 1936. A Contribution to the Analysis of the Negative Therapeutic Reaction. *Int. J. Psycho-Anal.* **17.**

ROSEN, J. N. 1946. The Method of Resolving Acute Catatonic Excitement. *Psychiat. Quart.* **20.**

—— 1947. The Treatment of Schizophrenic Psychoses by Direct Analytic Therapy. *Psychiat. Quart.* **21.**

—— 1950. The Survival Function of Schizophrenia. *Bull. Menninger Clinic* **14.**

—— 1962. *Direct Psychoanalytic Psychiatry.* New York: Grune & Stratton.

ROSENFELD, HERBERT, A. 1958. Some Observations on the Psychopathology of Hypochondriacal States. *Int. J. Psycho-Anal.* **39.**

—— 1965. Psychotic States: a Psychoanalytic Approach. Hogarth: London.

RUSSELL, BERTRAND. 1925. *The A.B.C. of Relativity.* London: Allen & Unwin; New York: Oxford University Press.

—— 1954. *Human Knowledge: its Scope and Limits.* London: Allen & Unwin.

RYCROFT, C. (ed.) 1966. *Psychoanalysis Observed.* London: Constable.

RYLANDER, G. 1948. Personal Analysis before and after Frontal Lobotomy. In: *The Frontal Lobes.* Baltimore: Williams & Wilkins.

RYLE, GILBERT. 1949. *The Concept of Mind.* London: Hutchinson.

SANDISON, RONALD & WHITELAW, J. D. A. 1957. Further Studies in the Therapeutic Value of LSD in Mental Illness. *J. ment. Sci.* **103.**

SANDISON, RONALD, WHITELAW, J. D. A., & SPENCER, A. M. 1957. Therapeutic Value of LSD in Mental Illness. *J. ment. Sci.* **100.**

SARGANT, WILLIAM. 1957. *Battle for the Mind.* London: Heinemann; London: Pan Books, 1959; New York: Doubleday.

SAUL, L. J. 1947. Some Observations on a Form of Projection. *Psychoanal. Quart.* **16.**

SAVAGE, CHARLES. 1952. LSD, a Clinical–Psychological Study. *Amer. J. Psychiat.* **108.**

—— 1955. Variations of Ego Feeling induced by LSD. *Psychoanal. Rev.* **42.**

SCHILLER, C. H. (ed.) 1964. *Instinctive Behaviour.* New York: International Universities Press.

SEGAL, H. 1950. Some Aspects of the Analysis of a Schizophrenic. *Int. J. Psycho-Anal.* **31.**

—— 1964. *Introduction to the Works of Melanie Klein.* London: Heinemann.

SLAVSON, S. R. 1950. *Analytic Group Psychotherapy.* New York: Columbia University Press.

SPITZ, R. 1958. On the Genesis of the Superego Components. *Psychoanal. Study Child* **13.**

SULLIVAN, H. S. 1931. The Modified Psychoanalytic Treatment of Schizophrenia. *Amer. J. Psychiat.* **11.**

SZASZ, T. S. 1957. *Pain and Pleasure: A Study of Bodily Feelings.* New York: Basic Books.

TAYLOR, F. K. 1961. *The Analysis of Therapeutic Groups.* London: O.U.P.

TERMAN, L. M. *et al.* 1929–59. *Genetic Studies of Genius.* Stanford, Calif.: Stanford University Press.

TINBERGEN, N. 1951. *The Study of Instinct.* Oxford: Clarendon Press.

—— 1953. *Social Behaviour in Animals.* London: Methuen.

TOULMIN, STEPHEN. 1953. *The Philosophy of Science.* London: Hutchinson.

WASSELL, B. B. 1959. *Group Psychoanalysis.* New York: Philosophical Library.

WEISSMAN, P. 1954. Ego and Superego in Obsessional Character and Neuroses. *Psychoanal. Quart.* **23.**

WINNICOTT, D. W. 1958. *Collected Papers: through Paediatrics to Psychoanalysis.* London: Tavistock; New York: Basic Books.

—— 1965. *The Maturational Processes and the Facilitating Environment.* London: Hogarth.

WISDOM, JOHN. 1953. *Philosophy and Psychoanalysis.* Oxford: Blackwell.

W

WISDOM, J. O. 1949. Hypothesis to explain Trauma-Re-enactment Dreams. *Int. J. Psycho-Anal.* **30.**

—— 1952. *Foundations of Inference in Natural Science.* London: Methuen.

—— 1956. Psychoanalytic Technology. *Brit. J. Philos. Sci.* May.

WITTGENSTEIN, L. 1953. *Philosophical Investigations.* Oxford: Blackwell; New York: Macmillan.

WOLF, A. & SCHARTZ, E. K. 1962. *Psychoanalysis in Groups.* New York: Grune & Stratton.

WOODGER, J. H. 1929. *Biological Principles.* London: Kegan Paul.

—— 1956. *Physics, Psychology and Medicine.* London: C.U.P.

YERKES, R. M. & YERKES, A. W. 1929. *The Great Apes.* New Haven, Conn.: Yale University Press.

ZUCKERMAN, S. 1932. *The Social Life of Monkeys and Apes.* London: Kegan Paul.

Name Index

Subject Index

(*n* refers to footnote entry)

ethics (*see also* intuitionism, ethical), 235–6, 252–3
  The Ethic of Honesty, 235–6
ethology, 47, 198, 206, 240–2, 250, 292–4, 296–7
evaluative utterances, *see* USES OF LANGUAGE
evolution, 16–17, 19, 33–4, 44, 61, 72, 83, 98, 108
exclusive disjunction, 12–13
'existential statements', 109
explanatory utterances, *see* USES OF LANGUAGE
extrapolation, 17, 34–5, 76, 235

FACT ANTITHESES
  fact-delusion, 190
  fact-explanation, 190–3
  fact-fiction, 190
  fact-illusion, 190
  fact-phantasy, 190
  fact-rumour, 190
  fact-surmise, 190
  fact-theory, 190–3
  factual-analytic, 190
  factual-explanatory, 161
  factual-legal, 161
  factual-psychological, 161
  factual-tendentious, 161, 190
  factual-theoretical, 190, 193
  factual-value judgements, 3
  factual-verbal, 190
Fact-finding Fallacy, *see* FALLACIES
'facts', 3–11, 28, 62–3, 86–8, 110, 159–63, 187–90, 203–4, 223
  'neutral', 159–64, 190
  public and private, 36–41, 43
  reallocation of, 8, 29, 187–8, 190–3
factual and verbal mistakes, 7, 41, 62
FALLACIES (*see also Chart, 218–21*)
  amphiboly, 154, 156, 201, 220–1
    definition of, 207
  Autonomy of Logic, 116–17, 201, 212–13, 215–16, 220–1
    definition of, 116–17, 204
  Behaviourist, 2, 30, 33, 80, 135, 137–41, 154–5, 200–1, 212, 216, 220–1, 239, 283
    definition of, 204–6

Epistemologist's, 30–1
equivocation, 137, 154, 156–8, 201, 220–1
  definition of, 207
Fact-finding, 30, 86–7, 163, 192, 201, 212–13, 215, 218–19
  definition of, 203–4
Fluctuating Rigour, 103–5, 110, 128, 153–4, 160, 196, 198, 200, 210, 212–13, 215, 217–19, 223, 226, 228, 248
  definition of, 103, 201
Fluctuating Scepticism, 128, 153–4, 171, 190, 198, 201, 210, 212–13, 215–19, 228, 256
  definition of, 202
Genetic, 112
Humean, 80
Iconoclastic, 142–3
ignoratio elenchi, 154, 201
  definition of, 207
Instrumentalist, 80
Intellectualist, 139
Kantian, 80, 129
Many Questions, 154, 201, 220–1
  definition of, 207
non causa pro causa, 82, 134–7, 154, 200–1, 210, 212, 216, 220–1
  definition of, 207
non sequitur, 154, 201
  definition of, 207
Operationalist, 34–5, 80–1
Overextensionism (Munroe's 'Reductionism'), 151–5, 201, 210, 212–13, 216, 220–1
  definition of, 155, 208
petitio principii, 154, 201
  definition of, 207
Phenomenalist, 80
post hoc ergo propter hoc, 154, 201
  definition of, 207
Pseudo-objectivity, 185–6, 201, 210, 212–13, 215–16, 218–19
  definition of, 202–3
Reductionist, 141–2
  definition of, 150–3, 155
Straw Man, 77, 111, 201, 210, 212, 215, 218–19, 228
  definition of, 203
Supra-controversy, 188, 193, 201,

Motive-producing Situation, 120, 237,
    247, 254, 282
Motives for Distortion, 115, 117–19,
    120–32, 144–5, 208, 223, 229, 233,
    235, 284
music, 199n
myth, 8, 86, 128

Natural Selection, 12
Nazi Party, 113
need, unconscious, and feeling of, 53–6,
    151, 209
'need-fulfilment', 54–6
Need Hypothesis, see HYPOTHESES
Neptune, 37–40, 42
neurology, 44, 167, 192, 198
neurosis, 57, 82, 131, 159
neutral utterances, see USES OF
    LANGUAGE
nightmares, 56, 71
non causa pro causa, see FALLACIES
Non-Commitment, see MECHANISMS
non sequitur, see FALLACIES
'normal', definition of, 258
normative utterances, see USES OF
    LANGUAGE
Nosopoietic Theory (Pavlov), 208,
    249, 283, 285

objectivity, 90–2, 185–6, 223, 228–30
object relationships, 20, 24, 69, 76
obsessional impulse, 178–9, 183
obsessional symptoms, 101, 202, 213,
    226–7
Oedipus complex, 64
'Oedipus effect', 90, 92–3
Omnipotence of Thought, 175n
Operationalism, see FALLACIES
oral level, regression to, 126
'other minds' problem, 128
Outsider, 132, 238
Overextensionism, see FALLACIES
overlapping language projections, see
    LANGUAGE PROJECTIONS

palaeontology, 34, 45–6
paradox, 7, 175–8, 188
    mind-dependence, 188–90
paranoia, 112, 124, 175, 180, 213, 234,
    255–7, 261

penicillin, 23–4, 70
penis envy, 123
perception, 42
perfectionism, 125
performative utterances, see USES OF
    LANGUAGE
perversion, 57–8
petitio principii, see FALLACIES
phallic level, of libidinal development,
    66, 126
pharmacology, 70–1, 240, 298
phenomenal world, 85
phlogiston, 45, 203
phobia, 101, 133, 213, 249
Physical Sciences (P) language projec-
    tion, see LANGUAGE PROJECTIONS
physics, 18–27, 29, 84–8, 91, 174, 189,
    241, 253
physiology, 38, 67, 70–1, 240, 242–3,
    245–6
play technique, 66, 242, 250, 282, 287
pleasure-need, 54–6
POINTS OF VIEW:
    common sense, 166–7, 186, 197
    controversial, 186
    genetic, 166
    incompatible, 162, 166–7
    legal, 161, 186
    psychoanalytic, 167, 185–6, 197
    scientific, 167
    shifts in, 197
    unfamiliar, 237
post hoc ergo propter hoc, see FALLACIES
pragmatics, 11–13, 112–14, 117, 227
Pragmatism, 203, 236
prediction, 16, 20, 59–60, 67–72, 94,
    97, 111, 116–17, 192
predictive hypotheses, see HYPOTHESES
Preformation theory, 71
prescriptive utterances, see USES OF
    LANGUAGE
Principle, General Testing, see Testing
    Principle, General
'privileged access', 134–7
probability of theories, 98–9
Progressive Affective Discrimination,
    145–8, 209, 215, 222
    definition of, 147
Projection, see MECHANISMS

projections, language, *see* LANGUAGE PROJECTIONS

proof, 17, 59, 71–2, 102–3, 129, 201, 207, 223

Pseudo-objectivity Fallacy, *see* FALLACIES

psychiatry, 123

psychic energy, 225, 227

psychoanalysis, applied, 22

psychodynamics, philosophy of (definition), 240–2, 251
   science of (definition), 239–41
   theory of, 249–50

psychokinesis, 201

psycholytic drugs, 240, 269–80, 287

'psychological research', 14

'psychologism', 109–10, 112, 203, 228, 236

psychology, academic, 31–2, 239–42, 281–3

psychopathic criminals, 104–5

Psychophysical Parallelism, 71

psychosis, 131, 175–6, 202, 286–7

public-private antithesis, 36–41, 43

punishment-need, 54–6

Quantum Theory, 99

radiation, 19, 83

'random', 12–13, 16, 102

rationality, 2, 120, 209, 211, 222, 224, 233–5, 297–8

Rationalization, *see* MECHANISMS

Reaction-formation, *see* MECHANISMS

reality, testing of, 24, 150

recidivism, 97

recommendatory utterances, *see* USES OF LANGUAGE

Rectilinear Propagation of Light, Principle of, 21, 71

Reductionism (*see also* FALLACIES: Overextensionism and Reductionist), 150–4

reflecting utterances, *see* USES OF LANGUAGE

refutation, 67–9, 75, 83–4, 89, 93

Regression, *see* MECHANISMS

relationships (required, avoided, calamity), 24, 109

relativity, theory of, 61, 86–8, 91, 98

Reparation, *see* MECHANISMS

Repression, *see* MECHANISMS

Repression, Reinforcement of, *see* MECHANISMS

research, scientific, 15–17, 20–1, 23–4

resistance, psychological, 235

responsibility, 223

'responsible', definition of, 174–7

retroprojection, 277

retrospective hypotheses, *see* HYPOTHESES

retrospection, 70, 137, 180

Reversal, *see* MECHANISMS

risk (risk-taking) utterances, *see* USES OF LANGUAGE

riskless utterances, *see* USES OF LANGUAGE

Rorschach tests, 32, 39, 240, 250, 255, 261–2, 287

Russian Revolution, 47–8

sadism, 58, 76, 142, 293

Saint Joan, 195

scepticism, 202
   tentative, 229

Scepticism, Fluctuating, *see* FALLACIES

Scepticism, Unrestricted, *see* FALLACIES

science of psychodynamics, definition of, 239–41

scientific language projections, *see* LANGUAGE PROJECTIONS

schizophrenia, 24, 175, 214, 286

Secondary Elaboration, 55

selection criteria (for training in psychodynamics), 261–2

semantics, 4–5, 11–13, 46–7, 60, 62, 117, 135, 196, 227

semiotic, 11

'sexual', Freud's concept of, 159

Snell's Law, 22, 24

Sophistication of Magical Thinking, *see* MECHANISMS

specialty distortion, 246–8

specificity, 69–70

spectrum, 77

speculative hypotheses, *see* HYPOTHESES

Splitting, *see* MECHANISMS

stammering, 217, 222

USES OF LANGUAGE—*cont.*

explanatory, 99, 102, 163, 193, 198, 236

focusing, 95, 100, 139, 190, 197–8, 237, 268

  definition of, 95

guarded, 237

informative, 94–5, 100, 198, 232, 236

neutral, 160–1, 163

normative, 95, 237

performative, 11–12, 163, 236

prescriptive, 95, 236

recommendatory, 13, 163, 236

reflecting, 189–90, 192, 224, 229–30, 237

risk (risk-taking), 114–15, 136, 237

riskless, 114–15, 224, 237

suggestive, 94, 96, 100, 198, 224, 232, 237

synthetic, 236

tendentious ('coloured'), 237

vagina dentata fear, 259

validation, 20–1, 40–2, 67–70

value judgement (*see also* USES OF LANGUAGE, appraising), 3, 163, 285

verifiability, 80

verification, *see* testing of hypotheses

Verification Principle, 225–8

'verificationism', 98, 228, 236

volcanology, 76

War and Peace, 195

warranted assertibility, theory of, 246

Will, Free, *see* Free Will

'Will, The', 168–86, 223

Will to Power (Nietszche), 130–2, 216

wish-fulfilment, 21–2, 54–8, 66, 71, 75, 115, 234, 287

wish-phantasy, 115

wit, 10, 292–4

  Freud's theory of, 227–8

Wittgensteinian Fallacy, *see* FALLACIES

zoology, 292

zoophobia, 52